Pine Island, Matlacha Pass, Island Bay, and Caloosahatchee National Wildlife Refuges

Comprehensive Conservation Plan

**U.S. Department of the Interior
Fish and Wildlife Service
Southeast Region**

October 2010

SUBMITTED BY: *Signed* DATE: 8/31/2010
PAUL TRITAIK, PROJECT LEADER

CONCUR: *Signed* DATE: 9/13/2010
ELIZABETH SOUHEAVER, REFUGE SUPERVISOR

CONCUR: *Signed* DATE: 9/15/2010
Acting Regional Chief (Acting)
Southeast Region

APPROVED BY: *Signed* DATE: SEP 16 2010
Cynthia K. Dohner, Regional Director
Southeast Region

COMPREHENSIVE CONSERVATION PLAN

PINE ISLAND, MATLACHA PASS, ISLAND BAY, AND CALOOSAHATCHEE NATIONAL WILDLIFE REFUGES
Charlotte and Lee Counties, Florida

**U.S. Department of the Interior
Fish and Wildlife Service**

Southeast Region
Atlanta, Georgia

October 2010

TABLE OF CONTENTS

COMPREHENSIVE CONSERVATION PLAN 1

I. BACKGROUND 1

    Introduction 1
    Purpose and Need for the Plan 1
    U.S. Fish and Wildlife Service 3
    National Wildlife Refuge System 3
    Legal and Policy Context 5
        Legal Mandates, Administrative and Policy Guidelines, and Other
        Special Considerations 5
        Biological Integrity, Diversity, and Environmental Health Policy 6
    National and International Conservation Plans and Initiatives 6
        North American Bird Conservation Initiative 7
        American Oystercatcher Conservation Plan 8
        National Wetlands Priority Conservation Plan 9
        Office of Ocean and Coastal Resource Management 9
    Relationship to State Wildlife Agency 10

II. REFUGE OVERVIEW 13

    Introduction 13
        Pine Island NWR 14
        Matlacha Pass NWR 14
        Island Bay NWR 17
        Caloosahatchee NWR 17
    History and Purposes of the Refuges 20
        History 20
        Purposes 21
    Special Designations 22
        Wilderness Area 22
        Marine Protected Area 23
        Outstanding Florida Waters 23
        State Aquatic Preserves and State Park 23
        Charlotte Harbor National Estuary Program 23
    Ecosystem Context 25
        Peninsular Florida Landscape Conservation Cooperative 25
        South Florida Ecosystem 27
    Regional Conservation Plans and Initiatives 35
        Charlotte Harbor National Estuary Program and Comprehensive Conservation and
        Management Plan 36
        South Florida Multi-Species Recovery Plan 36
        South Florida Ecosystem Plan 37
        Gulf of Mexico Program 37
        Comprehensive Everglades Restoration Plan 37
        Northern Everglades and Estuaries Protection Program 38
        State Wildlife Action Plan 39
        Florida's Endangered and Threatened Species Management and Conservation Plan 40
        Florida Natural Areas Inventory 40
        Surface Water Improvement and Management Programs 40

State Aquatic Preserves 41
State Parks and Preserves 42
Wild and Scenic Rivers 42
Area Climate Change Plans 43
Ecological Threats and Problems..44
Water Quality, Quantity, and Timing 46
Exotic, Invasive, and Nuisance Species 46
Potential Effects of Climate Change 47
Physical Resources...50
Climate...50
Climate Change and Global Warming 53
Geology and Topography 55
Soils 59
Hydrology...60
Air Quality 63
Water Quality and Quantity..64
Biological Resources 69
Habitat 69
Wildlife 79
Exotic, Invasive, and Nuisance Species 83
Cultural Resources..85
Socioeconomic Environment...86
Regional Demographics and Economy..86
Recreation and Tourism...90
Refuge Administration and Management 92
Land Protection and Conservation 92
Visitor Services 93
Personnel, Operations, and Maintenance..93

III. PLAN DEVELOPMENT..95

Summary of Issues, Concerns, and Opportunities..95
Wildlife and Habitat Management..96
Resource Protection 98
Visitor Services 98
Refuge Administration 98
Wilderness Review..99
Public Review and Comment 99

IV. MANAGEMENT DIRECTION 103

Introduction 103
Vision 103
Goals, Objectives, and Strategies...104
Wildlife and Habitat Management..104
Resource Protection 118
Visitor Services 121
Refuge Administration 124

V. PLAN IMPLEMENTATION 129
Introduction 129
Proposed Projects 129
    Wildlife and Habitat Management 130
    Resource Protection 132
    Visitor Services 135

APPENDICES 139

APPENDIX A. GLOSSARY 139
Acronyms and Abbreviations 147

APPENDIX B. REFERENCES AND LITERATURE CITATIONS 151

APPENDIX C. RELEVANT LEGAL MANDATES AND EXECUTIVE ORDERS 169

APPENDIX D. PUBLIC INVOLVEMENT 181
Summary of Public Scoping Comments 181
Summary of Public Comments on the Draft CCP/EA and the Service's Responses 182
    Affiliations of Commenters 183
    Summary of Concerns and the Service's Responses 183

APPENDIX E. APPROPRIATE USE DETERMINATIONS 205

APPENDIX F. COMPATIBILITY DETERMINATIONS 211

APPENDIX G. INTRA-SERVICE SECTION 7 BIOLOGICAL EVALUATION 219

APPENDIX H. WILDERNESS REVIEW 235

APPENDIX I. REFUGE BIOTA 237
Birds of the J.N. "Ding" Darling National Wildlife Refuge Complex 237
Amphibians and Reptiles of J.N. "Ding" Darling National Wildlife Refuge Complex 241
Mammals in the Vicinity of J.N. "Ding" Darling National Wildlife Refuge Complex 243
Fish in the Vicinity of J.N. "Ding" Darling National Wildlife Refuge Complex 244

APPENDIX J. BUDGET REQUESTS 245

APPENDIX K. LIST OF PREPARERS 247

APPENDIX L. CONSULTATION AND COORDINATION 249

APPENDIX M. FINDING OF NO SIGNIFICANT IMPACT 255

LIST OF FIGURES

Figure 1.	J.N. "Ding" Darling NWR Complex.	2
Figure 2.	Pine Island NWR.	15
Figure 3.	Matlacha Pass NWR.	16
Figure 4.	Island Bay NWR.	18
Figure 5.	Caloosahatchee NWR.	19
Figure 6.	Landscape Conservation Cooperatives.	26
Figure 7.	South Florida Ecosystem.	28
Figure 8.	Area conservation lands.	29
Figure 9.	Historic and current surface water flows, South Florida Ecosystem.	35
Figure 10.	Land cover types for the area.	45
Figure 11.	Temperature and precipitation data, Fort Myers Federal Aviation Administration Airport, Florida, 1971-2000.	52
Figure 12.	Geologic map of the State of Florida.	57
Figure 13.	Geological map of the southern peninsula of the State of Florida.	58
Figure 14.	Ground water aquifers and lithology of Charlotte and Lee counties.	62
Figure 15.	Shellfish harvesting in Lower Charlotte Harbor.	67
Figure 16.	Vegetation for Pine Island NWR.	71
Figure 17.	Vegetation for Matlacha Pass NWR.	72
Figure 18.	Vegetation for Island Bay NWR.	73
Figure 19.	Vegetation for Caloosahatchee NWR.	74
Figure 20.	Seagrass beds in the Refuge Complex area.	76
Figure 21.	Manatee abundance and Critical Habitat in the Refuge Complex area.	77
Figure 22.	Current organizational chart for the J.N. "Ding" Darling NWR Complex.	94
Figure 23.	Proposed organizational chart for the J.N. "Ding" Darling NWR Complex.	126

LIST OF TABLES

Table 1. National parks, national wildlife refuges and state parks in Collier,
Lee and Charlotte counties designated as lands containing Outstanding Florida Waters. 24
Table 2. Types of natural communities in the Charlotte Harbor Basin. 30
Table 3. Imperiled animal species of the Charlotte Harbor National Estuary
Program study area. 33
Table 4. Nationwide Rivers Inventory, Florida segments near the refuges. 43
Table 5. Temperature, Precipitation, and Snowfall Summary, Fort Myers
Federal Aviation Administration Airport, Florida (083186) 51
Table 6. Vegetation for Pine Island NWR. 69
Table 7. Vegetation for Matlacha Pass NWR. 70
Table 8. Vegetation for Island Bay NWR. 70
Table 9. Vegetation for Caloosahatchee NWR. 70
Table 10. Nonnative plants found at Pine Island, Matlacha Pass, Island Bay,
and Caloosahatchee NWRs. 84
Table 11. Demographics of the Charlotte Harbor region. 88
Table 12. Employment projections, 2007-2015. 89
Table 13. Recreational visits to the J.N. "Ding" Darling NWR Complex, 2004. 91
Table 14. Visitor recreation expenditures at the J.N. "Ding Darling" NWR Complex,
2004 (in thousands of dollars). 91
Table 15. Wildlife watching activities in Florida by U.S. residents. Wildlife Watching
(observing, photographing, or feeding wildlife) 92
Table 16. Minimum staffing priorities identified in 2008 by the J.N. "Ding" Darling
NWR Complex for Pine Island, Matlacha Pass, Island Bay, and Caloosahatchee NWRs....99
Table 17. Step-down management plans to be developed during the
15-year life of the CCP. 138

COMPREHENSIVE CONSERVATION PLAN

I. Background

INTRODUCTION

Located along Florida's southwest Gulf coast in Lee and Charlotte counties, the J.N. "Ding" Darling National Wildlife Refuge (NWR) Complex includes Pine Island, Matlacha Pass, Island Bay, Caloosahatchee, and J.N. "Ding" Darling NWRs (Figure 1). The Pine Island, Matlacha Pass, Island Bay, and Caloosahatchee refuges were each established with the primary purpose as a preserve and breeding ground for native birds. These four refuges currently cover a total of about 1,201 acres (486 hectares [ha]), as follows: Pine Island – 602.24 acres (243.72 ha); Matlacha Pass – 538.25 acres (217.82 ha); Island Bay – 20.24 acres (8.19 ha); and Caloosahatchee – 40 acres (16.19 ha). Located within an estuarine system consisting predominantly of mangrove swamps, these four refuges provide a diversity of habitats that include mangrove islands and shorelines; saltwater marshes and ponds; tidal flats; and upland hardwood forests. They also provide protection for 13 federally listed and 25 state-listed species, as well as many species of wading birds, waterbirds, raptors and birds of prey, nearctic-neotropical migratory birds, shorebirds, and seabirds.

This Comprehensive Conservation Plan (CCP) for Pine Island, Matlacha Pass, Island Bay, and Caloosahatchee NWRs was prepared to guide the refuges' future management actions and direction over the next 15 years. Fish and wildlife conservation will receive first priority in refuge management; wildlife-dependent recreation will be allowed and encouraged as long as it is compatible with, and does not detract from, the missions of the refuges or the purposes for which they were established.

The U.S. Fish and Wildlife Service (Service) developed a range of alternatives that best met the goals and objectives of the refuges and that could be implemented within the 15-year planning period. The four refuges' Draft Comprehensive Conservation Plan and Environmental Assessment (Draft CCP/EA) described the Service's proposed plan, as well as other alternatives that were considered and their effects on the environment. The Draft CCP/EA was made available to state and federal government agencies, conservation partners, and the general public for review and comment during May-July, 2010. Comments from all entities were considered in the development of this final CCP. The public comments that were received and the Service's reponses to them are summarized in Appendix D, Public Involvement.

PURPOSE AND NEED FOR THE PLAN

The purpose of the CCP is to fully develop a management action that best achieves the refuges' purposes; attains the vision and goals developed for the refuges; contributes to the mission of the National Wildlife Refuge System (Refuge System); addresses key problems, issues, and relevant mandates; and is consistent with sound principles of fish and wildlife management.

Specifically, the plan is needed to:

- provide a clear statement of the refuges' management direction;
- provide refuge neighbors, visitors, and government officials with an understanding of the Service's management actions on and around the refuges;

Figure 1. J.N. "Ding" Darling NWR Complex.

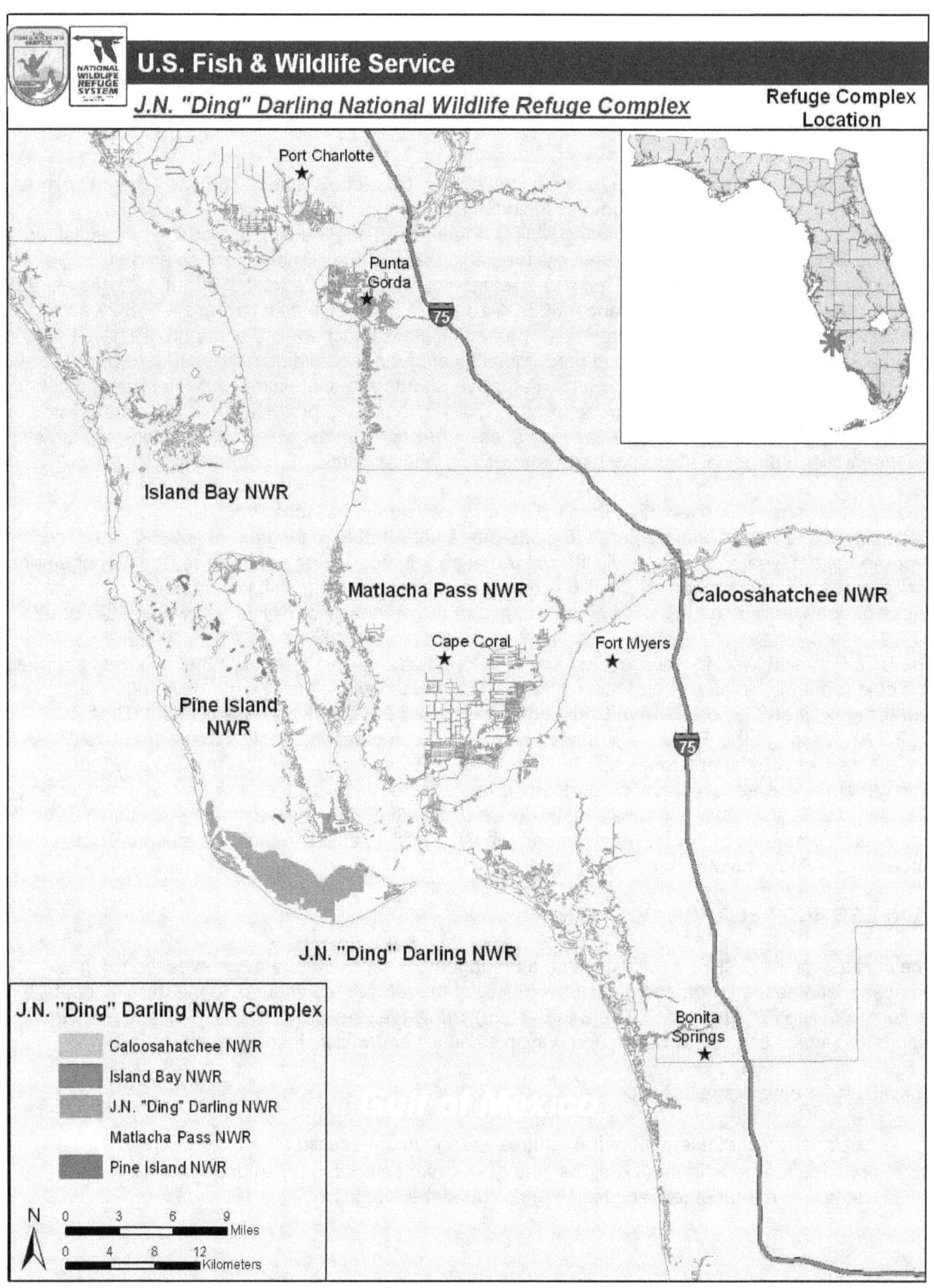

- ensure that the Service's management actions, including land protection and recreation and education programs, are consistent with the mandates of the National Wildlife Refuge System; and
- provide a basis for the development of budget requests for operations, maintenance, and capital improvement needs.

U.S. FISH AND WILDLIFE SERVICE

The U.S. Fish and Wildlife Service traces its roots to 1871 with the establishment of the Commission of Fisheries involved with research and fish culture. The once-independent commission was renamed the Bureau of Fisheries and placed under the Department of Commerce and Labor in 1903.

The Service also traces its roots to 1886 through the establishment of a Division of Economic Ornithology and Mammalogy in the Department of Agriculture. Research on the relationship of birds and animals to agriculture shifted to delineation of the range of plants and animals, so the name was changed to the Division of the Biological Survey in 1896.

The Department of Commerce's Bureau of Fisheries was combined with the Department of Agriculture's Bureau of Biological Survey on June 30, 1940, and transferred to the Department of the Interior as the Fish and Wildlife Service. The name was changed to the Bureau of Sport Fisheries and Wildlife in 1956, and finally to the Fish and Wildlife Service in 1974.

The Fish and Wildlife Service, working with others, is responsible for conserving, protecting, and enhancing fish and wildlife and their habitats for the continuing benefit of the American people through federal programs relating to wild birds, endangered species, certain marine mammals, fisheries, aquatic resources, and wildlife management activities (142 DM 1.1).

As part of its mission, the Service manages 551 national wildlife refuges and other units of the Refuge System covering 150 million acres (60.7 million ha). These areas comprise the National Wildlife Refuge System, the world's largest collection of lands and waters set aside specifically for fish and wildlife. The majority of these lands, 77 million acres (31 million ha), is in Alaska, while 54 million acres (21.8 ha) are part of three marine national monuments in the Pacific Ocean. The remaining acres/hectares are spread across the other 49 states and several United States territories. In addition to refuges, the Service manages thousands of small wetlands, 37 wetland management districts, 70 national fish hatcheries, 65 fishery resource offices, and 81 ecological services field stations. The Service enforces federal wildlife laws, administers the Endangered Species Act, manages migratory bird populations, restores nationally significant fisheries, conserves and restores wildlife habitat, and helps foreign governments with their conservation efforts. It also oversees the Federal Aid program that distributes hundreds of millions of dollars in excise taxes on fishing and hunting equipment to state fish and wildlife agencies.

NATIONAL WILDLIFE REFUGE SYSTEM

The mission of the National Wildlife Refuge System, as defined by the National Wildlife Refuge System Improvement Act of 1997, is:

> "... to administer a national network of lands and waters for the conservation, management, and where appropriate, restoration of the fish, wildlife and plant resources and their habitats within the United States for the benefit of present and future generations of Americans."

The National Wildlife Refuge System Improvement Act of 1997 (Improvement Act) established, for the first time, a clear legislative mission of wildlife conservation for the Refuge System. Actions were initiated in 1997 to comply with the direction of this new legislation, including an effort to complete comprehensive conservation plans for all refuges. These plans, which are completed with full public involvement, help guide the future management of refuges by establishing natural resources and recreation/education programs. Consistent with the Improvement Act, approved plans will serve as the guidelines for refuge management for the next 15 years. The Improvement Act states that each refuge shall be managed to:

- fulfill the mission of the National Wildlife Refuge System;
- fulfill the individual purposes of each refuge;
- consider the needs of wildlife first;
- fulfill the requirement of preparing a comprehensive conservation plan for each unit of the Refuge System;
- maintain the biological integrity, diversity, and environmental health of the Refuge System;
- recognize that wildlife-dependent recreation activities including hunting, fishing, wildlife observation, wildlife photography, and environmental education and interpretation are legitimate and priority public uses; and
- retain the authority of refuge managers to determine compatible public uses.

The following describes a few examples of the Service's national network of conservation lands. Pelican Island National Wildlife Refuge, the first refuge, was established in 1903 for the protection of colonial nesting birds in Florida, such as the snowy egret and brown pelican. Western refuges were established for American bison (1906), elk (1912), prong-horned antelope (1931), and desert bighorn sheep (1936) after overhunting, competition with cattle, and natural disasters decimated the once-abundant herds. The drought conditions of the Dust Bowl during the 1930s severely depleted breeding populations of ducks and geese. Refuges established during the Great Depression focused on waterfowl production areas, such as those that protected prairie wetlands in America's heartland. The emphasis on waterfowl continues today but also includes protection of wintering habitat in response to a dramatic loss of bottomland hardwoods. By 1973, the Service had begun to focus on establishing refuges for threatened and endangered species.

National wildlife refuges connect visitors to their natural resource heritage and provide them with an understanding and appreciation of fish and wildlife ecology to help them understand their role in the environment. Wildlife-dependent recreation on refuges also generates economic benefits to local communities. According to the report, *Banking on Nature 2006: The Economic Benefits to Local Communities of National Wildlife Refuge Visitation*, approximately 35 million people visited national wildlife refuges in 2006, generating almost $1.7 billion in total economic activity and creating almost 27,000 private sector jobs, producing about $543 million in employment income (Carver and Caudill 2007). Additionally, recreational spending on refuges generated nearly $185.3 million in tax revenues at the local, county, state, and federal levels (Carver and Caudill 2007). As the number of visitors grows, significant economic benefits are realized by local communities. In 2006, 87 million people, 16 years and older, fished (30 million), hunted (12.5 million), or observed wildlife (71 million), generating $120 billion (U.S. Department of the Interior, Fish and Wildlife Service, and U.S. Department of Commerce, U.S. Census Bureau 2007). In a study completed in 2002 on 15 refuges, visitation had grown 36 percent in 7 years. At the same time, the number of jobs generated in the surrounding communities grew to 120 per refuge, up from 87 jobs in 1995, pouring more than $2.2 million into local economies. The 15 refuges in the study were Chincoteague (Virginia); National Elk (Wyoming); Crab Orchard (Illinois); Eufaula (Alabama); Charles M. Russell (Montana); Umatilla (Oregon); Quivira (Kansas); Mattamuskeet (North Carolina); Upper Souris (North Dakota); San Francisco Bay (California);

Laguna Atacosa (Texas); Horicon (Wisconsin); Las Vegas (Nevada); Tule Lake (California); and Tensas River (Louisiana) the same refuges identified for the 1995 study. Other findings also validate the belief that communities near refuges benefit economically. Expenditures on food, lodging, and transportation grew to $6.8 million per refuge, up 31 percent from $5.2 million in 1995. For each federal dollar spent on the Refuge System, surrounding communities benefited with $4.43 in recreation expenditures and $1.42 in job-related income (Caudill and Laughland unpublished data).

Volunteers continue to be a major contributor to the success of the Refuge System. In 2006, over 36,000 volunteers contributed nearly 1.5 million hours on refuges nationwide. The value of their labor was more than $26 million; their in-kind services the equivalent of 696 full-time employees.

The wildlife and habitat vision for national wildlife refuges stresses that wildlife comes first; that ecosystems, biodiversity, and wilderness are vital concepts in refuge management; that refuges must be healthy and growth must be strategic; and that the Refuge System serves as a model for habitat management with broad participation from others.

The Improvement Act stipulates that comprehensive conservation plans be prepared in consultation with adjoining federal, state, and private landowners and that the Service develop and implement a process to ensure an opportunity for active public involvement in the preparation and revision (every 15 years) of the plans.

All lands of the Refuge System will be managed in accordance with an approved comprehensive conservation plan that will guide management decisions and set forth strategies for achieving refuge unit purposes. The CCP will be consistent with sound resource management principles, practices, and legal mandates, including Service compatibility standards and other Service policies, guidelines, and planning documents (602 FW 1.1).

LEGAL AND POLICY CONTEXT

LEGAL MANDATES, ADMINISTRATIVE AND POLICY GUIDELINES, AND OTHER SPECIAL CONSIDERATIONS

Administration of national wildlife refuges is guided by the mission and goals of the Refuge System, congressional legislation, presidential executive orders, and international treaties. Policies for management options of refuges are further refined by administrative guidelines established by the Secretary of the Interior and by policy guidelines established by the Director of the Fish and Wildlife Service. The treaties and laws relevant to the administration of the Refuge System and management of national wildlife refuges are summarized in Appendix C.

These treaties, laws, administrative guidelines, and policy guidelines assist the refuge manager in making decisions pertaining to soil, water, air, flora, fauna, and other natural resources; historical and cultural resources; research and recreation on refuge lands; and provide a framework for cooperation between the Pine Island, Matlacha Pass, Island Bay, and Caloosahatchee NWRs and their partners and adjoining private landowners.

Lands within the Refuge System are closed to public use unless specifically and legally opened. No refuge use may be allowed unless it is determined to be compatible. A compatible use is a use that, in the sound professional judgment of the refuge manager, will not materially interfere with or detract from the fulfillment of the mission of the Refuge System or the purposes of the particular refuge in question. All programs and uses must be evaluated based on mandates set forth in the Improvement Act. Those mandates are to:

- contribute to ecosystem goals, as well as refuge purposes and goals;
- conserve, manage, and restore fish, wildlife, and plant resources and their habitats;
- monitor the trends of fish, wildlife, and plants;
- manage and ensure appropriate visitor uses as those uses benefit the conservation of fish and wildlife resources and contribute to the enjoyment of the public; and
- ensure that visitor activities are compatible with refuge purposes.

The Improvement Act further identifies six priority wildlife-dependent recreational uses. These uses are hunting, fishing, wildlife observation, wildlife photography, and environmental education and interpretation. As priority public uses of the Refuge System, they receive priority consideration over other public uses in planning and management.

BIOLOGICAL INTEGRITY, DIVERSITY, AND ENVIRONMENTAL HEALTH POLICY

The Improvement Act directs the Service to ensure that the biological integrity, diversity, and environmental health of the Refuge System are maintained for the benefit of present and future generations of Americans (601 FW3). The Biological Integrity Policy is an additional directive for refuge managers to follow while achieving refuge purpose(s) and the Refuge System mission. It provides for the consideration and protection of the broad spectrum of fish, wildlife, and habitat resources found on refuges and associated ecosystems. When evaluating the appropriate management direction for refuges, refuge managers will use sound professional judgment to determine their refuges' contributions to biological integrity, diversity, and environmental health at multiple landscape scales. Sound professional judgment incorporates field experience, knowledge of refuge resources, the refuge's role within an ecosystem, applicable laws, and best available science, including consultation with others both inside and outside the Service.

NATIONAL AND INTERNATIONAL CONSERVATION PLANS AND INITIATIVES

Multiple partnerships have been developed among government and private entities to address the environmental problems affecting regions. A large amount of conservation and protection information defines the role of refuges at the local, national, international, and ecosystem levels. Conservation initiatives include broad-scale planning and cooperation between affected parties to address declining trends of natural, physical, social, and economic environments. The conservation guidance described below, along with issues, problems, and trends, was reviewed and integrated where appropriate into the CCP.

The CCP supports several key national and international conservation plans and initiatives, including the North American Bird Conservation Initiative (including the North American Waterfowl Management Plan, the Partners in Flight Bird Conservation Plan, North American Waterbird Conservation Plan, and the U.S. Shorebird Conservation Plan); the Western Hemisphere Shorebird Reserve Network; American Oystercatcher Conservation Plan; the National Wetlands Priority Conservation Plan; and the efforts and activities of the Office of Ocean and Coastal Resource Management.

NORTH AMERICAN BIRD CONSERVATION INITIATIVE

Started in 1999, the North American Bird Conservation Initiative is a coalition of government agencies, private organizations, academic institutions, and private industry leaders in the United States, Canada, and Mexico working to ensure the long-term health of North America's native bird populations. The initiative fosters an integrated approach to bird conservation to benefit all birds in all habitats. The four international and national bird initiatives include the North American Waterfowl Management Plan; the Partners in Flight Bird Conservation Plan; the North American Waterbird Conservation Plan; and the U.S. Shorebird Conservation Plan.

North American Waterfowl Management Plan

The North American Waterfowl Management Plan (NAWMP) is an international action plan to conserve migratory birds throughout the continent. The plan's goal is to return waterfowl populations to their 1970s' levels by conserving wetland and upland habitat. Canada and the United States signed the plan in 1986 in reaction to critically low numbers of waterfowl. Mexico joined in 1994, making it a truly continental effort. The NAWMP is a partnership of federal, provincial, state, and municipal governments, nongovernmental organizations, private companies, and many individuals, all working towards achieving better wetland habitat for the benefit of migratory birds, other wetland-associated species and people. Its purpose is to provide a forum for discussion of major, long-term international waterfowl issues and to make recommendations to directors of the participating countries' national wildlife agencies. The plan's projects are international in scope, but implemented at regional levels. These projects contribute to the protection of habitat and wildlife species across the North American landscape.

Partners in Flight Bird Conservation Plan

Managed as part of the Partners in Flight (PIF) Bird Conservation Plan, the Subtropical Florida physiographic area represents a scientifically based land bird conservation planning effort that ensures long-term maintenance of healthy populations of native land birds, primarily nongame land birds. Nongame land birds have been vastly underrepresented in conservation efforts, and many are exhibiting significant declines. This plan is voluntary and nonregulatory, and focuses on relatively common species in areas where conservation actions can be most effective, rather than the frequent local emphasis on rare and peripheral populations. Plans for the refuges include providing suitable nesting, foraging, and/or resting habitats for many priority species identified for the peninsular and subtropical physiographic areas, including the mangrove cuckoo (*Coccyzus minor*); Florida prairie warbler (*Dendroica discolor paludicola*); palm warbler (*Dendroica palmarum*); gray kingbird (*Tyrannus dominicensis*); black-whiskered vireo (*Vireo altiloquus*); wood stork (*Myctria americana*); reddish egret (*Egretta rufescens*); white ibis (*Eudocimus albus*); mottled duck (*Anas fulvigula*); American kestrel (*Falco sparverius*); and the short-tailed hawk (*Buteo brachyurus*).

Northern American Waterbird Conservation Plan

The North American Waterbird Conservation Plan (NAWCP) provides a framework for the conservation and management of 210 species of waterbirds in 29 nations. Threats to waterbird populations include destruction of inland and coastal wetlands, introduced predators and invasive species, pollutants, mortality from fisheries and industries, disturbance, and conflicts arising from abundant species. Particularly important habitats of the southeast region include pelagic areas, marshes, forested wetlands, and barrier and sea island complexes. Fifteen species of waterbirds are federally listed, including breeding populations of wood storks, Mississippi sandhill cranes (*Grus*

Canadensis pulla), whooping cranes (*Grus americana*), interior least terns (*Sterna antillarum*), and Gulf Coast populations of brown pelicans (*Pelecanus occidentalis*). A key objective of this plan is the standardization of data collection efforts to better recommend effective conservation measures.

The Southeastern U.S. Waterbird Conservation Plan stresses protection of nesting and foraging habitats for both colonial and noncolonial waterbirds. Charlotte Harbor and these four refuges support or could potentially support important colonies of beach-nesting species such as the sandwich tern (*Sterna sandvicencis*), royal tern (*Sterna maxima*), least tern, black skimmer (*Rynchops niger*), and laughing gull (*Larus atricilla*), and provide important mangrove nesting habitat for the brown pelican, anhinga (*Anhinga anhinga*), and most long-legged wading species such as reddish egrets.

U.S. Shorebird Conservation Plan

The U.S. Shorebird Conservation Plan is a partnership effort throughout the United States to ensure that stable and self-sustaining populations of shorebird species are restored and protected. The plan was developed by a wide range of agencies, organizations, and shorebird experts for separate regions of the country, and identifies conservation goals, critical habitat conservation needs, key research needs, and proposed education and outreach programs to increase the awareness of shorebirds and the threats they face. Primary objectives of this plan are the development of a scientifically-sound monitoring system to provide practical information to researchers and land managers; the identification of principles upon which management plans can integrate shorebird habitat conservation with multiple species strategies; and the design of a strategy for increasing public awareness and information concerning wetlands and shorebirds. The refuges are part of the Southeastern Coastal Plains and Caribbean Region, which is important for breeding shorebirds, as well as for supporting transient species during both northbound and southbound movements. Breeding species of highest regional priority include the American oystercatcher (*Haematopus palliatus*), snowy plover (*Charadrius alexandrinus*), Wilson's plover (*Charadrius wilsonia*), and piping plover (*Charadrius melodus*). The refuges provide breeding habitat for the American oystercatcher, snowy plover, and Wilson's plover and critical habitat for wintering piping plovers.

WESTERN HEMISPHERE SHOREBIRD RESERVE NETWORK

The mission of the Western Hemisphere Shorebird Reserve Network is to conserve shorebirds and their habitats through a network of key sites across the Americas. Sites are designated and managed to sustain all native shorebird species and their current populations throughout the Americas. The Network works to build a strong system of sites used by shorebirds throughout their migratory ranges; develop science and management tools that expand the scope and pace of habitat conservation at each site within the Network; establish local, regional and international recognition for sites, raising new public awareness and generating conservation funding opportunities; and, serve as an international resource, convener and strategist for issues related to shorebird and habitat conservation. Although the refuges are not currently a member of the Western Hemisphere Shorebird Reserve Network, they do play an important role for shorebirds in the Western Hemisphere.

AMERICAN OYSTERCATCHER CONSERVATION PLAN

The *American Oystercatcher Conservation Plan for the Atlantic and Gulf Coasts of the United States* (Schulte et al. 2006) focuses on *Haematopus palliatus* in the United States, referred to as the American oystercatcher or simply as oystercatchers. The present plan addresses only the populations on the East and Gulf coasts and summarizes current knowledge of the life history, distribution, and population trends of the species; describes current threats; lists research and management needs; and outlines recommended conservation actions. Conservation activities recommended to address these threats include the identification and protection of existing habitat; creation of new habitat through carefully designed use of dredge-spoil materials; management of existing protected areas to reduce predation and disturbance; and control of predator populations, especially in the nesting season. American oystercatchers are found on the refuges and the refuges provide breeding habitat for them.

NATIONAL WETLANDS PRIORITY CONSERVATION PLAN

The objective of the National Wetlands Priority Conservation Plan (NWPCP) is to assist agencies in focusing their acquisition efforts on the more important, scarce and vulnerable wetlands in the Nation. The NWPCP may also be used to establish priorities for wetlands protection that do not involve acquisition. In general, wetlands given priority consideration for acquisition will be those that provide a high degree of public benefits, that are representative of rare or declining wetland types within an ecoregion, and that are subject to identifiable threats of loss or degradation. Threshold criteria to be considered in determining acquisition priorities include functions and values of wetlands, historic wetland losses, and threat of future wetland losses. The NWPCP considers the following:

- Estimated proportion remaining of the respective types of wetlands which existed at the time of European settlement.
- Estimated current rate of loss and threat of future losses of the respective types of wetlands.
- Contributions of the respective types of wetlands to:
    - wildlife, including endangered and threatened species, migratory birds, and resident species;
    - commercial and sport fisheries;
    - surface and groundwater quality and quantity, and flood control;
    - outdoor recreation; and
    - other areas or concerns which are considered appropriate. These areas include natural areas, education, research, scenic, archaeological, historical and open space.

When a wetland site is added to the list of wetland sites warranting priority consideration for acquisition, it does not mean that the wetland necessarily will be acquired; rather, it means that the site qualifies for acquisition consideration. Any subsequent decision to purchase property must rely on additional data, funding availability, policies, and conditions that are not a part of the NWPCP. Any listing of wetlands for acquisition consideration has no direct bearing on federal regulatory programs or the evaluation of wetlands for regulatory purposes.

The refuges play a role in the NWPCP by protecting three of the most threatened wetlands in the nation, according to the National Wetlands Inventory. These wetlands are (1) estuarine intertidal forested scrub-shrub (93.2 percent lost between 1954 and 1974); (2) marine intertidal (57.5 percent lost between 1954 and 1974); and (3) palustrine scrub-shrub (56.7 percent lost between 1954 and 1974). The NWPCP has identified Florida as one of the coastal areas where the declining wetland types warrant priority consideration for protection and federal and state acquisition.

OFFICE OF OCEAN AND COASTAL RESOURCE MANAGEMENT

The Office of Ocean and Coastal Resource Management (OCRM) of the National Oceanic and Atmospheric Administration (NOAA) provides national leadership, strategic direction, and guidance to state and territory coastal programs and estuarine research reserves. The OCRM oversees six major programs. Each program has a national reach, but is designed to focus on local resources and needs. The OCRM works with state and territory coastal resource managers to develop a scientifically based, comprehensive national system of marine protected areas (MPAs) and supports effective management and sound science to protect, sustain and restore coral reef ecosystems.

These activities are mandated by the Coastal Zone Management Act (CZMA), the Marine Protected Area (MPA) Executive Order, and the Coral Reef Conservation Act. Numerous refuge management activities fall under the CZMA and the MPA designation for three of the refuges.

RELATIONSHIP TO STATE WILDLIFE AGENCY

A provision of the Improvement Act, and subsequent agency policy, is that the Service shall ensure timely and effective cooperation and collaboration with other state fish and game agencies and tribal governments during the course of acquiring and managing refuges. State wildlife management areas and national wildlife refuges provide the foundation for the protection of species, and contribute to the overall health and sustainment of fish and wildlife species in the State of Florida. For these four refuges, the primary state partners include the Florida Fish and Wildlife Conservation Commission (FWC); the Florida Department of Environmental Protection (FDEP); and the Southwest (SWFWMD) and South Florida (SFWMD) water management districts. These state agencies are charged with enforcement responsibilities relating to migratory birds, trust species, fisheries, and wetlands, as well as with management of the state's natural resources.

The FWC's mission is to manage fish and wildlife resources for their long-term well-being and the benefit of people. It protects and manages more than 575 species of wildlife, more than 200 native species of freshwater fish, and more than 500 native species of saltwater fish; while balancing these species' needs with the needs of more than 18 million residents (U.S. Census Bureau 2007) and the nearly 84 million annual visitors (Florida Department of Transportation and University of South Florida 2008) who share the land and water with Florida's wildlife. The FWC's responsibilities include:

- Law Enforcement – to protect fish and wildlife, keep waterways safe for millions of boaters and cooperate with other law enforcement agencies providing homeland security.
- Research – to provide information for the FWC and others to make management decisions based on the best science available involving fish and wildlife populations, habitat issues and the human-dimension aspects of conservation.
- Management – to manage the state's fish and wildlife resources based on the latest scientific data to conserve some of the most complex and delicate ecosystems in the world along with a wide diversity of species.
- Outreach – to communicate with a variety of audiences to encourage participation, responsible citizenship and stewardship of the state's natural resources.

Both the FWC and FDEP manage state lands and waters. The FWC manages 4.3 million acres (1.7 million ha) of public lands and 220,000 acres (89,030 ha) of private lands for recreation and conservation purposes. The FDEP manages 150 state parks covering nearly 600,000 acres (242,811 ha) and 46 coastal and aquatic managed areas, totaling over 5 million acres (2 million ha) of submerged lands and coastal uplands. The SWFWMD and SFWMD are two of Florida's five water management agencies. They are responsible for managing ground and surface water supplies in all or part of southwest and south Florida. These two water management districts include all or parts of 29 counties and cover a total area of almost 28,000 square miles (17.9 million acres or 7.25 million ha), largely consisting of wetlands or historically wet areas. The area is managed for the purposes of regional flood control, water supply and conservation, water quality protection, and ecosystem restoration. Of less acreage, but not of less importance, are upland areas managed by the water management districts. These areas preserve wetlands, waters, and wildlife and provide critical buffers between rapidly encroaching development and important wetland areas.

The State of Florida's participation and contribution throughout this planning process will provide for ongoing opportunities and open dialogue to improve the ecological sustainment of fish and wildlife in Florida. An essential part of comprehensive conservation planning is the integration of common mission objectives, where appropriate.

II. Refuge Overview

INTRODUCTION

The Pine Island, Matlacha Pass, Island Bay, and Caloosahatchee NWRs are administered as part of the J.N. "Ding" Darling NWR Complex (Figure 1). The Refuge Complex is part of the largest undeveloped mangrove ecosystem in the United States, and is world famous for its spectacular wading bird populations. Nesting and roosting islands make up the majority of the lands in these four satellite refuges of the Refuge Complex. The rare, threatened, and endangered species of management concern to the refuges include the wood stork (*Myctria americana*); roseate spoonbill (*Platalea ajaja*); roseate tern (*Sterna dougallii dougallii*); black skimmer (*Rynchops niger*); American oystercatcher (*Haematopus palliatus*); snowy plover (*Charadrius alexandrinus*); Wilson's plover (*Charadrius wilsonia*); red knot (*Calidris canutus*); piping plover (*Charadris melodus*); bald eagle (*Haliaeetus leucocephalus*); mangrove cuckoo (*Coccyzus minor*); black-whiskered vireo (*Vireo altiloquus*); gray kingbird (*Tyrannus dominicensis*); Florida prairie warbler (*Dendroica discolor paludicola*); Florida bonneted bat (*Eumops floridanus*); West Indian manatee (*Trichechus manatus*); ornate diamondback terrapin (*Malaclemys terrapin macrospilota*); loggerhead sea turtle (*Dermochelys coriacea*); green sea turtle (*Chelonia mydas mydas*); Kemp's ridley sea turtle (*Lepidochelys kempii*); hawksbill sea turtle (*Eretmochelys imbricata*); gopher tortoise (*Gopherus polyphemus*); American alligator (*Alligator mississippiensis*); American crocodile (*Crocodylus acutus*); eastern indigo snake (*Drymarchon corais couperi*); Gulf sturgeon (*Acipenser oxyrinchus desotoi*); and smalltooth sawfish (*Prisits pectinata*). Beyond rare, threatened, and endangered species, the refuges are also important for wading birds, waterbirds, raptors and birds of prey, nearctic-neotropical migratory birds, shorebirds, and seabirds. All four satellite refuges are closed to the public.

The four refuges cover a total of approximately 1,201 acres (486 ha).

- **Pine Island NWR** is approximately 602.24 acres (243.72 ha) with 18 mangrove islands and little upland habitat located in Pine Island Sound. The acquisition boundary is held in fee title with several islands covered under Bureau of Land Management (BLM) withdrawals.
- **Matlacha Pass NWR** is approximately 538.25 acres (217.82 ha) encompassing 31 islands and peninsulas and the Terrapin Creek Tract near the Sanibel Causeway at Bunche Beach. Piping plover critical habitat is designated on the refuge. The acquisition boundary is held in fee title with several islands covered under BLM withdrawals.
- **Island Bay NWR** consists of six undeveloped and roadless tracts of land on five small islands totaling approximately 20.24 acres (8.19 ha), is predominantly upland hardwood forests, and is located in the Cape Haze area of Charlotte Harbor. The acquisition boundary is held in fee title.
- **Caloosahatchee NWR** is 40 acres (16.19 ha) on four mangrove islands, located on the Caloosahatchee River, in Fort Myers.

The J.N. "Ding" Darling NWR is covered in a separate CCP. This CCP focuses on the four satellite refuges of the Refuge Complex: Pine Island, Matlacha Pass, Island Bay, and Caloosahatchee. The CCP for the four refuges contains concepts to guide further development and implementation of land use and management programs and any associated facilities and management structures for the next 15 years. Consideration of the refuges' physical, biological, and cultural resources, along with the socioeconomic environment and refuge management and administration, are taken into account and analyzed to produce an overview of the refuges and the challenges they face.

PINE ISLAND NWR

Pine Island NWR (Figure 2) is located on the southwest coast of Florida, north of Sanibel Island in Pine Island Sound in Lee County. The 602.24-acre (243.72-ha) refuge includes 18 islands and consists of densely forested red (*Rhizophora mangle*) and black (*Avicennia germinans*) mangroves with little uplands habitat. Mangrove swamp is the dominant cover type on 89% of the refuge, while less than 10% is upland hardwood forests. Whoopee, Benedict, and Patricio islands are the only islands within Pine Island NWR able to support upland vegetation, due to higher elevated upland sand ridges or shell mounds.

Pine Island NWR is managed as a natural area and is closed to the public. The refuge's islands consist primarily of mangrove forests needing little manipulation or physical management. Periodic biological and wildlife population surveys are conducted by the partners and by Refuge Complex staff to assess wildlife communities utilizing the area. The refuge's uplands and wetlands are maintained in their natural condition in order to provide undisturbed habitat for birds, fish, invertebrates, and other animals. Law enforcement patrols are routinely conducted for the protection of wildlife species. Occasionally, upland habitats, primarily on Patricio Island, are treated for exotic plants using prescribed burns, chemical treatment, and/or hand pulling. Colonial bird roost surveys are conducted quarterly on Bird Island and the nearby Broken Islands (off the refuge). Colonial bird nest surveys are conducted monthly from January to October on Broken Islands, Hemp Key, and several other refuge and state-owned islands in Matlacha Pass and Pine Island Sound.

MATLACHA PASS NWR

Matlacha Pass NWR (Figure 3) is located within the Matlacha Pass estuary in Lee County, Florida, approximately 8 miles northwest of Fort Myers. This refuge encompasses 31 islands and peninsulas and the Terrapin Creek Tract, totaling about 538.25 acres (217.82 ha) and consisting primarily of tidally influenced wetlands with low sand and shell ridges. Mangrove swamp is the dominant cover type on 88% of the refuge, while upland hardwood forests represent 10% of the refuge. The vegetation of many of the islands is almost exclusively red mangrove, but on some islands the interior wetlands are dominated by black mangroves, often mixed with white mangroves (*Laguncularia racemosa*) and buttonwood (*Conocarpus erectus*). The sand and shell ridges are vegetated with cabbage palms (*Sabal palmetto*) and tropical species, such as seagrape (*Coccoloba uvifera*), strangler fig (*Ficus aurea*), and gumbo limbo (*Bursera simaruba*).

Matlacha Pass NWR's uplands and wetlands are maintained in their natural condition to provide undisturbed habitat for birds, fish, invertebrates, and other animals. Periodic biological and wildlife population surveys are conducted by the partners and by Refuge Complex staff to assess wildlife communities utilizing the area. Occasionally, the upland habitats on Skimmer Island are treated for exotic plants, primarily Australian pines (*Casuarina equisetifolia*), using prescribed burns, chemical treatment, and/or hand pulling. Skimmer Island has been managed to try and attract nesting black skimmers and least terns away from construction sites on the mainland. Colonial bird nesting surveys are conducted annually from April through August on Lower Bird Key, Upper Bird Key, and Lumpkin Key. Colonial bird roost surveys are conducted quarterly on Lower Bird Key. Law enforcement patrols are routinely conducted for the protection of wildlife species and Calusa Indian sites. All the islands of Matlacha Pass NWR are closed to public access due to the fact that they are roosting and nesting islands for a variety of birds. Access to the waters surrounding these islands is only by boat, although navigation is difficult because of numerous oyster bars, seagrass beds, and shallow back bay/estuary waters. The refuge can be viewed by boat from the Intracoastal Waterway south of Charlotte Harbor between the eastern boundary of Pine Island and western boundary of Cape Coral.

Figure 2. Pine Island NWR.

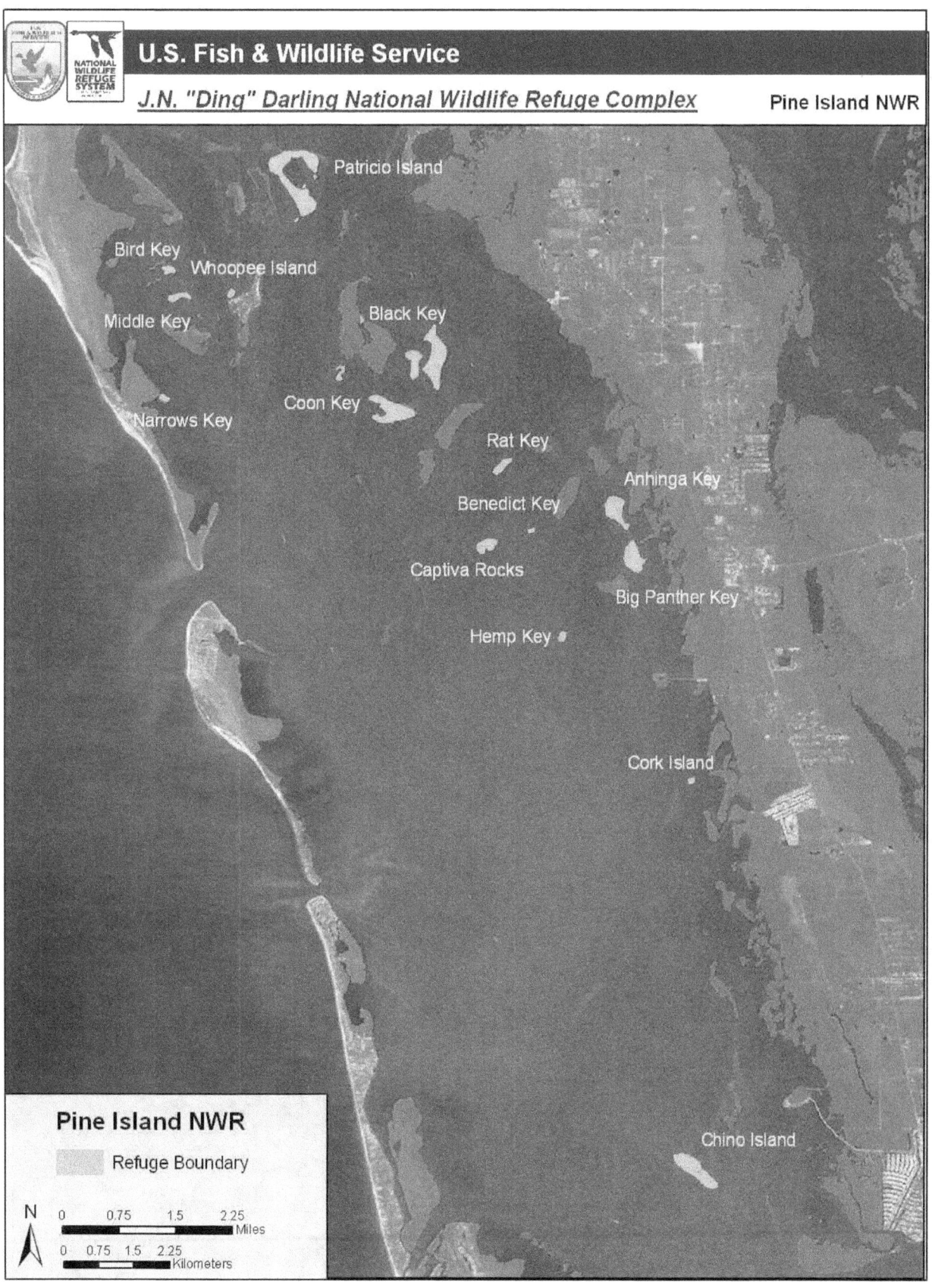

Figure 3. Matlacha Pass NWR.

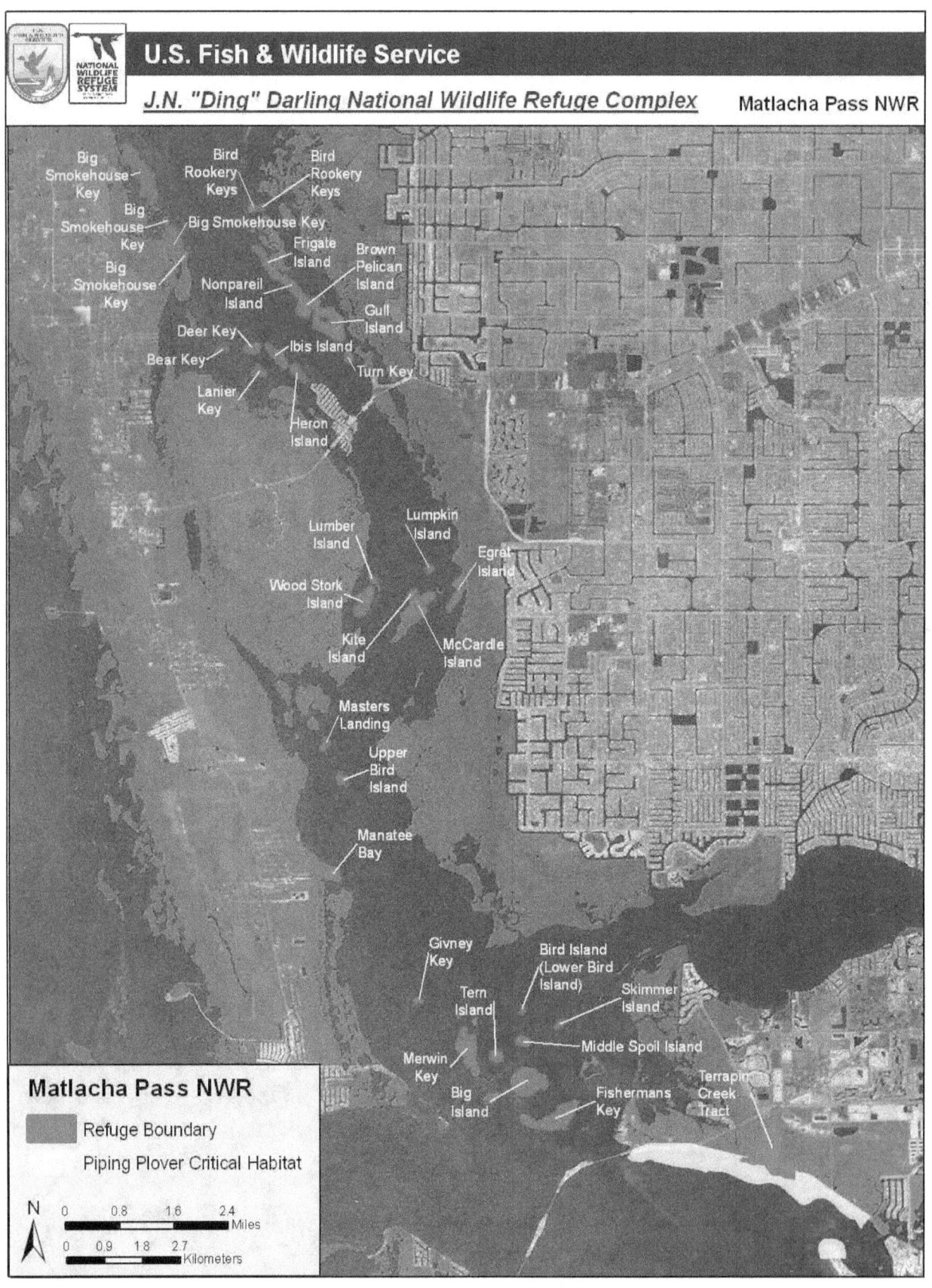

ISLAND BAY NWR

Island Bay NWR (Figure 4) is located in the Cape Haze area of Charlotte Harbor, in Charlotte County, Florida, southwest of Punta Gorda. By boat, this refuge is located on the north side of Charlotte Harbor in Turtle Bay. The nearest population centers are Port Charlotte, lying approximately 15 miles to the east and Fort Myers, roughly 23 miles to the southeast. Located in a vast complex of mangrove islands and brackish waters, Island Bay NWR consists of six undeveloped, roadless tracts of land totaling 20.24 acres (8.19 ha) occupying the higher portions of several islands and their mangrove shorelines. Upland hardwood forests represent the dominant cover type on 73% of the refuge, while mangrove swamp represents 19%. The refuge's islands include Gallagher Key, Bull Key, and two unnamed keys located between Bull and Turtle bays. Two other tracts, the Cash and John Quiet mounds, are located on the edge of Turtle Bay, reaching heights of 10 to 20 feet above sea level. The entire refuge is designated as a wilderness area and is closed to public access.

The Refuge Complex's staff manages Island Bay NWR as a natural area. Periodic biological and wildlife population surveys are conducted by the partners and by Refuge Complex staff to assess wildlife communities utilizing the area. Law enforcement patrols are routinely conducted for the protection of wildlife species and Calusa Indian artifact sites. Occasionally, the refuge staff chemically treats Brazilian pepper (*Schinus terebinthifolius*), an invasive exotic plant that threatens the overall plant community. Access to the waters surrounding the islands that make up the Island Bay NWR is only by boat. Navigation in these areas is difficult because of the existence of numerous oyster bars, seagrass beds, and shallow back bay/estuary waters.

CALOOSAHATCHEE NWR

Caloosahatchee NWR (Figure 5) is located in Lee County on the Caloosahatchee River within the city of Fort Myers, adjacent to the Florida Power and Light Company's Orange River Power Plant and the Orange River's outflow, and under the bridge where Interstate 75 crosses the Caloosahatchee River. This refuge includes 40 acres (16.19 ha), where 18.26 acres (7.39 ha) are spread across four islands with mangrove shorelines containing red, black, and white mangroves, and with upland island habitats covered with a variety of fresh and brackish water vegetation. The remaining 21.74 acres (8.8 ha) remain to be resolved and are not included in Figure 5. Mangrove swamp is the dominant cover type on 67% of the refuge, while upland hardwood forests represent the remaining 33%.

Caloosahatchee NWR is managed as a natural area. Periodic biological and wildlife population surveys are conducted by the partners and by Refuge Complex staff to assess wildlife communities utilizing the area. The refuge's uplands and wetlands are maintained in their natural condition in order to provide undisturbed habitat for birds, fish, invertebrates, and other animals. Occasionally, the Refuge Complex staff chemically treats Brazilian pepper, an invasive exotic plant that threatens the overall plant community. Law enforcement patrols are routinely conducted for the protection of wildlife species, including the endangered West Indian manatee which is commonly seen in the waters surrounding the refuge. A manatee viewing area is located adjacent to the refuge and is managed through a partnership with Lee County Manatee Park. Access to the waters surrounding these islands is only by boat, although navigation is difficult because of numerous oyster bars, seagrass beds, and shallow back bay/estuary waters. By boat, the refuge includes Buzzard Roost, an adjacent smaller island, the island that is located directly under the I-75 bridge as one heads up the Caloosahatchee River, and an adjacent smaller island for a total of four islands. Speed restrictions are strictly enforced for the protection of the West Indian manatee.

Figure 4. Island Bay NWR.

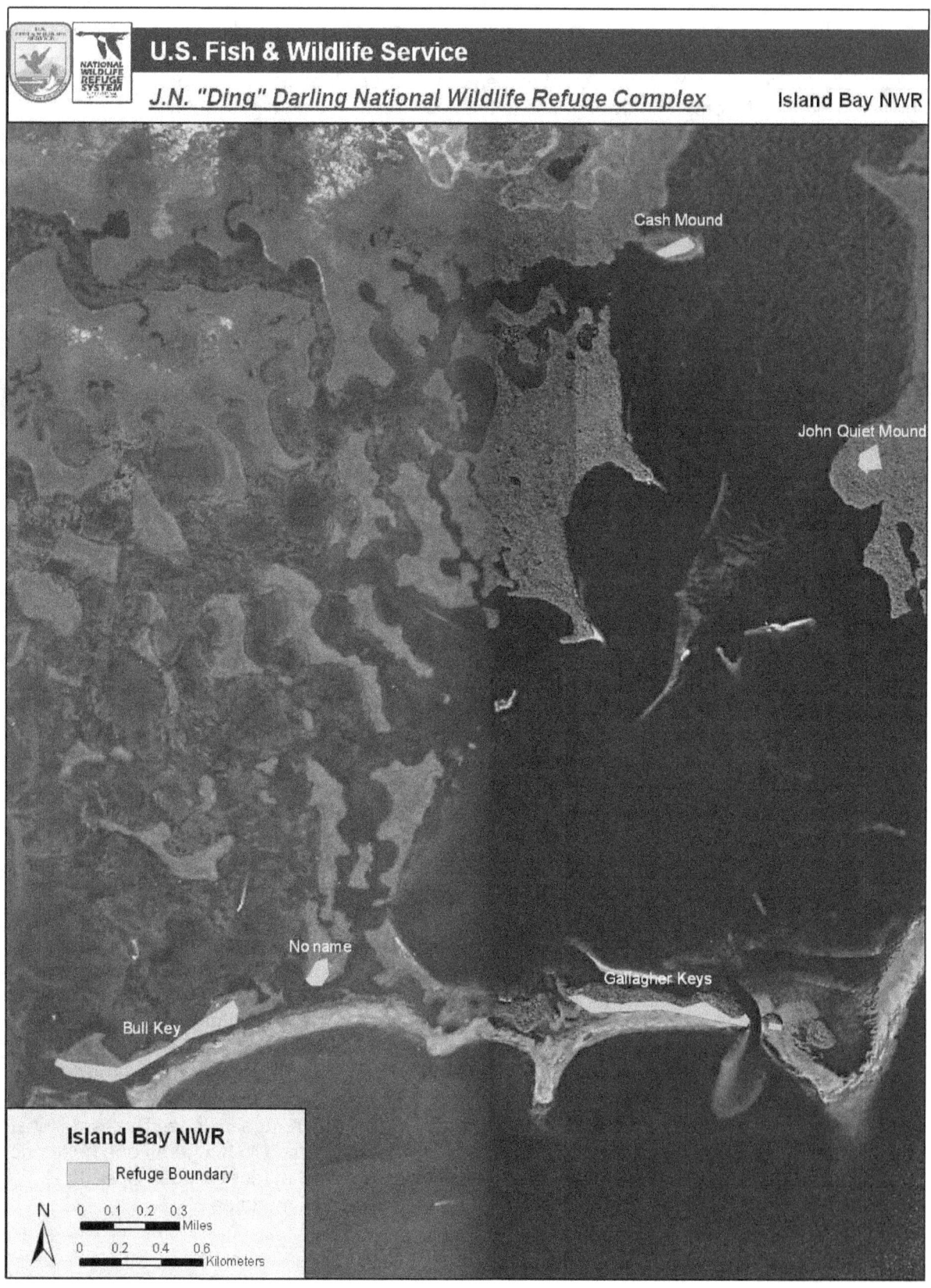

18 Pine Island, Matlacha Pass, Island Bay, and Caloosahatchee National Wildlife Refuges

Figure 5. Caloosahatchee NWR.

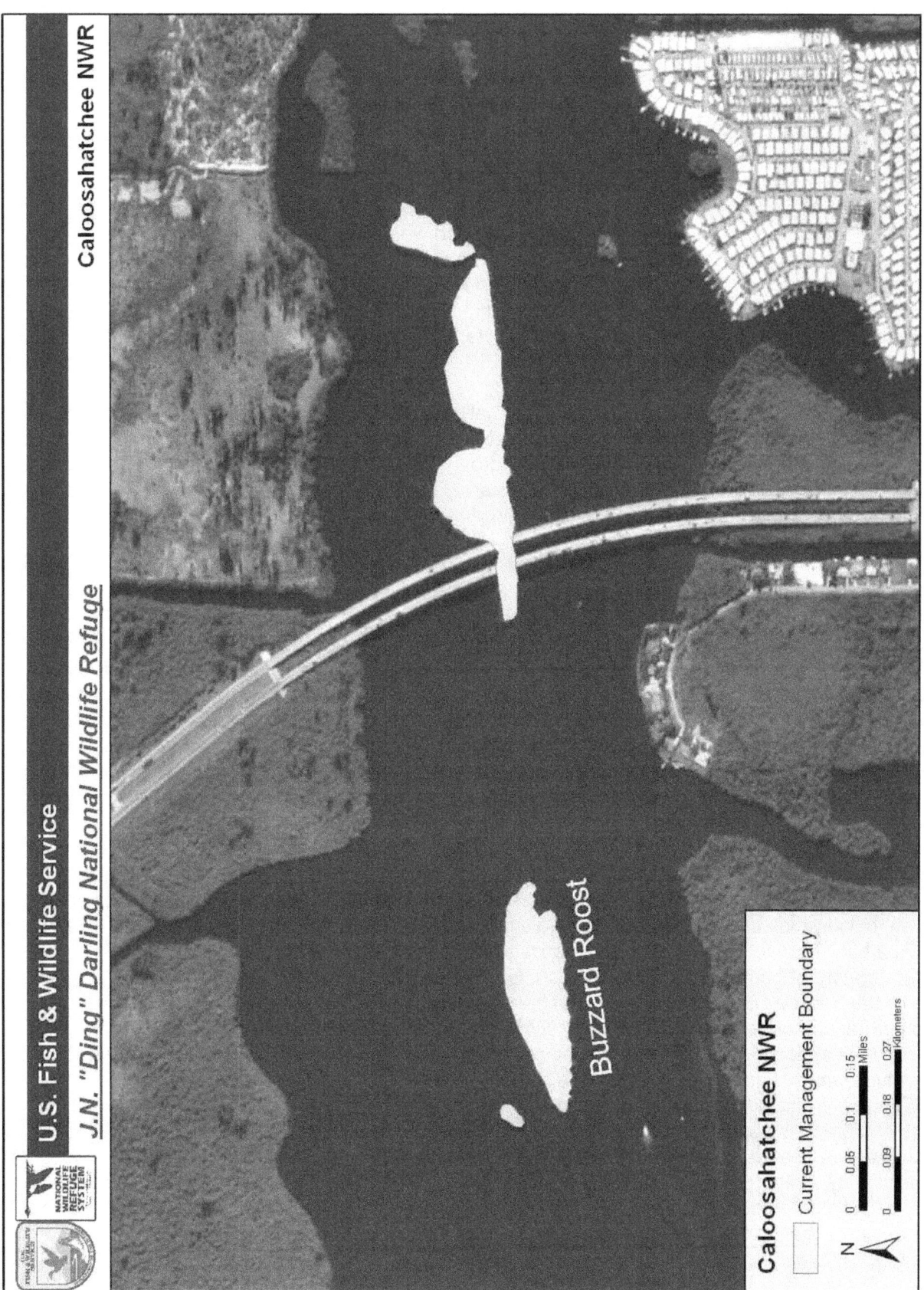

Comprehensive Conservation Plan

HISTORY AND PURPOSES OF THE REFUGES

HISTORY

About 24.5 million years ago, the Gulf barrier islands of Florida rose, as did Florida, from the receding seas. It is not known when man first arrived, but skeleton remains have been unearthed dating back about 6,000 years. Archaeological evidence shows that the Florida coastline was inhabited by mound builders some 3,000 years ago. These inhabitants are believed to be the Calusa warrior tribes, seafarers who created the first canals south of Charlotte Harbor, many of which are still visible today.

In 1513, Ponce de Leon set out to explore the east and west coasts of Florida. During this exploration, he returned to the Charlotte Harbor area to establish a colony. Several years later, the American mainland was opened for European settlement by the Hernando DeSoto expedition of 1539-42. According to various historical documents, Pedro Menendez D'Aviles built a mission-fort named San Antonio somewhere in the Charlotte Harbor region following his establishment of the first American colony at St. Augustine, Florida, in 1565.

The Spanish lost control of Florida to the British between 1763 and 1783, giving the English colonists a chance to leave their mark. Europeans populated the Charlotte harbor area in the 19th century with small fishing settlements. They named the mangrove-lined harbor for British Queen Charlotte. During that time, Seminoles also migrated to the area as the Calusa died out due to illness and years of war against European settlers and as the Calusa left with the Spanish.

All four refuges were originally established as a preserve and breeding ground for native birds. Three of the refuges (Pine Island, Matlacha Pass, and Island Bay) were established in 1908 through executive orders by President Theodore Roosevelt. These three refuges (or bird reservations as they were known then) were recommended for protection by the National Association of Audubon Societies (precursor to the National Audubon Society), particularly from T. Gilbert Pearson (then Secretary and eventual President of the Audubon Societies), who visited these islands while travelling to Key West to buy a home for murdered Audubon warden Guy Bradley's widow and children. Pearson documented the status of these islands as some of the last remaining rookeries of pelicans and wading birds on the Gulf Coast of Florida. Pearson recruited a local bird lover, Columbus McLeod, to protect these islands as an Audubon warden. Tragically, McLeod was murdered like Guy Bradley shortly after these islands became federal bird reservations.

Shell mounds within Pine Island NWR show evidence of Native American habitation. Originally, Matlacha Pass NWR was established with just three small islands. But since then, the refuge has grown to 31 islands and peninsulas and the Terrapin Creek Tract, encompassing about 538.25 acres (217.82 ha). The most recent addition of lands to Matlacha Pass NWR was in 1991, when approximately 312 acres (126.26 ha) of public lands were withdrawn from surface entry and mining for use by the Service. Fisherman Key, one of the largest islands of Matlacha Pass, once had fish camps and permanent residents on it. Island Bay NWR consists of six undeveloped tracts of land (about 20.24 acres/8.19 ha) occupying the higher portions of several islands and their mangrove shorelines. In 1970 the refuge was designated as a wilderness area. It also protects archaeological sites. Caloosahatchee NWR presently includes four islands with mangrove shorelines and upland covered with a variety of fresh and brackish vegetation. It was established in 1920 by Executive Order of President Woodrow Wilson and is located near the mouth of the Caloosahatchee River. This refuge was recommended for protection by winter residents, Thomas Alva Edison and his wife, Mina Miller Edison, who was active with the National Audubon Society. Much of the refuge's original dimensions have been changed due to the channelization effects of the river.

These four refuges are located within the barrier island and estuarine system of the Charlotte Harbor area. Two important rivers flow into this system near the refuges: the Caloosahatchee and Peace rivers. Created by overland flow through swamps and marshes, the Caloosahatchee River was connected to Lake Okeechobee in 1881 by the U.S. Army Corps of Engineers (USACE), linking the refuges to Lake Okeechobee and the Everglades (Charlotte Harbor National Estuary Program 2008). Today, the freshwater of the Caloosahatchee River is separated from the salt water of the estuary by Franklin Lock in eastern Lee County, far to the east of the refuges (Charlotte Harbor National Estuary Program 2008). Originating in the Green Swamp, the Peace River is located further north and is the largest contributor of fresh water to Charlotte Harbor (Charlotte Harbor National Estuary Program 2008). Historically, both rivers helped to create the rich and productive estuary in which the refuges exist. And, today, both help to deliver threats and impacts to the refuges.

PURPOSES

Designation of the refuges followed on the heels of protection of other nesting areas for birds from feather and plume hunters and egg collectors that began with the 1903 designation by President Theodore Roosevelt of Pelican Island NWR, the nation's first national wildlife refuge.

Pine Island NWR

Pine Island NWR was established "… as a preserve and breeding ground for native birds" by President Theodore Roosevelt through Executive Order 939 in 1908 to protect the thousands of herons, egrets, and pelicans that were being hunted to support the plume trade in the early 1900s. Two secondary purposes have also been applied to the refuge, as listed.

> "… suitable for (1) incidental fish and wildlife-oriented recreational development, (2) the protection of natural resources, (3) the conservation of endangered species or threatened species" 16 U.S.C. 460k-1 (Refuge Recreation Act) "… the Secretary…may accept and use…real…property. Such acceptance may be accomplished under the terms and conditions of restrictive covenants imposed by donors" 16 U.S.C. 460k-2 (Refuge Recreation Act)

> "…for the development, advancement, management, conservation, and protection of fish and wildlife resources" 16 U.S.C. 742f(a)(4) (Fish and Wildlife Act) "… for the benefit of the United States Fish and Wildlife Service, in performing its activities and services. Such acceptance may be subject to the terms of any restrictive or affirmative covenant, or condition of servitude" 16 U.S.C. 742f(b)(1) (Fish and Wildlife Act)

Matlacha Pass NWR

Three small islands were established as Matlacha Pass NWR by President Theodore Roosevelt through Executive Order 943 on September 26, 1908, again as a "… preserve and breeding ground for native birds." Since then, the refuge has grown to 31 islands and peninsulas and the Terrapin Creek Tract. Some of the most recent additions occurred on April 10, 1991, when Public Land Order 6843 withdrew approximately 312 acres (126.26 ha) of public lands from surface entry and mining for 40 years for use by the Service.

Island Bay NWR

Spanning 20.24 acres (8.19 ha) on six tracts on several islands, Island Bay NWR was established as a "preserve and breeding ground for native birds" on October 23, 1908, through Executive Order 958 signed by President Theodore Roosevelt. Later, on October 23, 1970, President Richard Nixon signed Public Law 91-504 establishing the refuge as a wilderness area. The wilderness designation conveys a secondary purpose to the refuge: "... wilderness areas...shall be administered for the use and enjoyment of the American people in such manner as will leave them unimpaired for future use and enjoyment as wilderness, and so as to provide for the protection of these areas, the preservation of their wilderness character, and for the gathering and dissemination of information regarding their use and enjoyment as wilderness..." 16 U.S.C. 1131 (Wilderness Act).

Caloosahatchee NWR

Caloosahatchee NWR was established by President Woodrow Wilson on July 1, 1920, through Executive Order 3299, also as a "... preserve and breeding ground for native birds." Much of the lands within the original refuge boundary, which included several mangrove islands, have been lost due to channelization of the Caloosahatchee River and deposition of dredged spoil upon the islands. The refuge now includes four islands totaling 40 acres (16.19 ha).

SPECIAL DESIGNATIONS

As part of the J.N. "Ding" Darling NWR Complex, these four refuges are part of the largest undeveloped mangrove ecosystem in the United States, and are famous for their spectacular migratory bird populations. Special designations for the refuges are: Island Bay NWR is designated as a wilderness area; three of the refuges are designated as marine protected areas; and all four refuges are designated as "Outstanding Florida Waters" and are part of the Gulf Ecological Management Sites program. Further, six state aquatic preserves are located in the larger landscape area, and the area is part of the Charlotte Harbor National Estuary Program.

WILDERNESS AREA

All six tracts of Island Bay NWR, which total 20.24 acres (8.19 ha), were designated as a national wilderness area (Public Law 91-504) on October 23, 1970, by President Richard Nixon. It is one of the smallest units in the National Wilderness Preservation System. The wilderness area designation provides an additional level of protection for the refuge. Comprised predominantly of mangrove swamp with small areas of tidal flats and upland hardwood forests, the Island Bay Wilderness Area is a closed area, protecting shorebirds, wading birds, waterbirds, and archaeological resources. Management activities within this wilderness area include boundary inspection and posting, law enforcement, and wildlife surveys and monitoring activities. Active management of these areas is restricted by guidelines contained in the Wilderness Act. Current management of the wilderness area is best described as minimum impact. As needed, the Service replaces boundary signs that designate the wilderness area. These refuge signs are the only authorized and maintained human material on the islands. No structures or facilities exist within the refuge's wilderness area.

Threats to the wilderness area include unauthorized access to the refuge; high public use levels and activities adjacent to the refuge in area waters; sea level rise; water quality degradation (including decreased dissolved oxygen, increased siltation, decreased water clarity, salinity imbalances, and increased chlorophyll a); contamination from local and regional freshwater discharges (including nitrogen, phosphorus, heavy metals, fecal coliform, pesticides, and pharmaceuticals); and invasive exotic plants and animals. Exemplifying current high waterway use, in 2006, Charlotte and Lee counties had over 71,000 registered recreational vessels (Florida Fish and Wildlife Conservation Commission 2007).

MARINE PROTECTED AREA

Internationally recognized for conserving natural, historical, and cultural marine resources, marine protected areas (MPAs) are intended to protect marine species and habitats, while also providing for sustainable recreation, sustainable commercial activities, enhanced research opportunities, and expanded educational opportunities. On December 1, 2000, all four refuges were listed as Candidate MPAs, as defined under Executive Order 13158 (signed on May 26, 2000). Under this executive order, an MPA is defined as "any area of the marine environment that has been reserved by Federal, State, territorial, tribal or local laws or regulations to provide lasting protection for part or all of the natural and cultural resources therein." Areas meeting this definition are intended to serve as the building blocks for a national MPA system. Such a system will form a network for addressing marine issues through pooled funding from the mix of MPA entities, shared research, increased available data, and enhanced protection across a system or throughout a species' range. The MPA system is expected to benefit marine species that utilize the refuges. A total of 225 nominations for the MPA were received, 99 of which are national wildlife refuges. Finding them to be eligible for the national system, the National Marine Protected Areas Center has accepted the nominations for 225 sites and placed them on the List of National System MPAs in April, 2009, including Pine Island, Matlacha Pass, and Island Bay NWRs.

OUTSTANDING FLORIDA WATERS

The Outstanding Florida Waters (OFWs) designation is given to waters that are "worthy of special protection due to their natural attributes" (§403.061, Florida Statutes); these waters are listed in Section 62-302.700, Florida Administrative Code (FAC). The intent of an OFW designation is to maintain ambient water quality. All permanent water bodies within national parks, national wildlife refuges, and state parks have been designated as OFWs. Other OFWs may also be designated as Special Waters based on a finding that the waters are of exceptional recreational or ecological significance and are identified as such in Rule 62-302, FAC. The OFW designation affords the highest protection possible under state water quality rules by prohibiting degradation of water quality from the conditions existing at the time of designation. Table 1 lists the national parks, national wildlife refuges, and state parks in Collier, Lee, and Charlotte counties that are designated as lands containing OFWs (Florida Department of Environmental Protection 2001, 2002, and 2003).

STATE AQUATIC PRESERVES AND STATE PARK

The refuges are adjacent to and surrounded by four Charlotte Harbor Aquatic Preserves: Pine Island Sound, Matlacha Pass, Cape Haze, and Gasparilla Sound-Charlotte Harbor. In addition, Lemon Bay Aquatic Preserve (also administered under the Charlotte Harbor Aquatic Preserves through the Florida Department of Environmental Protection's Office of Coastal and Aquatic Managed Areas) is near Island Bay NWR and Estero Bay Aquatic Preserve is near Matlacha Pass NWR. One large state buffer preserve, Charlotte Harbor Preserve State Park, is located north and east of Island Bay NWR.

CHARLOTTE HARBOR NATIONAL ESTUARY PROGRAM

Charlotte Harbor is recognized as an "estuary of national significance" and was added to the National Estuary Program (NEP) in 1995. The Charlotte Harbor basin supports a great diversity of subtropical plant and animal life. In 1990, 86 federally and state-protected plant and animal species were identified in the Charlotte Harbor NEP (CHNEP) area (Florida Department of Environmental Protection 2002a). The entire watershed of the greater Charlotte Harbor watershed has a total area of approximately 4,468 square miles. The estuary itself is the second largest open water estuary in the state. It is 30 miles long and seven miles wide with a total area of 270 square miles. Three rivers feed freshwater into the estuary: the Myakka, Peace, and Caloosahatchee rivers. This estuary is bordered by two counties and several local governments and the watershed contains at least portions of six additional counties and numerous local governments. The watershed is subdivided by a multitude of federal, state, and regional agencies with regulatory authorities. A series of resource management efforts have been conducted in the region over the past 25 years (Charlotte Harbor National Estuary Program, undated and 2008).

Table 1. National parks, national wildlife refuges and state parks in Collier, Lee and Charlotte counties designated as lands containing Outstanding Florida Waters.

Charlotte County:
- Stump Pass Beach State Park
- Cape Haze Aquatic Preserve (and Lee County)
- Charlotte Harbor Preserve State Park (and Lee County)
- Don Pedro Island State Park
- Gasparilla Sound-Charlotte Harbor State Aquatic Preserve (and Lee County)
- Island Bay National Wildlife Refuge
- Lemon Bay Estuarine System (Special Waters)
- Lemon Bay State Aquatic Preserve
- Port Charlotte Beach State Recreation Area

Lee County:
- Cayo Costa State Park
- Estero Bay Preserve State Park
- Gasparilla Island State Park
- J.N. "Ding" Darling National Wildlife Refuge
- Josslyn Island (Conservation and Recreation Lands)
- Matlacha Pass National Wildlife Refuge
- Matlacha Pass State Aquatic Preserve
- Pine Island National Wildlife Refuge
- Pine Island Sound State Aquatic Preserve
- Caloosahatchee National Wildlife Refuge
- Koreshan State Historic Site (and Mound Key Archeological State Park)
- Estero Bay State Aquatic Preserve
- Estero Bay (Special Waters)
- Estero Bay Tributaries and Acquisitions
- Lovers Key State Recreation Area

Collier County:
- Barefoot Beach Acquisitions
- Delnor-Wiggins Pass State Recreation Area
- Wiggins Pass/Cocohatchee River System (Special Waters)
- Rookery Bay State Aquatic Preserve
- Rookery Bay National Estuarine Research Reserve
- Rookery Bay Acquisitions
- Collier-Seminole State Park

- Cape Romano-Ten Thousand Islands State Aquatic Preserve
- Fakahatchee Strand State Preserve
- Florida Panther National Wildlife Refuge
- Ten Thousand Islands National Wildlife Refuge

Sources: Florida Department of Environmental Protection 2001, 2002, and 2003

ECOSYSTEM CONTEXT

PENINSULAR FLORIDA LANDSCAPE CONSERVATION COOPERATIVE

Throughout the nation, Landscape Conservation Cooperatives (LCCs) are currently under development. Figure 6 shows the LCCs for the continental U.S., while additional LCCs are under development for the Pacific Islands, Alaska, and the Caribbean. LCCs are applied conservation science partnerships between the U.S. Fish and Wildlife Service and other federal agencies, states, tribes, nongovernmental organizations, universities, and other stakeholders within a geographically defined area. LCCs will help inform resource management decisions and actions to address landscape-scale planning and management. Collectively, LCCs will comprise a seamless national network of planning and adaptive science capacity, connecting site-specific protection, restoration, and management efforts to larger goals supporting fish and wildlife populations and the natural systems that sustain them. One of the major functions of LCCs will be to ensure that all of the partners, including the Service, have access to existing data, science, expertise, and resources to limit duplication and provide an effective use of limited financial resources. LCCs will provide a more centralized venue to pull together the resources needed to research a problem; plan a response; identify and pool the needed skills, abilities, and funding to address the problem; take action; and evaluate the results, thus implementing Strategic Habitat Conservation within the landscape across partners.

Pine Island, Matlacha Pass, Island Bay, and Caloosahatchee NWRs are located within the Peninsular Florida LCC (Figure 6, label 12). Although Florida is part of three separate LCCs, much of the state is covered by the Peninsular Florida LCC. The Service is working with the State of Florida, the Miccosukee and Seminole tribes of Florida, and other partners to develop the Peninsular Florida LCC to enhance decision-making, planning, and management across the landscape to better serve wildlife and habitat resources found in this area. The Peninsular Florida LCC will complement Florida's Wildlife Action Plan and other landscape-level conservation strategies to restore, manage, and conserve the biodiversity of the region in the face of both climate change and intense development pressure associated with a rapidly growing human population.

The Peninsular Florida area is unique and complex, connecting subtropical and temperate climate zones and featuring a mosaic of more than 40 habitat types. This biologically diverse region encompasses hundreds of miles of beach and dune habitats, the St. Johns River watershed, xeric scrub uplands of the Lake Wales Ridge, the freshwater marshes of the Kissimmee River and Lake Okeechobee, vast sawgrass and cypress wetlands of the Everglades, extensive coastal mangroves and salt marsh, expanses of seagrass beds, and the unique pine rocklands and tropical hardwood hammocks of the Florida Keys. Offshore, it includes the only living coral reef ecosystem in the continental United States. This region is home to approximately 700 species of mammals, birds, amphibians, and reptiles; over 1,000 species of freshwater and marine fish; over 4,000 species of plants; and about 50,000 species of invertebrates. More than 100 of these species are federally listed as endangered or threatened, and the State of Florida considers nearly 1,000 of them as species of greatest conservation need (SGCN). Public interest in species conservation is intense

Figure 6. Landscape Conservation Cooperatives.

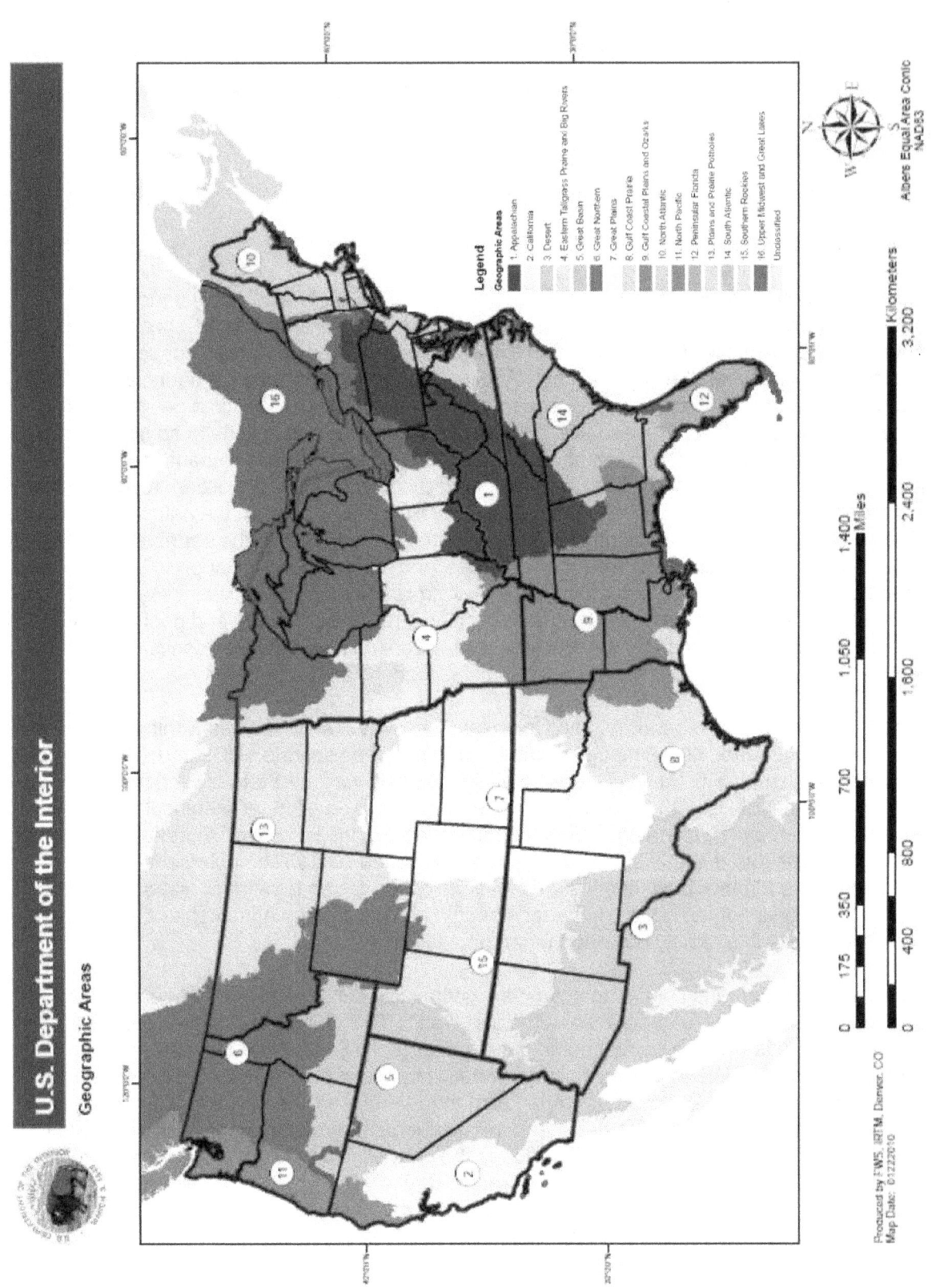

regarding species such as the Florida manatee, Florida panther, wood stork, Florida scrub-jay, and several species of sea turtles. The primary conservation challenges include habitat destruction and conversion, invasive species, and management of fire and natural hydrological processes. However, the most critical challenge is time. Florida faces intense pressure from development and Peninsular Florida is extremely vulnerable to the impacts of sea level rise, saltwater intrusion, and aquifer depletion. An area the size of Vermont may be developed in Florida over the next 50 years and millions of human residents may be displaced by the impacts of climate change and sea level rise by the turn of the century. The effectiveness of the Peninsular Florida LCC will have far-reaching implications.

SOUTH FLORIDA ECOSYSTEM

An ecosystem is a geographical area that includes and interconnects all the living (biotic) organisms, their physical (abiotic) surroundings, and the natural cycles that sustain them. The Outer Coastal Plain Ecological Province encompasses a large portion of the southeastern, coastal United States (Bailey 1978; U.S. Department of Agriculture [USDA] Forest Service 2008a and 2008b). The Outer Coastal Plain Ecological Province is an area of gentle slopes with abundant water resources. Estuaries, swamps, marshes, rivers, and lakes are abundant and provide habitat for a wide variety of plant and animal life. The Pine Island, Matlacha Pass, Island Bay, and Caloosahatchee NWRs are located in the southern part of the Outer Coastal Plain Ecological Province, in an area designated as the South Florida Ecosystem, which is now fully contained in the Peninsular Florida LCC.

The South Florida Ecosystem (Figure 7) currently encompasses approximately 26,000 square miles, of which 77 percent is land and 23 percent is water, covering the 19 southernmost Florida counties. The Ecosystem encompasses the Kissimmee River-Lake Okeechobee-Everglades drainage and the Peace River drainage, separated by the Lake Wales Ridge - the highest topographic feature of the Florida peninsula. The Ecosystem includes more than 10 major physiographic provinces (see Geology and Topography discussion in Chapter II. Refuge Overview, Physical Resources). The South Florida Ecosystem includes over 20 areas managed by the federal government (not including the Brighton, Miccosukee, and Seminole Indian reservations). These include 16 national wildlife refuges (including these four refuges); Big Cypress National Preserve; Biscayne National Park; Dry Tortugas National Park; Everglades National Park; and Florida Keys National Marine Sanctuary. Various other local and state conservation areas are also located within the South Florida Ecosystem (U.S. Fish and Wildlife Service 1998a). Figure 8 shows the conservation lands in the area.

The South Florida Ecosystem represents a mixture of Caribbean-subtropical, southern temperate, and local influences resulting in a wide variety of habitats that support substantial ecological, community, taxonomic, and genetic diversity. The Charlotte Harbor region of the ecosystem In the vicinity of the refuges is characterized by cypress and hardwood hammocks and extensive areas of poorly drained marshes. The central and southern regions of the ecosystem include marsh, dry and wet prairies, pine flatwoods, and estuaries. Mesic flatwoods support a wide diversity of animals and represent the third highest species richness of vegetative communities in Florida. Dry prairie is one of the most widespread upland vegetative communities in the Charlotte Harbor region. Coastal areas contain seagrass beds, mangroves, and coastal strand communities providing a variety of habitats and resources for a diversity of flora and fauna. The South Florida Ecosystem serves a variety of native wildlife, including over 65 federally listed species, as well as interjurisdictional fishes, neotropical migratory birds, nongame waterbirds, waterfowl, and state-listed species. Table 2 describes the acreage and types of natural communities in the Charlotte Harbor watershed and Table 3 lists the imperiled animal species in the Charlotte Harbor study area (Florida Department of Environmental Protection 2002a).

Figure 7. South Florida Ecosystem.

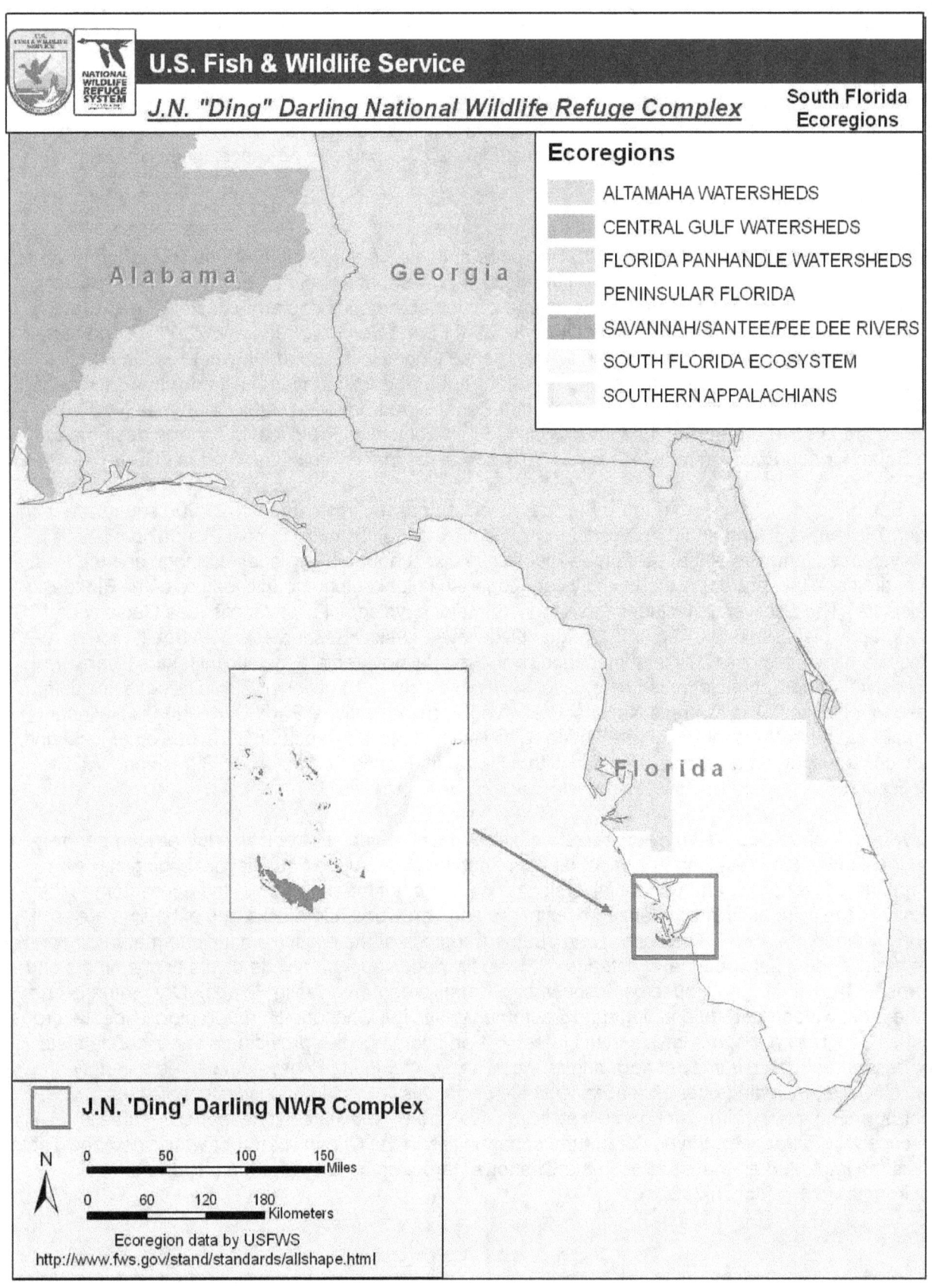

28 Pine Island, Matlacha Pass, Island Bay, and Caloosahatchee National Wildlife Refuges

Figure 8. Area conservation lands.

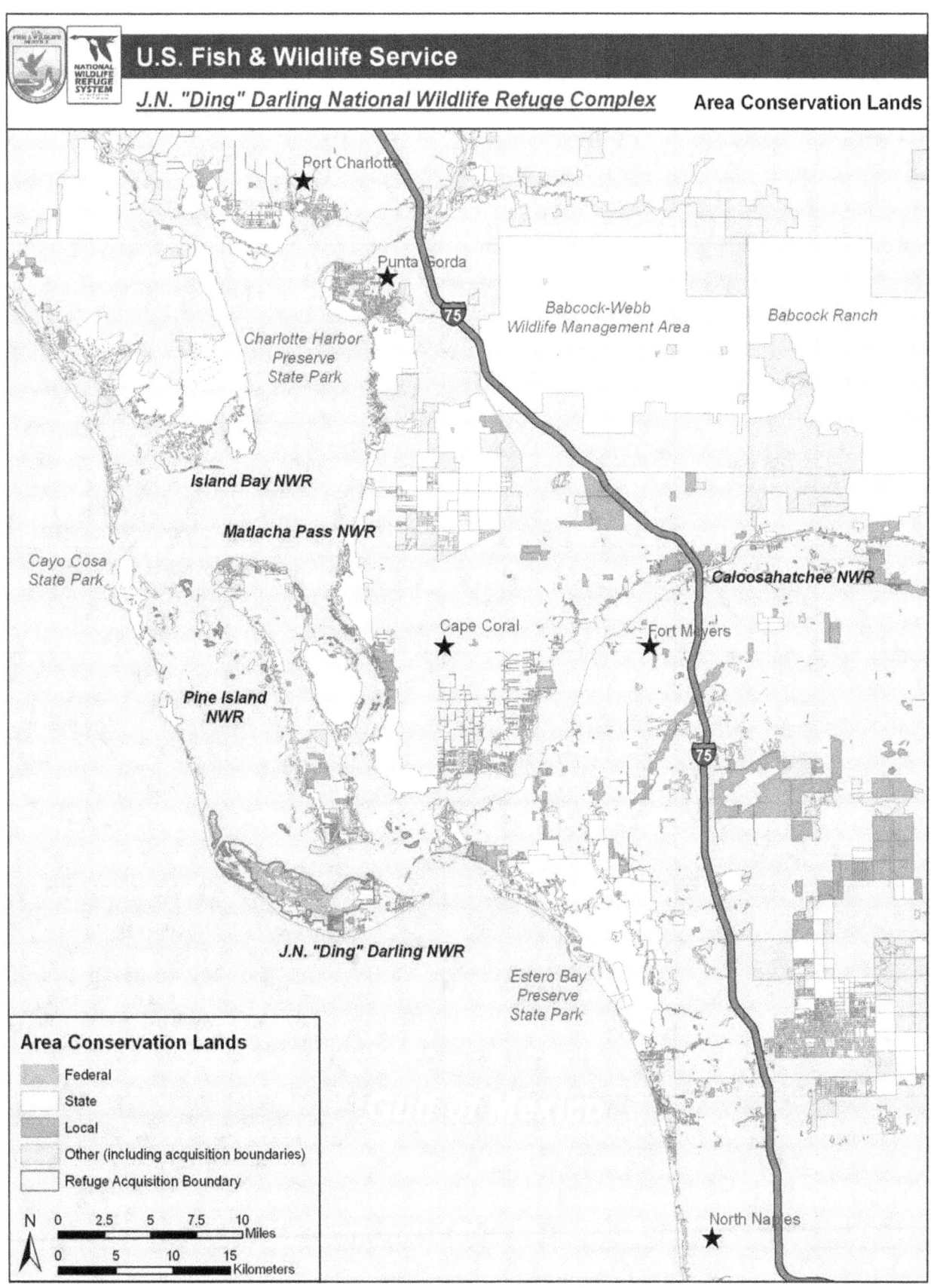

Comprehensive Conservation Plan

Table 2. Types of natural communities in the Charlotte Harbor Basin.

Category	Community Type	Area in Acres	Area in Hectares	Total Area (%)	Characteristics
Upland		87,840.8	35,547.9	20.60	
1	Coastal strand	493.6	199.8	0.12	Occurs on well drained sandy coastlines and includes typically zoned vegetation of upper beach, nearby dunes, or coastal rock formations.
2	Dry prairie	26,864.7	10,871.8	6.30	Large treeless grasslands and shrub lands on very flat terrain interspersed with scattered cypress domes, cypress strands, isolated freshwater marshes, and hammocks.
3	Pinelands	47,797.4	19,342.9	11.21	Includes north and south Florida pine flatwoods, south Florida pine rocklands, scrubby flatwoods, and commercial pine plantations. Cypress domes, bayheads, titi swamps, and freshwater marshes are commonly interspersed in isolated depressions.
6	Oak scrub	224.4	90.8	0.05	Hardwood community consisting of clumps of low growing oaks interspersed with white sand. Occurs in areas of deep, well-washed sterile sand.
7	Mixed hardwood pine	1,441.6	583.4	0.34	Southern extension of the Piedmont southern mixed hardwoods, occurring mainly on clay soils of the northern Panhandle. Also includes upland forests in which a mixture of conifers and hardwoods dominate over story.
8	Hardwood hammock	7,933.4	3,210.5	1.86	Includes major upland hardwood associations that occur statewide on fairly rich sandy soils.
9	Tropical hammock	3,085.7	1,248.7	0.72	Cold-intolerant hardwood community with very high plant diversity that occurs on coastal uplands in extreme south Florida. Characterized by tropical trees and shrubs at the northern edge of their range, which extends into the Caribbean.
Wetland		61,912.1	25,054.9	14.52	
10	Coastal salt marsh	9,135.4	3,697.0	2.14	Herbaceous and shrubby wetland communities that include cordgrass, needlerush, and transitional or high salt marshes, occurring statewide in brackish waters along protected low energy estuarine shorelines.

Category	Community Type	Area in Acres	Area in Hectares	Total Area (%)	Characteristics
11	Freshwater marsh	10,353.1	4,189.8	2.43	Wetland communities dominated by wide assortment of herbaceous plant species growing on sand, clay, marl, and organic soils in areas where water depths and inundation regimes vary.
12	Cypress swamp	4,251.3	1,720.4	1.00	Regularly inundated communities that form forested buffer along large rivers, creeks, and lakes, or occur in depressions as circular domes or linear strands. Strongly dominated by bald cypress or pond cypress.
13	Hardwood swamp	1,170.6	473.7	0.27	Association of wetland adapted trees, composed either of pure stands of hardwoods or hardwood cypress mixture. Occurs on organic soils and forms forested floodplain of nonalluvial rivers, creeks, and broad lake basins.
15	Shrub swamp	93.2	37.7	0.02	Dominated by low-growing, woody shrubs or small trees, usually found in wetlands changed by natural or human perturbations such as altered hydroperiod, fire, clear-cutting or land clearing, and siltation.
16	Mangrove swamp	36,908.5	14,939.3	8.65	Dense, brackish water swamps, usually dominated by red, black, and white mangroves, that occur along low-energy shorelines and in protected, tidally influenced bays of southern Florida. Comprises freeze-intolerant tree species that are distributed south of a line from Cedar Key on the Gulf coast to St. Augustine on the Atlantic coast.
Open Water		177054.0	71,651.2	41.51	
18	Water	177,054.0	71,651.2	41.51	Open water areas of inland lakes, ponds, rivers, and streams and brackish and saline waters of estuaries, bays, and tidal creeks.
Disturbed		99,677.0	40,337.9	23.37	
19	Grass and agricultural land	23,645.9	9,569.2	5.54	Upland communities with very low-growing grasses and forbs. Intensively managed sites such as improved pastures, lawns, golf courses, road shoulders, cemeteries, or weedy fallow agricultural fields.

Category	Community Type	Area in Acres	Area in Hectares	Total Area (%)	Characteristics
20	Shrub and brush	8,749.4	3,540.8	2.05	Includes different situations where natural upland communities have recently been disturbed and are recovering through natural successional processes.
21	Exotic plant communities	2,837.8	1,148.4	0.67	Upland and wetland areas dominated by invasive nonnative trees that have invaded native plant communities.
22	Barren and Urban land	64,443.9	26,079.5	15.11	Unvegetated areas such as roads, beaches, active strip mines, borrow areas, cleared land on sandy soils, and urban areas (rooftops, parking lots, etc.).
TOTAL		426,483.9	172,591.9	100.00	

Source: Florida Department of Environmental Protection 2002a

Table 3. Imperiled animal species of the Charlotte Harbor National Estuary Program study area.

Common Name	Scientific Name	Federal Status	State Status
Fish			
Mangrove rivulus	*Rivulus marmoratus*		Special Concern
Gulf sturgeon	*Acipenser oxyrinchus desotoi*	Threatened	Special Concern
Smalltooth Sawfish	*Prisits pectinata*	Endangered	
Amphibians and Reptiles			
American crocodile	*Crocodylus acutus*	Threatened	Endangered
Atlantic green turtle	*Chelonia mydas mydas*	Endangered	Endangered
Atlantic hawksbill turtle	*Eretmochelys imbricata*	Endangered	Endangered
Kemp's ridley turtle	*Lepidochelys kempii*	Endangered	Endangered
Atlantic leatherback turtle	*Dermochelys coriacea*	Endangered	Endangered
Atlantic loggerhead turtle	*Caretta caretta caretta*	Threatened	Threatened
Eastern indigo snake	*Drymarchon corais couperi*	Threatened	Threatened
Gopher tortoise	*Gopherus polyphemus*	Threatened	Threatened
American alligator	*Alligator mississippiensis*	Threatened (s/a)	Special Concern
Florida gopher frog	*Rana capito*		Special Concern
Diamondback terrapin	*Malaclemys terrapin*	Special Concern	
Birds			
Wood stork	*Myctria americana*	Endangered	Endangered
Florida Everglades (snail) kite	*Rostrhamus sociabilis plumbeus*	Endangered	Endangered
Kirtland's warbler	*Dendroica kirtlandii*	Endangered	Endangered
Florida grasshopper sparrow	*Ammodtramussavannarum floridanus*	Endangered	Endangered
Piping Plover	*Charadris melodus*	Threatened	Threatened
Audubon's crested caracara	*Caracara cheriway auduboni*	Threatened	Threatened
Roseate tern	*Sterna dougallii dougallii*	Threatened	Threatened
Florida scrub jay	*Aphelocoma coerulescens coerulescens*	Threatened	Threatened
Southeastern American kestrel	*Falco sparverius paulus*	Special Concern	Threatened
Florida sandhill crane	*Grus canadensis pratensis*		Threatened
Least tern	*Sterna albifrons*		Threatened
Cuban snowy plover	*Charadrius alexandrinus tenuirostris*		Threatened
Red-cockaded woodpecker	*Picoides borealis*	Endangered	Special Concern
Reddish egret	*Dichromanassa rufescens*	Special Concern	Special Concern
American oystercatcher	*Haematopus palliatus*	Special Concern	Special Concern
Brown pelican	*Pelecanus occidentalis s*		Special Concern
Little blue heron	*Florida caerulea*		Special Concern
Snowy egret	*Egretta thula*		Special Concern
Tricolored heron	*Hydranassa tricolor*		Special Concern
Roseate spoonbill	*Ajaia ajaja*		Special Concern
Limpkin	*Aramus guarauna pictus*		Special Concern
Florida burrowing owl	*Athena cunicularia floridana*		Special Concern
Marian's marsh wren	*Cistothorus palustris marianae*		Special Concern
White ibis	*Eudocimus albas*		Special Concern
Mammals			
Florida manatee	*Trichechus manatus latirostris*	Endangered	Endangered
Florida panther	*Felis concolor coryi*	Endangered	Endangered
Mangrove fox squirrel	*Sciurus niger avicennia*		Threatened
Florida black bear	*Ursus americanus floridanus*		Threatened
Everglades mink	*Mustela vision-evergladensis*		Threatened
Sherman's fox squirrel	*Sciurus niger shermani*	Special Concern	Special Concern
Florida mouse	*Peromyscus floridanus*	Special Concern	Special Concern
Sanibel Island Rice Rat	*Oryzomys palustris sanibeli*		Special Concern

Source: Florida Department of Environmental Protection 2002a

For 5,000 years, the greater South Florida Everglades' ecosystem flourished, nurtured by sun and frequent rain. Runoff from the pinewoods and prairies of the Kissimmee River Basin flowed into Lake Okeechobee. The water then spilled over the south shore of the lake and flowed south in shallow sheets through vast stretches of sawgrass in a slow journey to Florida Bay. The Caloosahatchee River collected runoff and funneled water west into the Gulf of Mexico. At the river's mouth, where fresh and salt water mixed, a large, lush estuary evolved, providing shelter and forage for an array of fish, shellfish, birds, and wildlife. In 1881, a Philadelphia developer, Hamilton Disston, purchased from the state some four million acres (1.6 million ha) around Lake Okeechobee and a year later he succeeded in cutting a canal that, for the first time, linked Lake Okeechobee to the Caloosahatchee River and the Gulf of Mexico, and opened the region to navigation and development. In the years since, the river's navigation channel has been enlarged and is now known as the C-43 canal, and for most purposes, the C-43 canal and Caloosahatchee River are one and the same (see Figure 9) (U.S. Army Corps of Engineers and South Florida Water Management District 2003).

Enhanced agricultural development due to the availability of irrigation water from the C-43 canal, urban development in the Fort Myers/Cape Coral area, and regulatory releases of freshwater from Lake Okeechobee have all been linked to significant water quality changes in the Caloosahatchee Estuary. When water is discharged from Lake Okeechobee into the Caloosahatchee River following a heavy rain, it moves down the river and is quickly released into Charlotte Harbor and the Gulf of Mexico. This surge of fresh water changes delicate estuarine salinity levels and harms brackish marine habitats in the Caloosahatchee Estuary. These releases of freshwater from Lake Okeechobee, increases in nonpoint source urban runoff associated with increased development, and agricultural runoff (drainage) are impacting the Caloosahatchee River and the Charlotte Harbor Estuary. Water quality parameters of concern include: salinity, nutrients, turbidity, trace organics, and metals. All of these negatively impact the flora and fauna of the area (U.S. Army Corps of Engineers 2007; South Florida Water Management District 2008).

Pine Island, Matlacha Pass, Island Bay, and Caloosahatchee NWRs are located in the Southwestern Florida Flatwoods Sub-ecoregion (Level IV, 75b) of the Southern Coastal Plain Ecoregion (Level III-75) (Loveland and Acevedo 2008; Drummond 2008; U.S. Environmental Protection Agency 2007a). Ecoregions denote areas of general similarity in ecosystems and in the type, quality, and quantity of environmental resources (U.S. Environmental Protection Agency 2007b). The Southern Florida Flatwoods Ecoregion is a nearly level coastal plain of pine flatwoods, extensive areas of pasture and rangeland, cabbage palm hammocks, and marshes. Streams and lakes are common and surface and ground water supplies are abundant. The land surface is about four meters above sea level. Most of the area is flat, but some hammocks rise about one meter above the general level landscape and low beach ridges and dunes rise two to three meters above the lower inland areas. Generally, elevations range from sea level to less than 25 meters moving inland. Its textured soils are wet, coarse, and sandy. The annual precipitation is the area is 44 to 60 inches, about 60% of which occurs from June through September as tropical storms. Late autumn and winter are relatively dry. Based on data from the Fort Myers Airport, annual average temperatures range from 64.6°F to 84°F, while monthly average temperatures range from 53.5°F in January to 91.4°F in August (Southeast Regional Climate Center 2007). Charlotte Harbor is one of the more prominent geographic features in the region. Population growth has been very rapid in recent years, and much of the coastal area is highly urbanized. Flatwood forest vegetation is primarily slash pine, longleaf pine, cabbage palm, and live oak. Saw palmetto, gallberry, and bluestems and wiregrasses characterize the understory. Land use in the Southern Florida Flatwoods is characterized as 7% cropland; 36% grassland; 22% forest; 17% urban developed; 13% open water; and 5% other (U.S. Department of Agriculture 2006a).

Figure 9. Historic and current surface water flows, South Florida Ecosystem.
(Lee County 2009)

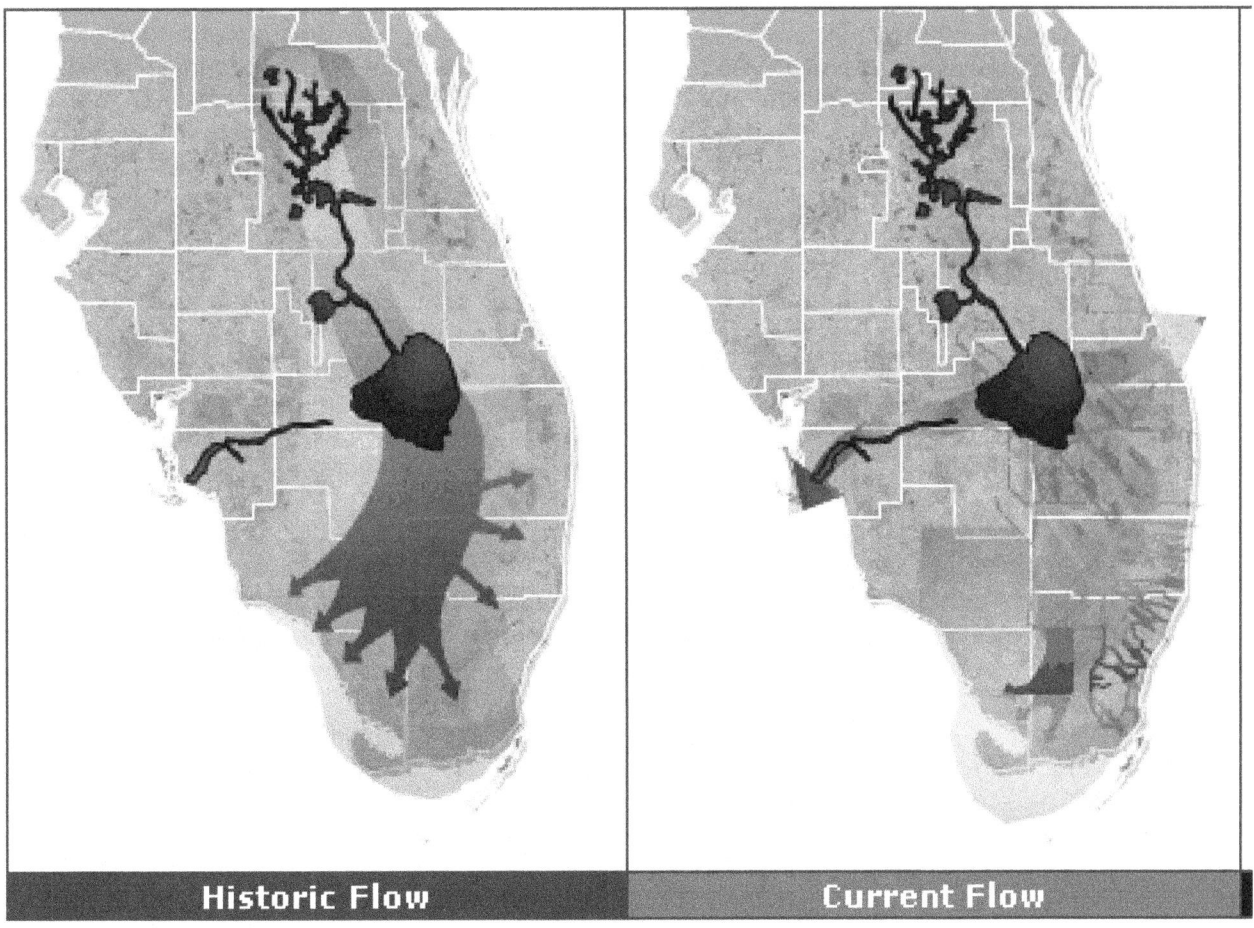

REGIONAL CONSERVATION PLANS AND INITIATIVES

Pine Island, Matlacha Pass, Island Bay, and Caloosahatchee NWRs are located along the Gulf coast and are part of the Southwestern Florida Flatwoods Sub-ecoregion, of the Southern Coastal Plain. As such, the refuges play a role in numerous regional conservation plans and initiatives, including the Charlotte Harbor National Estuary Program and Comprehensive Conservation and Management Plan; South Florida Multi-Species Recovery Plan; South Florida Ecosystem Plan; the Gulf of Mexico Program; the Comprehensive Everglades Restoration Plan, including the Caloosahatchee River (C-43) West Basin Storage Reservoir Project and the Southwest Florida Feasibility Study; the Northern Everglades and Estuaries Protection Program; State Wildlife Action Plan; Florida's Endangered and Threatened Species Management and Conservation Plan; Florida Natural Areas Inventory; and the SWFWMD's and SFWMD's Surface Water Improvement and Management programs. Further, the refuges are in the Charlotte Harbor area, which also contains the Charlotte Harbor National Estuary Program, state aquatic preserves, state parks, and a state preserve. The National Park Service has identified four Wild and Scenic River segments in the area. Further, area climate change-related plans are important regional initiatives for future management. The four refuges are located outside of the Coastal Barrier Resources System.

CHARLOTTE HARBOR NATIONAL ESTUARY PROGRAM AND COMPREHENSIVE CONSERVATION AND MANAGEMENT PLAN

The National Estuary Program (NEP) was established as part of the 1987 amendments to the Clean Water Act (CWA) and seeks to protect and restore estuaries of national significance that are deemed to be threatened by pollution, development, or overuse. The Charlotte Harbor National Estuary Program (CHNEP) is one of the seven estuary programs in the Gulf of Mexico. Other NEP programs in the immediate area of the refuges are the Tampa Bay NEP and the Sarasota Bay NEP. Several federal agencies participate in planning and assessment efforts related to these NEPs, including the EPA, NOAA, U.S. Geological Survey (USGS), Department of Interior (DOI), and the USDA.

The Charlotte Harbor region supports a great diversity of semitropical plant and animal life. In 1990, 86 federal and state-protected plant and animal species were identified in the Charlotte Harbor area (Florida Department of Environmental Protection 2002a). In 1995 Charlotte Harbor was designated as an "estuary of national significance." The CHNEP covers the Greater Charlotte Harbor Watershed from Venice to Bonita Springs to Winter Haven. It is a partnership of citizens, elected officials, resource managers, and commercial and recreational resource users who work to improve the water quality and ecological integrity of the CHNEP study area. A cooperative decision-making process is used to address diverse resource management concerns in the 4,700-square-mile CHNEP study area. The 2008 update of CHNEP's Comprehensive Conservation and Management Plan (CCMP) outlines four priority problems: **hydrologic alterations, water quality degradation, fish and wildlife habitat loss, and stewardship gaps.** The refuges are located within the CHNEP Pine Island Sound subbasin, which has several key concerns, including freshwater inflows from Cape Coral; Caloosahatchee River outflows, especially concerns related to timing; water quality; salinity; water volumes; and impacts to seagrass beds, oyster beds, and other plants and animals. The CCMP contains six major goals for preserving and restoring Charlotte Harbor. These goals are: improve the environmental integrity of the Charlotte Harbor study area; preserve, restore and enhance seagrass beds, coastal wetlands, barrier beaches, and functionally related uplands; reduce point and nonpoint sources of pollution to attain desired used of the estuary; provide the proper fresh water inflow to the estuary to ensure a balanced and productive ecosystem; develop and implement a strategy for public participation and education; and develop and implement a formal Charlotte Harbor management plan with a specified structure and process for achieving goals for the estuary (Charlotte Harbor National Estuary Program 2008).

The concerns of the CHNEP are also the refuges' resource concerns. The Refuge Complex staff coordinates with CHNEP partners on a regular basis.

SOUTH FLORIDA MULTI-SPECIES RECOVERY PLAN

The South Florida Multi-Species Recovery Plan is one of the first recovery strategies specifically designed to meet the needs of multiple species that do not occupy similar habitats. It is also one of the first designed to approach recovery by addressing the needs of entire watersheds: the Kissimmee-Okeechobee-Everglades watershed, the Caloosahatchee River-Big Cypress watershed, and the Peace-Myakka River watershed. The refuges play a role in the recovery of several federally listed species, including the wood stork (endangered), piping plover (threatened), West Indian manatee (endangered), and loggerhead sea turtle (threatened).

SOUTH FLORIDA ECOSYSTEM PLAN

The Service's South Florida Ecosystem Plan (U.S. Fish and Wildlife Service 1998a) seeks to better manage federal trust resources, such as migratory birds, threatened and endangered species, freshwater wetlands, interjurisdictional fisheries, mangrove forests, estuaries and estuarine wetlands, seagrasses, hardbottom, and coral reefs in the South Florida Ecosystem (Figure 7). The ecosystem encompasses the Kissimmee River, Lake Okeechobee, the Everglades, Peace River, Charlotte Harbor, Caloosahatchee River, Big Cypress Basin, Florida Keys, and the upper and lower east coast of Florida. The seven goals of the South Florida Ecosystem Plan are:

- Protect and manage National Wildlife Refuge System units and other national interest lands.
- Protect migratory birds and protect, restore, and manage their habitats.
- Protect, restore, and manage candidate, threatened, and endangered species and their habitats.
- Protect, restore, and manage wetlands and other freshwater habitats.
- Protect, manage, and restore fish and other aquatic species, and their habitats.
- Protect, restore, and enhance coastal and estuarine habitats.
- Protect, restore, and manage for biodiversity.

GULF OF MEXICO PROGRAM

The Gulf of Mexico Program (GMP) (U.S. Environmental Protection Agency, undated-a) was formed in 1988 by the Environmental Protection Agency as a nonregulatory, inclusive partnership to provide a broad geographic focus on the major environmental issues in the Gulf. The program provides a tool to leverage the resources of 18 different federal agencies; a variety of environmentally-minded agencies from the states of Alabama, Florida, Louisiana, Mississippi, and Texas; and numerous public and private organizations. Under the umbrella of the GMP is Florida's Gulf Ecological Management Site (GEMS) Program (Florida Department of Environmental Protection 2008), which through the cooperation of federal, state, local, and private programs, resources, and mechanisms is identifying special ecological sites and providing information for each site in an informational database. All four refuges are part of the GEMS Program.

COMPREHENSIVE EVERGLADES RESTORATION PLAN

Starting in the 1940s, the Central and South Florida Project—constructed in partnership between the USACE and the SFWMD—is an elaborate and effective water management system providing flood protection and water supply for South Florida. The system caused unintended environmental impacts to the South Florida ecosystem. In 1992 and 1996, Congress authorized the Restudy of the Central and South Florida Project to assess the measures necessary to restore the South Florida ecosystem. The Comprehensive Everglades Restoration Plan (CERP) was completed in 1999. CERP was included in the Water Resources Development Act of 2000. Nearly 70 agencies and organizations came forward to support the implementation of CERP, with the USACE and the SFWMD taking the lead roles as the federal and local sponsors. The refuges of the J.N. "Ding" Darling NWR Complex participate in CERP and Southwest Florida Feasibility Study planning, coordination, and implementation activities (U.S. Army Corps of Engineers and South Florida Water Management District 2006).

The Caloosahatchee River (C-43) West Basin Storage Reservoir Project

A major CERP project related to the refuges is the Caloosahatchee River (C-43) West Basin Storage Reservoir Project. The purpose of the project is to improve the timing and quantity of fresh water flows to the Caloosahatchee River Estuary. The West Basin Storage Reservoir will store fresh water from Lake Okeechobee and storm water runoff that will be released slowly, as needed, to ensure a more natural, consistent flow of fresh water to the estuary. This will help to restore the estuary by eliminating salinity changes and improving the ecological health of flora and fauna on the refuges (U.S. Army Corps of Engineers 2003 and 2007; U.S. Army Corps of Engineers and South Florida Water Management District 2006). (See the discussion of *Freshwater Releases from the Caloosahatchee Watershed and Lake Okeechobee* in the Water Quality section below.)

Southwest Florida Feasibility Study

CERP and the Southwest Florida Feasibility Study (SWFFS) (U.S. Army Corps of Engineers, South Florida Water Management District, and Water Resources Advisory Commission 2006) provide a framework and guide to restore, protect, and preserve the water resources of central and southern Florida, including the Everglades. The goal of CERP and SWFFS is to capture fresh water that now flows unused to the Atlantic Ocean and the Gulf of Mexico and redirect it to areas that need it most. The majority of the water will be devoted to environmental restoration, reviving a dying ecosystem. The remaining water will benefit cities and farmers by enhancing water supplies for the South Florida economy. The USACE, in partnership with the South Florida Water Management District and numerous other federal, state, local, and tribal partners, has developed this plan to save the Everglades. This study will provide a framework to improve water quality and address the health of aquatic ecosystems; water flows; water supply; wildlife, biological diversity, and natural habitat along the Gulf coast of southern Florida—all of which are important issues to the refuges (U.S. Army Corps of Engineers 2006; U.S. Army Corps of Engineers and South Florida Water Management District 2006).

NORTHERN EVERGLADES AND ESTUARIES PROTECTION PROGRAM

The Northern Everglades and Estuaries Protection Program recognizes the importance and connectivity of the entire Everglades ecosystem, both north and south of Lake Okeechobee. Implementation of this program will improve the quality, quantity, timing, and distribution of water to the natural system and reestablish salinity regimes suitable for maintaining healthy, naturally diverse, and well-balanced estuarine ecosystems. The health of the Northern Everglades will be enhanced by improving land management to reduce nutrient runoff, by constructing treatment wetlands to improve water quality, and by completing water storage projects to better connect, manage and distribute water to the natural system. Under this program, the State of Florida recognized the importance of protection and restoration of the Lake Okeechobee watershed and the Caloosahatchee and St. Lucie rivers and estuaries. The South Florida Water Management District, Florida Department of Environmental Protection, and Florida Department of Agriculture and Consumer Services, in cooperation with Lee and Martin counties and other affected municipalities, developed the Caloosahatchee and St. Lucie River Watershed Protection Plans. The Caloosahatchee River Watershed Protection Plan includes three components: a Construction Project; a Pollutant Control Program; and a Research and Water Quality Monitoring Program. The Construction Project and Pollutant Control Program include water quality projects, along with agricultural and urban best management practices (BMPs), to maximize nutrient loading reductions to meet Total Maximum Daily Loads (TMDLs) as they are established for the Caloosahatchee River Estuary. In addition, it includes water storage projects for improving quantity, timing, and distribution of water in the estuary and to re-establish salinity regimes suitable for maintaining a healthy, naturally diverse and well-balanced estuarine ecosystem. The Research and Water Quality Monitoring Program describes the current state of knowledge regarding hydrology, water quality, aquatic habitat, and effects of Lake Okeechobee on delivery of water to the Caloosahatchee River Estuary. It builds upon the existing monitoring, research, and modeling efforts and makes recommendations and modifications to these efforts to better achieve and assess the water quality and quantity targets of the Caloosahatchee River Watershed Protection Plan (South Florida Water Management District 2009a and 2009b).

STATE WILDLIFE ACTION PLAN

As a requirement for participating in the federal State Wildlife Grants Program, each state and territory has created a Comprehensive Wildlife Conservation Strategy for conservation of a broad array of fish and wildlife. Throughout the development process, the objectives were to identify SGCN and their habitats and to develop high priority conservation actions to abate problems for those species and habitats. These objectives have been developed in a prudent effort to prevent declines before species become imperiled, thereby saving millions of tax dollars. In addition, the matching requirement has encouraged partnerships and cooperation among conservation partners. To meet the intent of the Service's State Wildlife Grants Program, the FWC created Florida's Wildlife Legacy Initiative. The goal of the initiative was to develop a strategic vision for conserving all of Florida's wildlife. Florida's Comprehensive Wildlife Conservation Strategy (FCWCS) was completed and approved in 2005. The FCWCS emphasizes the building of partnerships with other agencies and the private sector, uses a habitat-based conservation approach, incorporates a broad definition of wildlife (to include invertebrates, aquatic species, and other species), and favors nonregulatory methods in its effort to reach conservation goals and objectives, many of which provided useful guidance in developing CCP benchmarks. A variety of species and habitats found on the refuges are listed in the FCWCS as needing special management protection. And, the predominant habitat type for all four refuges, mangrove swamp, is one of nine marine habitat categories that were identified as having the highest relative threat status (Florida Fish and Wildlife Conservation Commission 2005). SGCN associated with mangrove swamps include the Pine Island marsh rice rat (*Oryzomys palustris planirostris*); magnificent frigatebird (*Fregata magnificens*); yellow-crowned night-heron (*Nyctanassa violacea*); black-crowned night-heron (*Nycticorax nycticorax*); bald eagle, mangrove cuckoo, black-whiskered vireo, gray kingbird, Florida prairie warbler, and ornate diamondback terrapin (Florida Fish and Wildlife Conservation Commission 2005).

Florida Coastal Wildlife Conservation Initiative

Florida's Coastal Wildlife Conservation Initiative is an FWC-led effort to develop an integrated approach that focuses on coastal wildlife and habitat needs, as well as on related socioeconomic issues. This integrated approach includes participation by partners and input from stakeholders to address the range of activities that impact coastal wildlife in a balanced fashion. The vision is to ensure the long term conservation of native wildlife in coastal ecosystems throughout Florida in balance with human activities (Florida Fish and Wildlife Conservation Commission 2010a).

Florida Bird Conservation Initiative

The Florida Bird Conservation Initiative (FBCI) is another wildlife initiative of the State of Florida. It was formed as a voluntary public-private partnership seeking to promote the sustainability of native Florida birds and their habitats through coordinated efforts that strategically address critical needs related to conservation planning, delivery of conservation programs, research and monitoring, education and outreach, and public policy. The FWC works with the Atlantic Coast Joint Venture and a wide variety of conservation partners in the State of Florida to serve FBCI goals. The FBCI will address bird conservation over the entire state, including two joint ventures and two bird conservation regions (BCRs 27 and 31) (Florida Fish and Wildlife Conservation Commission 2010b).

FLORIDA'S ENDANGERED AND THREATENED SPECIES MANAGEMENT AND CONSERVATION PLAN

Florida's Endangered and Threatened Species Management and Conservation Plan (Florida Fish and Wildlife Conservation Commission 2004), as required under Section 5 of the Florida Endangered and Threatened Species Act of 1977 (§372.072 Florida Statutes) is a plan for management and conservation of species listed by the State of Florida. In addition to those species listed by the federal government, several state-listed species of management concern to the refuges occur on and near the refuges, including the roseate spoonbill (species of special concern); black skimmer (species of special concern); American oystercatcher (species of special concern); snowy plover (threatened); gopher tortoise (threatened); Sanibel Island rice rat (*Oryzomys palustris sanibeli*) (species of special concern); reddish egret (species of special concern); brown pelican (species of special concern), little blue heron (*Egretta caerulea*) (species of special concern); snowy egret (*Egretta thula*) (species of special concern); tricolored heron (*Egretta tricolor*) (species of special concern); white ibis (species of special concern); and least tern (threatened) (Florida Fish and Wildlife Conservation Commission 2009a).

FLORIDA NATURAL AREAS INVENTORY

The Florida Natural Areas Inventory (FNAI) is a nonprofit organization dedicated to gathering, interpreting, and disseminating information critical to the conservation of Florida's biological diversity. The Inventory was founded in 1981 as a member of The Nature Conservancy's international network of natural heritage programs. The databases and expertise of FNAI facilitate environmentally sound planning and natural resource management to protect the plants, animals, and communities that represent Florida's natural heritage. The Florida Natural Areas Inventory is the primary source of information on Florida's conservation lands. The Inventory databases include boundaries and statistics for more than 1,600 federal, state, local, and privately managed areas, all provided directly by the managing agencies (Florida Natural Areas Inventory 2009).

FNAI includes sites and sightings on the four refuges (Florida Natural Areas Inventory undated).

SURFACE WATER IMPROVEMENT AND MANAGEMENT PROGRAMS

In the late 1980s, it was determined that Florida had to do more to protect and restore its surface waters. While point sources (sewage and industrial wastes) were being controlled, nonpoint sources (pollutants that enter water bodies in less direct ways) were still a major concern. In 1987, the Florida Legislature created the Surface Water Improvement and Management (SWIM) program to address nonpoint pollutant sources. The SWIM program is the only program that addresses a waterbody's needs as a system of connected resources, rather than isolated wetlands or water bodies. To accomplish this, SWIM meshes across governmental responsibilities, forging important partnerships in water resource management. While the state's five water management districts and the Florida Department of Environmental Protection are directly responsible for the SWIM program, they work in concert with federal, state, and local governments, as well as with the private sector. The refuges fall under two water management districts and two SWIM programs.

Charlotte Harbor is sixth on the SWFWMD's SWIM priority list. The Charlotte Harbor SWIM Plan reflects the CHNEP Comprehensive Conservation and Management Plan.

Lower Charlotte Harbor (LCH) is defined as the basins of Pine Island Sound, Matlacha Pass, East and West Caloosahatchee, Estero Bay, and the lower portion of Charlotte Harbor proper. The Plan's basic strategy is one of restoring, protecting, and managing the surface water resources of the Lower Charlotte Harbor Watershed. The Lower Charlotte Harbor SWIM Plan focuses on six primary initiatives (South Florida Water Management District 2008):

- Water Quality – the utilization of water quality monitoring data to evaluate sources of pollutants; the application of water quality models to evaluate the fate of water quality constituents; and the implementation of prioritized water quality enhancements for both 303(d) listed surface waters and other degraded waters.
- Stormwater Quantity – the reduction of sheet flow and the periodic discharge of large quantities of fresh stormwater runoff into the major river systems in the LCH results in ecologically damaging changes in salinity throughout the estuarine areas of the watershed. This plan focuses on mechanisms to reduce these excess flows and restore more natural timing and quantity of freshwater inflows to the watershed.
- Watershed Master Planning and Implementation – an evaluation of stormwater management and identification of problem areas, with detailed remedial actions generally derived using hydrologic models simulating water volumes and flows under a range of climatic conditions.
- Habitat Assessment, Protection and Restoration – evaluate ancillary data needed to identify and provide habitat protection and restoration in the LCH. Additional data collection efforts for parameters such as benthic organism diversity, submerged aquatic vegetation distribution, and shellfish areas will be evaluated and implemented as necessary.
- Outreach – the LCH watershed encompasses a diverse region of urban, agricultural and environmental lands, and it is managed and regulated by numerous agencies and municipalities. Outreach, including both communication and coordination, is vital tool for the South Florida Water Management District (SFWMD) to efficiently and effectively meet the differing needs of these entities, while also meeting LCH SWIM goals. Through outreach, SFWMD can provide leadership with both the public and local governments.
- Funding – the need for long-term dedicated funding to reach plan goals. It also serves to coordinate funding within and across district areas of responsibility, as well as within each of the other initiatives in the LCH SWIM Plan.

Both the Lower Charlotte Harbor SWIM Plan and the Charlotte Harbor NEP's CCMP identified hydrologic alterations; water quality degradation; and, fish and wildlife habitat loss as significant management issues. The goals of the Lower Charlotte Harbor SWIM Plan are consistent with the goals identified by the Charlotte Harbor NEP and the SWIM Plan's management strategies for protecting and restoring Charlotte Harbor are based on the Charlotte Harbor NEP's CCMP.

STATE AQUATIC PRESERVES

In 1975, Florida adopted the Aquatic Preserve Act to protect state-owned submerged lands for those areas with exceptional biological, aesthetic, and scientific value to set them aside forever as aquatic preserves or sanctuaries for the benefit of future generations. Today, Florida has 46 aquatic preserves on nearly 2 million acres (809,371 ha) (Florida Department of Environmental Protection 2009a). Four aquatic preserves totaling over 157,000 acres (63,536 ha) are located in the area of the four refuges: Pine Island Sound (designated in 1970, 54,000 acres, 21,853 ha); Matlacha Pass (designated in 1972, 12,500 acres, 5,059 ha); Cape Haze (designated in 1978, 11,000 acres, 4,452 ha); and Gasparilla Sound/Charlotte Harbor (designated in 1979, 80,000 acres, 32,375 ha) (Florida Department of Environmental Protection 2009a). Covering the Cape Haze, Gasparilla Sound, Matlacha Pass, and Pine Island Sound aquatic preserves, the Charlotte Harbor Aquatic Preserves

Management Plan was approved in 1983 (Florida Department of Natural Resources 1983a). The Charlotte Harbor Aquatic Preserves Management Plan covers over 200 square miles, which is 90% of the surface water area in the Charlotte Harbor system (Florida Department of Natural Resources 1983a). These four aquatic preserves were designated and are managed as wilderness preserves to maintain their wilderness condition (Florida Department of Natural Resources 1983a). Beyond these four aquatic preserves, two additional aquatic preserves totaling about 19,000 acres (7,689 ha) are located nearby: Lemon Bay (designated in 1986, 8,000 acres, 3,237 ha) and Estero Bay Aquatic Preserve (designated in 1983, 11,000 acres, 4,452 ha) (Florida Department of Environmental Protection 2009a). Covering 7,667 acres (3,103 ha) and as outlined in its management plan, the Lemon Bay Aquatic Preserve was established to preserve marine and estuarine areas in essentially natural or restored conditions so that the aesthetic, biologic, and scientific values shall endure for the enjoyment of present and future generations (Florida Department of Natural Resources 1992). Covering over 15 square miles of surface water area, the Estero Bay Aquatic Preserve was designated and is managed as a wilderness preserve to maintain the wilderness condition (Florida Department of Natural Resources 1983b). The resources of the four refuges benefit from protection and management of all of these aquatic preserves.

STATE PARKS AND PRESERVES

Management plans for Cayo Costa State Park, Gasparilla Island State Park, and Charlotte Harbor Preserve State Park also relate to and benefit the four refuges. Located north of North Captiva Island between Pine Island Sound and the Gulf of Mexico, Cayo Costa State Park is near Pine Island NWR and includes portions of four islands, totaling 2,656 acres (1,075 ha) (Florida Department of Environmental Protection 2005a). Cayo Costa State Park is designated as a public outdoor recreation site (Florida Department of Environmental Protection 2005a). Located just north of Cayo Costa State Park between Charlotte Harbor and the Gulf of Mexico and north of Boca Grande Pass, Gasparilla Island State Park is near Island Bay NWR and is 128 acres (52 ha) in size (Florida Department of Environmental Protection 2002c). Gasparilla Island State Park is also designated as a public outdoor recreation site (Florida Department of Environmental Protection 2002c). Encompassing 42,598 acres (17,239 ha) along Charlotte Harbor, Charlotte Harbor Preserve State Park is close to Island Bay NWR with portions in Punta Gorda and Cape Coral (Florida Department of Environmental Protection 2007). Designated for public outdoor recreation and conservation, Charlotte Harbor Preserve State Park includes 70 miles of shoreline and numerous islands (Florida Department of Environmental Protection 2007).

WILD AND SCENIC RIVERS

Public Law 90-542 (Wild and Scenic Rivers Act of 1968) requires the identification of potential wild, scenic, and recreational river areas within the nation. Section 5(d) of the Wild and Scenic Rivers Act (16 U.S.C. 1271-1287) requires that "In all planning for the use and development of water and related land resources, consideration shall be given by all Federal agencies involved to potential national wild, scenic and recreational river areas." It further requires that "the Secretary of the Interior shall make specific studies and investigations to determine which additional wild, scenic and recreational river areas.....shall be evaluated in planning reports by all Federal agencies as potential alternative uses of water and related land resources involved". The National Park Service has identified four Wild and Scenic River segments in the J.N "Ding" Darling NWR Complex area: three in Lee County (Estero River, Hendry Creek, and Orange River) and one in Charlotte County (Shell Creek). Details for these river segments are provided in Table 4 (National Park Service 2007).

Table 4. Nationwide Rivers Inventory, Florida segments near the refuges.

River	County	Reach	Length (miles)	ORVs	Description
Estero River	Lee	RM 0, Estero Bay, to RM 8, US 41 and Koreshan State Park	8	S, R, F, W, H, C	Established canoe/nature trail; Koreshan State Historic Site, flows through mangrove swamp.
Hendry Creek	Lee	RM 0, Estero Bay, to RM 5, FL 865 and Gladiolus Drive	5	S, R, F, W	Diverse estuarine ecosystem.
Orange River	Lee	RM 0, confluence with Caloosahatchee River, to RM 9, Lehigh Acres	9	S, R, F, W	State Endangered Manatee Marine Mammal Sanctuary.
Shell Creek	Charlotte	RM 3, US 17/FL 35 bridge, to RM 20, east of FL 31 bridge	17	S, R, H, C	Scenic stream with excellent water quality.

Outstandingly Remarkable Values (ORVs): Scenery (S); Recreation (R); Geology (G); Fish (F); Wildlife (W); Prehistory (P); History (H); Cultural (C); Other Values (O).

Source: National Park Service 2007

AREA CLIMATE CHANGE PLANS

The Service and the partners recognize the need to respond to the impacts of climate change, including through the development of the Peninsular Florida LCC, the development and refinement of various modeling efforts, and the development of management plans. The Charlotte Harbor National Estuary Program and the Southwest Florida Regional Planning Council have several very recent climate change related plans that are useful for the refuges, including the Comprehensive Southwest Florida/Charlotte Harbor Climate Change Vulnerability Assessment (Beever et al. 2009a), Charlotte Harbor Regional Climate Change Vulnerability Assessment (Charlotte Harbor National Estuary Program and Southwest Florida Regional Planning Council 2010), and City of Punta Gorda Adaptation Plan (Beever et al. 2009b). Further, Lee County is currently working on a Climate Change Vulnerability Report and a Climate Change Resiliency Plan. The Service is committed to working with these and other partners to understand and ameliorate the impacts of climate change in the Charlotte Harbor area.

Comprehensive Southwest Florida/Charlotte Harbor Climate Change Vulnerability Assessment

The Comprehensive Southwest Florida/Charlotte Harbor Climate Change Vulnerability Assessment examined climate change in Southwest Florida, identifying 246 climate change adaptations that could be utilized to address various vulnerabilities in the region. The document emphasizes the need for monitoring, especially to establish threshold indicators; prescriptive actions that can be adaptively managed as additional information becomes available; and the need to act now to avoid, mitigate, minimize, and adapt to the negative effects of climate change (Beever et al. 2009a).

The Refuge Complex assisted the Charlotte Harbor Climate Change Vulnerability Assessment by participating in the selection of climate change indicators as part of the Climate Change Indicators Workgroup.

Charlotte Harbor Regional Climate Change Vulnerability Assessment

The Charlotte Harbor Regional Climate Change Vulnerability Assessment addresses potential climate changes in air and water and the effects of those changes on climate stability, sea level, hydrology, geomorphology, natural habitats and species, land use changes, economy, human health, human infrastructure, and variable risk projections, in the Charlotte Harbor Region. The assessment identifies priority vulnerabilities facing the Charlotte Harbor region, including changes related to drought, flood, hurricane severity, land area, habitats, biological cycles, and uncertainty in environmental models (Charlotte Harbor National Estuary Program and Southwest Florida Regional Planning Council 2010).

City of Punta Gorda Adaptation Plan

The EPA named Charlotte Harbor one of six Climate Ready Estuary pilot programs. The City of Punta Gorda Adaptation Plan is part of this pilot and identifies alternative adaptations that could be undertaken to address the identified climate change vulnerabilities for the City of Punta Gorda, including adaptive management and subsequent monitoring. Eight major areas of climate change vulnerability were identified for the City of Punta Gorda: fish and wildlife habitat degradation; inadequate water supply; flooding; unchecked or unmanaged growth; water quality degradation; education and economy and lack of funds; fire; and availability of insurance. The top agreed-upon adaptations for each area of vulnerability include: protecting and restoring seagrass; using xeriscaping and native plant landscaping; explicitly indicating in the comprehensive plan which areas will retain natural shorelines; constraining locations for certain high risk infrastructure; restricting fertilizer use; promoting green building alternatives through education, taxing incentives, and green lending; and conducting drought preparedness planning (Beever et al. 2009b).

ECOLOGICAL THREATS AND PROBLEMS

The refuges face numerous threats and various challenges all related to growth of the human population and development of the landscape. The area's developed nature is evident in the land cover types depicted in Figure 10. The Charlotte Harbor National Estuary Program outlines the ecological threats and problems for this area (Charlotte Harbor National Estuary Program 2008):

- Hydrologic alterations: Adverse changes to amounts, locations and timing of freshwater flows, the hydrologic function of floodplain systems and natural river flows.
- Water quality degradation: Pollution from agricultural and urban runoff, point source discharges, septic systems and wastewater treatment systems, atmospheric deposition, ground water and other sources.
- Fish and wildlife habitat loss: Degradation and elimination of headwater streams and other habitats, conversion of natural shorelines caused by development, cumulative impacts of docks and boats, invasion of exotic species and cumulative and future impacts.
- Stewardship gaps: Limitations in people's knowledge of choices and management decisions that will lead to sustainability within their community. These gaps include over arching issues such as public outreach, advocacy and data management.

Figure 10. Land cover types for the area.

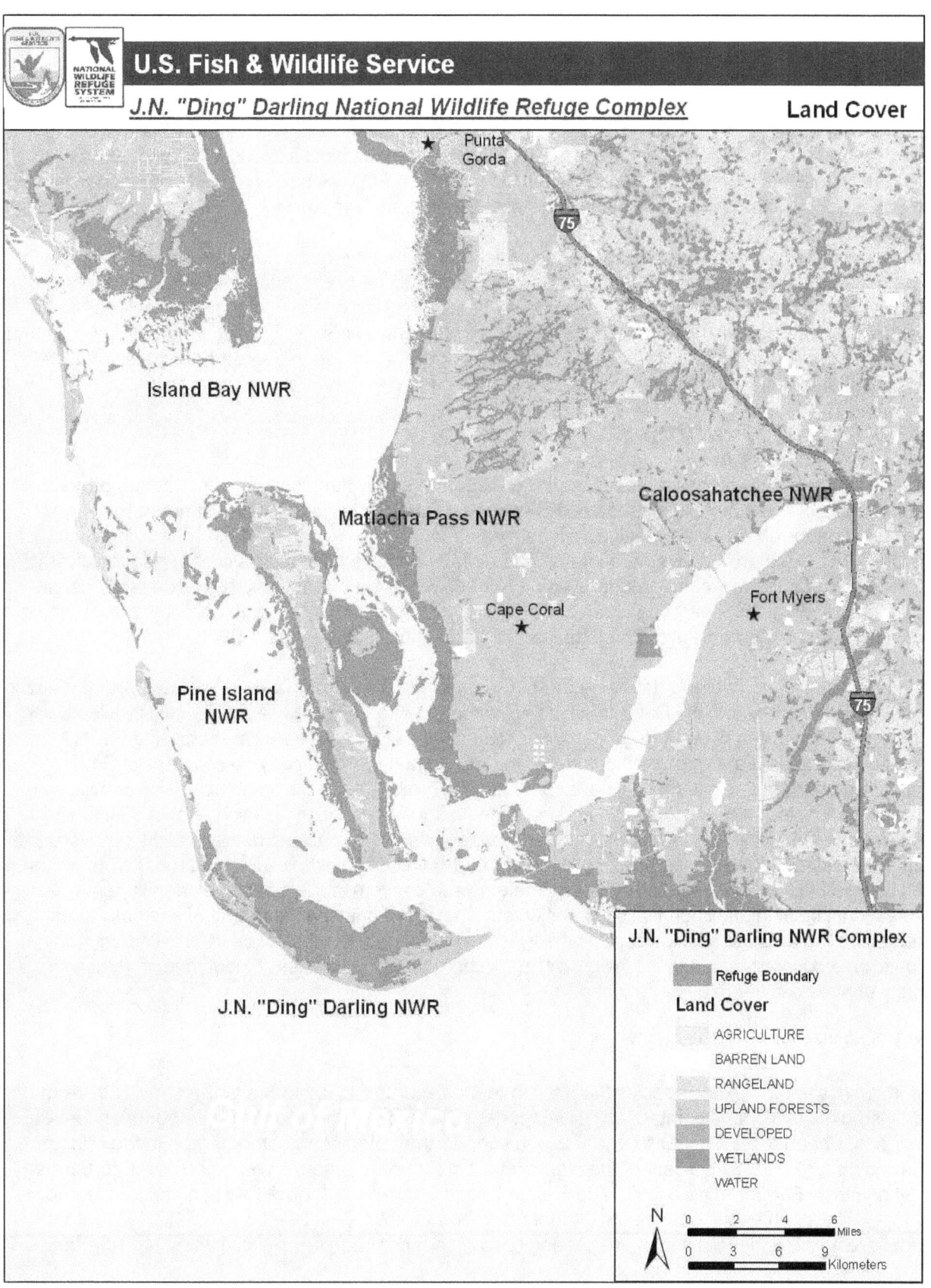

Comprehensive Conservation Plan 45

Specific to Pine Island, Matlacha Pass, Island Bay, and Caloosahatchee NWRs, the most important ecological threats and problems are directly related to those of the larger Charlotte Harbor, including the growing human population and associated use and development of the landscape. Within the 15-year life of the CCP and by 2025, Charlotte County is expected to grow 26 percent to 224,577 (gaining about 47,000 people during the 15 years), while Lee County is expected to grow 36 percent to 838,209 (gaining 220,000 people during the 15 years) (Zwick and Carr 2006). By 2060, Charlotte County is expected to reach 335,713 (increasing 2.4 times since 2000 and 1.9 times since 2010), while Lee County would be nearly 1.4 million (more than tripling since 2000 and more than doubling since 2010) (Zwick and Carr 2060). It is anticipated that Lee County will be built out before 2060 as part of a nearly continuous band of urban development along Florida's southwest coast (Zwick and Carr 2006).

The key ecological threats and problems include altered quantity, quality and timing of freshwater flows, including freshwater flows from the Caloosahatchee River and watershed and regulatory releases from Lake Okeechobee. These altered flows effect salinity levels and nutrient loads in the Charlotte Harbor Estuary, which impact seagrasses, oysters, and other habitat types and the fish and wildlife resources that use those habitats. Additional threats include the spread of exotic, invasive, and nuisance species and the impacts of climate change.

WATER QUALITY, QUANTITY, AND TIMING

The ecological health of the Refuge Complex's estuarine ecosystem is linked directly to the health of Charlotte Harbor and the Caloosahatchee River watershed (inclusive of the Kissimmee River and Lake Okeechobee watersheds). Coastal southwest Florida is one of the fastest urbanizing regions in the U.S. The rapid urban development that has already occurred has radically changed the character and ecology of coastal waters. Mangroves have been removed or cut back; red tide events cause public health warnings; seagrass areas have declined or been damaged; and groundwater pumping has reached its maximum limit (Charlotte Harbor National Estuary Program 2008).

Beyond the ongoing use and development of the landscape, hydrologic modifications and the timing of hydrologic releases into the Caloosahatchee River from Lake Okeechobee are specific problems and concerns for the health of the Refuge Complex. Manmade canals and levees crisscrossing South Florida have altered the natural hydrology that formed and maintained the wetlands and estuaries of South Florida. Residential and commercial development along the bays and Caloosahatchee River have adversely impacted wildlife and habitat and increased point and nonpoint pollution (e.g., nutrients and turbidity) into the waterways. As a result of the hydrologic modifications, the quality, timing, duration, and volume of water releases from Lake Okeechobee into the Caloosahatchee River and runoff from within the Caloosahatchee watershed are specific problems and concerns for the health of the refuges. Recreational boating and sport fishing has affected fish populations and the quality of seagrass beds, threatening Endangered species such as the West Indian manatee and sea turtles. In short, the rapid population, economic, and agricultural growth in southern and southwestern Florida has brought with it a variety of threats to the refuges (Cox et al. 1994).

EXOTIC, INVASIVE, AND NUISANCE SPECIES

Florida's invasion by exotic species began with the first European explorers in the early 16th century. Because of its mild climate, international seaports, cultural diversity, and lenient importation laws, Florida has been the epicenter for more exotic species than almost any other region in the country. Currently, more than 31 percent of the plants found in Florida are nonnative, as are over 26 percent of all animals (Ferriter et al. 2005). The Florida Exotic Pest Plant Council has outlined 67 Category I and 71 Category II exotic pest plants for Florida (Florida Exotic Pest Plant Council 2007). Category I plants are invasive exotics which are altering native plant communities by displacing native species, changing community structures or ecological functions, or hybridizing with natives. This definition does not rely on the economic severity or geographic range of the problem, but on the documented ecological damage caused. Category II plants are invasive exotics that have increased in abundance or frequency, but have not yet altered Florida plant communities to the extent shown by Category I species. These species may become ranked Category I, if ecological damage is demonstrated.

The Charlotte Harbor NEP CCMP (Charlotte Harbor National Estuary Program 2008) provides a partial list of out-of-control exotic, invasive, and nuisance species, as follows:

- Australian pine (*Casuarina equisetifolia*): Pine-like trees introduced a century ago for windbreaks and erosion control along coastlines; toppled by winds; displaces coastal vegetation and spreads easily.
- Brazilian pepper (*Schinus terebinthifolius*): Holly look-alike brought to Manatee and Charlotte counties in the 1920s; irritant sap; forms dense stands; displaces wildlife and native plants; encroaches into wetlands; easily spread by wildlife.
- Punk tree or melaleuca (*Melaleuca quinquenervia*): Fast-growing, white-barked tree intended for windbreaks and draining of wetlands; forms dense thickets, displacing wildlife; very common throughout southwest Florida and the Everglades and is spreading northward; eradication effort is a constant battle.
- Hydrilla (*Hydrilla verticillata*): Aquatic plant that entered Tampa in 1950s; grows dense strands of whorled leaves that choke waterways and deplete oxygen; displaces native plants and fish; control efforts making steady progress.
- Water hyacinth (*Eichhornia crassipes*): Large floating plant with dark green leaves and lavender flowers; introduced in the 1800s; slows water flow and boats; depletes oxygen; increasingly managed, which also assists hydrilla control.
- Air potato (*Dioscorea bulbifera*): Introduced through agriculture in 1905; covers native trees, shading out understory vegetation; eliminates habitat.
- Cogongrass (*Imperata cylindrica*): Introduced in 1911 for cattle forage and soil stabilization; found not to be good forage for cattle; can increase fire intensity; invades native habitats, agricultural forests, roadsides, phosphate mining lands and altered pinelands; takes over large areas, crowding out native species.
- Nile monitor lizard (*Varanus niloticus*): First identified in Cape Coral as a problem after the adoption of the CCMP in 2000; a nuisance animal that can prey on native animals and small pets.

Native wildlife and habitats in and around the refuges have been impacted by the growing human population; the Caloosahatchee River; and exotic, invasive, and nuisance species, including through direct loss of wildlife and habitats, as well as fragmentation of habitats, decreasing the sustainability of many species. Further, large snakes are posing more and more of a problem for this area, including the Burmese python (*Python molurus bivittatus*).

POTENTIAL EFFECTS OF CLIMATE CHANGE

Department of the Interior Secretarial Order 3226 states that there is a consensus in the international community that global climate change is occurring and that it should be addressed in governmental decision-making. This order ensures that climate change impacts are taken into account in connection with Departmental planning and decision-making. Additionally, it calls for the incorporation of climate change considerations into long-term planning documents such as the CCP. Projecting the impacts of climate change is hugely complex. The effects of climate change on populations and range distributions of wildlife are expected to be species specific and highly variable, with some effects considered negative and others considered positive.

Meteorological and climatological events, such as hurricanes (e.g., No-name storm and Hurricane Charley) and sea level rise, pose challenges for refuge management. Further, climate change related stressors will likely enhance the negative impacts of other stressors. Climate change may exacerbate shoreline erosion due to rising seas (Doyle 1998; Natural Resources Defense Council 2001; Zhang et al. 2004; Bindoff et al. 2007; Holland and Webster 2007; Nicholls et al. 2007) and may result in an increase in the intensity and frequency of tropical cyclones (Emanuel 1987; Emanuel 2005; Webster et al. 2005; Mann and Emanuel 2006). Low-lying islands will face impacts from global climate change, particularly rising sea level and coastal storms. Such effects have already been experienced in the past; however, these events may become more frequent and severe within the 15-year time period covered by this CCP, based on recent projections by the Intergovernmental Panel on Climate Change (Intergovernmental Panel on Climate Change 2007). Saline intrusion into the subsurface freshwater lens from sea level rise and saltwater inundation of surface freshwaters from storm surges can alter coastal ecosystems and freshwater marshes resulting in more salt-tolerant aquatic plant communities. The most immediate action that the Service can take is to gather the best scientific data possible for understanding natural processes in their current state, modeling possible impacts and subsequent changes from sea level rise, and developing adaptive management strategies for future conservation needs.

A report by the Florida Oceans and Coastal Council summarized climate change drivers, effects, and potential results in relation to Florida's ocean and coastal resources. Increasing greenhouse gases are expected to result in increases in ocean acidification, which may result in the potential for shifts in marine ecosystem structure and dynamics and declines in or disappearance of important fisheries habitats, such as coral reefs. Increasing air temperature and water vapor is expected to result in altered rainfall and runoff patterns and altered frequency and intensity of tropical storms and hurricanes. Altered rainfall and runoff patterns may result in the potential for increased frequency of extreme rainfall events, exacerbating already altered and stressed conditions in estuaries and the potential for decreasing rainfall in highly urbanized landscapes. Altered frequency and intensity of tropical storms and hurricanes may result in the potential for more frequent and severe hurricanes. As sea surface temperatures continue to increase, already stressed coastal and marine environments will experience more adverse impacts and ocean currents may shift. Increasing ocean temperature is expected to result in increases in coral bleaching and disease; increases in fish diseases, sponge die-offs, and loss of marine life; changes in the distribution of native and exotic species; changes in nutrient supply, recycling, and food webs; harmful algal blooms, and hypoxia. Increases in coral bleaching and disease may result in the potential for the damage and/or loss of some coral species due to exceedance of thermal tolerance limits, increased occurrence and severity of coral bleaching events, increased algal blooms, increased diseases for corals and associated organisms, major shifts in coral reef communities, and decreased biodiversity. Increases in fish diseases, sponge die-offs, and loss of marine life may result in the potential for more frequent die-offs of marine fauna that cannot move to cooler water, which will be exacerbated by increased nutrients, pollution, and algal blooms. Changes in the distribution of native and exotic species may result in drastic changes in species compositions in marine and estuarine systems, increased exotic species, range shifts and/or extirpation for many species, increased diseases, and loss of some species. Changes in nutrient supply, recycling, and food webs may result in less efficient food webs, resulting in decreased productivity, including of economically important fish and other species. More frequent and intense harmful algal blooms may disrupt marine and estuarine systems, result in more frequent fish kills, and adversely impact people. Increased hypoxia due to increased nutrients running off into coastal systems may result in longer and/or recurring hypoxic events and negative impacts to bottom-dwelling and feeding organisms. Increasing sea level is expected to result in changes in estuaries, tidal wetlands, and tidal rivers; changes in beaches, barrier islands, and inlets; and reduced coastal water supplies. Changes in estuaries, tidal wetlands, and tidal rivers may result in loss of some tidal wetlands and some lowland coastal forests; loss of over half saltmarsh, shoals, and mud flats, negatively impacting fishes and birds; replacement of high diversity wetlands with low diversity wetlands; increases in open waters; increased risk to shallow water dependent fish species; and the loss of many coastal systems that currently buffer storm impacts. Changes in beaches, barrier islands, and inlets may include increased erosion; migration landward of barrier islands; and loss of some barrier islands, altering or eliminating marshes and estuaries. Reduced coastal water supplies may mean increased competition for water, potential for increased saltwater intrusion, and increased threats to surficial aquifers (Florida Oceans and Coastal Council 2009).

In the Comprehensive Southwest Florida/Charlotte Harbor Climate Change Vulnerability Assessment, the Southwest Florida Regional Planning Council and the Charlotte Harbor National Estuary Program examine current and ongoing climate change. Southwest Florida is currently experiencing climate change. The natural setting of southwest Florida coupled with extensive overinvestment in the areas closest to the coast have placed the region at the forefront of geographic areas that are among the first to suffer the negative effects of a changing climate. More severe tropical storms and hurricanes with increased wind speeds and storm surges have already severely damaged both coastal and interior communities of southwest Florida. Significant losses of mature mangrove forest, water quality degradation, and barrier island geomorphic changes have already occurred. Longer, more severe dry season droughts coupled with shorter duration wet seasons consisting of higher volume precipitation have generated a pattern of drought and flood impacting both natural and man-made ecosystems. Even in the most probable, lowest impact future climate change scenario predictions, the future for southwest Florida will include increased climate instability; wetter wet seasons; drier dry seasons; more extreme hot and cold events; increased coastal erosion; continuous sea level rise; shifts in fauna and flora with reductions in temperate species and expansions of tropical invasive exotics; increasing occurrence of tropical diseases in plants, wildlife and humans; destabilization of aquatic food webs including increased harmful algae blooms; increasing strains upon and costs in infrastructure; and increased uncertainty concerning variable risk assessment with uncertain actuarial futures (Beever et al. 2009a).

Because the refuges lack even baseline data, measured impacts to refuge resources are currently unknown. Likely changes and stressors include alterations in wildlife populations and ranges, increased storm intensity, increased drought severity and persistence, and increased density and diversity of exotic and invasive species. And, these are likely to exacerbate other stressors, resulting in decreased water quality, altered water quantity and timing of flows, and increased pollution. The prospect of global climate change could result in a wide variety of changes to the natural resources in and around Pine Island, Matlacha Pass, Island Bay, and Caloosahatchee National Wildlife Refuges. The full range and degree of the direct and indirect effects would be very difficult to predict, but conjectures can be made. The many small mangrove islands and marshes of the refuges with low elevation topography would be more likely to experience higher rates of coastline erosion. Rises in sea levels could shift marshes inland (Field et al. 2001) and transition intertidal marshes into subtidal marshes (Galbraith et al. 2002) or open water. Sea level rise would also increase salt water intrusion resulting in the alteration of plant communities and result in declines in mangrove and seagrass communities (Twilley et al. 2001). Changes to climate patterns could elevate sea surface temperatures resulting in increased storm frequencies and intensities (Erwin et al. 2004). If storms and hurricanes occur more frequently, besides increased local damage to mangrove forests, there would be temporary increases in sediments and organic material discharged to coastal waters around the refuges (Twilley et al. 2001). Elevated air temperatures could also lead to increased drought durations resulting in altered and more intense fire seasons (Twilley et al. 2001). These changes would also present conditions likely to increase the incidence of algal blooms and red tide events and increase the spread of exotic and invasive species (Ogden et al. 2005), and negatively change the refuges' ecologically important diverse plant species (Browder et al. 2005). This would potentially increase the number of threatened and endangered species and further imperil those already at risk. Populations of native plants and animals—already stressed and greatly reduced in their ranges—

could experience further stress from warmer temperatures, putting those species at increased risk for loss of local populations or even complete extinction (Harris and Cropper 1992). The potential effects of changing climate on these rather isolated refuges could be substantial because of the limited opportunities for natural species to migrate (Twilley et al. 2001).

In 2006 and 2008, respectively, the Sea Level Affecting Marshes Model (SLAMM) was run for Pine Island NWR (McMahon 2006) and Island Bay NWR (Clough 2008). The model for Pine Island NWR led to results for 2100 showing the loss of uplands, tidal flats, and estuarine beaches; the transition of habitats to salt marsh; a 15 percent loss of mangroves; and a 263 percent increase in open estuarine waters (McMahon 2006). The various scenarios for Island Bay NWR led to results ranging from no change in mangroves and a shift of tidal flats to open estuarine waters to the conversion of mangroves and tidal flats to open estuarine waters by 2100 (Clough 2008). Although limited data were used to develop this model, the model does indicate trends. Increased data, increased coordination with the partners, improved climate change and other modeling efforts [e.g., Sea, Lake, and Overland Surges from Hurricanes (SLOSH) models accurately model area flooding levels under storm scenarios], and refinement of the SLAMM with more accurate baseline data would help increase its predictability, providing better information to enhance decision-making for the refuges.

PHYSICAL RESOURCES

CLIMATE

The climate in the area of the refuges is subtropical and humid, with temperature extremes of both the summer and winter being tempered by the marine influence of the Gulf of Mexico. Much of peninsular Florida is in a latitudinal band that, globally, is desert. However, Florida and the Refuge Complex area are saved from this fate by being surrounded by water. Rising air, caused by heating of the Florida peninsula land surface, causes moist sea breezes to flow in from the coasts toward the center of the State, triggering thunderstorms and causing a summer rainy season. During the winter and spring months, when water off the coast is warm relative to the land and less heating of the ground surface occurs, the effect of the water is actually reversed, and rainfall tends to be suppressed causing a distinct dry season. Cold northern air passing over water is warmed; hence the peninsula is also protected from the extremes of cold temperatures during the winter.

Based on data from the Fort Myers Airport, the annual average temperature is about 74 degrees Fahrenheit (°F), while annual average temperatures range from 64.6°F to 84°F and monthly average temperatures range from 53.5°F in January to 91.4°F in August. Annual rainfall averages about 54-55 inches. Almost two-thirds of the average annual rainfall occurs during the wet season (June-September), mostly the result of localized convective thunderstorms. Most summer thunderstorms are triggered by air rising off of the heated land surface and they often occur in the afternoon, especially where the sea breezes from the east and west coasts meet. The average temperature and rainfall data are presented in Table 5 and Figure 11.

Winters are mild, with many bright, warm days and moderately cool nights. There are frequent long periods during the winter when only very light, or no rain falls. Occasional cold snaps bring temperatures in the 30s°F, but only rarely do temperatures drop into the 20s°F. The lowest recorded temperature in the area of the refuges (at the Fort Myers weather station) was 26°F in December of 1962. Frost occurs on only a few occasions each year, and usually is light and scattered. In the summer, temperatures have reached 100°F, but these occurrences are very rare. The highest recorded temperature in the area was 103°F in June of 1981.

Table 5. Temperature, Precipitation, and Snowfall Summary, Fort Myers Federal Aviation Administration Airport, Florida (083186)
Period of Record Monthly Climate Summary: 1/1/1931 to 6/30/2007

	Jan	Feb	Mar	Apr	May	Jun	Jul	Aug	Sep	Oct	Nov	Dec	Annual
Average Max. Temperature (°F)	74.7	76.1	79.9	84.2	88.6	90.5	91.1	91.4	89.7	85.7	80.2	76.0	84.0
Average Min. Temperature (°F)	53.5	54.6	58.4	62.4	67.5	72.5	74.2	74.5	73.9	68.3	60.5	55.2	64.6
Average Total Precipitation (in.)	1.83	2.11	2.76	2.02	3.54	9.56	8.97	8.89	8.45	3.38	1.50	1.52	54.54
Average Total Snowfall (in.)	0.0	0.0	0.0	0.0	0.0	0.0	0.0	0.0	0.0	0.0	0.0	0.0	0.0
Average Snow Depth (in.)	0	0	0	0	0	0	0	0	0	0	0	0	0

Source: Southeast Regional Climate Center 2007

Summer thunderstorms are frequent. From June through September they occur on two out of every three days on an average. Most rain during the summer occurs as late afternoon or early evening thunderstorms, which bring welcome cooling on hot summer days. These showers seldom last long, even though they yield large amounts of rain. During the late summer or fall, tropical storms or hurricanes may pass nearby and result in heavy downpours that may reach torrential proportions. Twenty-four-hour amounts from six to over 10 inches may occur. The highest one-day total at the Fort Myers weather station was 7.78 inches in September of 1962.

The area in and around these four refuges is hit periodically by tropical storms and by minor and major hurricanes (categories 3-5). The landscape has repeatedly been sculpted by wind and waves from tropical cyclones. Hurricanes are most likely in September and October, when the ocean temperature is warmest and humidity highest. Annually, over a hundred tropical waves develop in the Atlantic, Caribbean, and Gulf of Mexico, although generally fewer than ten develop into tropical storms, and only a handful become hurricanes. Several major hurricanes have occurred in the area since 1900. The Great Miami Hurricane of 1926 first devastated Miami as a Category 4 storm, then passed over San Carlos Bay and Captiva Island as a Category 3 storm. In 1944, an unnamed Category 3 storm passed west of the area, making landfall near the Sarasota County line. In 1960, Hurricane Donna made landfall as a Category 4 Hurricane near Naples and cut a path north to Fort Myers and across the peninsula to re-enter the Atlantic Ocean near Daytona Beach. The storm track of the eye of Donna was east of the refuge, but the size of the storm was immense, and the Charlotte Harbor area was subjected to hurricane force winds for over four hours. Category 4 Hurricane Charley pounded the area in 2004. The right eyewall of Charley passed over North Captiva Island and severed it into two parts (Meyers et al. 2006).

Figure 11. Temperature and precipitation data, Fort Myers Federal Aviation Administration Airport, Florida, 1971-2000.

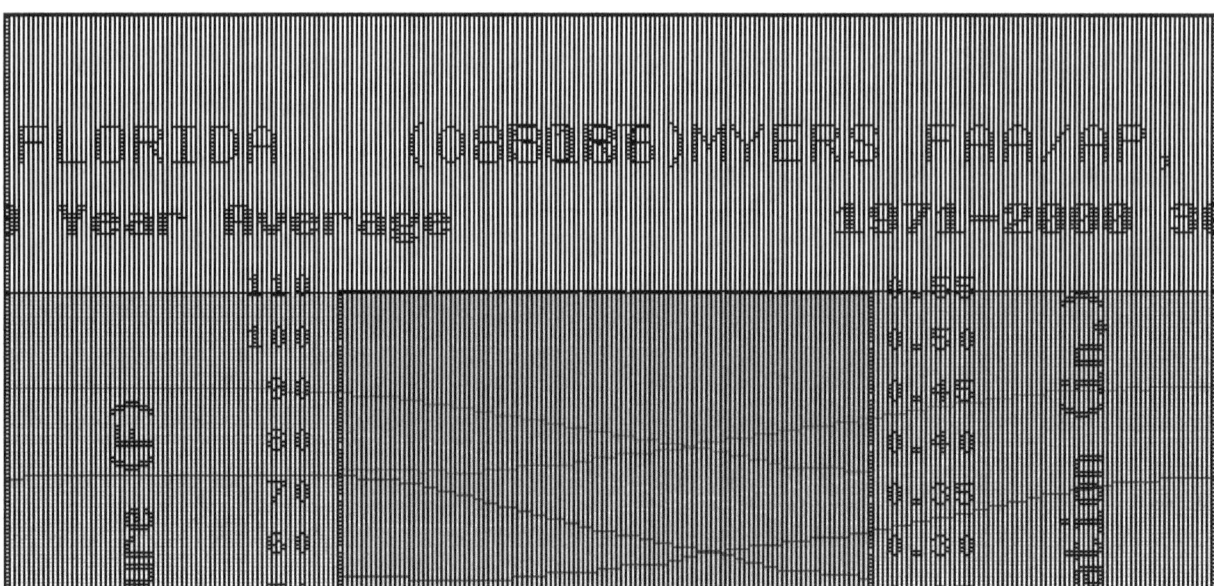

- Maximum (Max) Temp. is the average of all daily maximum temperatures recorded for the day of the year
- Average (Ave) Temp. is the average of all daily average temperatures recorded for the day of the year
- Minimum (Min) Temp. is the average of all daily minimum temperatures recorded for the day of the year
- Precipitation is the average of all daily total precipitation recorded for the day of the year

Source: Southeast Regional Climate Center, undated

The prevailing wind direction is normally from the east and, and except during the passage of tropical storms, high velocities are usually not experienced. During the winter and spring a few days may have 20- to 30-mile per hour (mph) winds and thunderstorms are sometimes accompanied by strong gusts for brief periods. Winds approximating 100 mph have been experienced with the passage of hurricanes during the fall months.

There is seldom a day without sunshine at some time. The sunniest months are April and May, with about a 75 percent chance of possible sunshine. Relative humidity is high during the night (~90 percent), dropping off in the middle of the day (~50 to 60 percent). Heavy fog is rather infrequent, occurring mostly in winter during the early mornings.

Measurable snowfall has never been recorded since records have been kept at Fort Myers, beginning in 1931.

CLIMATE CHANGE AND GLOBAL WARMING

According to data from the National Oceanic and Atmospheric Administration (NOAA) and National Aeronautics and Space Administration (NASA), the Earth's average surface temperature has increased by about 1.2 to 1.4°F since 1900 (U.S. Environmental Protection Agency 2009b). In January 2008, NOAA reported that seven of the eight warmest years on record have occurred since 2001, part of a rise in temperatures of more than 0.6 degrees Celsius (°C) (1°F) since 1900. Within the past three decades, the rate of warming in global temperatures has been approximately three times greater than the century scale trend (National Oceanic and Atmospheric Administration 2008). If greenhouse gases, primarily carbon dioxide, methane, and nitrous oxide, continue to increase, climate models predict that the average temperature at the Earth's surface could increase from 3.2 to 7.2°F above 1990 levels by the end of this century. (U.S. Environmental Protection Agency 2009a)

The effects of climate change and global warming are anticipated to result in changes in weather/rainfall patterns, decreases in snow and ice cover, rising sea levels, and stressed ecosystems. For the southeastern U.S. and Gulf coast, this could result in a variety of impacts, including increased loss of barrier islands and wetlands; increased risk of shoreline flooding due to sea level rise, storm surge, and extreme precipitation events; greater likelihood of warmer/dryer summers and wetter/reduced winter cold; and alterations of ecosystems and habitats due to these changes in weather patterns. Resultant changes in ranges for wildlife and plants would likely allow for increased invasion and spread of exotic, invasive, and nuisance species; would likely limit the ability of plants to respond to the need to move in response to shifting ranges, making them less likely to be sustained in place; and may disrupt natural vegetation-wildlife relationships.

Global warming, resulting in melting of glaciers and ice sheets, will cause sea levels to rise. NASA estimates that yearly, 50 billion tons of ice are melting from the Greenland ice sheet (National Aeronautics and Space Administration 2000). NASA aerial surveys show that more than 11 cubic miles of ice is disappearing from the Greenland ice sheet annually (Krabill et al. 2000). New satellite measurements reveal that the Greenland and West Antarctic ice sheets are shedding about 125 billion tons of ice per year (NASA 2009). Considering that land less than 10 meters above sea level contains two percent of the world's land surface, but 10 percent of its population, major impacts in the U.S. will be felt by large numbers of people living on the low lying coastlands, particularly along the Gulf coast. Worldwide measurements of sea level show a rise of about 0.17 meters (0.56 feet) during the twentieth century (National Aeronautics and Space Administration 2009).

The effects of rising sea levels are even more dramatic in Florida. Because of Florida's natural land subsidence, south Florida's sea level has risen about 0.31 meters (1.0 feet) since 1846 and it is still rising today, at a rate that is equivalent to 0.20 to 0.40 meters (0.67 to 1.33 feet) per century (Ning et al. 2003; U.S. Environmental Protection Agency undated-b). This rate is 6 to 10 times faster than the average rate of sea level rise along the south Florida coast during the past 3,000 years. If the current trend continues without any additional global warming, the sea along the south Florida coast would climb another 7.6 centimeters (3 inches) by 2025 and 25.4 centimeters (10 inches) by 2100. But, global warming is expected to accelerate this sea level rise. During the next 25 years, the sea is likely to rise 12.7 centimeters (5 inches), rather than 7.6 centimeters (3 inches) (U.S. Environmental Protection Agency undated-b). By 2100, the best available science indicates that south Florida seas will be approximately 20 inches higher than they were in 1990 (Ning et al. 2003; U.S. Environmental Protection Agency undated-b). At the very least, these rising sea levels will likely result in the loss of some refuge habitats, with the transition of many refuge habitats to more open estuarine waters (Clough 2008) with increased beach erosion.

Consensus does not exist on how global warming might affect the frequency and severity of hurricanes and tropical storms, or change the frequency and strength of El Niño and La Niña events. Models suggest that tropical regions will probably receive less rain, but rain events will tend to be more intense. In Florida, rainfall patterns have changed in the last 100 years with rainfall declining in parts of south Florida, while increasing in central Florida and the Panhandle; while El Nino events have coincided with periods of drought (U.S. Environmental Protection Agency undated-b). Scientists are also not certain how global warming will affect the salinity of bays and estuaries. Warmer temperatures would increase evaporation, making them more saline. But if precipitation increases, more freshwater runoff would result in less salinity. Under either scenario, seagrasses, mangroves, and other native plants and animals on the refuges would likely be adversely impacted (U.S. Environmental Protection Agency undated-b).

In addition to the rising seas, loss of wetlands, increased beach erosion, and changes in temperature and precipitation are also likely to affect south Florida's plants and wildlife. To survive the climbing temperatures, both marine and land-based plants and animals have started to migrate towards the poles and towards higher elevations. Those species that cannot migrate or adapt face extinction. The Intergovernmental Panel on Climate Change (IPCC) estimates that 20-30 percent of plant and animal species will be at risk of extinction if temperatures climb more than 1.5° to 2.5°C (NASA 2009). Computer models suggest that the overall climate of Florida may warm, resulting in more frequent extremely hot summer days and a longer growing season (U.S. Environmental Protection Agency undated-b).

A warmer climate could allow heat-loving exotic plant species, such as the invasive Melaleuca, Chinese tallow, and Australian pine to expand their ranges. Rapid sea level rise could harm low-lying mangrove communities. Florida's mangrove forests also provide food, nesting, and nursery areas for many animals—including more than 220 species of fish, 24 reptile and amphibian species, 18 species of mammals, and 181 bird species (U.S. Environmental Protection Agency undated-b). In general, the response of mangroves to sea level rise depends on the type of mangroves, their environmental setting, the amount of freshwater available to maintain root growth, and the sediment supply. Mangrove communities in south Florida already are affected by a number of stressors, including invasive Brazilian pepper plants, hurricanes, agricultural runoff, and human development. Climate change and a rise in sea level pose new stresses to these ecosystems, already in danger (U.S. Environmental Protection Agency undated-b). In addition, the potential increased frequency of hurricanes or wildfires could accelerate the invasion of exotic, invasive, and nuisance species (Twilley et al. 2001). However, warmer winters lead to fewer frosts; consequently, tropical plants and trees that are vulnerable to cold temperatures may also benefit.

Warmer air or water temperatures can also impact animal species. Evidence suggests that the gender of sea turtles is determined by the surrounding temperature at critical stages in development, with warmer temperatures producing more females. Warmer temperatures could thus create reproductive problems for an already declining species (Mrosovsky and Provancha 1992). The majority of Florida's native fish species are temperate species existing near the southern limit of their distribution range. However, almost all of the 28 exotic species established in Florida waters in recent years were subtropical or tropical (Courtenay 1994). A recent study of the effects of climate change on eastern U.S. bird species concluded that as many as 78 species of birds could decrease by at least 25 percent, while as many as 33 species could increase in abundance by at least 25 percent due to climate and habitat changes (Matthews et al. 2004).

GEOLOGY AND TOPOGRAPHY

Geology

Florida's environment and ecology are based on its geologic history, which is primarily based upon changing sea levels (Allen and Main 2005). The Florida Plateau formed from volcanic activity and marine sedimentation about 530 million years ago (Allen and Main 2005). Over 40 million years ago the Florida Plateau acted as a marine shelf at the bottom of the ocean (Cervone 2003). As sea levels rose and fell, this shallow shelf collected the remains of sea creatures, creating a limestone bedrock that formed the basis of the Florida peninsula as sea levels eventually set at current levels (Cervone 2003).

The basement rocks of the Florida Plateau include Precambrian-Cambrian igneous rocks, Ordovician-Devonian sedimentary rocks, and Triassic-Jurassic volcanic rocks. Florida's igneous and sedimentary foundation separated from the African Plat when the super-continent Pangaea rifted apart in the Triassic and sutured to the North American craton (continent).

A thick sequence of mid-Jurassic to Holocene sediments (unlithified to well lithified) lies upon the eroded surface of the basement rocks. Carbonate sedimentation predominated from mid-Jurassic until at least mid-Oligocene on most of the Florida Plateau. In response to renewed uplift and erosion in the Appalachian highlands to the north and sea-level fluctuations, siliciclastic sediments began to encroach upon the carbonate-depositing environments of the Florida Plateau. Deposition of siliciclastic-bearing carbonates and siliciclastic sediments predominated from mid-Oligocene to the Holocene over much of the Plateau. Numerous disconformities formed in response to nondeposition and erosion resulting from sea-level fluctuations occurring within the stratigraphic section.

The oldest Florida sediments exposed at the modern land surface are Middle Eocene carbonates of the Avon Park Formation, which crop out on the crest of the Ocala Platform in west-central Florida. Much of the State is blanketed by Pliocene to Holocene siliciclastic-bearing sediments that were deposited in response to late Tertiary and Quaternary sea-level fluctuations (Figure 12) (Scott et al. 2001).

Florida experienced cycles of sediment deposition and erosion in response to sea level changes throughout the Cenozoic Era (the last 65 million years). Florida's Cenozoic-aged sediments include two major groups: the Paleogene and Neogene-Quaternary. During the Paleogene, carbonate sediments formed due to biological activity and are mostly made up of whole or broken fossils including foraminifera, bryozoa, molluscs, corals and other forms of marine life. Very little siliciclastic sediment (quartz sands, silts, and clays) was able to reach Florida because the "Gulf Trough" separated the Florida Plateau from the siliciclastic source area of the Appalachian Mountains. In the late Paleogene, the Appalachians were uplifted, erosional rates increased, and siliciclastic sediments filled the Gulf Trough. Siliciclastic sediments then encroached upon the carbonate depositing environments. Thus, the sediments deposited during the Neogene were primarily quartz sands, silts and clays with varying amounts of limestone, dolomite and shell. In southern Florida, carbonate sediments still predominated because most of the siliciclastic sediments, moving south with the coastal currents, were funneled offshore. The area of the modern-day Everglades was a shallow marine bank where calcareous sediments and bryozoan reefs accumulated. These sediments compacted and eventually formed the limestone that floors the Everglades today (Florida Department of Environmental Protection 2006b).

Island Bay, Pine Island, Matlacha Pass, and Caloosahatchee NWRs are located in the Southern Florida Flatwoods Major Land Resource Area (MLRA), which is a young marine plain underlain by Tertiary-age rocks, including very fine grained shale, mudstone, and limestone beds. A sandy marine deposit of Pleistocene age occurs at the surface in most of this MLRA (USDA National Resources

Conservation Service 2006), with Holocene age sediments in evidence along the southwest Gulf coast shoreline (Figure 13). The Holocene sediments occur near the west coast of Florida at elevations generally less than 1.5 meters. The sediments include quartz, sands, carbonate sands and muds, and organics (Scott 2001). The land mass that is now Southwest Florida remained shallowly submerged beneath the ocean until the Miocene and Pleistocene epochs. Most of Collier and eastern Lee counties emerged during the Miocene Epoch, about 15 million years ago. Not until the Pleistocene Epoch, slightly more than 1 million years ago, did the coastal areas from southern Sarasota County to southern Collier County emerge and begin evolving into the coastline known today. (Most of Glades and Hendry counties also emerged during this epoch.) The process of emergence and submergence of the Florida peninsula is believed to have been cyclic, occurring throughout known geologic time. The emergence, characteristic of the Miocene and Pleistocene epochs, was caused principally by declining sea levels. Evidence exists, however, that the global sea level has been rising since then.

The deposits at and near the surface include sand, shells, clay, and limestone generally less than 120 feet thick. Below these deposits is the Tamiami Formation of Pliocene Age which consists chiefly of gray and green clay and sandy clay. Thin beds of sandstone, sand, or limestone occur locally in the Tamiami and phosphorite is a common accessory mineral. Both formations consist predominantly of gray and gray-white phosphatic limestone with interbedded marl or calcareous clay. Phosphorite is abundant with major concentrations in the lower part of the Hawthorn Formation. Below the Tampa Limestone, the Suwannee Limestone is usually penetrated 600 to 700 feet below land surface. This formation consists predominantly of tan limestone (Boggess and O'Donnell 1982).

Southwest Florida can be divided into ten major physiographic provinces. Four of these physiographic provinces surround and dominate the geology of the Refuge Complex area, as listed (Southwest Florida Regional Planning Council 2002).

- **Gulf Barrier Chain:** The Gulf Barrier Chain is a string of barrier islands from Longboat Key to Cape Romano. It is believed that these islands formed as dune ridges and spits from sand supplied by coastal headlands, rivers, and formerly emergent areas of the continental shelf. As sea level rose during glacial retreat (beginning 6,000 to 8,000 years ago and ending between 3,000 and 5,000 years ago), the area flooded. Prior to this flooding the sea level was 100 meters lower than present and land extended 150 kilometers or more farther west. When the rise in sea level began to slow 4,000 to 5,000 years ago, this sand was acted upon by winds, currents, and waves to form islands parallel to the shoreline. Pine Island NWR, as well as Sanibel Island and the western parts of Matlacha NWR, lie entirely in this province, and are believed to have formed from deltaic Holocene sediments and deposits composed chiefly of mollusk shells and is thought to be only 5,000 years old (Clark, 1976).
- **Gulf Coastal Lowlands:** Found in northwest Lee County, the Gulf Coastal Lowlands are composed primarily of marine sands and sediments, and are separated from the DeSoto Plain (to the north and east) by marine terraces that developed on the south side of the Peace River Valley. The transition from upland to shoreline occurs as a broad, gently southwestward sloping plain composed of depositional sediments of marine origin. These sediments are aligned generally parallel to the coastline, an arrangement that indicates their formation by marine forces. The province ranges in elevation from sea level to about 50 feet above sea level. The generally flat lowland areas are characterized by wetlands interspersed with pine-palmetto flatwoods. The soils are deep and poorly drained. Streams and rivers are known as blackwaters (tea-colored) because of the presence of tannins (tannic acids) found in surface runoff due to local vegetation (including cypress, hardwood hammocks, flatwoods, and swamp and marsh vegetation) (Fernald and Purdum 1998). Island Bay NWR lies entirely in the Gulf Coastal Lowlands as well as eastern parts of Matlacha NWR.

Figure 12. Geologic map of the State of Florida.
(Scott 2000)

Figure 13. Geological map of the southern peninsula of the State of Florida.
(Scott et al. 2001)

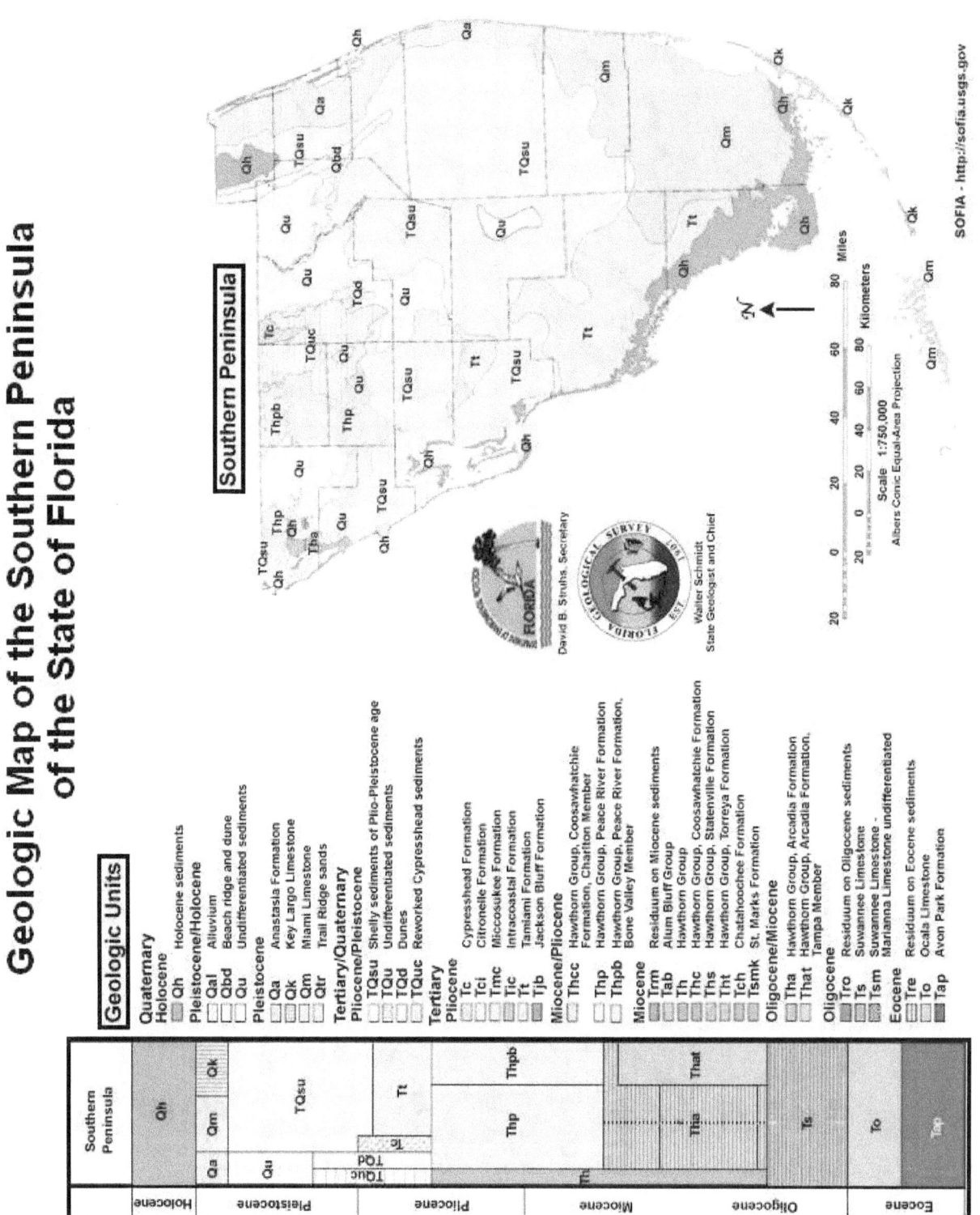

- **Caloosahatchee Valley:** The Caloosahatchee Valley Province divides Lee County with the Gulf Coastal Lowlands province to the north and the Southwestern Slope Province to the south. It rises less than 15 feet in elevation. It extends east to west from Lake Okeechobee to the Lee County shoreline. It is underlain by clay, shell, and limestone deposits. The northern extent is marked by the descending scarp of the DeSoto Plain. Caloosahatchee NWR lies entirely within this physiographic province, as well as the southern parts of Matlacha NWR.
- **Southwestern Slope:** Southern Lee County is included in the Southwestern Slope Province. The slope most likely originated as a marine terrace during periods of higher sea level. It varies in elevation from a high of 25 feet to sea level. The surface consists of shells, marls, and organic material underlain by limestone (Southwest Florida Regional Planning Council 2002).

Topography

Topography is the result of natural forces acting upon regional geologic formations from ancient times until the present. It is an important aspect of a region's character and determines drainage patterns, flood limits, soil types, settlement history and potential, and vegetation and wildlife ranges. The region's topography is quite flat, ranging from sea level to a maximum elevation of about 90 feet. The islands of the Refuge Complex are mostly comprised of classical dune ridge and swale topography, with a maximum elevation of less than 20 feet, and usually less than 10 feet.

SOILS

Each type of soil is an indicator of preexisting conditions: (1) climate and (2) living organisms acting on (3) parent materials over (4) time as conditioned by (5) relief. In central and south Florida, the soils or uppermost sediments are geologically young and are surficial. The soil profiles reflect changes in sediment types rather than development of chemically or mechanically produced horizons. One is likely to observe sands layered over marsh-produced calcareous marl, particularly in coastal areas. The taxonomic classification system of the U.S. Department of Agriculture's Natural Resources Conservation Service categorizes soil types by order, suborder, great group, subgroup, family, and soil series (U.S. Department of Agriculture 2008). Nationwide, there are 12 orders of soil, five of which dominate Florida's landscape: *Entisols* (7.5 million acres, 3 million ha); *Spodosols* (8.4 million acres, 3.4 million ha); *Ultisols* (6.9 million acres, 2.8 million ha); *Alfisols* (4.6 million acres, 1.9 million ha); and *Histosols* (4.0 million acres, 1.6 million ha) (Collins 2003).

Spodosols (and to a lesser extent, *Entisols*) is the dominant soil order in the Charlotte Harbor area. The soils in this area have a hyperthermic soil temperature regime, an aquic soil moisture regime, and siliceous mineralogy. The soils are generally deep or very deep, poorly drained or very poorly drained, and loamy or sandy. Narrow to broad bands of Sulfaquents and Hydraquents (both great groups of *Entisols*) and Sulfihemists (a great group of *Histosols*) occur along and near the coast of Florida. Moderately well drained, sandy Haplohumods (a great group of *Spodosols*), having dark organic stained subsoil; and excessively drained, sandy Quartzipsamments (a great group of *Entisols*) are found on low old beach ridges and dunes. More inland, poorly drained, sandy Haplaquods (a great group of *Spodosols*) have a dark organic stained subsoil at a depth of two to four feet; and poorly drained Psammaquents (a great group of *Entisols*) are sandy throughout. Most of the coastline of southwest Florida is dominated by nearly level to sloping sandy beaches and adjacent sand dunes; and level, very poorly drained coastal marshes and swamps of variable-textured mineral and organic soils subject to frequent tidal flooding, primarily used for recreation and wildlife.

HYDROLOGY

The southwestern Florida coast bordering the Gulf of Mexico is a low-energy, microtidal (less than 0.5 m tidal amplitude) region that is constantly changing as a result of active coastal processes that are directly linked to meteorological events. Wind-driven waves and tidal currents are the most important geological agents controlling sediment transport and evolution of the Gulf and bay shores. Astronomical tides in the Gulf of Mexico are mixed and typically have a range of less than one meter. More specifically, the tides in Charlotte Harbor are a mixture of lunar (semidiurnal) and solar (diurnal) gravitational effects. Two unequal high and low tides occur daily, with an average range from about two to three feet. Water levels vary only about 0.5 m between high and low tide during a normal tidal cycle. Tide records around the Gulf since the turn of the century all show the same general variations in sea level that coincide with droughts and periods of abnormally high rainfall. Averaging of the tide records shows that some areas, such as the west coast of Florida, are relatively stable because of the hard limestone substrates. Nonstorm waves in the eastern Gulf of Mexico are normally less than 0.3 meters high, and wave energy decreases to the north where the Gulf shore consists of marsh. Hurricane Charley in 2004 resulted in peak storm surges between four and six feet (1.5 to 2 meters), mainly on the Lee County barrier Islands. The surface water-ground water hydrology of large barriers islands, such as Sanibel Island, is complex. Only larger barrier islands have freshwater marshes in dune swales.

Surface Water

Because of the nearly instantaneous infiltration of rainwater, few barrier islands develop a natural type of channelized interior drainage system. The islands of the refuges are no different with little or no surface water retained, since most of it percolates or runs off into estuarine waters. The exception to this is at the Terrapin Creek Tract in Matlacha Pass NWR. Terrapin Creek is a small drainage the empties into the estuary. The Terrapin Creek Tract also contains a couple of ephemeral ponds.

Groundwater

Figure 14 illustrates characteristics of the groundwater systems in Charlotte and Lee counties. There is an unconfined surficial water-table aquifer which is closely underlain by a shallow artesian aquifer in the Pleistocene Limestone. Collectively these two shallow aquifers are referred to as the Surficial Aquifer System (SAS). These shallow aquifers are underlain by at least two deep artesian aquifers: the Lower Hawthorn aquifer, and the underlying and the underlying Suwannee aquifer. Collectively these two deep aquifers are referred to as the Floridan Aquifer System (FAS). Each of these aquifers is discussed below.

- Unconfined, surficial water-table aquifer – The saturated part of this layer is termed the surficial water-table aquifer. The uppermost 20 to 25 feet of sediment is unconfined, consisting of quartz sand, shell, and some minor percentages of carbonate mud in the lower beds. Climatic factors primarily control water table fluctuations. The water table rises in response to recharge, and declines when water is withdrawn or discharged from the aquifer. The only natural source of freshwater recharge on the refuges' islands is rainfall. In the absence of freshwater recharge, saline water may recharge the aquifer laterally from the sea or from the underlying shallow artesian aquifer. Natural discharge from the aquifer includes evaporation, evapotranspiration, groundwater discharge to the sea, (and discharge to streams or lakes if any are present). When the water table is high, fresh water is stored, and the wetland areas are filled. When the water table is low, the quantity of water in storage decreases and wetland areas tend to dry. The freshwater stored in the water-table aquifer has a great natural variation in quality. Even small perturbations can result in upward pluming or other saline intrusions, and tidal overtopping sometimes occurs. Without an adequate

quantity of fresh water stored within the water-table aquifer, the present flora and fauna on many of the islands could not exist.
- The top of the shallow artesian aquifer occurs between 25 and 30 feet below mean sea level in the Pleistocene Limestone. It is normally separated from the overlying surficial water-table aquifer by a heterogeneous mud stratum, and separated from the lower artesian aquifers by carbonate clay beds in the Tamiami Formation. There are some areas where the upper confining bed is extremely thin, or does not exist. Leakage between the shallow artesian and the surficial water-table aquifers is possible in these areas. Water levels in the shallow artesian aquifer fluctuate daily with the tides. The range of these fluctuations is a function of the distance to the nearest tidal water body, and the permeability of the aquifer. Water levels in the shallow artesian aquifer are not greatly responsive to seasonal water level variations in the overlying water-table aquifer. Water quality varies considerably in the shallow artesian aquifer, but the entire aquifer is saline. Chloride values often exceed concentrations in seawater, usually about 19,000 mg/l in the vicinity of Sanibel Island. These high chloride waters may have formed when the strata were originally deposited, or through downward leakage and selective osmotic differentiation. The lower chloride concentrations may be the result of partial flushing during deposition, or recent flushing. There is no known recharge to the shallow artesian aquifer other than possible downward leakage, which occurs only under special conditions. Leakage of water between the shallow artesian aquifer and the water-table aquifer is strictly a function of head differential and vertical permeability. During high tide periods, the water level in the shallow artesian aquifer usually stands above the water table, and potential leakage is upward.
- During the low part of the tidal cycle, the water level in the shallow artesian aquifer usually drops below the water table, and possible leakage is downward. When the water table is high for an extended period, such as after heavy rainfall, the water table may remain above the artesian water level through numerous tidal cycles. To some degree, leakage between the two aquifers occurs continuously. The vertical permeability of the mud stratum is the primary control of the quantity leaked.
- Two deep artesian aquifers underlying the area and yield significant quantities of water: the Lower Hawthorn aquifer and the Suwannee aquifer. Neither aquifer is directly recharged from refuges' islands. Regionally, the intermediate Lower Hawthorn aquifer is the primary ground water resource in the Charlotte Harbor basin (Sarasota, Charlotte and Lee Counties). The Lower Hawthorn aquifer is positioned near the contact between the Hawthorn Formation and the underlying Tampa Limestone, while the Suwannee aquifer lies near the contact between the Tampa Limestone and the underlying Suwannee Limestone. Artesian head pressure within these lower aquifers ranges from 16 to 32 feet above mean sea level. Daily fluctuations of 1 to 2 feet occur due to tidal and atmospheric pressure variations. The Lower Hawthorn and Suwannee aquifers generally contain saline water—or water that has at least 1,000 milligrams per liter (mg/l) of dissolved solids. The water in the upper part of the Lower Hawthorn aquifer is highly saline. A relatively thin zone of freshwater, containing 600 mg/l to 1,000 mg/l of dissolved chloride, occurs near the base of the Lower Hawthorn aquifer. Dissolved chloride concentrations in the Suwannee aquifer are nearly 1,000 mg/l at the top of the aquifer, and increase progressively with depth. Extreme variations of water quality in each aquifer occur from well to well on the island. The freshwater zone occurs at different depth intervals in nearly every well, and sometimes does not occur at all. Little is known about other characteristics of these aquifers, such as transmissivity, storage coefficient, sustained yield, draw-down, or permanence of quality.

Figure 14. Ground water aquifers and lithology of Charlotte and Lee counties.

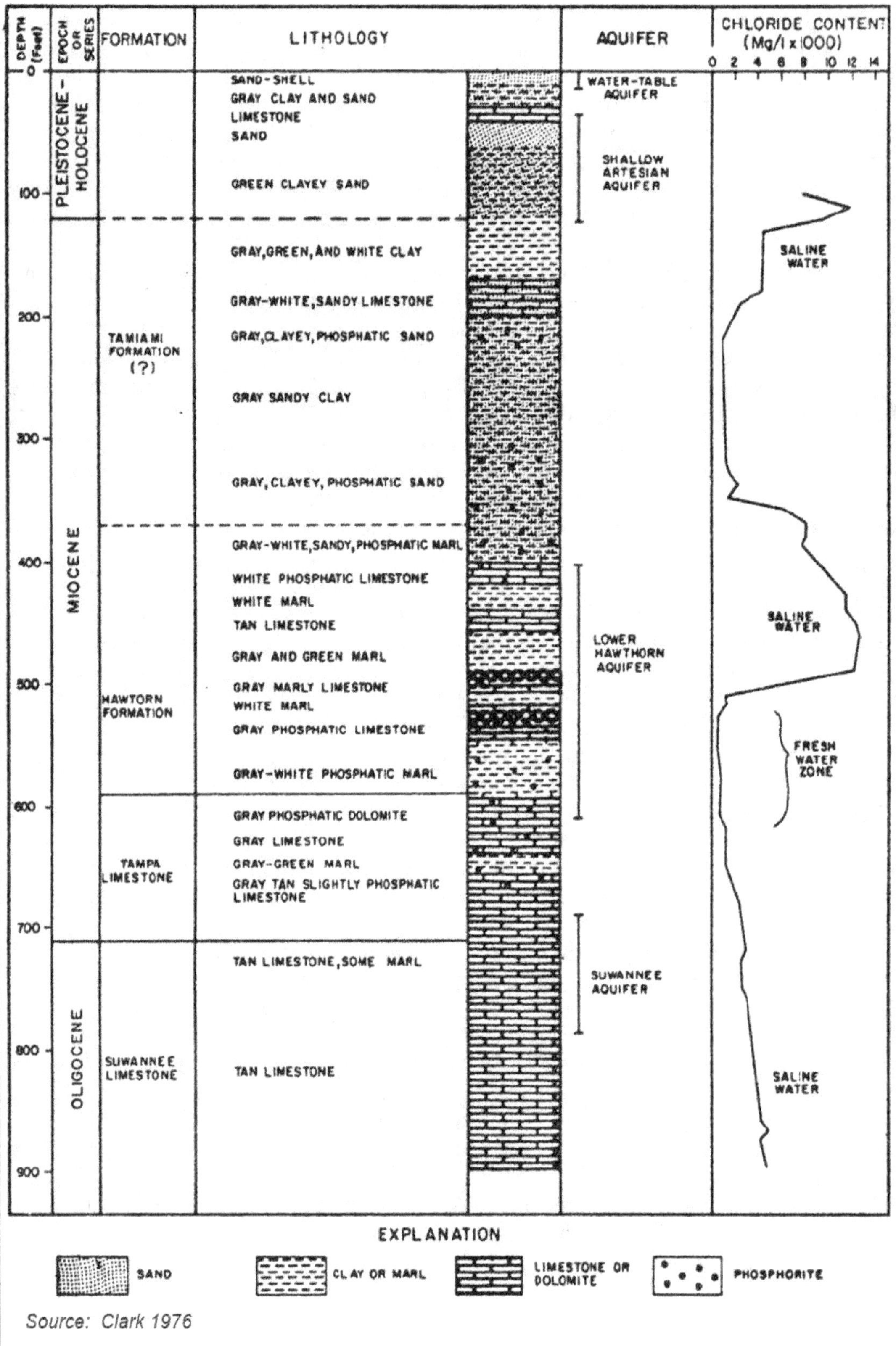

Depth (Feet)	Epoch or Series	Formation	Lithology	Aquifer	Chloride Content (Mg/l x 1000)
0–125	Pleistocene–Holocene		Sand-shell; Gray clay and sand; Limestone; Sand; Green clayey sand	Water-table aquifer; Shallow artesian aquifer	Saline water
125–370	Miocene	Tamiami Formation (?)	Gray, green, and white clay; Gray-white, sandy limestone; Gray, clayey, phosphatic sand; Gray sandy clay; Gray, clayey, phosphatic sand		
370–600	Miocene	Hawthorn Formation	Gray-white, sandy, phosphatic marl; White phosphatic limestone; White marl; Tan limestone; Gray and green marl; Gray marly limestone; White marl; Gray phosphatic limestone; Gray-white phosphatic marl	Lower Hawthorn aquifer	Saline water; Fresh water zone
600–720	Miocene	Tampa Limestone	Gray phosphatic dolomite; Gray limestone; Gray-green marl; Gray tan slightly phosphatic limestone		
720–900+	Oligocene	Suwannee Limestone	Tan limestone, some marl; Tan limestone	Suwannee aquifer	Saline water

EXPLANATION: Sand; Clay or marl; Limestone or dolomite; Phosphorite

Source: Clark 1976

AIR QUALITY

The Clean Air Act of 1970 (as amended in 1990 and 1997), required the EPA to implement air quality standards to protect public health and welfare. National Ambient Air Quality Standards (NAAQS) were established based on protecting health (primary standards) and preventing environmental and property damage (secondary) for six pollutants commonly found throughout the United States: lead, ozone, nitrogen oxides (NO_x), carbon monoxide (CO), sulfur dioxide (SO_2), and particulate matter less than 10 and 2.5 microns in diameter (PM_{10} and $PM_{2.5}$).

The Florida Division of Air Resource Management operates National Ambient Monitoring Stations (NAMS) and State and Local Ambient Monitoring Stations (SLAMS) to measure ambient concentrations of these pollutants. In 2006, ambient air quality data were collected by 216 monitors (in 34 counties) strategically placed throughout the State (Florida Department of Environmental Protection 2006a). Areas that meet the NAAQS are designated attainment areas, while areas not meeting the standards are termed nonattainment areas. While no pollutant monitoring data are being collected on the refuges per se, air quality is monitored on a regular basis by four monitors in the Charlotte Harbor (Lee County) area, and by 25 monitors in the counties within 100 miles of the refuge. Florida's 2006 monitoring results indicate that all of the Charlotte Harbor area (in fact all of Southwest Florida) qualifies as an attainment area for all monitored pollutants (Florida Department of Environmental Protection 2006a).

The Air Quality Index (AQI) is a summary index developed by EPA for reporting daily air quality. It tells how clean or polluted the air is and what associated health effects might be of concern. The AQI focuses on health effects that may be experienced within a few hours or days after breathing polluted air. EPA calculates the AQI for five major air pollutants regulated by the Clean Air Act: ground-level ozone, particle pollution (also known as particulate matter), carbon monoxide, sulfur dioxide, and nitrogen dioxide. (Lead is also considered a major air pollutant under the Clean Air Act. However, because all areas of the United States are currently attaining the NAAQS for lead, the AQI does not specifically address lead.) For each of these pollutants, EPA has established national air quality standards to protect public health (AirNow 2009). Between 1999 and 2006, the Charlotte Harbor (Lee County) area averaged 337 days each year with good or better air quality, better than 80 percent of the counties where monitoring is now conducted. In addition the air quality index data show that air quality has been improving during these last several years (Florida Department of Environmental Protection 2006a).

The current sources of air pollution in southwest Florida are area-wide resulting primarily from automobiles in urban areas and land clearing activities. Auto emissions per car are down, but the number of cars is increasing. Fortunately the number of large industrial polluters is limited in Southwest Florida. Although the area has a small number of industrial smokestacks, there is considerable pollution from automobiles and smaller licensed emitters throughout the region.

WATER QUALITY AND QUANTITY

Water Quality

Water quality concerns relate to freshwater releases from the Caloosahatchee watershed and from Lake Okeechobee, shellfish harvesting and red tides, and cultural eutrophication, as well as to impaired water bodies, mercury contamination, and pesticides and polychlorinated biphenyls.

Freshwater Releases from the Caloosahatchee Watershed and Lake Okeechobee

The South Florida Water Management District and the U.S. Army Corps of Engineers manage the releases of freshwater from Lake Okeechobee into the Caloosahatchee River to reduce flooding during the wet season, to manage the availability of water for agricultural and public water supply needs during the dry season, and to protect the health of the Caloosahatchee River and Estuary. However, the quantity, quality, and timing of these freshwater discharges from Lake Okeechobee into the River and Estuary are dramatically impacting the ecosystems in Matlacha Pass, San Carlos Bay, and Pine Island Sound.

The water quality of Lake Okeechobee is impacted by more than 40 years of untreated stormwater runoff from dairy farms and agricultural fields, both north and south of the lake. Urban sprawl throughout the watershed has added to the problem. The combined effect has adversely impacted the lake's water quality and the quality of the water released. A similar situation exists within the Caloosahatchee Basin, where commercial and residential development has occurred at a rapid pace, particularly along the coast. Freshwater releases from Lake Okeechobee in the Matlacha Pass, San Carlos Bay, and Pine Island Sound area have degraded and damaged over 10,000 acres (4,047 ha) of seagrass beds near the mouth of the Caloosahatchee River. This negatively impacts habitat federally designated as critical to the Endangered West Indian manatee and the Endangered smalltooth sawfish, as well as negatively impacting sea turtles and numerous fisheries, including pink shrimp (*Penaeus duorarum*), seatrout (*Cynoscion nebulosus*), blue crab (*Callinectes sapidus*), and grouper; as well as destroying oyster beds, commercial clam beds, and virtually all other filter feeding organisms ranging from barnacles to sponges and corals (City of Sanibel 2009a).

During the wet season, when water levels in Lake Okeechobee are high, excessive releases from the lake are made as a flood-control measure. However, these wet season releases, combined with runoff from the Caloosahatchee River Basin, contain high levels of nitrogen and phosphorus -- nutrients which promote algal blooms in the coastal areas and estuaries. The high flows also carry high levels of suspended material and sediments that block sunlight, which is necessary for growth of seagrasses.

But just as too much freshwater can cause problems, in the dry season, a lack of rain, watershed runoff, and discharges from Lake Okeechobee permit saltwater from the Gulf of Mexico to migrate into brackish estuaries and up the Caloosahatchee River, thus raising the salinities of San Carlos Bay and the waters of the refuges. To offset these increased salinities, small quantities of water must be released from Lake Okeechobee to lower salinity levels for freshwater organisms.

> ### A Case in Point
>
> Releases of freshwater from Lake Okeechobee occurred at rates of up to 22,000 cubic feet per second (cfs), into the Caloosahatchee River and subsequently into Matlacha Pass, San Carlos Bay, and Pine Island Sound, occurred in 2004. The average discharge of freshwater from the Caloosahatchee River is approximately 2,000 cfs. Discharges greater than approximately 4,500 cfs lower salinity concentrations to 20 parts per thousand (ppt) or below in San Carlos Bay – lower than optimum for shoal grass and turtle grass survival. The 2004 freshwater releases from Lake Okeechobee not only lowered the salinity of Matlacha Pass, San Carlos Bay, and Pine Island Sound, but also increased the nutrient levels (nitrogen and phosphorus) in waters of the refuges. The lower salinities reduced seagrass cover and higher nutrient concentrations initiated red, green, and blue-green algal blooms. The decomposition of dead and decaying algae and seagrasses lowered the dissolved oxygen concentrations in the water, resulting in the loss of fish habitat. In addition, nutrient induced algae blooms and the resulting hypoxia caused extensive fish kills in the Caloosahatchee River and Matlacha Pass, San Carlos Bay, and Pine Island Sound. The carpet of filamentous red and green algae is not only unsightly on sandbars, beaches, mudflats, and seagrass beds, but in the long term the loss of habitat could adversely impact the refuges' bird, fish, and shellfish populations.
>
> (City of Sanibel 2006a and 2009b)

Control of salinity, nutrient, and sediment concentrations to protect the habitat diversity and the health of aquatic ecosystems of San Carlos Bay and the refuges is complex. Ecosystems consist of literally hundreds of thousands of species of plants and wildlife that are interconnected in a complicated dance of life. Any man-made intervention can potentially have a domino effect on the entire system. All of which means there are no simple solutions to the effects of freshwater releases from Lake Okeechobee. The quantity, quality, and timing of releases from Lake Okeechobee and the subsequent effects must all be considered and management plans developed to address a variety of weather (wet and dry) conditions and coordinated with and amongst a variety of partners.

Shellfish Harvesting and Red Tides

Most of San Carlos Bay is closed to shellfish harvesting because of the risk of bacterial contamination from pollutants carried in runoff from the land and the Caloosahatchee River, Figure 15. Consuming shellfish from such waters could result in a variety of illnesses, ranging from diarrhea to infectious hepatitis. To protect public health, it is against the law to possess shellfish such as oysters or clams taken from waters that are closed to shellfish harvesting. Two areas of lower Charlotte Harbor, Pine Island Sound and parts of Matlacha Pass, are conditionally approved for shellfish harvesting; however, these areas are typically closed to harvesting following heavy rains, which wash bacteria-laden pollutants into the waters. Information about the status of these two conditionally approved harvesting areas is available by calling the State (Florida Department of Agriculture and Consumer Services 2004).

Red tides occur in the Gulf of Mexico almost every year, generally in the late summer or early fall. They are most common off the central and southwestern coasts of Florida. The Florida red tide organism, *Karenia brevis*, produces a toxin that can kill marine animals and affect humans. Scientists have studied this organism for more than 50 years. The Florida red tide organism was identified in 1947, but anecdotal reports of the effects of red tide in the Gulf of Mexico date back to the 1530s. Most blooms last 3 to 5 months and may affect hundreds of square miles. Occasionally, however, blooms continue sporadically for as long as 18 months and may affect thousands of square miles. Red tides can kill fish, birds, and marine mammals; cause health problems for humans; and adversely affect local economies. When *K. brevis* reaches cell counts of 5,000 cells per liter of seawater, shellfish beds in the area are closed, sometimes for months at a time, until it is safe to harvest again. A protracted and intense red tide (*K. brevis*) bloom affected the west coast of Florida from Tampa to Fort Meyers and surrounding waters during 2005 (Florida Fish and Wildlife Conservation Commission Undated).

Cultural Eutrophication

The entire Charlotte Harbor watershed is contributing to the cultural eutrophication of the Harbor's estuarine waters. The explosive population growth in the watershed has stimulated economic growth, resulting in stormwater runoff from residential development, intensive agriculture practices, and phosphate mining activities. Estuarine water quality in the Pine Island Sound-San Carlos Bay area has been impacted. Median concentrations of total nitrogen, ammonia ion-NH_4, organic nitrogen, and chlorophyll-a are all greater than statewide medians (Florida Department of Environmental Protection 2002b). Eutrophication links an array of ecological problems, including algal blooms, loss of seagrass, fish kills, and shellfish and benthic organism declines – all contributing to a serious disruption of the entire estuarine food web of flora and fauna (fish, birds and mammals). Information collected during 2002 in EPA's National Estuary Program Coastal Condition Report rated the overall condition of Charlotte Harbor as fair, based on three indices. The water quality index rated poor; the sediment quality index rated good; and, the benthic quality index rated fair. The water quality index, which rated poor, was based on five indicators: nitrogen, phosphorus, chlorophyll a, water clarity, and dissolved oxygen. Elevated phosphorus and poor water clarity contributed to the Harbor's poor water quality condition. The Report noted declines in dissolved oxygen levels and major increases in total suspended solids in the southern portion of the Harbor (U.S. Environmental Protection Agency 2007c).

Impaired Water Bodies

Section 303(d) of the Clean Water Act (CWA) requires the State of Florida to list waters that do not meet applicable water quality standards so as to protect human health and aquatic life. In addition, the CWA requires the establishment of Total Maximum Daily Loads (TMDLs) for those waters on a prioritized schedule. Water bodies that do not meet water quality standards are identified as "impaired" for the particular pollutants of concern (e.g., nutrients, bacteria, and mercury). For impaired water bodies, TMDLs are developed to establish the maximum amount of a pollutant that a water body can assimilate without causing exceedances of water quality standards. As such, development of TMDLs is an important step toward restoring waters to their designated uses. In order to achieve the water quality benefits intended by the CWA, it is critical that TMDLs, once developed, be implemented as soon as possible.

Figure 15. Shellfish harvesting in Lower Charlotte Harbor.
(Florida Department of Agriculture and Consumer Services, Division of Aquaculture 2004)

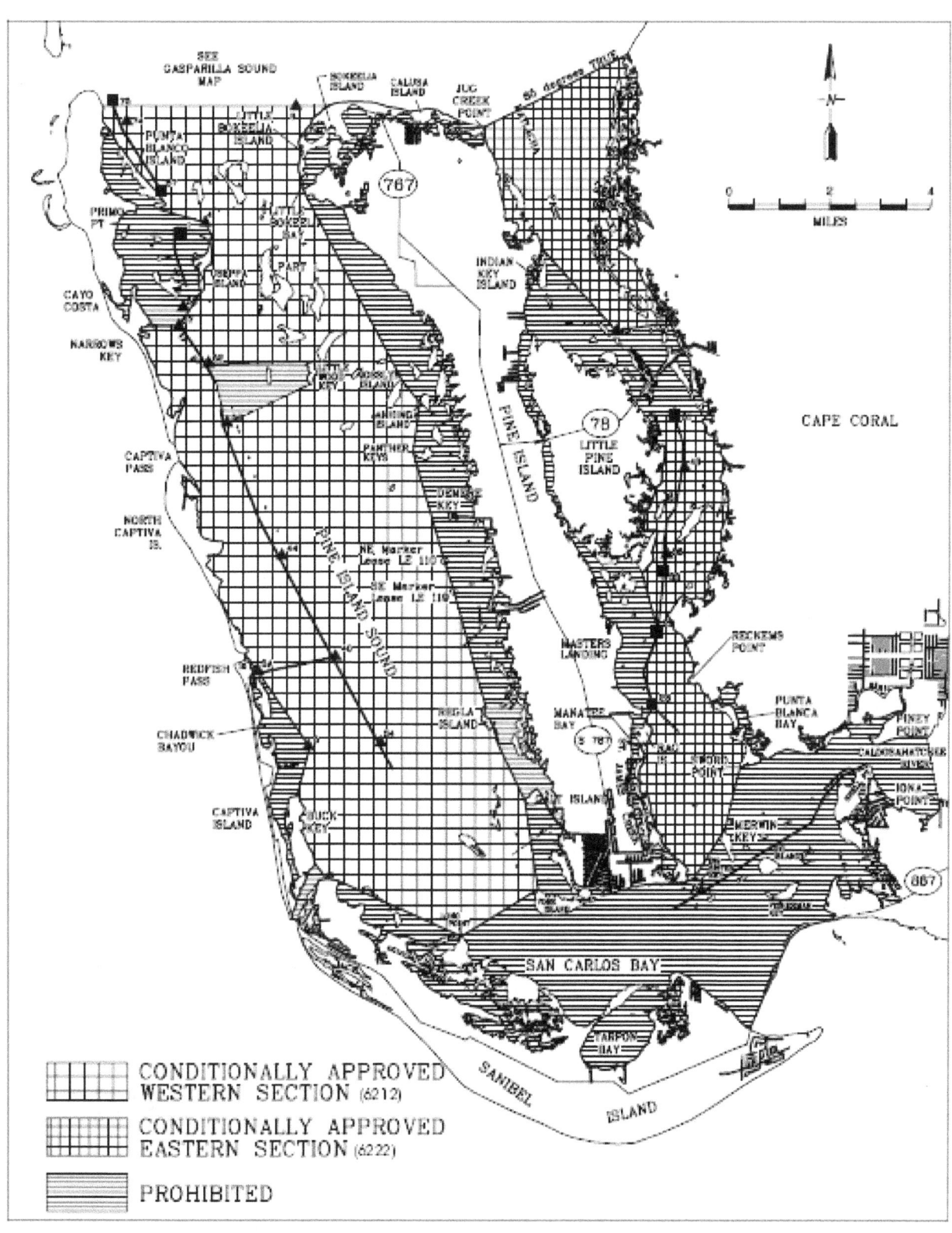

The quality of the waters of the four refuges is impacted by the impaired upstream releases from Lake Okeechobee and the flows and runoff from the Caloosahatchee River watershed (as discussed above). Sections of Charlotte Harbor, Pine Island Sound, Matlacha Pass, Pine Island, and the Florida Gulf Coast, as well as segments of the Caloosahatchee River basin and Estuary and Lake Okeechobee, are also listed by the State of Florida as water quality impaired. TMDL development for Lower Charlotte Harbor Basin was initiated in 2008 for all of the parameters, except for mercury which is planned for 2011. TMDL development in the Caloosahatchee Basin was initiated in 2008 for nutrients and dissolved oxygen, and all other parameters in 2009. TMDL plans for phosphorous were initiated in 2001 for Lake Okeechobee.

Mercury Contamination

The evidence of mercury contamination in fish and wildlife in South Florida freshwater and terrestrial ecosystems is extensive. Trends in mercury accumulation in South Florida, as evidenced by sediment profiles, show that atmospheric mercury deposition has increased approximately fivefold since 1900 (Rood et al. 1995). The deposition rate of mercury by rainfall measured today is at least double that of other remote sites in North America (Guentzel et al. 1995). Piscivorous freshwater sport fish and alligators in many watersheds, especially in the Everglades, have high mercury levels in their tissues (Ware et. al. 1990, Eisler 1987). High mercury levels have been detected in the Endangered wood stork and in other birds (Sundlof et al. 1994). There is concern that the 50-year decline in wading bird numbers in South Florida partially may be partially a result of increased mercury exposure; intensive studies are underway to further define this concern (U.S. Fish and Wildlife Service 1999).

Excessive concentrations of mercury have been found in all of Florida's coastal waters affecting commercial and sport-fishing interests. A much better understanding of local, regional, and global sources; amounts; and effects of mercury on Florida waters and fisheries is needed. Most Florida seafood contains low to medium levels of mercury. As a result, the State of Florida has issued human health advisories regarding consumption of fish for several species. "Do not Eat" advisories have been issued for all of Florida coastal and marine waters (including Lower Charlotte Harbor) for king mackerel (*Scomberomorus cavalla*), all sharks, blackfin tuna (*Thunnus atlanticus*), cobia (*Rachycentron canadum*), jack crevalle (*Caranx hippos*), great barracuda (*Sphyraena barracuda*), and little tunny (*Euthynnus alletteratus*). Moderate risk and low risk fish consumption advisories have also been issued for a number of other marine and estuarine fish species. (More detailed information is available at the Florida Department of Health's website, http://doh.state.fl.us/floridafishadvice/.)

Pesticides and Polychlorinated Biphenyls

Pesticides have also been widely used in agricultural and urban areas in South Florida for more than 50 years to control insects, fungi, weeds, and other undesirable organisms. Because of year round warm temperatures and a moist climate, Florida agriculture requires vigorous pest control, thus while Florida agricultural production ranks approximately 30th in the U.S., pesticide usage per acre is in the top five (U.S. Fish and Wildlife Service 1999). The compounds used vary in their toxicity, persistence, and transport. Since the late 1960s, persistent organochlorine pesticides have been detected in fish that are part of the Everglades food chain. Some more persistent pesticides, such as dichlorodiphenyltrichloroethane (DDT), Chlordane, Dieldrin, and Aldrin have been banned for use in the State, but their residues still occur in the environment. Although pesticides are usually applied to specific areas and directed at specific organisms, these compounds often become widely distributed and are potentially hazardous to nontarget species. Herbicides, including Atrazine, Bromocil, Simazine, 2-4-D, and Diuron, which have the highest rates of application, are among the most frequently detected pesticides in Florida's surface waters. By far the most frequently detected insecticides in surface waters are the chlorinated hydrocarbon ones that are no longer used in the State, such as dichlorodiphenyldichloroethane (DDD), dichlorodiphenyldichloroethylene (DDE), DDT, Dieldrin, and Heptachlor. These insecticides are also the most frequently detected pesticides in bottom sediments. Chlorinated chemicals such as polychlorinated biphenyls (PCBs), dioxins, and furans, which are generated and used primarily in urban and industrial areas, pose serious concerns to fish, wildlife, and human populations. Although most uses of PCBs have been banned since the late 1970s, these persistent chemicals are still found in the environment and continue to pose potential threats to fish, wildlife, and humans. In recent years, many organochlorine pesticides and PCBs have been linked to hormone disruption and reproductive problems in aquatic invertebrates, fishes, birds, and mammals (U.S. Fish and Wildlife Service 1999).

BIOLOGICAL RESOURCES

HABITAT

Island Bay, Pine Island, Matlacha Pass, and Caloosahatchee NWRs provide a representation of a coastal subtropical barrier island system within an intertidal estuarine wetland system that encompasses approximately 1,201 total acres (458.92 ha) of important vegetative communities (including predominantly mangrove swamps with saltwater marshes and ponds, tidal flats, and upland hardwood forests) that attract and support a wide variety of wildlife, including migratory birds (for roosting, nesting, migrating, and wintering) and 13 federally and 25 State listed species. These habitats comprise a diverse system that contains a mixture of temperate, subtropical, and tropical woody plants, supporting rare, threatened, and endangered species. Mangroves provide nursery areas for aquatic species and nesting and resting areas for birds. The beaches and shores of the refuges provide loafing and foraging sites for shorebirds, gulls, and terns. The surrounding shallow bays provide valuable foraging areas for wading birds and waterbirds.

All four refuges are predominantly mangrove swamps that exist in an estuarine system. Pine Island NWR also includes small areas of saltwater marsh and ponds (Table 6 and Figure 16). Matlacha Pass NWR also includes small areas of saltwater ponds and tidal flats (Table 7 and Figure 17). Island Bay NWR also includes small areas of upland hardwood forests and tidal flats (Table 8 and Figure 18). All of Caloosahatchee NWR is classified as mangrove swamp (Table 9 and Figure 19).

Table 6. Vegetation for Pine Island NWR.

Vegetation Type	Acres	Hectares
Mangrove Swamp	538.93	218.10
Saltwater Marsh	11.67	4.72
Saltwater Ponds	4.68	1.90
Upland Hardwood Forests	46.96	19.00
Total	602.24	243.72

Table 7. Vegetation for Matlacha Pass NWR.

Vegetation Type	Acres	Hectares
Mangrove Swamp	471.97	191.00
Saltwater Ponds	6.80	2.75
Tidal Flats	6.41	2.59
Upland Hardwood Forests	53.07	21.48
Total	**538.25**	**217.82**

Table 8. Vegetation for Island Bay NWR.

Vegetation Type	Acres	Hectares
Mangrove Swamp	3.91	1.58
Tidal Flats	1.53	0.62
Upland Hardwood Forests	14.80	5.99
Total	**20.24**	**8.19**

Table 9. Vegetation for Caloosahatchee NWR.

Vegetation Type	Acres	Hectares
Mangrove Swamp	4.95	2.00
Upland Hardwood Forests	13.31	5.39
Acres to be Resolved (not mapped)	21.74	8.80
Total	**40.00**	**16.19**

Figure 16. Vegetation for Pine Island NWR.

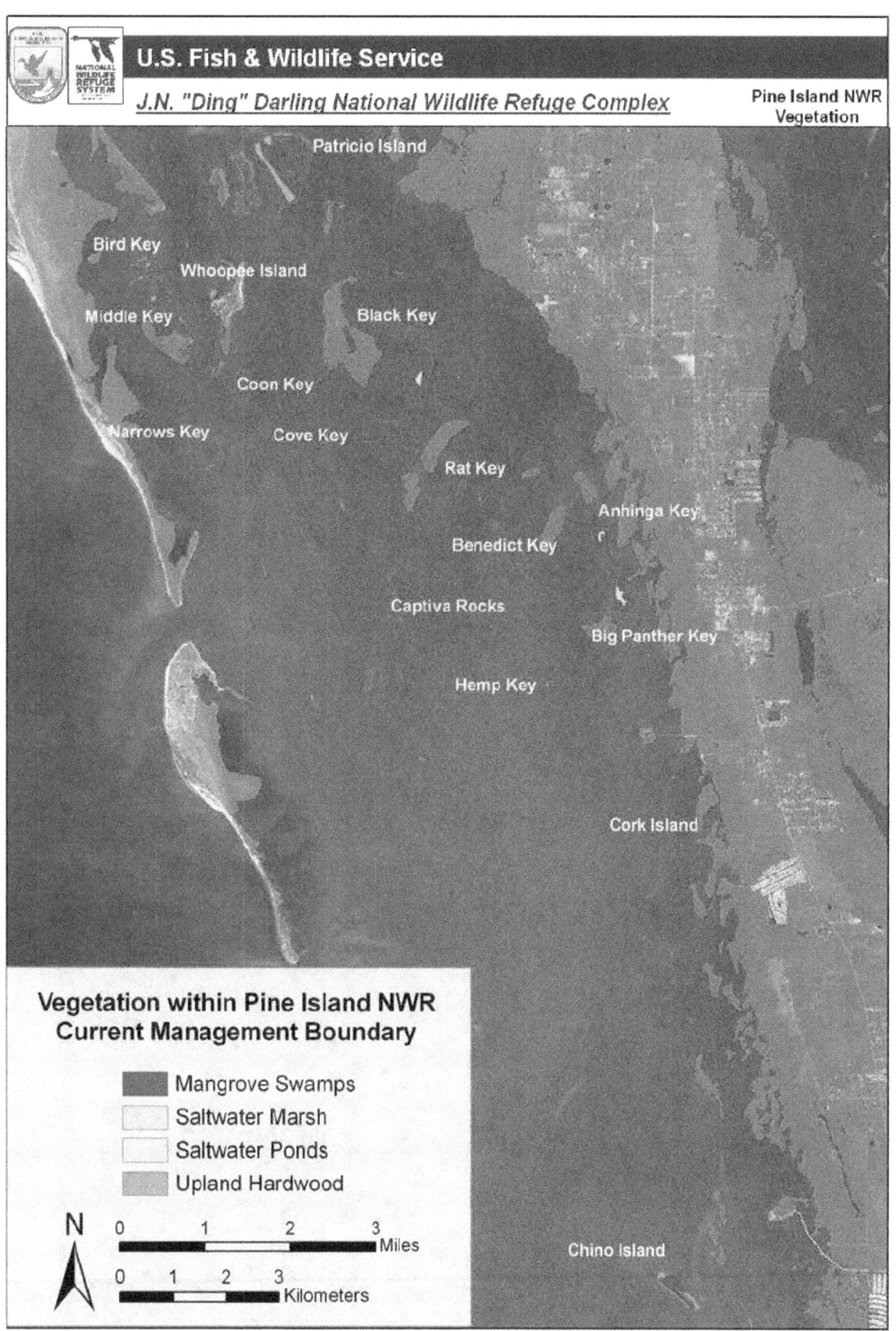

Comprehensive Conservation Plan

Figure 17. Vegetation for Matlacha Pass NWR.

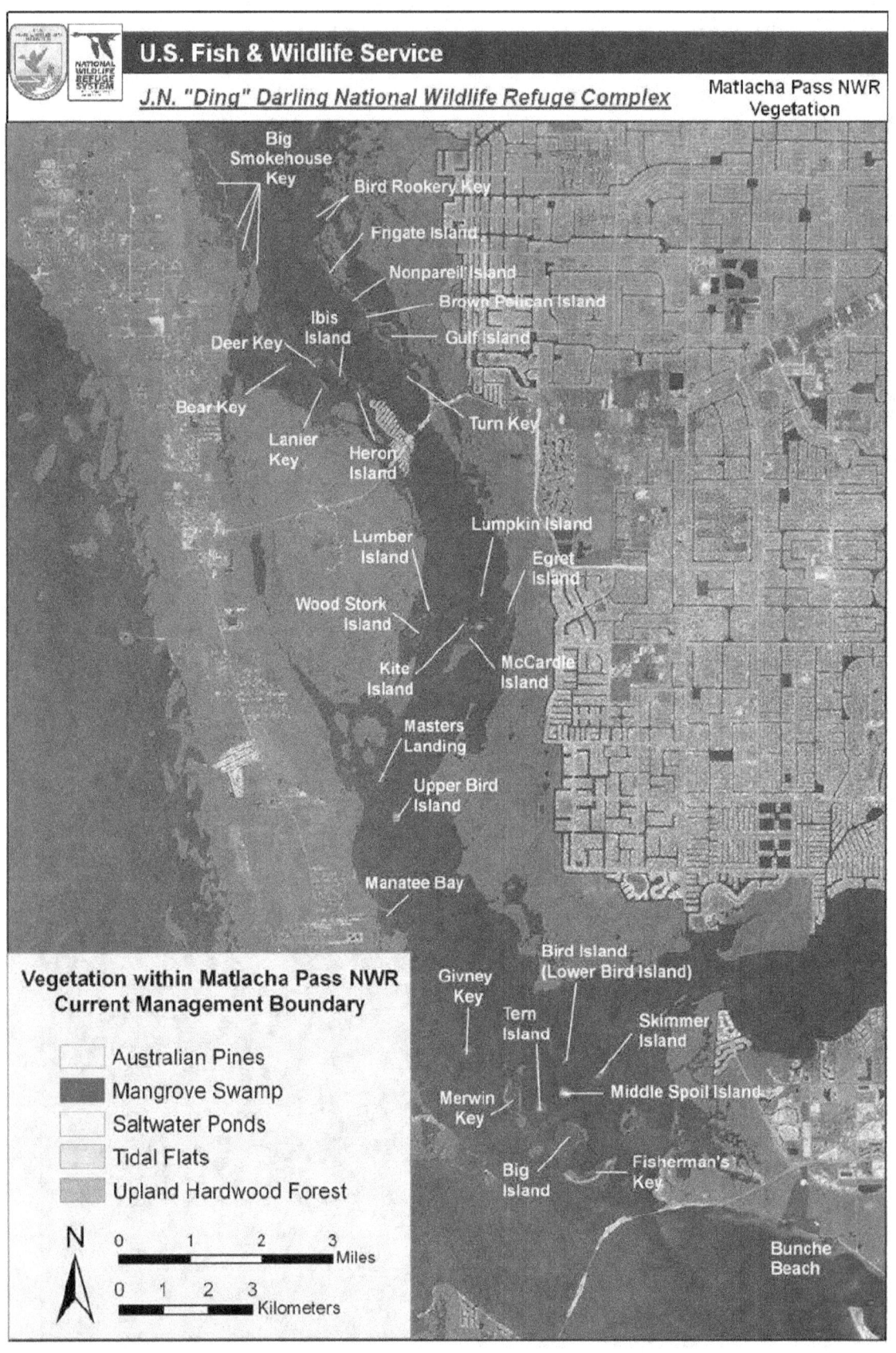

Figure 18. Vegetation for Island Bay NWR.

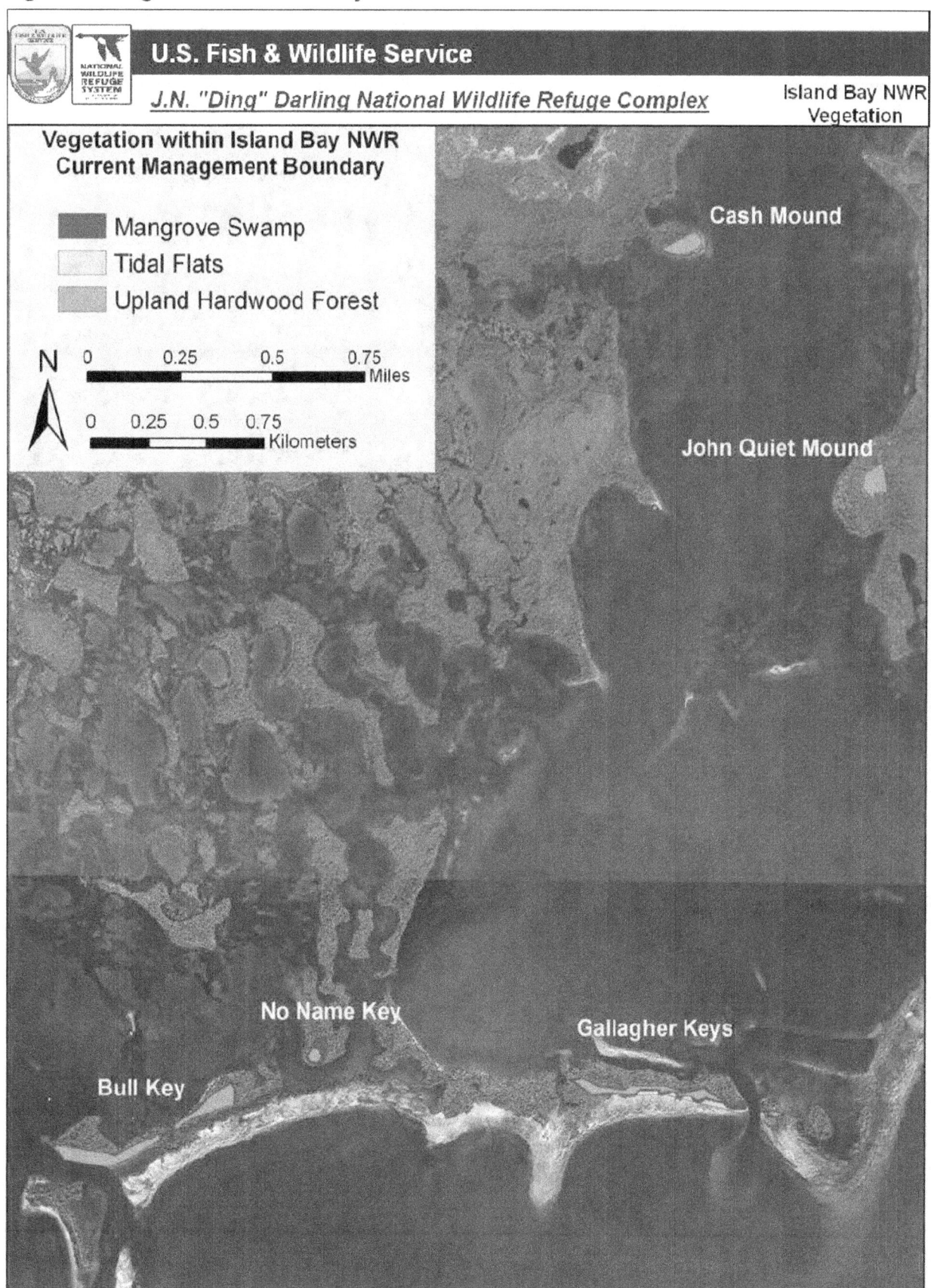

Comprehensive Conservation Plan 73

Figure 19. Vegetation for Caloosahatchee NWR.

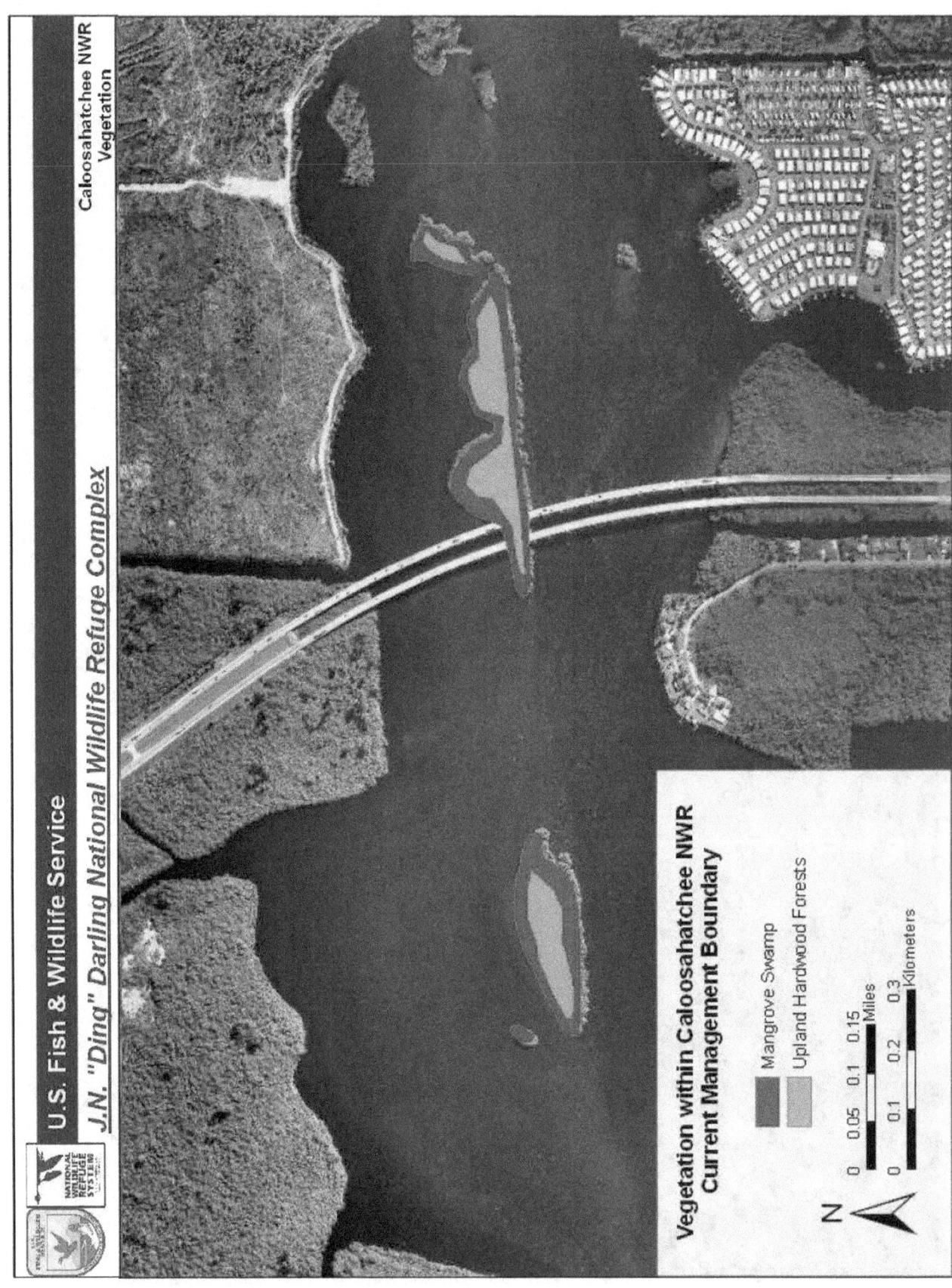

Estuary

The four refuges are located within an estuary, an area where salt and fresh water mix. Estuaries create some of the most nutritionally rich habitat for thousands of species of plants and animals in an intricate food web. The basis of this food web in South Florida is the extensive mangrove forests and productive seagrass beds. Microorganisms thrive on the decaying leaves of seagrasses and mangroves, providing additional food for other animals. Rich in marine life, these shallow waters attract thousands of fish, shrimp, crabs, and snails, which are preyed upon by the numerous wading birds of the refuges. Seagrass beds and mangrove forests serve as shelter, nursery, and feeding areas for many fish species, such as mullet, snook (*Centropomus undecimalis*), red drum, and snapper, as well as for other marine organisms. Waters surrounding the refuges provide important habitat for fish that help to support the world-class sportfishing of this estuary. Healthy seagrass beds are essential to grazing species, such as the Endangered West Indian manatee and the endangered green sea turtle. The estuary is also important to thousands of shorebirds, such as red knots, dunlin (*Caldris alpine*), and Western sandpipers (*Calidris mauri*) that use the area as resting and feeding grounds during their migrations. Great blue herons (*Ardea Herodias*), reddish egrets, roseate spoonbills, and other wading birds use the many islands as roosting sites, and many nest on the rookery islands found in the estuary.

Seagrass Beds

Although none occur within the refuges, seagrass beds are important foraging habitat for a variety of species, including manatees and green sea turtles, and cover substantial areas around the islands of the Refuge Complex, primarily in the shallow depths of the waterways (less than one to six feet) (Figure 20). Since 1950 the State of Florida has experienced over a 50 percent decline of seagrasses. As of 1995, large sections of seagrasses in Lee County were rated as degraded with light to severe scarring from propeller cuts of boats operating in the shallow waters. Areas of scarred seagrass are scattered throughout the area. These seagrass beds support seasonally variable growths of submerged aquatic macrophytes, mostly consisting of four species: turtle grass (*Thalassia testudinum*), shoal grass (*Halodule wrightii*), manatee grass (*Syringodium filiforme*), and widgeon grass *(Ruppia maritima)* in areas with low salinity. Seagrass is one of the most productive natural communities in the world and it is a principal contributor to the marine food web (U.S. Fish and Wildlife Service 2002). Aerial survey data from the late 1990s show that the distribution of manatees correlates fairly well with the distribution of seagrass (Figure 21) (Meyers et al. 2006).

Tidal Flats

Very small amounts of Island Bay and Matlacha Pass NWRs are tidal flats. Tidal flats are unvegetated areas of sand or mud protected from wave action and composed primarily of mud transported by tidal channels. An important characteristic of the tidal flat environment is its alternating tidal cycle of submergence and exposure to the atmosphere. Tidal flats support a variety of species of wading birds, waterbirds, waterfowl, shorebirds, sea birds, fish, reptiles, and invertebrates of conservation concern to the Service and to the State of Florida. The most important threats and stressors to tidal flats are altered water quality, altered species composition, habitat destruction and disturbance, altered hydrological regime, and altered weather regime and sea level rise predominantly from coastal development; incompatible industrial operations; incompatible recreational activities; roads, bridges, and causeways; inadequate stormwater management; management activities (e.g., beach nourishment); invasive animals; pollution and spills; incompatible releases of water (including water quality, water quantity, and timing); solid waste; disruption of longshore transport of sediment; climate variability; channel modification; surface and groundwater withdrawals; vessel impacts; and harmful algal blooms (Florida Fish and Wildlife Conservation Commission 2005).

Figure 20. Seagrass beds in the Refuge Complex area.

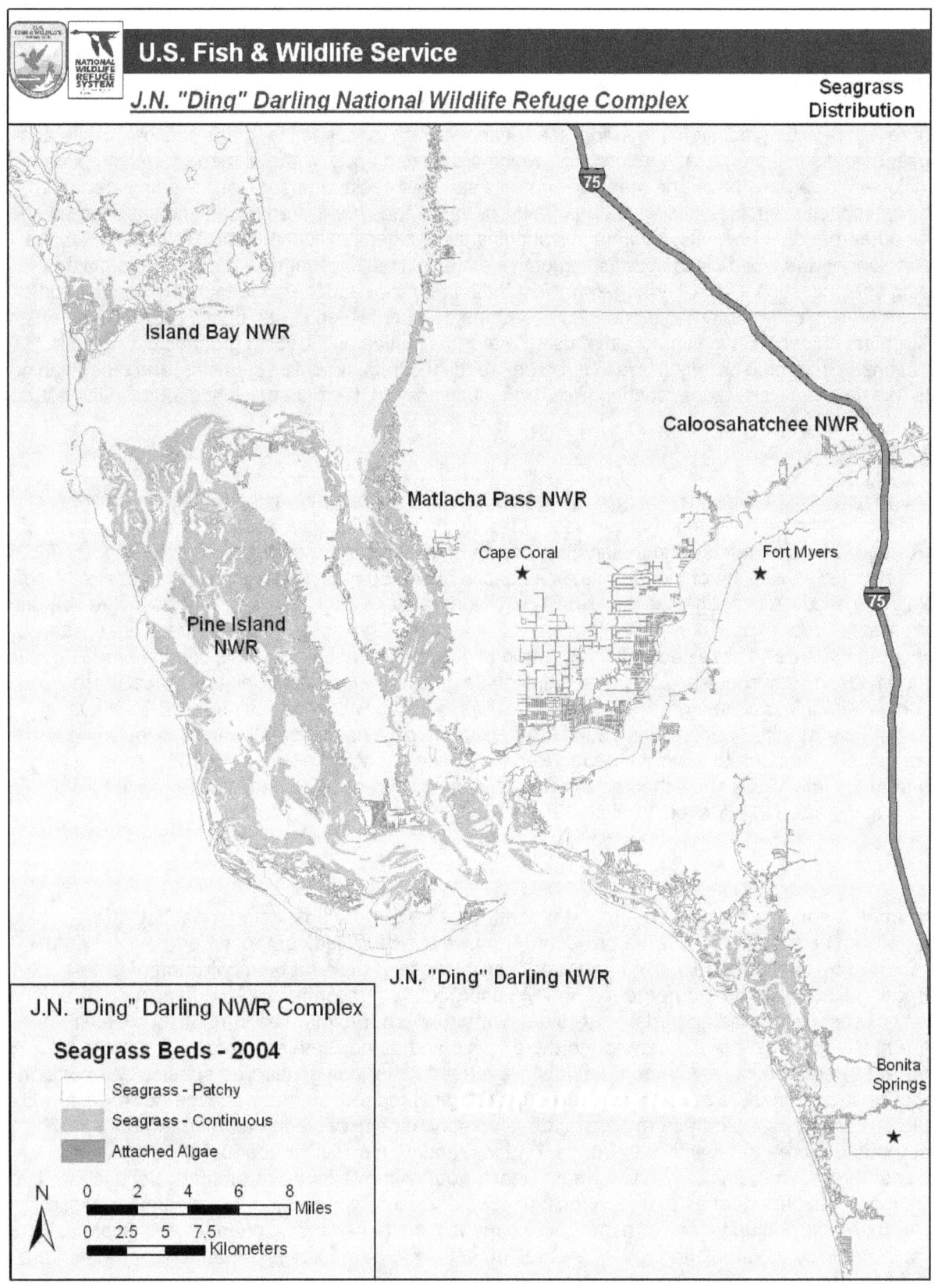

Figure 21. Manatee abundance and Critical Habitat in the Refuge Complex area.

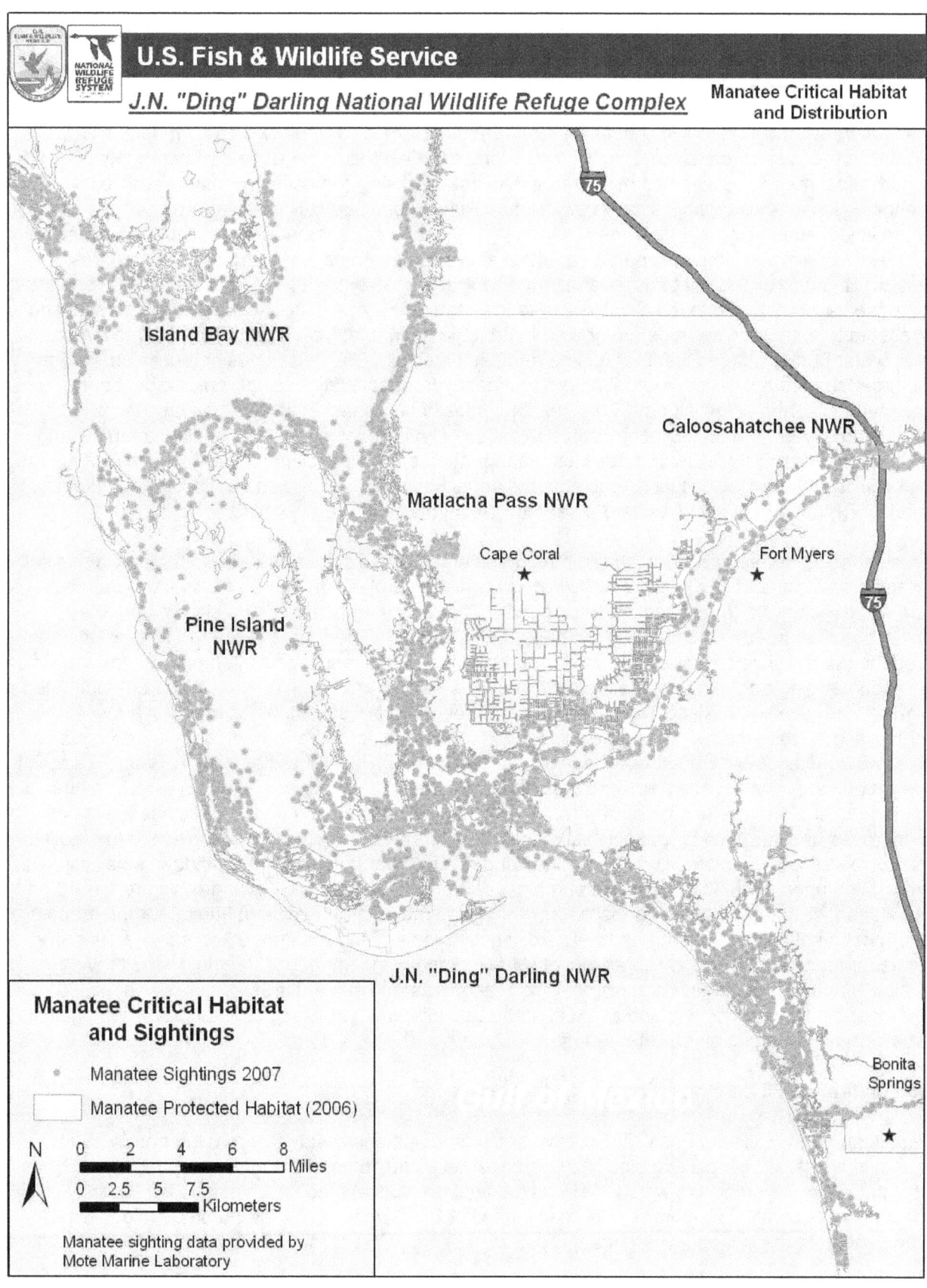

Comprehensive Conservation Plan

Mangrove Swamp

Pine Island, Matlacha Pass, and Caloosahatchee NWRs are predominantly mangrove swamp. Mangroves form dense, brackish-water swamps along low-energy shorelines and in protected, tidally influenced bays of southern Florida. This community type is composed of freeze sensitive tree species and, with some limited exceptions, mangroves which are distributed south of Cedar Key on the Gulf coast and south of St. Augustine on the Atlantic coast. These swamp communities are usually composed of red, black, and white mangroves. Depending on slopes and amounts of disturbance, mangrove swamps may progress in zones of single species from seaward (red mangrove) to landward (white mangrove) areas. Buttonwoods usually occur in areas above high tide. Often vines, such as rubber vines and morning-glory, clamber over mangroves, especially at swamp edges. Mangrove swamps support a variety of species of mammals, wading birds, waterbirds, waterfowl, mangrove forest birds, nearctic-neotropical migratory birds, fish, reptiles, and invertebrates of conservation concern to the Service and to the State of Florida. The most important threats and stressors to mangrove swamps are altered hydrologic regime, habitat destruction, altered structure, alter water quality, altered weather regime and sea level rise, altered species composition, habitat disturbance, and habitat fragmentation predominantly from coastal development; roads, bridges, and causeways; harmful algal blooms; incompatible industrial operations; invasive plants; shoreline hardening; invasive animals; incompatible releases of water (including water quality, quantity, and timing); incompatible wildlife and fisheries management strategies; climate variability; parasites and pathogens; channel modification; incompatible aquaculture operations; and pollution and nutrient loading. (Florida Fish and Wildlife Conservation Commission 2005)

Three species of trees dominate this subtropical forest and are specially adapted to grow in this salty, swampy environment: red mangrove (*Rhizophora mangle*), black mangrove (*Avicennia germinans*), and white mangrove (*Languncularia racemosa*). The red mangrove is the most common and distinctive mangrove in the Refuge Complex. The twisted, tangled roots of the red mangrove give credence to the claim, the tree that walks. Large dart shaped seedlings, called propagules, can often be seen hanging from the branches of this tree. Islands that are low in elevation and are inundated at high tide are overwash islands dominated by red mangrove trees. The black mangrove thrives a little further ashore than the red mangrove. The black mangroves breathe through specialized roots called pneumatophores, which thrust upwards through black marshy soil. Further from the water's edge is the white mangrove. These trees excrete salt from pores in their leaves. Mangroves play a vital role in the food chain of this marine environment. Microorganisms thriving on the decaying leaves of mangroves become food for animals such as shrimp, crabs, snails, and worms. Rich in marine life, the surrounding salt and freshwater marshes and shallow waters attract thousands of small fish which are preyed upon by the numerous wading birds of the Refuge Complex. Mangroves are the foundation for the detritus-based food web, which also make them excellent habitat for the breeding and roosting of colonial wading birds. The distinctive roots of the mangrove tree serve as nursery areas for many fish species such as mullet (*Mugil*), snook, and snapper (*Lutjanus*), and provide shelter for numerous marine organisms. The mangroves and salt and freshwater marshes also reduce the effects of flooding and serve to stabilize sediments, providing coastal protection against erosion and damaging stormwater runoff.

Salt Marsh – Saltwater Marshes and Saltwater Ponds

Pine Island and Matlacha Pass NWRs have small amounts of saltwater marsh and ponds. Salt marsh is vegetated almost completely by herbaceous plants, primarily grasses, sedges, and rushes. This community type occurs within the intertidal zone of coastal areas and may be infrequently (high marsh) to frequently (low marsh) inundated by salt or brackish water. Salt marsh develops where wave energies are low and where mangroves are absent. Within salt marsh, plant species are often distributed unevenly, especially in transitional areas. Species distributions are affected by biotic and abiotic variables such as elevation, substrate type, degree of slope, wave energy, competing species, and salinity. The salt marsh habitat is among the most productive communities in the world. Primary production is greatly affected by soil salinity and tidal frequency. Salt marshes support a variety of species of wading birds, waterbirds, waterfowl, shorebirds, sea birds, fish, reptiles, and invertebrates of conservation concern to the Service and to the State of Florida. The most important threats and stressors to salt marsh habitats are habitat destruction and fragmentation, sedimentation, altered structure, altered water quality, altered water quantity, altered weather regime and sea level rise, erosion, altered hydrologic regime, altered primary production, and altered species composition predominantly from coastal development, incompatible releases of water (including water quality, water quantity, and timing), climate variability, inadequate stormwater management, surface water withdrawals, channel modification, management activities (e.g., beach nourishment), disruption of longshore transport of sediment, and invasive plants (Florida Fish and Wildlife Conservation Commission 2005).

Hardwood Hammock Forest – Upland Hardwood Forests

Upland hardwood forests comprise the majority of Island Bay NWR and a third of Caloosahatchee NWR. The hardwood hammock forest class includes the major upland hardwood associations that occur statewide on fairly rich sandy soils. Variations in species composition and the local or spatial distributions of these communities are due in part to differences in soil moisture regimes, soil type, and geographic location within the State. The upland hardwood forests of Island Bay NWR include a mixture of temperate, subtropical, and tropical woody plants and are characterized by cabbage palm, gumbo limbo, seagrape, and strangler fig. The refuge's upland hardwood forests support nearctic-neotropical migratory birds and reptiles of conservation concern to the Service and the State of Florida. The most important threats and stressors to upland hardwood forests are habitat destruction; altered species composition and dominance; altered hydrologic regime; altered community structure; and fragmentation of habitats, communities, and ecosystems predominantly by development and roads, surface water withdrawals, and invasive plants (Florida Fish and Wildlife Conservation Commission 2005).

WILDLIFE

The refuges serve a variety of wildlife, especially migratory birds and wading birds, and they provide important nesting sites for a variety of birds. The estuary, mangroves, and seagrasses surrounding the refuges attract many species of fish, such as mullet, snook, red drum, and snapper. Appendix I contains a list of wildlife species of concern and/or importance for management of the refuges. Periodic wildlife surveys are conducted by the partners at the four refuges to assess wildlife communities utilizing the area. However, the refuges lack sufficient data to determine status and trends. Further, Refuge Complex personnel also employ other management methods to protect and enhance the refuge's resources, including controlling exotic plants. Refuge management activities include partnerships with local agencies, organizations, and groups; education and interpretation classes; and law enforcement activities.

Thirteen federally listed and 25 state-listed species occur on and around the refuges. The rare, threatened, and endangered species of management concern to the refuges include the wood stork, roseate spoonbill, roseate tern, black skimmer, American oystercatcher, snowy plover, Wilson's plover, red knot, piping plover, bald eagle, mangrove cuckoo, black-whiskered vireo, gray kingbird, Florida prairie warbler, Florida bonneted bat, West Indian manatee, ornate diamondback terrapin, loggerhead sea turtle, green sea turtle, Kemp's ridley sea turtle, hawksbill sea turtle, gopher tortoise, American alligator, American crocodile, eastern indigo snake, Gulf sturgeon, and smalltooth sawfish.

The wood stork is listed by both the Service and the State of Florida (Florida Fish and Wildlife Conservation Commission 2009a) as an endangered species. Wood storks are known to use all four refuges for roosting and foraging, while nesting is known to occur on Caloosahatchee NWR at Buzzard Roost.

The roseate spoonbill is listed as a species of special concern by the State of Florida due to its vulnerability to habitat modification, environmental alteration, human disturbance, or human exploitation which, in the foreseeable future, may result in its becoming a state-listed threatened species unless appropriate protective or management techniques are initiated or maintained and due to the fact that it has not sufficiently recovered from past population depletion (Florida Fish and Wildlife Conservation Commission 2009a). The roseate spoonbill is known to use the refuges.

The roseate tern is listed by both the Service and the State of Florida (Florida Fish and Wildlife Conservation Commission 2009a) as a threatened species. Roseate terns have been observed in the vicinity Pine Island, Matlacha Pass, and Island Bay NWRs.

The black skimmer is listed as a species of special concern by the State of Florida due to its vulnerability to habitat modification, environmental alteration, human disturbance, or human exploitation which, in the foreseeable future, may result in its becoming a state-listed threatened species unless appropriate protective or management techniques are initiated or maintained (Florida Fish and Wildlife Conservation Commission 2009a). Black skimmers historically nested on Skimmer Island in Matlacha Pass NWR, but no nesting of skimmers is known to currently occur on any of the four refuges.

The American oystercatcher is listed as a species of special concern by the State of Florida due to its vulnerability to habitat modification, environmental alteration, human disturbance, or human exploitation which, in the foreseeable future, may result in its becoming a state-listed threatened species unless appropriate protective or management techniques are initiated or maintained and due to the fact that it may already meet certain criteria for designation as a state-listed threatened species, but for which conclusive data are limited or lacking (Florida Fish and Wildlife Conservation Commission 2009a). American oystercatchers are known to use the refuges.

Snowy plovers, Wilson's plovers, and red knots are known to use all four refuges. Snowy plovers and other shorebirds nest along the beaches of Terrapin Creek at Matlacha Pass NWR. Snowy plovers are listed by the State of Florida as threatened (Florida Fish and Wildlife Conservation Commission 2009a). The Service considers snowy and Wilson's plovers as species of management concern due to their dependence on vulnerable or restricted habitats. In August 2006, the red knot was designated as a candidate species for consideration for listing under the Endangered Species Act.

In Florida, the piping plover is listed by both the Service and the State of Florida as a threatened species (Florida Fish and Wildlife Conservation Commission 2009a). Approximately 4,000 feet (1,200 meters) of critical habitat within Matlacha Pass NWR was designated in 2001 by the Service for wintering piping plovers along the shoreline of the Terrapin Creek Tract, adjacent to the county's Bunche Beach (Figure 3).

Although the bald eagle was delisted in 2007, it is still protected under various acts and treaties, including the Bald and Golden Eagle Protection Act, the Lacey Act, and the Migratory Bird Treaty Act. Bald eagles are known to use and occasionally nest in the vicinity of the refuges.

Important mangrove forest birds using the refuges include the mangrove cuckoo, black-whiskered vireo, gray kingbird, and Florida prairie warbler. The black-whiskered vireo and the Florida prairie warbler are considered by the Service to be species of management concern due to the small population or limited distribution of the black-whiskered vireo and due to the documented or apparent population decline of the Florida prairie warbler.

The Florida bonneted bat is listed by the State of Florida as an endangered species (Florida Fish and Wildlife Conservation Commission 2009a) and is listed as a candidate species for listing under the Endangered Species Act. A colony of Florida bonneted bats is known to occur in Cape Coral and they are suspected to occur on and around the refuges.

The West Indian manatee is listed by the Service and the State of Florida as an endangered species (Florida Fish and Wildlife Conservation Commission 2009a). Critical habitat for the manatee has been designated in the area (Figure 21). The Southwest manatee subpopulation, which includes all four refuges, represents about 41 percent of the state's manatee population. To help provide protection for and limit threats to this species, numerous federal manatee protection areas are located near the refuges. In 2008, three manatee deaths in nearby Charlotte County were attributed to watercraft, while 14 manatee deaths in Lee County were attributed to watercraft (Florida Fish and Wildlife Conservation Commission 2009c). The Refuge Complex coordinates with the partners to conduct regular law enforcement patrols in the area. High numbers of manatees occur regularly around all four refuges for much of the year. A manatee viewing deck in located at Lee County's Manatee Park, adjacent to Caloosahatchee NWR, where manatees congregate during winter months around the refuge.

The ornate diamondback terrapin has been considered a status review species by the Service for over a decade. In part, its conservation status has remained unchanged because most states have little information concerning current population trends. Issues are further complicated by the fact that many states cover terrapin regulations under fisheries units, while state wildlife agencies typically oversee conservation status listings. According to the State of Florida, the status of the ornate diamondback terrapin is unknown and the population is considered declining (Florida Fish and Wildlife Conservation Commission 2005). Ornate diamondback terrapins are known to occur on Matlacha Pass NWR at Terrapin Creek.

Under the Endangered Species Act, loggerhead sea turtles are listed as threatened and Kemp's ridley, green, and hawksbill sea turtles are listed as endangered. The Mote Marine Laboratory has monitored in-water populations of sea turtles in the greater Charlotte Harbor area since 2003. The Mote Marine Laboratory and its partners have been conducting set netting and visual surveys of the Charlotte Harbor area, including Island Bay, Pine Island, and Matlacha Pass NWRs, to evaluate species composition, developmental migrations, habitat use, and feeding ecology. So far, the survey results have yielded sightings and captures of loggerheads, Kemp's ridleys, and greens. In order of abundance, loggerheads are typically found near tidal passes; ridleys congregate close to creek or bay mouths; and greens are often observed in seagrass pastures in 6 to 8 feet of water.

The eastern indigo snake is listed by the Service and the State of Florida as a threatened species (Florida Fish and Wildlife Conservation Commission 2009a). There is recent and historic evidence of gopher tortoise activity on islands in Island Bay, Pine Island, and Caloosahatchee NWRs, which are commensal with eastern indigo snakes. The Terrapin Creek Tract of Matlacha Pass NWR is also expected to support gopher tortoises and possibly eastern indigo snakes.

The American alligator is listed by the Service as a threatened species by similarity of appearance and as a species of special concern by the State of Florida (Florida Fish and Wildlife Conservation Commission 2009a). Alligators are commonly found in the vicinity of the refuges.

The American crocodile is listed by the Service as a threatened species and by the State of Florida as an endangered species (Florida Fish and Wildlife Conservation Commission 2009a). The American crocodile was federally reclassified from endangered to threatened in 2007. There is one known American crocodile in the vicinity of the refuges, which is commonly seen at nearby J.N. "Ding" Darling NWR.

Gopher tortoises are under review for listing in Florida by the Service under the Endangered Species Act and are listed by the State of Florida as a threatened species (Florida Fish and Wildlife Conservation Commission 2009a). In 1975, the gopher tortoise was listed by the state as a threatened species. In 1979, due to changes in the state's listing criteria, the species was downlisted to species of special concern. Between 2002 and 2006, the state recognized the need to uplist the gopher tortoise to threatened. In 2008 it was uplisted by the state to threatened. There is recent and historic evidence of gopher tortoise activity on islands in Island Bay, Pine Island, and Caloosahatchee NWRs. The Terrapin Creek Tract of Matlacha Pass NWR is expected to support gopher tortoises.

The Gulf sturgeon is listed by the Service as a threatened species and by the state as a species of special concern (Florida Fish and Wildlife Conservation Commission 2009a). The Gulf sturgeon's historic range has included the Charlotte Harbor area.

The smalltooth sawfish is listed by the Service as an endangered species, but is not listed by the state. The smalltooth sawfish has designated critical habitat in the Charlotte Harbor area.

Beyond rare, threatened, and endangered species, the refuges are also important for wading birds, waterbirds, raptors and birds of prey, nearctic-neotropical migratory birds, shorebirds, and seabirds. The refuges were specifically established to protect native birds and they include numerous rookery islands, as well as numerous sites used by a variety of birds for foraging, roosting, and resting. The Refuge Complex's partners currently conduct rookery surveys from January through October on Matlacha Pass NWR and in Pine Island Sound (Charlotte Harbor Aquatic Preserves). The partners also started conducting annual aerial surveys of the rookeries in 2008, expanding to include all four refuges in 2009. The refuges have limited information regarding raptors and birds of prey. The refuges also lack information regarding the mix of nearctic-neotropical migratory birds, shorebirds, and seabirds.

Pine Island NWR

Pine Island NWR has several islands that are used by over 2,000 wading birds and waterbirds as foraging, resting, roosting, and nesting sites. Great (*Ardea alba*), reddish, snowy, and cattle (*Bubulcus ibis*) egrets; great blue, little blue, tricolored, and green herons (*Butorides virescens*); black-crowned and yellow-crowned night herons; wood storks; white ibises; brown pelican; double-crested cormorant (*Phalacrocorax auritus*); and magnificent frigatebirds can be commonly found on and around these islands. It is common to see a mix of birds on Hemp Island and Bird Key. Raccoons (*Procyon lotor elucus*) are the primary mammal found on the islands. Dolphins (*Tursiops truncatus*) and manatees can be seen in the surrounding waters. Small colonies of gopher tortoises may be found on some of the larger islands. Endangered and threatened species using the refuge and its surrounding waters include wood storks, sea turtles, and manatees.

Matlacha Pass NWR

Several islands of Matlacha Pass NWR are used as foraging, resting, roosting, and nesting sites by 1,000 to 2,500 wading birds and waterbirds. Great, reddish, snowy, and cattle egrets; great blue, little blue, tricolored, and green herons; black-crowned and yellow-crowned night herons; wood storks; white ibises; brown pelicans; and magnificent frigatebirds can be commonly found on and around these islands. The beaches and shores provide loafing, feeding, and nesting areas for migratory waterfowl, shorebirds, gulls, and terns. Ospreys (*Pandion haliaetus*) can be observed nesting and feeding in the Matlacha Pass area. Skimmer Island has been managed for the purpose of attracting nesting black skimmers and least terns away from construction sites on the mainland. Several endangered and threatened species benefit from the habitats on and around the refuge, including wood storks, sea turtles, and manatees.

Island Bay NWR

The beaches and shores of Island Bay NWR provide loafing and feeding sites for shorebirds, gulls, and terns. The surrounding shallow bays provide valuable feeding areas for wading and water birds. Other vertebrates known to use the refuge or surrounding waters include raccoons, manatees, and sea turtles.

Caloosahatchee NWR

Numerous birds nest, rest, and forage on and around the islands of Caloosahatchee NWR. A wood stork rookery is located on Buzzard Roost. The endangered West Indian manatee is commonly seen around refuge islands and a viewing area is located adjacent to the refuge. The warm water outflow from the Orange River Power Plant is a major wintering area for the West Indian manatee and the nearshore and riverine areas provide interjurisdictional fish species habitat. A gopher tortoise burrow is known to occur on the refuge.

EXOTIC, INVASIVE, AND NUISANCE SPECIES

All four refuges are impacted by a variety of exotic, invasive, and nuisance species, which may be contributing to or causing the partial or total failure of some rookeries. Priority exotic, invasive, and nuisance species of current management concern include Brazilian pepper; Australian pine; seaside mahoe (*Thespesia populnea*); air potato; carrotwood (*Cupaniopsis anacardioides*); earleaf acacia (*Acacia auriculiformis*); lead tree (*Leucaena leucocephala*); natal grass [*Melinis repens* (=*Rhynchelytrum repens*)]; black rats (*Rattus rattus*); green iguanas (*Iguana iguana*); feral hogs (*Sus scrofa*); Savannah monitor lizards (*Varanus exanthematicus*); and Nile monitor lizards. The green mussel (*Perna viridis*) was recently discovered nearby in Tarpon Bay on J.N. "Ding" Darling NWR and the Chinese mysterysnail (*Cipangopaludina chinensis malleate*) has been found nearby in a Cape Coral canal (Loren Coen, personal communications, 2009). Further, large snakes are posing more and more of a problem for this area, including the Burmese python (*Python molurus bivittatus*). Table 10 includes 22 nonnative plant species found on the refuges, where 12 are classified by the Florida Exotic Pest Plant Council (FLEPPC) as Category I and five are Category II.

Table 10. Nonnative plants found at Pine Island, Matlacha Pass, Island Bay, and Caloosahatchee NWRs.

Common Name	Scientific Name	FLEPPC Category
Australian pine	*Casuarina equisetifolia*	I
Beach naupaka	*Scaevola sericea*	I
Brazilian pepper	*Schinus terebinthifolius*	I
Carrotwood	*Cupaniopsis anacardioides*	I
Coconut palm	*Cocos nucifera*	
Council tree	*Ficus altissima*	II
Earleaf acacia	*Acacia auriculiformis*	I
Guava	*Psidium guajava*	I
Guinea grass	*Panicum maximum*	II
Lantana	*Lantana camara*	I
Laurel fig	*Ficus microcarpa*	I
Lead tree	*Leucaena leucocephala*	II
Life plant	*Kalanchoe pinnata*	II
Madagascar periwinkle	*Catharanthus roseus*	
Melaleuca	*Melaleuca quinquenervia*	I
Papaya	*Carica papaya*	
Rosary pea	*Abrus precatorius*	I
Royal poinciana	*Delonix regia*	
Sansevieria	*Sansevieria hyacinthoides*	II
Seaside mahoe	*Thespesia populnea*	I
Sicklepod	*Senna obtusifolia*	
Surinam cherry	*Eugenia uniflora*	I

Initial exotic plant control treatments were conducted during 2007 to 2009 for Pine Island, Island Bay, and Caloosahatchee NWRs. Both initial and follow-up exotic plant sweeps have been conducted from 2006 to 2008 on six islands of Matlacha Pass NWR (i.e., Fisherman's Key, Givney Key, Merwin Key, Big Island, Skimmer Island, and Tern Island) and at Terrapin Creek by contractors, Service staff, or through Challenge Cost Share grants with Lee County. However, initial exotic plant control efforts have not been started for Matlacha Pass NWR. Exotic plant removal operations on several islands have also been conducted to reduce the impacts from Hurricane Charley in 2004. Beyond addressing plants, the refuges have conducted small mammal trapping and have euthanized black rats.

CULTURAL RESOURCES

Southwest Florida has had a long, rich, and colorful history over the past 8,000 years. As many as 6,000 years ago, Native Americans inhabited the coastal region. The shell mounds that occur along the coast of both Lee and Charlotte counties were once utilized by pre-Columbian people, the fore bearers of one of the most powerful and complex Native American societies. Dating as far back as 2,500 years, the native Calusa Indians were the first-known residents of the islands of the area. The Calusa skillfully transformed the waterways around the islands into abundant riches of food and tools. Whelks, conchs, clams, oysters, and other seafood were used for food, and their empty shells were crafted into tools. The Calusa proved to be skilled builders and craftsmen, perching their huts high atop shell mounds to provide protection from storm tides. Some of their shell mounds, which were also used for ceremonial, ritual and burial sites, remain intact today. Specifically, two smaller tracts of the Island Bay NWR, Cash Mound and John Quiet Mound, which are located on the edge of Turtle Bay, are of historical interest because a large Native American mound is the dominating feature on each of them. Also, shell mounds located on Benedict Island of the Pine Island NWR show evidence of Calusa Indians once inhabiting this island at the time of European exploration (U.S. Fish and Wildlife Service 1998).

The presence and extent of cultural resources are basically unknown for the refuges. A Bay of Pigs training site is known to occur in the area, on or near Pine Island NWR. However, information about this site is unknown and undocumented. Pine Island and Matlacha Pass NWRs may include historic homesites. Pine Island, Matlacha Pass, and Island Bay NWRs are known to have Indian mounds.

The Spanish explorer Juan Ponce de Leon is believed to have landed in the area and discovered Sanibel Island, which he named Santa Isybella after Queen Isabella, in 1513 while searching for his "Fountain of Youth." He and his Spanish seamen battled the hostile Calusas for years, and Ponce de Leon eventually suffered a fatal arrow attack at their hands in 1523, at which time he retreated to Cuba and died. The Spanish were unsuccessful in establishing any permanent settlement. However, their infiltration introduced European disease and slavery to the area, and overcome by yellow fever, tuberculosis and measles, the Calusa population all but became extinct by the late 1700s. In the 1800s, the Florida Seminole Indians (Seminole means "wild people") opposed the Spaniards trying to colonize Sanibel and Captiva islands. The long-lasting Seminole Indian wars were brutal by any standard (as many as 1,500 to 2,000 U.S. soldiers were killed) and discouraged any permanent settlements in Florida for many decades.

Legend has it that the barrier islands soon became a haven for pirates. The "Buccaneer Coast" attracted the notorious Jose Gaspar to the region in the early 1800s, where it was rumored that he buried his stolen treasure on Sanibel, and then built a prison on Isle de los Captivas, or Captiva Island, where he kept his female prisoners captive for ransom. Gaspar himself was captured in 1821 by the U.S. Navy, but wrapped himself in chains and jumped overboard off his ship, rather than face imprisonment.

Europeans populated the area in the 19th century with small fishing settlements (especially Sanibel Island, but Fisherman Key of Matlacha Pass NWR also once had fish camps and permanent residents on it). The area's islands provided ample food in the form of wildlife and fish for its residents during that century, including a large feral hog population on Sanibel Island as early as 1831. After extensive exploration and surveying, Sanibel Island was purchased in 1831 by the Florida Peninsular Land Company (a group of New York investors) as a settlement site because of its good harbor, climate, and general amenities. The first settlers, who arrived in 1833, lived temporarily in palmetto-thatched huts with floors of shell and sand. These early settlers envisioned the Island as a paradise for recreation and health recuperation. But the settlement did not prosper. Most of the settlers deserted; many left because of a final series of Indian raids in 1836 (Clark 1976). Only two persons registered in the 1870 U.S. Census.

In 1845, Florida was admitted to the Union and became the 27th state. In 1850, Fort Casey was erected on the site of a former settlement on Sanibel Island. A hurricane destroyed much of the fort on October 6, 1873. The area became populated again after the Civil War when the military increased its presence on Sanibel Island and as a result it was deemed safe for settlers.

About 100 years ago, a tragedy at Island Bay was instrumental in changing the face of conservation politics. Audubon warden Columbus McLeod, while protecting the area's wading birds, was ax-murdered there by plume hunters. Columbus McLeod was not the only one. During a three-year period, three other Audubon wardens, hired at rates of one to thirty dollars per month, were all murdered. The first was Guy Bradley, an Everglades warden who was killed in July 1905, widely considered the first martyr of conservation. In September 1908, L. P. Reeves, an Audubon warden in South Carolina, was also murdered, allegedly by fish pirates. Columbus McLeod's bloody hat and sunken patrol boat were found in November of 1908. Plume hunters of the day provided for the fashion centers of New York and Europe. Ladies of the day wore plumes of egrets on their hats and used roseate fans of spoonbill tail feathers. McLeod's death instigated a movement to ban the feather trade market and a movement to hire state wardens, and was a catalyst for the American conservation movement (Stout 2008).

SOCIOECONOMIC ENVIRONMENT

REGIONAL DEMOGRAPHICS AND ECONOMY

Although Native Americans inhabited the area about 6,000 years ago and although more modern settlement of the area began to prosper in the 1850s, much of the development of the area did not occur until the post-World War II period with the influx of war veterans. The four refuges are located on Florida's southwest Gulf coast in Lee and Charlotte counties. Close to 10 million people—about two-thirds of the State of Florida's 2000 Census population—live within a 150-mile radius of Lee County, and that number is expected to increase to more than 13 million by the year 2010 (Bureau of Economic and Business Research 1999).

Pine Island, Matlacha Pass, Island Bay, and Caloosahatchee NWRs are surrounded by three metropolitan areas (Lee County, Collier County, and Charlotte County). The populations of Lee and Charlotte counties have grown to be currently estimated at about 796,000, with an additional nearly 381,000 for Collier County (Zwick and Carr 2006). Lee County encompasses the entire Cape Coral-Fort Myers, Florida Metropolitan Statistical Area (MSA); Collier County encompasses the entire Naples-Marco Island MSA; and Charlotte County encompasses the entire Punta Gorda MSA. All three counties are highly developed, with 88-90 percent of their populations living in urban areas (City-Data.com 2008). The U.S. Census Bureau, in its 2006 American Community Survey, estimated that the populations of these MSAs were as follows (U.S. Department of Commerce, U.S. Census Bureau 2006a):

- Cape Coral-Fort Myers, Florida MSA – 571,344
- Naples-Marco Island MSA – 314,649
- Punta Gorda MSA – 154,438

Within the 15-year life of the CCP and by 2025, Charlotte County is expected to grow 26 percent to 224,577 (gaining about 47,000 people during the 15 years), while Lee County is expected to grow 36 percent to 838,209 (gaining 220,000 people during the 15 years) and Collier County is expected to grow 45 percent to 553,762 (Zwick and Carr 2006). By 2060, Charlotte County is expected to reach 335,713 (increasing 2.4 times since 2000 and 1.9 times since 2010), while Lee County would be nearly 1.4 million (more than tripling since 2000 and more than doubling since 2010) and Collier County would reach 963,051 (increasing 3.8 times since 2000 and 2.5 times since 2010) (Zwick and Carr 2006). The entire State of Florida is anticipated to reach a population of 21 million by 2015, nearly 26 million by 2030, and nearly 36 million by 2060 (Zwick and Carr 2006).

Florida's population growth is the state's primary engine of economic growth, fueling both employment and income growth (Florida Legislature 2007). From 1960 to 2008, the population in the State of Florida increased from just fewer than 5 million to over 18 million, an increase of over 260 percent. In addition, the J.N. "Ding" Darling Refuge Complex area of coastal southwest Florida is one of the fastest-urbanizing regions in the United States. Between 1960 and 2000, the area's population increased from 90,000 to 900,000, a 10-fold increase (Main and Allen 2007). The U.S. Census Bureau estimates that of the 25 U.S. counties with the largest numerical increases in population from 2000 to 2006, six of them are Florida counties. Between 2000 and 2006, Lee County's population increase of over 130,000 (an approximate 30 percent increase in population) ranked 25th nationally in terms of numerical population growth (U.S. Department of Commerce, U.S. Census Bureau 2006b). During the same six-year period, the population of Collier and Charlotte counties increased just over 25 percent and 9 percent, respectively.

The three counties' per-capita incomes are above state and national averages. Approximately 9 percent, 9.7 percent, and 7.5 percent of individuals live at or below the poverty level in Lee, Collier, and Charlotte counties, respectively, which are lower than the state (12.6 percent) and national (13.3 percent) rates (Table 11).

Unemployment levels in Lee, Collier, and Charlotte counties recently have risen above the national average. In September 2007, unemployment rates for Lee, Collier, and Charlotte counties were 5.2 percent, 5.3 percent, and 5.9 percent, respectively, compared to the state and national unemployment rates of 4.3 percent and 4.7 percent, respectively (Florida Gulf Coast University, Regional Economic Research Institute 2007). Other demographic and economic information for the three counties is given in Table 11.

Table 11. Demographics of the Charlotte Harbor region.

Characteristic	Lee County[b]	Collier County[c]	Charlotte County[d]	State of Florida	United States
Demographic					
Population, 2006	571,344	314,649	154,438	18,089,888	299,398,485
Total Land Area (square miles)	803.6	2,025.3	693.6	53,926.8	3,537,438.0
Population Increase (%), since 2000	29.6%	25.2%	9.1%	13.2%	6.4%
Population Density (population/square mile)	711	155	223	335	85
Race/Ethnicity (% of Population)					
White	84.6	83.7	90.5	76.1	73.9
Black/African American	7.3	5.5	5.5	15.4	12.4
Hispanic/Latino (of any race)	16.1	25.2	4.7	20.1	14.8
Asian	1.3	1.0	0.9	2.2	4.4
Education (% of population over 25)					
High School degree	85.6	83.8	88.6	84.1	84.1
College degree	24.1	29.0	21.1	27.0	27.0
Economic					
Median Household Income	$ 48,553	$ 55,888	$ 44,166	$ 45,495	$ 48,451
Per capita Income	$ 29,069	$ 34,650	$ 26,538	$ 25,297	$ 25,267
Families below poverty level (%)	6.0%	6.3%	5.6%	9.0%	9.8%
Individuals below poverty level (%)	9.0%	9.7%	7.5%	12.6%	13.3%

[a] Source: U.S. Department of Commerce, U.S. Census Bureau 2006a and 2006b
[b] The Cape Coral-Fort Myers, Florida Metropolitan Statistical Area (MSA)
[c] The Naples-Marco Island, Florida Metropolitan Statistical Area (MSA)
[d] The Punta Gorda, Florida Metropolitan Statistical Area (MSA)

The economy of Lee County is large and diversified. Once a retirement haven, Lee County is now dominated by working-age people. The service industry (33 percent); retail trade (14 percent); construction (13 percent); government (federal, state, and local) (12 percent); and financial activities (5 percent) are the five largest employment sectors (Southwest Florida Economic Development Office 2009). Although these statistics show a low percentage of residents being employed in the commercial fishing industry and the recreational sportfishing business, they directly and indirectly affect several other employment sectors because they have a positive impact on the area's tourism.

Table 12 shows the growth rates and industry employment projections for Lee, Charlotte, and Collier counties, among others, from 2007 to 2015.

Table 12. Employment projections, 2007-2015.

Industry (Lee County)	Employment 2008	Employment 2016	Annual Growth Rate, %
Agriculture, Forestry, Fishing and Hunting	1,560	1,480	-0.64
Construction	24,604	34,113	4.83
Manufacturing	5,942	6,728	1.65
Trade	45,240	53,916	2.34
Transportation	3,084	3,463	1.54
Information	4,144	4,612	1.41
Financial Activities	13,125	16,279	3.00
Professional and Business Services	29,358	35,036	2.42
Education and Health Services	21,929	28,386	3.68
Leisure and Hospitality	30,281	36,035	2.38
Other Services (Except Government)	9,803	11,682	2.40
Federal Government	2,423	2,532	0.56
State Government	4,481	5,341	2.40
Local Government	29,818	36,056	2.62
Self-Employed and Unpaid Family Workers	23,721	28,337	2.43
Totals	249,653	304,138	2.73

Industry (Charlotte, Collier, Glades, Hendry, and Lee Counties)	Employment 2008	Employment 2016	Annual Growth Rate
Agriculture, Forestry, Fishing and Hunting	11,217	10,345	-0.97%
Construction	43,816	60,625	4.80%
Manufacturing	10,771	11,227	0.53%
Trade	79,691	94,312	2.24%
Transportation and Warehousing	5,031	5,652	1.54%
Information	6,740	7,486	1.38%
Financial Activities	24,151	29,879	2.96%
Professional and Business Services	49,526	58,767	2.33%
Education and Health Services	47,834	60,592	3.33%
Leisure and Hospitality	59,895	71,189	2.36%
Other Services (Except Government)	17,758	21,094	2.35%
Federal Government	3,462	3,603	0.51%
State Government	6,817	7,701	1.62%
Local Government	50,244	59,515	2.31%
Self-Employed and Unpaid Family Workers	48,262	56,265	2.07%
Totals	465,515	558,527	2.50%

Source: Southwest Florida Economic Development Office 2009

RECREATION AND TOURISM

Not only does Florida have a high number of residents and high growth rates, it also experiences high tourism. Nearly 84 million people visited Florida in 2006 (Florida Department of Transportation and University of South Florida 2008). Given the growth, proximity, and the socioeconomic impacts of the MSAs, strong development pressures are being felt by the refuges. An estimated 3.6 million tourists visit the three-county area and spend an estimated 2.1 billion dollars each year, based on 2005 data for Lee and Charlotte counties and 2003 data for Collier County (Lee County Visitors and Convention Bureau 2005; Charlotte County Visitors Bureau 2005; Collier County Tourist Development Council 2003).

Popular area recreational activities include boating, swimming, sunbathing, and fishing. In addition to the economic activity provided by recreation and tourism, other activities such as commercial fishing, citrus agriculture and beef cattle production, and phosphate mining are of economic importance in the three-county area. The 1996 dollar estimates of these four economic activities in the Charlotte Harbor NEP study area are shown below (Hazen and Sawyer 1998):

Tourism and Recreation	$2,196.9 million
Agriculture	$671.6 million
Mining	$270.3 million
Commercial Fishing	$22.6 million

Although the four refuges are closed to the public except for rare excursions taken during the annual "Ding Darling Days" celebration, the nearby J.N. "Ding" Darling NWR hosts an estimated 700,000 visitors a year. Table 13 provides details of the recreation visits there in 2004 where the estimated 723,365 visitors accounted for 1.5 million visits participating in various activities on the refuge. Nonconsumptive activities (e.g., hiking and observing wildlife) account for about 94 percent of total recreation visits. About 25 percent of recreation visits are undertaken by area residents, while about 75 percent of recreation visits were by nonresidents. Total expenditures by visitors to the J.N. "Ding" Darling NWR were almost 32 million dollars in 2004, with nonresidents accounting for 92 percent of these expenditures (Caudill and Henderson 2005). Nonconsumptive activities accounted for about 91 percent of these expenditures, with the remaining 9 percent of these expenditures for fishing (Caudill and Henderson 2005). Table 14 provides recreation expenditure information.

Outdoor Recreational Economics

Although the four satellite refuges of the Refuge Complex are closed to the public and access to the waters immediately surrounding these satellite refuge islands is difficult, the wildlife resources of the area in general, including the J.N. "Ding" Darling NWR Complex, are economically important. In addition to commercial and recreational fishing, ecotourism, including wildlife viewing, photography, and environmental interpretation, is increasingly being seen as economically important to local businesses. As the population increases and the number of places left to enjoy wildlife decreases, the Refuge Complex area is anticipated to become even more important to the local community. It benefits the community directly by providing recreational and employment opportunities for the local population and indirectly by attracting tourists from outside the area to generate additional income to the local economy. Table 15 presents this information and summarizes the economic value of wildlife watching in Florida by U.S. residents.

Table 13. Recreational visits to the J.N. "Ding" Darling NWR Complex, 2004.

Activity	Residents	Nonresidents	Total
Nonconsumptive:			
Nature Trails	130,794	523,174	653,968
Observation Platforms	24,352	137,995	162,347
Other Wildlife Observation	49,397	279,350	328,647
Beach /Water Use	1,538	13,839	15,377
Other Recreation	140,441	140,441	280,882
Hunting:			
Big Game	0	0	0
Small Game	0	0	0
Migratory Birds	0	0	0
Fishing:			
Freshwater	210	52	262
Saltwater	44,837	44,837	89,674
Total Visitation	**391,468**	**1,139,689**	**1,531,156**
Total Visitors			**723,365**

Source: Caudill and Henderson 2005

Table 14. Visitor recreation expenditures at the J.N. "Ding Darling" NWR Complex, 2004 (in thousands of dollars).

Activity	Residents	Nonresidents	Total
Nonconsumptive:	$1,664.3	$27,118.1	$28,782.4
Hunting:			
Big Game	—	—	—
Small Game	—	—	—
Migratory Birds	—	—	—
Total Hunting	—	—	—
Fishing:			
Freshwater	$0.9	$2.5	$3.5
Saltwater	$727.9	$2,245.7	$2,973.5
Total Fishing	$728.8	$2,248.2	$2,977.0
Total Expenditures	***$2,393.1***	***$29,366.3***	***$31,759.4***

Source: Caudill and Henderson 2005

Table 15. Wildlife watching activities in Florida by U.S. residents.
Wildlife Watching (observing, photographing, or feeding wildlife)

Total wildlife-watching participants	4,240,000
Away-from-home participants	1,560,000
Around-the-home participants	3,274,000
Days of participation away from home	16,551,000
Average days of participation away from home	11
Total expenditures	$3,081,496,000
Trip-related	$887,942,000
Equipment and other	$2,193,554,000
Average per participant	$720
Average trip expenditure per day	$54
Total trip and equipment expenditures by nonresidents in Florida	$653,278,000
Average per nonresident participant	$858
Average trip expenditure per day	$104

U.S. Fish and Wildlife Service and U.S. Department of Commerce, U.S. Census Bureau 2006

REFUGE ADMINISTRATION AND MANAGEMENT

The headquarters for the Refuge Complex and all Refuge Complex staff are housed at the J.N. "Ding" Darling NWR on Sanibel Island.

LAND PROTECTION AND CONSERVATION

Pine Island NWR was established on September 15, 1908, and includes approximately 602.24 acres (243.72 ha) within Pine Island Sound in Lee County (Figure 2). Matlacha Pass NWR was established on September 26, 1908 and now includes approximately 538.25 acres (217.82 ha) within Matlacha Pass in Lee County (Figure 3). Island Bay NWR was established on October 23, 1908 and includes 20.24 acres (8.19 ha) in Charlotte County (Figure 4). Caloosahatchee NWR was established on July 1, 1920 and now includes approximately 40 acres (16.19 ha) in Lee County, adjacent to Fort Myers (Figure 5). An estimated 18.26 acres (7.39 ha) are included on the four islands in Figure 5, while the remaining 21.74 acres (8.8 ha) remain to be resolved and are not included in Figure 5. Some of the most recent additions to Pine Island and Matlacha Pass NWRs occurred on April 10, 1991, through a public land order which withdrew 98.86 acres (40.01 ha) of public lands for Pine Island and 312.92 acres (126.63 ha) of public lands for Matlacha Pass from surface entry and mining for 40 years for use by the Service. The acquisition boundary and the management boundary are the same for Pine Island, Matlacha Pass, and Island Bay NWRs. The boundary for Caloosahatchee NWR has undergone many changes since its inception in 1920. The current management boundary for Caloosahatchee NWR only includes the four islands identified on Figure 5.

In a 2002 Final Environmental Assessment and Land Protection Plan (EA/LPP), the Service proposed boundary expansions for each of the refuges. However, this EA/LPP never received final approval.

VISITOR SERVICES

Although Pine Island, Matlacha Pass, Island Bay, and Caloosahatchee NWRs are closed to the public, boat access to the adjacent waters provide limited public use opportunities related to the refuges, including saltwater fishing, wildlife observation, and wildlife photography. The refuges are part of the Great Calusa Blueway. Additionally, the Caloosahatchee NWR, because of its location on the river within the city of Fort Myers, has fishing, canoeing and kayaking, and a manatee viewing area adjacent to the refuge. All state fishing laws apply for saltwater and freshwater fishing and crabbing. Boating is allowed only in designated areas and several waters are slow speed/minimum wake zones. The Island Bay NWR Wilderness Area is a closed area.

Although the refuges are closed, the Refuge Complex staff has offered programs in Pine Island, including regular interpretive programs at the Pine Island Library starting in 2006 and a centennial event on Pine Island in 2008. Further, train-the-teacher workshops and the Summer Teachers Assisting Refuge (STAR) program kicked off at J.N. "Ding" Darling NWR in 2009, benefitting the surrounding communities.

Many educational and recreational opportunities are available on the nearby J.N. "Ding" Darling NWR, including fishing, boating, kayaking, canoeing, bicycling, nature photography, birdwatching, and environmental education and interpretative programs and tours. The four refuges are frequently included in these programs and activities. Occasionally, special tours are conducted specifically to the areas surrounding the four refuges. For example, in October 2008 during the celebration known as the "Ding" Darling Days, the tour boat companies Captiva Cruises, Tropic Star, and Island Girl, along with Tarpon Bay Explorers and other kayak outfitters, partnered with the Refuge Complex to offer cruises into Roosevelt Channel and Pine Island Sound to watch wildlife on and around the islands of Pine Island NWR, including Narrows Key, Bird Key, Middle Key, Whoopee Island, Patricio Island, Part Island, Coon Key, Black Key, and Cove Key.

PERSONNEL, OPERATIONS, AND MAINTENANCE

Although the four refuges are unstaffed, they are managed as part of the J.N. "Ding" Darling NWR Complex. Covering all five refuges in the Complex, the J.N. "Ding" Darling NWR staff includes 14.5 permanent full-time employees (FTEs), three temporary full-time employees, five student interns, nine seasonal/temporary employees, and three student employees (Figure 22). Another five seasonal interns are housed at the Refuge Complex's Maintenance Shop. In addition, over 240 volunteers annually contribute services equivalent to an additional 10 full-time employees.

Located near the J.N. "Ding" Darling NWR Visitor/Education Center and Administration Headquarters on Sanibel Island, the Refuge Complex's Maintenance Shop has earth-moving, vegetation control, and water management machinery and equipment; staff housing; equipment and boat storage; and maintenance facilities that are vital to fulfilling the purposes of the refuges. The annual budget of the Refuge Complex varies, but has averaged about $2,500,000 over the past few years.

Community partnerships play an important part in the daily operations of the Refuge Complex. Locally the Service provides fiscal support for Partners for Fish and Wildlife projects that restore fish and wildlife habitat. Also, the Refuge Complex has cooperative agreements with the City of Sanibel and the Sanibel-Captiva Conservation Foundation (SCCF) that allow for the sharing of equipment, personnel, and material for the restoration of fish and wildlife habitat on and off the refuges. The Refuge Complex also has a cooperative agreement with the "Ding" Darling Wildlife Society. The Society assists with funding projects that directly contribute to the purposes, vision, goals, and objectives of the Refuge Complex.

Figure 22. Current organizational chart for the J.N. "Ding" Darling NWR Complex.

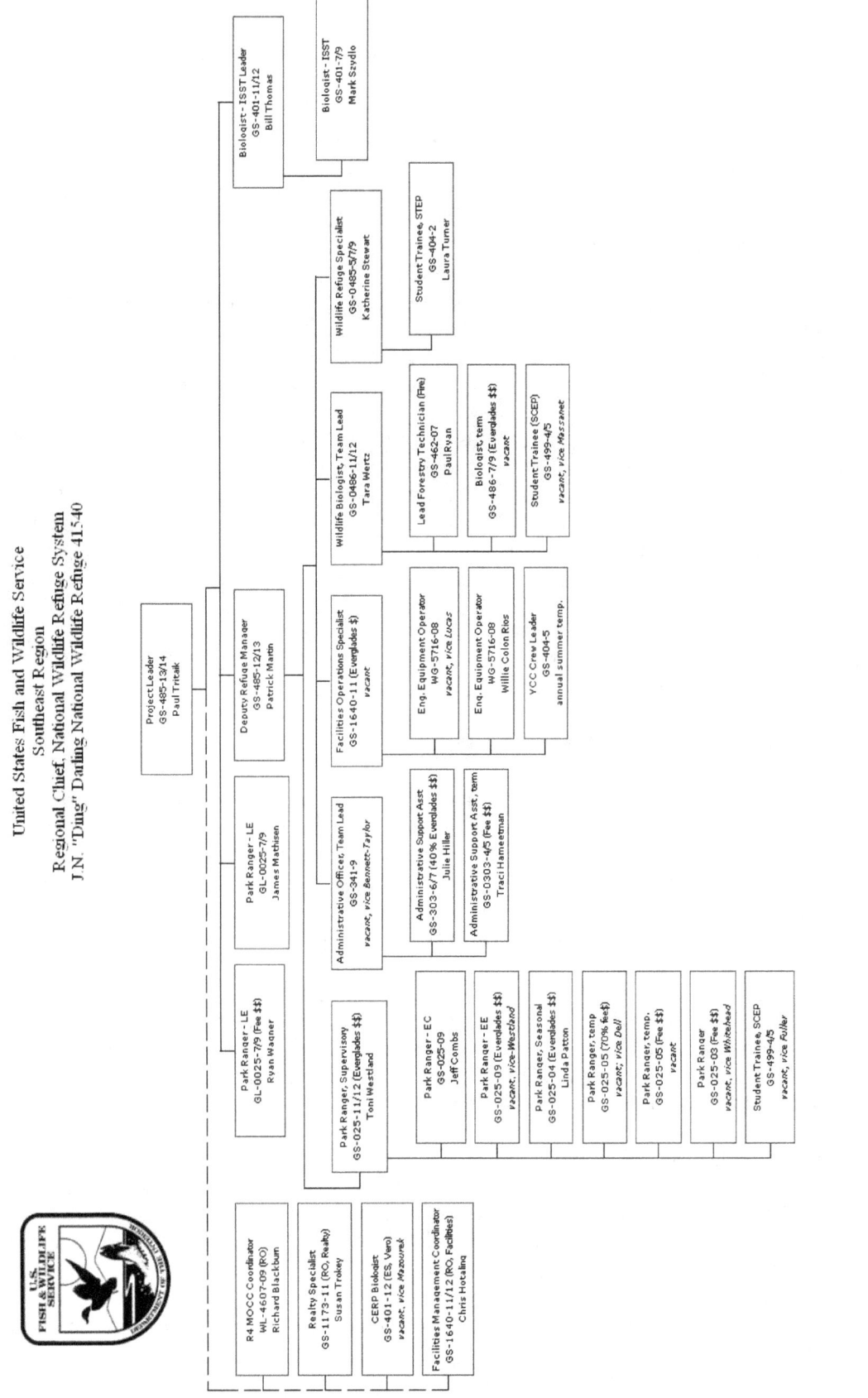

Pine Island, Matlacha Pass, Island Bay, and Caloosahatchee National Wildlife Refuges

III. Plan Development

SUMMARY OF ISSUES, CONCERNS, AND OPPORTUNITIES

The comprehensive planning process officially began in February 2007. A Service Core Planning Team was assembled and began preplanning activities such as gathering data and information and meeting with J. N. "Ding" Darling NWR staff. This process started in January 2008 with visioning and preparation for the public scoping phase of the planning process. To include the governmental partners in the planning process, an Intergovernmental Coordination meeting was held on April 7, 2008, and included representatives from the Seminole Tribe of Florida, Florida Fish and Wildlife Conservation Commission, Florida Department of Environmental Protection, Florida Department of Agriculture and Consumer Services, South Florida Water Management District, Southwest Florida Regional Planning Council, Lee County, Lee County Mosquito Control District, and the city of Sanibel. The Intergovernmental Coordination Planning Team identified items such as existing and needed data, refuge resources, issues, concerns, affected members of the public, vision ideas, and public participation issues. As a group, this Intergovernmental Team prioritized its top issues to be addressed by the refuges over the 15-year life of the plan. Appendix D provides a summarized list of these issues.

Public scoping began in the spring of 2008, including a notice that was published in the *Federal Register* on April 2, 2008 and coverage in local newspapers. Additional information about the planning process and public scoping was provided through informational flyers, planning updates, several articles published in local newspapers, and postings on the Refuge Complex's Internet website (http://www.fws.gov/dingdarling/CCP/CCP.html). Information was also included in the Ding Darling Wildlife Society newsletter. Given the proximity of the refuges, several shared issues, and many overlapping interested parties, joint public meetings were held for the satellite refuges ((i.e., Pine Island, Matlacha Pass, Island Bay, and Caloosahatchee NWRs) and J.N. "Ding" Darling NWR. Using the Refuge Complex's growing CCP public mailing list, as well as public mailing lists from various governmental partners, informational flyers were mailed out to interested parties. This flyer invited participation in the planning process through a variety of means, including public meetings, letters, faxes, telephone calls, e-mail messages, and personal visits. The flyer also announced the times and locations of the public meetings, provided other information, and described the purposes of the five refuges. Three neighborhood public meetings were conducted during the week of April 7, 2008: on April 8th at the Sanibel School, Sanibel Island, Florida; on April 9th at Cypress Lake Middle School, Fort Myers, Florida; and on April 10th at Pine Island Elementary School, Pine Island, Florida.

The public scoping meetings were attended by a total of over 40 individuals representing a variety of interests and organizations. Beyond the verbal comments recorded at these public meetings, over 90 written comments were also submitted by individuals, organizations, and governmental entities submitted comments regarding future management of these five refuges. Letters, faxes, email messages, and phone calls were received from across the country. Appendix D, Public Involvement, summarizes the comments that were submitted at the public scoping meetings.

Experts from the Service, Florida Fish and Wildlife Conservation Commission, Lee County, Indian River County Mosquito Control District, City of Sanibel, and the Sanibel-Captiva Conservation Foundation participated in a wildlife and habitat management review of the Refuge Complex in 2001. A wilderness review for the Refuge Complex was updated in 2008. The information garnered from these reviews helped the planning team analyze and develop recommendations for the CCP and the Draft CCP/EA.

During the preplanning and public scoping phases of CCP development, a myriad of issues, concerns, and opportunities were raised by the public, local businesses, organizations, the Service, and other governmental agencies. The identification of issues was a major factor in determining the refuges' future management goals and objectives, as well as future projects. In addition to the general public scoping meetings, another meeting was conducted with federal, state, and local governmental agencies. Coordination with the governmental partners and the public is essential to ensure support for the CCP and the identified projects. While some of the issues and concerns raised during scoping are important to the future of the refuges, many are not within the Service's management jurisdiction or authority, and some are outside of its control. Several opportunities raised during scoping are addressed by the Service in this CCP. The Service evaluated the long list of issues raised, identified the priority issues to be addressed over the next 15 years, evaluated steps to rectify these issues and resource needs, and measured the impact of implementing the CCP. From these priority issues, the Service developed the list of goals, objectives, and strategies to shape management of the refuges for the 15-year life of the CCP. The priority issues for the refuges to address during the 15-year life of the CCP are:

- Increasing and changing human population, development of the landscape, recreational uses and demands, and associated impacts.
- Issues and impacts associated with water quality, water quantity, and timing of flows.
- Invasion and spread of exotic, invasive, and nuisance species.
- Climate change impacts.
- Need for long-term protection of important resources.
- Declines in and threats to rare, threatened, and endangered species.
- Insufficient baseline wildlife and habitat data and lack of comprehensive habitat management plan.
- Insufficient staff and resources to address refuge needs.

These management priorities were identified in response to the challenges facing these island refuges. Although some of the challenges span more than one category, the priority issues are divided into four management categories: wildlife and habitat management, resource protection, visitor services, and refuge administration. The issues of the increasing and changing human population, development of the landscape, recreational uses and demands, and associated impacts span all four categories. Lee and Charlotte counties had an estimated 725,782 residents in 2006 (U.S. Census Bureau 2007). Population growth projections estimate these counties to grow to over 1 million by 2025 and over 1.7 million by 2060 (Zwick and Carr 2006). These two counties are expected to be built out before 2060 as part of a nearly continuous band of urban development along Florida's southwest coast (Zwick and Carr 2006). Further, exemplifying current high waterway use in and around the refuge, in 2006, Charlotte and Lee counties had over 71,000 registered recreational vessels (Florida Fish and Wildlife Conservation Commission 2007). This growth in the population and use of the landscape will continue to impact the refuges into the future.

WILDLIFE AND HABITAT MANAGEMENT

The refuges and their fish and wildlife resources have also been affected by increasing development pressure and associated habitat loss; altered quality, quantity, and timing of freshwater flows; the spread of exotic, invasive, and nuisance species; sea level rise and climate change; and the declines in and threats to rare, threatened, and endangered species.

The refuges are unable to evaluate the status and trends of many fish and wildlife species and their habitats within the refuges due to the lack of sufficient baseline data and the lack of a comprehensive habitat management plan to help guide management, monitor results, and adapt management as necessary to achieve outlined goals and objectives. Additionally, the demand for recreational uses adjacent to the refuges and the resultant impacts on fish and wildlife resources within the refuges are increasing and changing along with changes in the human population and development.

Altered water quality, quantity, and timing of freshwater flows also affect these island refuges. Management of the Caloosahatchee River directly affects the Caloosahatchee and Matlacha Pass NWRs. Freshwater flows in the Caloosahatchee River releases deviate from the historical quality, quantity, and timing of freshwater flows. Impacts include extreme variations in salinity levels, increased nutrients and sedimentation, decreased light attenuation, and increased contaminants from upstream and their effects on seagrasses, oyster beds, and algal blooms within and adjacent to the refuges. In addition, alterations of natural drainage patterns as a result of development and canal dredging in Cape Coral have similar effects on the quality, quantity, and timing of freshwater flows to Matlacha Pass NWR. Likewise, development and agricultural development on Pine Island has affected water quality and timing of flows to Matlacha Pass and Pine Island NWRs.

The refuges are currently and will continue to be affected by the spread of exotic, invasive, and nuisance plants and animals. Key exotic, invasive, and nuisance species of concern for these island refuges include Brazilian pepper, Australian pine, seaside mahoe, beach naupaka [*Scaevola taccada* (=*Scaevola sericea, S. frutescens*)], sicklepod (*Senna obtusifolia*), umbrella tree [*Schefflera actinophylla* (=*Brassaia actinophylla*)], earleaf acacia, Nile monitor lizard, feral hogs, and possibly the green iguana and black rat.

The rare, threatened, and endangered species of management concern to the refuges include the wood stork, roseate spoonbill, roseate tern, black skimmer, American oystercatcher, snowy plover, Wilson's plover, red knot, piping plover, bald eagle, mangrove cuckoo, black-whiskered vireo, gray kingbird, Florida prairie warbler, West Indian manatee, ornate diamondback terrapin, loggerhead sea turtle, green sea turtle, Kemp's ridley sea turtle, hawksbill sea turtle, gopher tortoise, American alligator, American crocodile, eastern indigo snake, Gulf sturgeon, and smalltooth sawfish. The refuges' rookeries and shorebird nesting islands and exotic, invasive, and nuisance species are primary management concerns. The rookery islands are experiencing ongoing disturbance by recreational users violating the closed areas and impacts from uses occurring adjacent to the refuges. Hurricane and storm events also impact the refuges.

Although the refuges are closed to public access and use, adjacent recreational activities do affect them, including increasing waterway traffic; increasing waterway access; increasing boat sizes; the proliferation of personal watercraft; disturbance to nesting and roosting birds; erosion of island shorelines; and discarded and abandoned monofilament line, cast nets, and crab traps from fishing activities, resulting in entanglement of various wildlife.

Further, Caloosahatchee NWR has Interstate 75 (I-75) running directly over the refuge, with an average daily traffic of 62,500 vehicles traversing over the refuge in 2007 (Florida Department of Transportation 2008). That represents nearly 23 million vehicles in 2007. Proposals exist to widen I-75 from the existing four lanes. The growing traffic and the proposed widening project, including the construction activities and the physical location of the support structures for the bridge on the refuge, have the potential for additional negative impacts to the refuge, including the abandonment of rookeries on the refuge.

Climate change factors also impact these island refuges, their resources, and future management, while also exacerbating the other wildlife and habitat management issues.

RESOURCE PROTECTION

Also impacted by the increasing human population and the associated impacts, key resource protection issues for the refuges include the need to ensure long-term protection of cultural resources and important habitats.

The presence and extent of cultural resources are basically unknown for these island refuges. A Bay of Pigs training site is known to occur in the area, on or near Pine Island NWR. However, information about this site is unknown and undocumented. Pine Island and Matlacha Pass NWRs may include historic homesites. Pine Island, Matlacha Pass, and Island Bay NWRs are known to have Indian mounds.

Further, boundary issues exist for the refuges. Due to erosion, accretion, dredging, and channelization activities, discrepancies exist regarding the number and location of those islands included under Caloosahatchee NWR. Island Bay NWR has some boundary posts, but lacks a complete posted boundary. Further shifting shorelines due to the fluid nature of the mean high tide line affect the shoreline boundaries and signage for all four satellite refuges.

With no regular Service law enforcement presence at these island refuges, resource protection is minimal. Although closed to public use and access, violations of closed areas are known to occur. Law enforcement response for these island refuges comes from Sanibel Island, over an hour away by boat, or from the Service's Zone Officer who could be located anywhere within the zone at any particular time, making for variable and long response times. The Service regularly relies on the law enforcement partners for these island refuges, specifically FWC, which enforces closed areas around rookeries and nearby speed zones and manatee zones.

VISITOR SERVICES

Although these island refuges are closed to public use and access, the surrounding waterways experience high use and traffic. In 2006, more than 71,000 recreational watercraft were registered in the two home counties of these four island refuges, Charlotte and Lee counties (Florida Fish and Wildlife Conservation Commission 2007). Public use activities occur in the waters and lands adjacent to the refuges and include fishing, canoeing, kayaking, motor boating, parasailing, windsurfing, ski tubing, using personal watercraft, and participating in wildlife observation and photography. These adjacent uses have associated wildlife and habitat impacts, as previously described. Further, the refuges face the potential for increasing demands to use them [e.g., although Caloosahatchee NWR only includes 40 acres (16.19 ha) of land, the Service has denied previous requests for bathrooms and resting areas along the 90-mile long Great Calusa Blueway Paddle Trail]. Thus, the priority visitor services management issues for the refuges are directly linked to the increasing and changing human population, development of the landscape, increasing recreational uses and demand for recreational and educational activities, and the associated wildlife and habitat impacts of all of these.

REFUGE ADMINISTRATION

Several refuge administration concerns arise when looking at the current and future management needs to serve the purposes, vision, and goals of the refuges. And given the location and nature of these island refuges, addressing the impacts will require coordination with the governmental partners, area residents, and users of adjacent areas. Key future management concerns relate to the insufficient staff and resources to address the needs of the four refuges, which were identified in 2008 by a Service minimum staffing exercise, including biological monitoring; law enforcement; and exotic, invasive, and nuisance species control. The Refuge Complex's identified minimum staffing priorities for the four refuges are listed in Table 16.

Table 16. Minimum staffing priorities identified in 2008 by the J.N. "Ding" Darling NWR Complex for Pine Island, Matlacha Pass, Island Bay, and Caloosahatchee NWRs.

Ranking	Refuge	Position	Full-Time Equivalent
2	Matlacha Pass	Biological Science Technician	1.0
4	Matlacha Pass	Law Enforcement Officer	1.0
5	Pine Island	Administrative Assistant	1.0
6	Pine Island	Park Ranger (environmental education and outreach)	0.5
7	Matlacha Pass	Maintenance Worker	1.0
8	Caloosahatchee	Hydrologist/Marine Scientist	1.0
9	Pine Island	Law Enforcement Officer	1.0
10	Pine Island	Biological Science Technician	1.0
11	Island Bay	Information Technology Specialist [Geographic Information System (GIS)]	0.5
11	Matlacha Pass	Information Technology Specialist (GIS)	0.5
12	Caloosahatchee	Law Enforcement Officer	1.0
13	Island Bay	Biological Science Technician	1.0
15	Caloosahatchee	Biological Science Technician	1.0
16	Island Bay	Law Enforcement Officer	1.0

The lack of Service visibility and presence at these island refuges and the poor Service image in the communities surrounding the refuges further impact the Service's ability to accomplish stated goals and objectives.

WILDERNESS REVIEW

Refuge planning policy requires a Wilderness Review as part of the comprehensive conservation planning process. A Wilderness Review for the Refuge Complex was updated in 2008. In summary, no areas or additional areas of the refuges were found to be suitable for designation as Wilderness at this time. The results of the Wilderness Review are provided in Appendix H.

PUBLIC REVIEW AND COMMENT

An early article about the comprehensive planning process appeared in the *Island Sun* newspaper, Sanibel, Florida, on March 28, 2007: "Refuges Begin Comprehensive Planning." In March and April, 2008, the Refuge Complex posted information regarding the comprehensive planning process inside the entrance to the Education Center at J.N. "Ding" Darling NWR in Sanibel. This information included an informational poster, mailing list request forms, comment forms, and a collection box for forms. On March 26, 2008, the Refuge Complex's web pages were updated to include background information on the refuges and their comprehensive conservation planning process, information about the upcoming public meetings, and updates:

- http://www.fws.gov/dingdarling;
- http://www.fws.gov/dingdarling/CCP/CCP.htm;
- http://www.fws.gov/dingdarling/CCP/PublicMeetings.htm; and
- http://www.fws.gov/dingdarling/CCP/Updates.htm.

On March 26, 2008 a "Ding on the Wing" email was sent to about 500 members of the "Ding" Darling Wildlife Society to notify them of the upcoming planning process. The spring 2008 edition of "Ding" Darling Wildlife Society's newsletter, *Society Pages*, Sanibel, Florida, included information about the planning process in "News from the Refuge." A Notice of Intent to prepare a Comprehensive Conservation Plan (CCP) for the four refuges was published in the *Federal Register* (volume 73, number 64) on April 2, 2008. Prior to the public meetings and in early April, a news article appeared in the *Pine Island-Eagle News*, Bokellia, Florida, "Input sought for refuge comprehensive plan" and a news article appeared in the *Island Reporter*, Sanibel, Florida, "Refuges to begin CCP process; public scoping to decide future." On April 7, 2008, a governmental scoping meeting was held at the Refuge Complex Headquarters in Sanibel. This was followed by three public scoping meetings: April 8, 2008 in Sanibel; April 9, 2008 in Fort Myers; and April 10, 2008 in Pine Island. Appendix D, Public Involvement, provides additional information about the public scoping process.

In early 2010 and prior to release of the four refuges' Draft Comprehensive Conservation Plan and Environmental Assessment (Draft CCP/EA) for public review and comment, postcards were mailed to individuals and entities on the CCP mailing list to announce the upcoming release of the document for public review and comment and to allow interested parties to request a compact disk (CD) and/or paper copies of the document for review. On March 19, 2010, the Refuge Complex's web pages were updated to announce the upcoming release of the document and to allow interested parties to request a CD and/or paper copies (http://www.fws.gov/dingdarling/CCP/CCP.html). This was followed by a "Ding on the Wing" email on April 2, 2010 to over 1,000 "Ding" Darling Wildlife Society members to announce the upcoming release of the Draft CCP/EA and to allow interested parties to request a CD and/or paper copies.

On May 19, 2010, the Draft CCP/EA was posted on the Service's Southeast Regional Office website http://www.fws.gov/southeast/planning/CCP/JNdingdarlingComplexDraftSinglePageDocument.html. On May 21, 2010, a notice was published in the *Federal Register* (volume 75, number 98) to announce the availability of the four refuges' Draft CCP/EA for public review and comment. Copies were provided to those who requested them. Copies were also provided to the State of Florida's Clearinghouse for review, as well as to other interested governmental agencies. The Draft CCP/EA was also made available to the public for review on the Internet and through the J.N. "Ding" Darling NWR Education Center.

Public comments were accepted from May 21, 2010 through June 22, 2010. The State Clearinghouse's comment period ran from May 21, 2010 through July 23, 2010. On May 24, 2010, the Refuge Complex's web pages were updated to provide information, post the public review and comment period, provide information on how copies of the Draft CCP/EA could be accessed or requested, and provide information on how to submit comments:

- http://www.fws.gov/dingdarling;
- http://www.fws.gov/dingdarling/CCP/CCP.html;
- http://www.fws.gov/dingdarling/CCP/UpdatesCCP.html; and
- http://www.fws.gov/dingdarling/NewsReleases.html.

At the end of the public review and comment period for the Draft CCP/EA, a total of 7 responses submitting comments were received. One was from a private citizen; one was from a nongovernmental organization; and five were from other governmental agencies. Appendix D, Public Involvement, summarizes the comments that were received on the Draft CCP/EA and the Service's responses to them.

IV. Management Direction

INTRODUCTION

The Service manages fish and wildlife habitats considering the needs of all resources in decision-making. But first and foremost, fish and wildlife conservation assumes priority in refuge management. The National Wildlife Refuge System Improvement Act requires the Service to maintain the ecological health, diversity, and integrity of refuges. Public uses are allowed if they are appropriate and compatible with wildlife and habitat conservation. The Service has identified six priority wildlife-dependent public uses. These uses are hunting, fishing, wildlife observation, wildlife photography, and environmental education and interpretation.

Described below is the Comprehensive Conservation Plan (CCP) for managing the refuges over the next 15 years. This management direction contains the goals, objectives, and strategies that will be used to achieve the refuges' vision and purposes.

Four alternatives for managing the refuges were considered: Alternative A, Current Management, (No Action); Alternative B, Native Wildlife and Habitat Diversity; Alternative C, Migratory Birds; and Alternative D, Rare, Threatened, and Endangered Species. Each of these alternatives was described in the Alternatives section of the Environmental Assessment (Section B of the Draft CCP/EA). The Service chose Alternative C, Migratory Birds, as the preferred management direction.

Implementing the management action would result in increased protection for breeding, nesting, resting, roosting, foraging, and migrating birds on the four refuges. Increased information on a variety of species, suites of species, and habitats would enhance decision-making for the refuges. Further benefits would be realized from increased control of exotic, invasive, and nuisance species. The refuges would coordinate with the partners to address concerns related to the impacts from water quality, quantity, and timing of flows and from climate change and sea level rise. Resource protection would be enhanced, including through increased information about cultural resources on the refuges; resolved boundary issues; additional special designations; improved management of the Island Bay Wilderness Area; improved coordination with the partners to increase awareness and understanding of area residents and area visitors of these closed refuges; and minimized impacts from adjacent uses. To achieve this, the refuges would work with governmental and nongovernmental partners, area communities, the "Ding" Darling Wildlife Society, and local businesses and the refuges would pursue the addition of refuge-specific staff to address management concerns.

VISION

Existing in an increasingly developed landscape, the refuges of Pine Island, Matlacha Pass, Island Bay, and Caloosahatchee will continue to provide sanctuary to a variety of migratory birds, nesting birds, and other wildlife. Visitors to the area will always be treated to vistas of undeveloped, protected coastal islands, berms, and waterways; tidal swamps; and sand flats, teeming with fish, birds, manatees, and dolphins. Despite high waterway recreational activities adjacent to these island, mangrove, and beach habitats, human impacts to these important resources will be minimized. Fulfilling their establishing purposes as preserves and breeding grounds for native birds, these island refuges will serve as shining examples of partnerships and intergovernmental coordination to manage the important resources of the larger landscape.

GOALS, OBJECTIVES, AND STRATEGIES

The goals, objectives, and strategies presented are the Service's responses to the issues, concerns, and needs expressed by the planning team, the Refuge Complex staff, governmental and nongovernmental partners, and the public and are presented in hierarchical format. Chapter V, Plan Implementation, identifies the projects associated with the various objectives and strategies.

The outlined goals, objectives, and strategies reflect the Service's commitment to achieve the mandates of the National Wildlife Refuge System Improvement Act of 1997, the mission of the National Wildlife Refuge System, and the purposes and vision of Pine Island, Matlacha Pass, Island Bay, and Caloosahatchee NWRs. The Service intends to accomplish these goals, objectives, and strategies within the next 15 years.

WILDLIFE AND HABITAT MANAGEMENT

Wildlife and habitat management activities would be expanded during the 15-year life of the CCP, including addressing rare, threatened, and endangered species; wildlife and habitat diversity; exotic, invasive, and nuisance species; water quality, quantity, and timing; and climate change. During the 15-year life of the CCP, numerous wildlife and habitat surveys would continue or be expanded and others would be added, while the refuges would work with the partners to increase the scientific rigor of these data collection and analysis efforts.

Discussion: Thirteen federally listed species and 25 state-listed species occur on and around Pine Island, Matlacha Pass, Island Bay, and Caloosahatchee NWRs. Further, the State of Florida identified 974 species of mammals, birds, amphibians, reptiles, fish, and invertebrates as those of greatest conservation need in the state (Florida Fish and Wildlife Conservation Commission 2005). The rare, threatened, and endangered species of management concern to the refuges include the wood stork, roseate spoonbill, roseate tern, black skimmer, American oystercatcher, snowy plover, Wilson's plover, red knot, piping plover, bald eagle, mangrove cuckoo, black-whiskered vireo, gray kingbird, Florida prairie warbler, West Indian manatee, ornate diamondback terrapin, loggerhead sea turtle, green sea turtle, Kemp's ridley sea turtle, hawksbill sea turtle, gopher tortoise, American alligator, American crocodile, eastern indigo snake, Gulf sturgeon, and smalltooth sawfish. Wildlife surveys conducted by the Refuge Complex staff have shown a decline in several wildlife populations in recent years. An up-to-date, geographically referenced, wildlife database inventory (including all four refuges' flora and fauna) needs to be developed and implemented to monitor long-term status and trends and to proactively protect the refuges' species and habitats, with particular attention to:

- migratory bird populations;
- habitat and land and water use, improvements, management practices, and changes;
- rare, threatened, and endangered species;
- native fish populations (as a food source for wildlife and to support recreational fishing); and
- exotic, invasive, and nuisance species.

Wildlife and Habitat Management Goal 1: Rare, Threatened, and Endangered Species

Minimize the threats to and promote the recovery of the rare, threatened, and endangered species occurring within Pine Island, Matlacha Pass, Island Bay, and Caloosahatchee NWRs.

Wildlife and Habitat Management Objectives 1.a. Wood Stork

Wildlife and Habitat Management Objective 1.a(1): Throughout the life of the CCP, continue conducting rookery surveys to determine the presence/absence of wood storks and within five years of CCP approval, work with the partners and foster research to monitor wood storks using Pine Island, Matlacha Pass, Island Bay, and Caloosahatchee NWRs and to identify wood stork colony origin and foraging range and locations for those wood storks using the refuges.

Discussion: The wood stork is listed by both the Service and the State of Florida (Florida Fish and Wildlife Conservation Commission 2009a) as an endangered species. The United States breeding population of wood storks declined from an estimated 20,000 nesting pairs in the 1930s to a low of around 5,000 nesting pairs in the late 1970s (Ogden et al. 1987). The lowest recorded annual total was 2,500 pairs in 1978, a result of poor nesting conditions in conjunction with the low population. From the 1960s to the mid-1980s, the wood stork nesting population declined in southern Florida and increased in northern Florida, Georgia, and South Carolina (Ogden et al. 1987). Prior to 1970, a majority (70 percent) of the population nested south of Lake Okeechobee and declined from 8,500 pairs in 1961 to fewer than 500 pairs in the late 1980s and early 1990s. More recently, synoptic surveys were completed in 1999 and 2001 to 2006. These surveys documented a population ranging between 5,560 and 11,279 pairs. The 2006 survey documented 11,279 pairs. This was the first time the nesting population was greater than 10,000 pairs since the early 1960s. Additionally, a majority of the population now breeds north of Lake Okeechobee (taken from wood stork recovery plan five-year review, U.S. Fish and Wildlife Service 2007a).

Wood storks are known to use all four refuges for roosting and foraging, while nesting is known to occur on Caloosahatchee NWR. The refuges would continue coordinating with the partners to survey rookeries to help support wood stork recovery. And the refuges would coordinate with the Service's lead on wood storks (at the Ecological Services Jacksonville Field Office) to help develop an understanding of the colony origin and the foraging range and locations for the wood storks using the refuges. Adaptive management activities could include assessing valuable foraging wetlands used by the wood storks for protection, assessing valuable roosting and nesting sites used by the wood storks for protection, and forming or enhancing collaboration with other agencies managing areas used by the wood storks. See Wildlife and Habitat Management Objective 2.a(1) for rookery surveys and Wildlife and Habitat Management Objective 2.a(2) and Resource Protection Objective 2.b(1) for implementation of closed area buffers to protect wood storks and other wading and water birds. Rodgers and Schwikert (2002) recommended a minimum buffer size for wood storks of 118 meters to minimize impacts from outboard-powered boats and personal watercraft. And the refuges would work with the partners to address water quality, quantity, and timing concerns to benefit a variety of resources, including wood storks.

Wildlife and Habitat Management Objective 1.a(2): Within five years of CCP approval, confirm ownership of the wood stork nesting island at Caloosahatchee NWR.

Discussion: Buzzard Roost of Caloosahatchee NWR includes a wood stork rookery. However, discrepancies exist in relation to the boundary of Caloosahatchee NWR. The Refuge Complex would work with the Service's Southeast Region Realty office, Bureau of Land Management, the State of Florida, and the Lee County Property Appraiser's office to confirm and recognize the proper boundary of Caloosahatchee NWR and Service ownership of the four remaining islands originally set aside by the executive order that established the refuge, including the known wood stork nesting island at the refuge.

Wildlife and Habitat Management Objective 1.b. Roseate Spoonbill

Wildlife and Habitat Management Objective 1.b(1): Throughout the life of the CCP, continue conducting rookery surveys to determine the presence/absence of roseate spoonbills and work with the partners and foster research to monitor roseate spoonbills using Pine Island, Matlacha Pass, Island Bay, and Caloosahatchee NWRs and to identify spoonbill colony origin and foraging range and locations for those spoonbills using the refuges.

Discussion: The roseate spoonbill is listed as a species of special concern by the State of Florida due to its vulnerability to habitat modification, environmental alteration, human disturbance, or human exploitation which, in the foreseeable future, may result in its becoming a state-listed threatened species unless appropriate protective or management techniques are initiated or maintained and due to the fact that it has not sufficiently recovered from past population depletion (Florida Fish and Wildlife Conservation Commission 2009a). Prior to the 1850s, thousands of spoonbills likely existed along the Gulf coast in Texas, Louisiana, and Florida. By 1920, plume hunting and colony disturbance largely depleted the spoonbill population in the United States. A 1999 survey of nesting populations estimated 408 pairs in Florida Bay in the Florida Keys, at Merritt Island, in Tampa Bay, and at two freshwater sites in the Everglades. The Florida Bay population represents the majority of the spoonbills that nest in the state. During the summer, roseate spoonbills are also found in Louisiana, Texas, Mexico, and Central and South America. Though plume hunting has ceased, spoonbills are still vulnerable today to habitat loss and alteration. In Florida Bay, freshwater inflows from the Everglades adversely affect the salinities of coastal wetlands and the populations of fish and other prey of spoonbills (taken from FWC roseate spoonbill overview, Florida Fish and Wildlife Conservation Commission 2009b).

To help protect roseate spoonbills using the refuges, the Refuge Complex would continue coordinating with partners to survey rookeries. Adaptive management activities could include assessing valuable foraging wetlands used by the spoonbills for protection, assessing valuable roosting and nesting sites used by the spoonbills for protection, and forming or enhancing collaboration with other agencies managing areas used by the spoonbills. As needed, the refuges would coordinate with the State to provide buffers around roosting sites. Rodgers and Schwikert (2002) recommended a minimum buffer size for roseate spoonbills of 98 meters to minimize impacts from outboard-powered boats and personal watercraft. And the refuges would work with the partners to address water quality, quantity, and timing of flow concerns.

Wildlife and Habitat Management Objectives 1.c. Black Skimmer

Wildlife and Habitat Management Objective 1.c(1): Throughout the life of the CCP, work with the U.S. Army Corps of Engineers (USACE) and other partners to continually create or enhance suitable nesting habitat for black skimmers during area dredge and spoil activities.

Wildlife and Habitat Management Objective 1.c(2): Within five years of CCP approval, work with the partners to minimize human disturbances and impacts to Skimmer Island on Matlacha Pass NWR or to any other site found to be used by black skimmers.

Wildlife and Habitat Management Objective 1.c(3): Within 10 years of CCP approval, monitor the Terrapin Creek tract of Matlacha Pass NWR for use by black skimmers.

Discussion: The black skimmer is listed as a species of special concern by the State of Florida due to its vulnerability to habitat modification, environmental alteration, human disturbance, or human exploitation which, in the foreseeable future, may result in its becoming a state-listed threatened species unless appropriate protective or management techniques are initiated or maintained (Florida Fish and Wildlife Conservation Commission 2009a). Black skimmers historically nested on Skimmer Island in Matlacha Pass NWR, but no nesting of skimmers is known to currently occur on any of the four refuges. Continue conducting surveys of rookeries to determine use and nesting by black skimmers. Coordinate with the USACE to benefit black skimmers, American oystercatchers, and roseate terns. Monitor beach profile changes over time in relation to climate change and sea level rise. Continue conducting prescribed burns and mechanical clearing on Skimmer Island to maintain potential black skimmer nesting habitat. As needed, coordinate with the state to provide buffers around black skimmer nesting sites. The refuges would adapt management as necessary to protect black skimmer nesting and to minimize human disturbances to black skimmers.

Wildlife and Habitat Management Objectives 1.d. American Oystercatcher and Roseate Tern

Wildlife and Habitat Management Objective 1.d(1): Throughout the life of the CCP, work with USACE and other partners to create or enhance suitable nesting and foraging habitats for American oystercatchers and roseate terns during area dredge and spoil activities.

Wildlife and Habitat Management Objective 1.d(2): Within five years of CCP approval, evaluate the development of a formal survey to monitor population status and trends for American oystercatchers using Pine Island, Matlacha Pass, Island Bay, and Caloosahatchee NWRs.

Wildlife and Habitat Management Objective 1.d(3): Within five years of CCP approval, work with the partners to document presence/absence of the roseate tern on Pine Island, Matlacha Pass, Island Bay, and Caloosahatchee NWRs.

Discussion: The American oystercatcher is listed as a species of special concern by the State of Florida due to its vulnerability to habitat modification, environmental alteration, human disturbance, or human exploitation which, in the foreseeable future, may result in its becoming a state-listed threatened species unless appropriate protective or management techniques are initiated or maintained and due to the fact that it may already meet certain criteria for designation as a state-listed threatened species, but for which conclusive data are limited or lacking (Florida Fish and Wildlife Conservation Commission 2009a). The roseate tern is listed by both the Service and the State of Florida (Florida Fish and Wildlife Conservation Commission 2009a) as a threatened species. Roseate terns have been observed in the vicinity of all four refuges.

To help protect American oystercatchers and roseate terns using the refuges, the Refuge Complex would conduct a variety of management actions. The refuges would continue coordinating with the partners to survey rookeries. And they would coordinate with USACE to benefit black skimmers, American oystercatchers, and roseate terns. Further, they would also monitor beach profile changes over time in relation to climate change and sea level rise. As needed, the refuges would coordinate with the State to provide buffers around nesting sites. Rodgers and Schwikert (2002) recommended a minimum buffer size for American oystercatchers of 103 meters to minimize impacts from outboard-powered boats and personal watercraft. The refuges would adapt management as necessary.

Wildlife and Habitat Management Objectives 1.e. Snowy Plover, Wilson's Plover, and Red Knot

Wildlife and Habitat Management Objective 1.e(1): During the life of the CCP, continue working with the partners to survey and monitor for presence/absence of snowy plover and within one year of CCP approval include Wilson's plover and red knot in these survey and monitoring activities at Pine Island, Matlacha Pass, Island Bay, and Caloosahatchee NWRs.

Wildlife and Habitat Management Objective 1.e(2): Within five years of CCP approval, work with the partners to minimize disturbances and impacts to snowy plovers, Wilson's plovers, and red knots at Pine Island, Matlacha Pass, Island Bay, and Caloosahatchee NWRs.

Discussion: Snowy plovers, Wilson's plovers, and red knots are known to use all four refuges. Snowy plovers and other shorebirds nest along the beaches of Terrapin Creek at Matlacha Pass NWR. Snowy plovers are listed by the State of Florida as threatened (Florida Fish and Wildlife Conservation Commission 2009a). The Service considers snowy and Wilson's plovers as species of management concern due to their dependence on vulnerable or restricted habitats. To help protect these species, the refuges would continue to work with the partners to conduct existing snowy plover surveys. Wilson's plovers and red knots would be included in these survey activities. Further, the refuges would work with the partners to minimize disturbances to nesting beaches (e.g., through activities such as implementation of buffers, increased signage, increased awareness of users, and increased patrol and enforcement). Support for the existing snowy plover banding project would continue. And the refuges would monitor beach profile changes over time in relation to climate change and sea level rise. As needed, the refuges would coordinate with the state to provide buffers around nesting sites.

Wildlife and Habitat Management Objectives 1.f. Piping Plover

Wildlife and Habitat Management Objective 1.f(1): During the life of the CCP, continue protecting the designated piping plover wintering critical habitat as a closed area at Terrapin Creek in Matlacha Pass NWR to support recovery of the species.

Wildlife and Habitat Management Objective 1.f(2): Within five years of CCP approval, develop a winter surveying program to document the presence/absence and abundance of piping plovers throughout Pine Island, Matlacha Pass, Island Bay, and Caloosahatchee NWRs.

Discussion: In Florida, the piping plover is listed by both the Service and the State of Florida as a threatened species (Florida Fish and Wildlife Conservation Commission 2009a). Approximately 4,000 feet (1,200 meters) of critical habitat within Matlacha Pass NWR was designated in 2001 by the Service for wintering piping plovers along the shoreline of the Terrapin Creek Tract, adjacent to Bunche Beach. The refuges would increase management activities to better serve piping plovers using them. The refuges would increase survey efforts to document presence, abundance, and locations used during the winter for all four refuges. All refuges would adapt management as necessary to minimize disturbances and support recovery of this species. The Refuge Complex would support recovery goals, including by conducting winter surveys, minimizing impacts and disturbances, and increasing public awareness. Minimize disturbances and impacts to piping plovers from humans and dogs on the beach. Minimize disturbances to beach habitats. And the refuges would monitor beach profile changes over time in relation to climate change and sea level rise. To provide better protection and to help minimize disturbance, the refuges would work with the partners to establish seasonal closed areas buffers around known piping plover roost areas. And the Refuge Complex would post boundaries for the piping plover critical habitat designated at Terrapin Creek at Matlacha Pass NWR.

Wildlife and Habitat Management Objective 1.g. Bald Eagle

Wildlife and Habitat Management Objective 1.g(1): During the life of the CCP, work with the partners to protect active and inactive bald eagle nest trees. Where nest sites are detected, minimize disturbance during the nesting season.

Discussion: Although the bald eagle was delisted in 2007, it is still protected under various acts and treaties, including the Bald and Golden Eagle Protection Act, the Lacey Act, and the Migratory Bird Treaty Act. The dramatic recovery of the bald eagle over the past 35 years has been one of the greatest conservation success stories of our nation. The bald eagle population increased from its 1963 low of 487 breeding pairs in the lower 48 states to 9,789 breeding pairs in 2007. The State of Florida conducts annual aerial surveys to identify bald eagle nest sites and Florida had 1,133 breeding pairs in 2007. When and where bald eagle nest sites are discovered on any of the refuges, the Refuge Complex would work with the partners to protect these sites by (1) keeping a distance between the activity and the nest (distance buffers); (2) maintaining preferably forested (or natural) areas between the activity and around nest trees (landscape buffers); and (3) avoiding certain activities during the breeding season. The buffer areas would serve to minimize visual and auditory impacts associated with human activities near nest sites. Ideally, the buffers would be large enough to protect existing nest trees and provide for alternative or replacement nest trees.

Wildlife and Habitat Management Objective 1.h. Mangrove Forest Birds

Wildlife and Habitat Management Objective 1.h(1): Within 10 years of CCP approval, begin surveys to assess population status and trends for mangrove forest birds and research the effectiveness of survey protocols with nesting cycles and timing to better determine the status of these birds on Pine Island, Matlacha Pass, Island Bay, and Caloosahatchee NWRs.

Discussion: Important mangrove forest birds using the refuges include the mangrove cuckoo, black-whiskered vireo, gray kingbird, and Florida prairie warbler. The black-whiskered vireo and the Florida prairie warbler are considered by the Service to be species of management concern due to the small population or limited distribution of the black-whiskered vireo and due to the documented or apparent population decline of the Florida prairie warbler. To help protect these mangrove forest birds using the refuges, the Refuge Complex would conduct a variety of management actions. The refuges would continue controlling exotic plants to improve the habitats for these birds. Further, the refuges would initiate call-back surveys as part of a Breeding Bird Survey, where feasible (e.g., at Terrapin Creek in Matlacha Pass NWR).

Wildlife and Habitat Management Objectives 1.i. West Indian Manatee

Discussion: The West Indian manatee is listed by the Service and the State of Florida as an endangered species (Florida Fish and Wildlife Conservation Commission 2009a). The greatest threats to manatee survival are collisions with boats and loss of warm water habitat. Other threats to manatees include declines in water and habitat quality; habitat loss; loss of natural springs and spring flows due to human development and demand for water; flood gates and canal locks; monofilament fishing line, abandoned cast nets and crab traps, and other discarded trash; red tide blooms; and harassment. A 2009 survey counted at least 3,800 manatees in Florida. Although population numbers are currently higher than previous surveys, over the long term the trend is anticipated to slowly decline. The southwest subpopulation, which includes all four refuges, represents about 41 percent of the state's manatee population. The primary factors causing mortality in the southwest subpopulation are collision with watercraft, which represent 32 percent of deaths in southwest Florida and red tide blooms, which represent 24-28 percent of deaths in southwest Florida. Key habitat-related concerns for the southwest subpopulation include manatee dependence on industrial warm-water discharges; storm-related impacts on habitat and adult survival; periodic red tide events; water quality and submerged aquatic vegetation; human disturbance; increasing boat traffic; and water control structure-related deaths. This subpopulation may be declining while other subpopulations seem to be increasing. To help provide protection for and limit threats to this species, numerous federal manatee protection areas are located near the refuges. (Taken from the West Indian manatee recovery plan five-year review, U.S. Fish and Wildlife Service 2007b.)

Wildlife and Habitat Management Objective 1.i(1): During the life of the CCP, continue working with the partners to conduct regular law enforcement patrols of speed zones to minimize threats and impacts to West Indian manatees in and around Pine Island, Matlacha Pass, Island Bay, and Caloosahatchee NWRs.

Discussion: In 2008, three manatee deaths in Charlotte County were attributed to watercraft, while 14 manatee deaths in Lee County were attributed to watercraft (Florida Fish and Wildlife Conservation Commission 2009c). To help minimize watercraft collisions with manatees, the refuges would continue to work with the partners to conduct regular law enforcement patrols of speed zones and no-motor zones, including the Service's Office of Law Enforcement, FWC, Lee County Sheriff's Office, and the Sanibel Police Department. The refuges would continue to participate in the Florida Marine Mammal Stranding Network – Southwest and with the Mote Marine Laboratory to facilitate quick response, care, and rehabilitation of injured manatees. Coordinate with the National Marine Fisheries Service (NMFS) and FWC on necropsies, potentially using the Gavin Site, if necessary. Critical habitat for manatees was designated by the Service in 1976 to include "all U.S. territorial waters adjoining the coast and islands of Lee County," which includes the waters around the Pine Island NWR and Matlacha Pass NWR islands (note: the waters around the Pine Island NWR islands are mostly unregulated, but the waters around the Matlacha Pass NWR islands are Slow Speed All Year, 25 mph in the channel); the "Charlotte Harbor north of the Charlotte – Lee County line," which includes the waters around the Island Bay NWR islands (note: these waters are a combination of unregulated, 25 mph, Idle Speed Zones); and the "Caloosahatchee River downstream from the Florida State Highway 31 bridge, Lee County," which includes the waters around the Caloosahatchee NWR islands (note: these waters are all regulated as Idle Speed Outside Channel All Year, Intracoastal Waterway Idle Speed November 15 - March 31, Intracoastal Waterway 25 mph April 1 - November 14).

Wildlife and Habitat Management Objective 1.i(2): Throughout the life of the CCP, continue working with the partners to support recovery of the West Indian manatee, including providing and supporting environmental education, interpretation, and outreach.

Discussion: To help develop public awareness, understanding, and appreciation for manatees and related management activities, the refuges would continue working with Lee County's Manatee Park by providing interpretive assistance on manatees and information on the refuges. Several objectives would help support this objective.

Wildlife and Habitat Management Objective 1.j. Ornate Diamondback Terrapin

Wildlife and Habitat Management Objective 1.j(1): Within five years of CCP approval, coordinate with the partners to initiate surveys to develop baseline data for the ornate diamondback terrapin and determine population status and trends, including nesting success and bycatch mortality, within Pine Island, Matlacha Pass (especially the Terrapin Creek Tract), Island Bay, and Caloosahatchee NWRs.

Discussion: The ornate diamondback terrapin has been considered a status review species by the Service for over a decade. In part, its conservation status has remained unchanged because most states have little information concerning current population trends. Issues are further complicated by the fact that many states cover terrapin regulations under fisheries units, while state wildlife agencies typically oversee conservation status listings. According to the State of Florida, the status of the ornate diamondback terrapin is unknown and the population is considered declining (Florida Fish and Wildlife Conservation Commission 2005). The International Union for the Conservation of Nature lists the diamondback terrapin as a near threatened species (International Union for the Conservation of Nature 2009). The Florida Natural Areas Inventory (FNAI) reports that for diamondback terrapins, "statewide population surveys and monitoring are sorely needed." Ornate diamondback terrapins are known to occur on Matlacha Pass NWR at Terrapin Creek. They are susceptible to illegal harvest, bycatch in abandoned crab traps (particularly smaller males and juvenile females), raccoon predation, and roadkill.

Wildlife and Habitat Management Objective 1.k. Sea Turtles

Wildlife and Habitat Management Objective 1.k(1): Throughout the life of the CCP, work with the partners to determine the relative abundance of in-water populations of juvenile sea turtles around the refuges and evaluate potential trends.

Discussion: In-water populations of sea turtles have been monitored in the greater Charlotte Harbor area since 2003 by the Mote Marine Laboratory. Mote Marine and its partners have been conducting set netting and visual surveys of the Charlotte Harbor area, including Island Bay, Pine Island, and Matlacha Pass NWRs, to evaluate species composition, developmental migrations, habitat use, and feeding ecology. So far, the survey results have yielded sightings and captures of loggerheads, Kemp's ridleys, and greens. In order of abundance, loggerheads are typically found near tidal passes; ridleys congregate close to creek or bay mouths; and greens are often observed in seagrass pastures in six to eight feet of water. Annual catch per unit effort rates for visual transect sightings range from 0.011 to 0.021 turtles/hour and sighting densities drop during the winter months (Eaton et al. 2008). Another goal of this project is to evaluate post-hurricane effects on turtle foraging ecology in Charlotte Harbor. Surveys conducted after Hurricane Charley in 2004 reported hypoxic conditions and a massive horseshoe crab die-off in that same area. Disturbances to seagrass beds and changes in crustacean populations after hurricanes are also being evaluated as having possible effects on sea turtle foraging ecology. This information would enable the refuges to adapt management as necessary to protect these turtles.

Wildlife and Habitat Management Objectives 1.l. Gopher Tortoise and Eastern Indigo Snake

Wildlife and Habitat Management Objective 1.l(1): Within 10 years of CCP approval, work with the partners to survey gopher tortoise and eastern indigo snake presence/absence on Pine Island, Matlacha Pass, Island Bay, and Caloosahatchee NWRs and estimate population density and habitat carrying capacity, where applicable.

Discussion: Gopher tortoises are under review for listing in Florida by the Service under the Endangered Species Act and are listed by the State of Florida as a threatened species (Florida Fish and Wildlife Conservation Commission 2009a). In 1975, the gopher tortoise was listed by the state as a threatened species. In 1979, due to changes in the state's listing criteria, the species was downlisted to species of special concern. Between 2002 and 2006, the state recognized the need to uplist the gopher tortoise to threatened. In 2008, it was uplisted by the state to threatened. There is recent and historic evidence of gopher tortoise activity on islands in Island Bay, Pine Island, and Caloosahatchee NWRs. And the Terrapin Creek Tract of Matlacha Pass NWR is expected to support gopher tortoises.

The eastern indigo snake is listed by the Service and the State of Florida as a threatened species (Florida Fish and Wildlife Conservation Commission 2009a). There is recent and historic evidence of gopher tortoise activity on islands in Island Bay, Pine Island, and Caloosahatchee NWRs, which are commensal with eastern indigo snakes. The Terrapin Creek Tract of Matlacha Pass NWR is also expected to support gopher tortoises and possibly eastern indigo snakes.

Wildlife and Habitat Management Objective 1.I(2): Throughout the life of the CCP, enhance upland habitat islands where gopher tortoises are known to occur.

Discussion: The refuges would continue to remove invasive exotic vegetation and thin understory where needed to benefit gopher tortoises and eastern indigo snakes, as well as other species.

Wildlife and Habitat Management Goal 2: Wildlife and Habitat Diversity

Conserve, restore, enhance, and manage the upland, transitional, and estuarine habitats of Pine Island, Matlacha Pass, Island Bay, and Caloosahatchee NWRs to maintain and enhance their biological integrity and to support species diversity and abundance of native plants and animals, with an emphasis on migratory birds.

Wildlife and Habitat Management Objectives 2.a. Wading Birds and Waterbirds

Wildlife and Habitat Management Objective 2.a(1): Throughout the life of the CCP, continue coordinating with the partners to survey all rookeries on Pine Island, Matlacha Pass, Island Bay, and Caloosahatchee NWRs.

Wildlife and Habitat Management Objective 2.a(2): Within five years of CCP approval, work with the State of Florida and other partners to establish appropriately sized closed area buffers around key nesting, roosting, and foraging areas within Pine Island NWR (e.g., Lower Bird Island and Hemp Key), Matlacha Pass NWR (e.g., Skimmer Island, Lumpkin Island, and Givney Key), Island Bay NWR, and Caloosahatchee NWR.

Discussion: The refuges were specifically established to protect native birds and they include numerous rookery islands, as well as numerous sites used by a variety of birds for foraging, roosting, and resting. The partners currently conduct rookery surveys from January through October on Matlacha Pass NWR and in Pine Island Sound (Charlotte Harbor Aquatic Preserves). The partners also started conducting annual aerial surveys of the rookeries in 2008, expanding to include all four refuges in 2009. To provide better protection for these sites and to minimize impacts to them, the refuges would work with the partners to minimize human disturbance and impacts to wading and water birds with the State of Florida and other partners to establish appropriately sized closed area buffers. Buffer sizes would depend on the species using the sites, based upon current research (e.g., Rodgers and Schwikert 2002). The refuges would work with the partners and volunteers to determine the areas and islands being utilized and the species present. The Service does not intend to create buffers around all islands and shorelines, but only those providing important functions for wading birds, water birds, shorebirds, and seabirds. Distances for proposed closed area buffers would be from refuge boundaries (which are identified at mean high water along shorelines) out into adjacent waterways. Through outreach activities and through the J.N. "Ding" Darling Education Center, the Refuge Complex would work to increase awareness and understanding of the impacts of disturbances to the birds using the refuges for nesting, resting, feeding, and roosting. Also benefitting wading and water birds, the refuges would work with the partners to address concerns related to water quality, quantity, and timing of flows.

Wildlife and Habitat Management Objective 2.b. Raptors and Birds of Prey

Wildlife and Habitat Management Objective 2.b(1): Within 10 years of CCP approval, coordinate with the partners to identify the nesting, breeding, roosting, and foraging habitat needs of raptors and birds of prey on Pine Island, Matlacha Pass, Island Bay, and Caloosahatchee NWRs to restore and maintain these habitats to support these birds.

Discussion: The refuges have limited information regarding raptors and birds of prey using them. To better provide for these birds, the refuges would expand refuge management activities, including identifying and managing for their habitat needs, surveying for their presence/absence during other surveys, and providing protection for any nests discovered for protection of bald eagle nests. Further, to also benefit raptors and birds of prey, the refuges would work with the partners to address concerns related to water quality, quantity, and timing of flows.

Wildlife and Habitat Management Objectives 2.c. Nearctic-Neotropical Migratory Birds

Wildlife and Habitat Management Objective 2.c(1): Within five years of CCP approval, coordinate with the partners to identify and manage for the habitat needs of the nearctic-neotropical migratory birds using Pine Island, Matlacha Pass, Island Bay, and Caloosahatchee NWRs.

Wildlife and Habitat Management Objective 2.c(2): Within 10 years of CCP approval, during habitat management and restoration activities work with the partners to select for certain shrubs and trees as food sources and potential migration and nesting habitats (e.g., in hardwood hammocks) on Pine Island, Matlacha Pass, Island Bay, and Caloosahatchee NWRs.

Discussion: The refuges lack information regarding the mix of nearctic-neotropical migratory birds using them. To better provide for these birds, the refuges would expand refuge management activities, including identifying and managing for their habitat needs, including selecting for certain shrubs and trees as food sources and potential migration and nesting habitat. Further, to increase information about these birds and to enhance decision-making, the refuges would survey for their presence/absence during other surveys. And the refuges would continue to conduct exotic plant control activities, also benefitting these birds.

Wildlife and Habitat Management Objectives 2.d. Shorebirds and Seabirds

Wildlife and Habitat Management Objective 2.d(1): During the life of the CCP, continue to record shorebird and seabirds nesting and use during rookery surveys of Pine Island, Matlacha Pass, Island Bay, and Caloosahatchee NWRs.

Wildlife and Habitat Management Objective 2.d(2): Within 10 years of CCP approval, work with USACE and other partners to continually create or enhance suitable nesting, resting, and foraging habitat for shorebirds and seabirds during area dredge and spoil activities.

Wildlife and Habitat Management Objective 2.d(3): Within five years of CCP approval, work with the partners to provide, manage, and protect beach nesting habitat, including creating and enforcing closed area buffers around nesting, resting, and foraging areas.

Wildlife and Habitat Management Objective 2.d(4): Within five years of CCP approval, coordinate with the partners to develop appropriately sized closed area buffers to minimize impacts to shorebirds and seabirds using the Terrapin Creek Tract of Matlacha Pass NWR.

Discussion: Although most shorebird and seabird use of the refuges would be noted during other surveys, separate surveys would be conducted to determine presence/absence of black skimmers; American oystercatchers; snowy plovers, Wilson's plovers, and red knots; and piping plovers. Several objectives seek to develop wildlife and habitat benefits from area dredge and spoil activities for black skimmers and for American oystercatchers and roseate terns. To minimize disturbance and impacts, closed area buffers are proposed under several objectives for wading and waterbirds, including wood storks, roseate spoonbills, and shorebirds and seabirds. To provide better protection for shorebirds and seabirds and to minimize impacts to them, the refuges would work with the State of Florida and other partners to establish appropriately sized closed area buffers. Buffer sizes would depend on the species using the sites, based upon current research (e.g., Rodgers and Schwikert 2002). The refuges would work with the partners and volunteers to determine the areas and islands being utilized and the species present. The Service does not intend to create buffers around all islands and shorelines, but only those providing important functions for wading birds, water birds, shorebirds, and seabirds. Potential buffer zones could include recently active islands, such as Skimmer Island, Lower Bird Island, Givney Key, Upper Bird Island, Lumpkin Island, East and West Bird Rookery Keys, Big Smokehouse Key, and Hemp Island. Distances for proposed closed area buffers would be from refuge boundaries (which are identified at mean high water along shorelines) out into adjacent waterways. The Terrapin Creek Tract serves a variety of birds and it includes critical habitat designated for wintering piping plovers.

Wildlife and Habitat Management Objectives 2.e. Refuge Habitats

Wildlife and Habitat Management Objective 2.e(1): Within five years of CCP approval, develop and annually maintain a vegetation GIS database that covers the acquisition boundaries for Pine Island, Matlacha Pass, Island Bay, and Caloosahatchee NWRs.

Discussion: The refuges lack specific enough vegetation data, including classification data with subcategory habitats and the variable mix of habitats by percent cover of dominant species. Although broad scale data do exist, they lack the detail necessary for refuge management, planning, and analysis. The development and maintenance of a vegetation database would enhance decision-making for all four refuges and would serve a variety of goals and objectives, including those benefitting shorebirds and seabirds, raptors and birds of prey, and nearctic-neotropical migratory birds, as well as exotic plant control activities.

Wildlife and Habitat Management Objective 2.e(2): Throughout the life of the CCP, continue to manage the mix of habitats making up Pine Island, Matlacha Pass, Island Bay, and Caloosahatchee NWRs.

Wildlife and Habitat Management Objective 2.e(3): During the life of the CCP, continue maintaining interior grassland and wetlands habitats on three islands: Skimmer, Middle Spoil, and Tern islands in Matlacha Pass NWR; using prescribed fire with a targeted 3- to 5-year burn rotation and employing selective mechanical removal of vegetation where necessary to maintain the quality of these islands for shorebird and seabird use.

Wildlife and Habitat Management Objective 2.e(4): Within five years of CCP approval, evaluate all habitats within the four refuges for potential restoration opportunities with a management focus on serving the needs of migratory birds.

Discussion: The habitats of primary management concern are the nesting, resting, roosting, and foraging islands and shorelines; island interior grasslands and wetlands; mangroves; and hammocks; as well as any seagrass beds and oyster beds located within any designated closed area buffers. Seagrass beds would also benefit from the lack of disturbance afforded by the closed areas. The refuges would expand exotic plant and animal control activities. The Refuge Complex would continue working with SCCF to plant mangroves on various islands and along certain shorelines to restore habitat. The refuges would evaluate all islands and the Terrapin Creek Tract for restoration opportunities, setting a priority for any work at Terrapin Creek. Further, the refuges would prioritize the needs of migratory birds in any restoration plans. During the life of the CCP, the refuges would develop inventories of species using each main habitat type. Habitat management techniques would include prescribed fire, exotic plant control, and selective mechanical removal of vegetation where necessary to maintain the quality of these habitats. The refuges would work with USACE and other partners to create or enhance suitable nesting and foraging habitats for black skimmers, American oystercatchers, roseate terns, and other shorebirds and seabirds, during area dredge and spoil activities. To benefit a variety of habitats and species, the refuges would also work with the partners to address concerns related to water quality, quantity, and timing of flows.

Wildlife and Habitat Management Objective 2.f. Proposed Interstate 75 Widening Project

Wildlife and Habitat Management Objective 2.f(1): During the planning phases for the proposed Interstate 75 widening project, work with partners to identify and address wildlife and habitat impacts associated with the proposed project.

Discussion: Interstate 75 passes directly over Caloosahatchee NWR. Further, the existing bridge stanchion is located on one of the islands of Caloosahatchee NWR. The Refuge Complex would work with the partners to resolve any ownership and jurisdictional issues associated with Interstate 75 and Caloosahatchee NWR. Further, the Refuge Complex would work with the Florida Department of Transportation, the Service's Vero Beach Ecological Service's Field Office, and other partners to ensure that wildlife and habitat values are conserved and protected in relation to this project. Numerous options may be considered, including the addition of lands and waters to Caloosahatchee NWR or other area refuges.

Wildlife and Habitat Management Goal 3: Exotic, Invasive, and Nuisance Species

Eradicate existing and future exotic, invasive, and nuisance species within Pine Island, Matlacha Pass, Island Bay, and Caloosahatchee NWRs to maintain and enhance the biological integrity of their upland, transitional, and estuarine habitats.

Wildlife and Habitat Management Objectives 3.a. Control of Exotic, Invasive, and Nuisance Plants

Wildlife and Habitat Management Objective 3.a(1): During the life of the CCP, continue working with the partners to annually inspect and re-treat as needed the exotic, invasive, and nuisance plants on all four refuges with a focus on priority habitats for migratory birds.

Wildlife and Habitat Management Objective 3.a(2): Within five years of CCP approval, work with the partners to identify and locate new infestations of Florida Exotic Pest Council Category I and Category II exotic, invasive, and nuisance plants on all four refuges, focusing initial attack on eradication.

Discussion: Exotic, invasive, and nuisance species have impacted most habitats of the refuges. Priority species of current management concern include Brazilian pepper, Australian pine, seaside mahoe, air potato, carrotwood, earleaf acacia, lead tree, and natal grass. The refuges would focus management efforts on those high-priority habitats serving migratory birds. Initial exotic plant control treatments were conducted during 2007 to 2009 for Pine Island, Island Bay, and Caloosahatchee NWRs. Both initial and follow-up exotic plant sweeps have been conducted from 2006 to 2008 on six islands of Matlacha Pass (i.e., Fisherman's Key, Givney Key, Merwin Key, Big Island, Skimmer Island, and Tern Island) and at Terrapin Creek by contractors, Service staff, or through Challenge Cost Share grants with Lee County. However, initial exotic plant control efforts have not been started for Matlacha Pass NWR. Exotic plant removal operations on several islands have also been conducted to reduce the impacts from Hurricane Charley in 2004. As new infestations are discovered, initial attack would be focused on eradication.

Wildlife and Habitat Management Objectives 3.b. Control of Exotic, Invasive, and Nuisance Animals

Wildlife and Habitat Management Objective 3.b(1): During the life of the CCP, continue to work with the partners to control and eradicate exotic, invasive, and nuisance animals threatening Pine Island, Matlacha Pass, Island Bay, and Caloosahatchee NWRs.

Wildlife and Habitat Management Objective 3.b(2): Within five years of CCP approval, work with the partners to increase education and awareness to build support for management activities to eradicate invasive exotic species and to minimize negative impacts from nuisance species.

Discussion: Exotic, invasive, and nuisance wildlife species currently impact all four refuges in some way and may be contributing to or causing the partial or total failure of some rookeries. Current priority exotic, invasive, and nuisance species for the four refuges include black rats, green iguanas, feral hogs, and Nile monitor lizards. The refuges have conducted small mammal trapping and have euthanized black rats. The refuges would work with the partners to control and eradicate exotic, invasive, and nuisance wildlife species, adapting management as necessary to respond to new species with an emphasis on eradication. The refuges would work with partners to increase education and awareness of the negative impacts of exotic, invasive, and nuisance animals. Further, the refuges would evaluate more effective means of trapping and euthanizing exotic, invasive, and nuisance animals. Focusing on eradication, the refuges need to be regularly informed and updated to be able to adapt management quickly to respond to new locations and species to minimize impacts to refuge resources, with an emphasis on protecting migratory birds. To help do this, the refuges would increase involvement and actively participate with the Southwest Florida Cooperative Invasive Species Management Area (SWFL CISMA), including creating an alert network to notify partners of the presence and spread of exotic, invasive, and nuisance species, focusing efforts on early detection and rapid response. Current information indicates that the range of the Burmese python has extended north to the Myakka River, potentially including the refuges (Skip Snow, personal communication, 2009). An active alert network would help to detect their presence. And the green mussel was recently discovered nearby in Tarpon Bay on J.N. "Ding" Darling NWR (Loren Coen, personal communication, 2009).

Wildlife and Habitat Management Goal 4: Water Quality, Quantity, and Timing of Flow

Work with the partners to address and resolve the water quality, quantity, and timing of flow concerns associated with the watersheds of Pine Island, Matlacha Pass, Island Bay, and Caloosahatchee NWRs; Lake Okeechobee releases to the west; and the Gulf of Mexico.

Wildlife and Habitat Management Objectives 4.a. Water Quality, Quantity, and Timing of Flow

Discussion: Water quality, quantity, and timing of flow issues impact all refuge resources. The following wildlife and habitat management objectives are also intended to specifically benefit wood storks, roseate spoonbills, black skimmers, American oystercatchers, roseate terns, other wading and water birds, other shorebirds and seabirds, bald eagles, other raptors and birds of prey, West Indian manatees, American crocodiles, American alligators, smalltooth sawfishes, and Gulf sturgeons, as well as mangroves, seagrass beds, and oyster beds.

Wildlife and Habitat Management Objective 4.a(1): Throughout the life of the CCP, continue working with the partners on Lake Okeechobee regulation schedules to optimize water quality, quantity, and timing of flow to support the estuarine ecosystem within which the refuges exist.

Discussion: Lake Okeechobee regulation schedules are set by USACE. The Service's Ecological Services Vero Beach Field Office coordinates regularly with the USACE on these regulation schedules. The refuges would increase efforts to work with the partners to address concerns related to water quality, quantity, and timing of flows, including coordinating with the Service's Ecological Services Vero Beach Field Office for Fish and Wildlife Coordination Act input on new regulation schedules for Lake Okeechobee to address management concerns on those activities impacting the refuges' ecology, with an emphasis on the needs of migratory birds and their habitats.

Wildlife and Habitat Management Objective 4.a(2): Within five years of CCP approval, work with the partners to expand the existing network of water quality monitoring stations, which provide data related to water quality, quantity, and timing of flows for the watersheds of Pine Island, Matlacha Pass, Island Bay, and Caloosahatchee NWRs.

Discussion: The partners already have water quality monitoring stations in and around the refuges. The refuges would work with the partners to evaluate the existing network of water quality monitoring stations and evaluate the need to expand this network to cover all four refuges. The refuges would continue the existing Service partnership with USGS to conduct a water quantity and quality study, which also includes Caloosahatchee NWR. Fish seining, seagrass surveys, and bird counts would be done in conjunction with the water sampling to document any correlations. Species that would be targeted for surveying would include juvenile species of tarpon (*Megalops atlantica*), snook, seatrout (*Megalops atlantica*), mangrove snapper (*Lutjanus griseus*), sheepshead (*Archosargus probatocephalus*), mullet, menhedan (*Brevoortia patronus*), pink shrimp, and blue crabs. Bird counts would target wading birds and shorebirds. Management concerns would be focused on those activities impacting migratory birds and their habitats. Increased information from the water quality network and the USGS study would enhance decision-making for the refuges and would benefit a variety of species.

Wildlife and Habitat Management Goal 5: Climate Change

Identify, understand, and ameliorate the impacts of climate change on the resources of Pine Island, Matlacha Pass, Island Bay, and Caloosahatchee NWRs to plan for and adapt management as necessary to protect the native wildlife; the upland, transitional, and estuarine habitats; and the cultural resources of the refuges.

Wildlife and Habitat Management Objective 5.a. Climate Change Impacts

Wildlife and Habitat Management Objective 5.a(1): During the life of the CCP, work with the partners to refine and run appropriate climate change models and foster needed research to understand the impacts on refuge resources, with a focus on the potential impacts on migratory birds.

Discussion: The impacts from climate change and sea level rise are already being seen around the globe. Since much of the refuges are islands and shorelines, understanding the impacts of climate change on refuge resources would be an important part of future management. The Refuge Complex would evaluate refuge management activities that could adapt to these changes and/or minimize their impacts. One key concept would be to build resilience/flexibility in natural systems to enable them and the wildlife that use them to better cope with a range of conditions that might occur. Finding ways to decrease vulnerability and increase adaptive capacity of these systems and wildlife are measures that would likely be employed in varying degrees. The strategies to accomplish this objective are outlined below.

Strategies:

- Work with the Service's South Florida Ecosystem Team and Massachusetts Institute of Technology to develop a climate change and sea level rise model.
- Partner with the SCCF Marine Lab to model climate change impacts to the refuges.
- Re-run the SLAMM model when high resolution Light Detecting and Ranging (LiDAR) data become available.
- Work with partners to establish benchmarks and monitoring in relation to sea level rise, shoreline change, saltwater intrusion, and habitat changes and shifts. Monitor beach profile changes over time as related to climate change and sea level rise. Monitor changes manifested in shoreline erosion, saltwater intrusion into aquifer, decreased vitality of mangroves and other edge species, increased prevalence of disease, increased level of pH in the marine environment, and increased frequency and duration of drought and fire.
- Use the Service's fire weather station located at J.N. "Ding" Darling NWR on Sanibel Island to compare changes in the local climate, especially with regard to rainfall and temperature.
- Work with Cornell University to track changes in migratory bird presence, timing of migration, and timing of breeding bird nesting, as well as the timing of associated flora.
- Work with the partners, particularly SCCF and Bailey-Matthews Shell Museum to monitor the pH of surrounding waters and any associated changes in shellfish organisms.
- Work with the partners to monitor subtle shifts in species abundance, productivity, range, and phenology.
- Anticipate increased invasion of exotic species.
- Monitor succession of natural communities to include more tropical dominant species.

RESOURCE PROTECTION

Resource Protection Goal 1: Cultural Resources

Protect the archaeological and historical resources of Pine Island, Matlacha Pass, Island Bay, and Caloosahatchee NWRs.

Resource Protection Objectives 1.a. Archaeological and Historic Resources

Resource Protection Objective 1.a(1): During the life of the CCP, continue evaluating cultural resource issues for all four refuges when projects are proposed and continue patrolling known cultural resource sites, addressing issues as they arise.

Resource Protection Objective 1.a(2): Within 15 years of CCP approval, coordinate with the Service's Regional Archaeologist and the State Historic Preservation Officer to develop a comprehensive survey of all cultural resources for these four refuges to update existing information.

Discussion: In addition to wildlife and habitats, the refuges also provide protection for cultural resources. However, the full extent of cultural resources is unknown for Pine Island, Matlacha Pass, Island Bay, and Caloosahatchee NWRs. The Refuge Complex's law enforcement staff currently patrols known cultural resource sites. The partners also generally patrol the refuges. Since the refuges are closed, any access that is detected by law enforcement is controlled. The refuges would adapt management as necessary to protect any newly identified sites.

Resource Protection Goal 2: Refuges' Boundaries, Management Agreements, and Special Designations

Work with the partners to acquire, manage, or otherwise protect all remaining properties within the acquisition boundaries of Pine Island, Matlacha Pass, Island Bay, and Caloosahatchee NWRs to protect their upland, transitional, and estuarine habitats.

Resource Protection Objectives 2.a. Refuges' Boundaries

Resource Protection Objective 2.a(1): Within five years of CCP approval, review and revise the refuges' existing management boundaries to ensure postable, identifiable, and defensible boundaries for all four refuges.

Resource Protection Objective 2.a(2): Within five years of plan approval, work with the Service's Southeast Region Realty Office to develop an accurate survey of the refuges' ownership boundaries.

Resource Protection Objective 2.a(3): Within five years of CCP approval, work with the partners to improve the posting of the piping plover critical habitat designated at Terrapin Creek on Matlacha Pass NWR.

Resource Protection Objective 2.a(4): Within five years of CCP approval, work with the partners to evaluate the other boundary and posting needs at Terrapin Creek on Matlacha Pass NWR.

Resource Protection Objective 2.a(5): Within five years of CCP approval, pursue the inclusion of Manatee Island from the "Ding" Darling Wildlife Society in Caloosahatchee NWR.

Discussion: Currently all four refuges have posted management boundaries. Over time, the refuges would repost these boundaries as needed. However, discrepancies are known to exist regarding boundaries and ownership (e.g., at Caloosahatchee NWR). The refuges need complete, clearly defined surveys to help minimize issues associated with ownership, encroachment from adjoining private properties, and expansion of adjacent rights-of-way. Due to various actions since the establishment of Caloosahatchee NWR in 1920 (e.g., dredging activities, shifting and erosion of islands, loss of islands, and islands claimed by the state), a Bureau of Land Management (BLM) survey is needed to confirm Service ownership of the four remaining islands set aside by Executive Order and identified as part of the refuge's boundary (Figure 5), as well as the total acreage of the refuge. The Refuge Complex would work with the Service's Southeast Region Realty office, BLM, the State of Florida, and the Lee County Property Appraiser's office to confirm and recognize the proper boundary of Caloosahatchee NWR. To help resolve boundary and ownership discrepancies, the Refuge Complex would work with BLM to conduct legal boundary surveys and historical research. And the Refuge Complex would evaluate the boundary and posting needs of the Terrapin Creek Tract of Matlacha Pass NWR. Under a Minor Expansion Proposal (MEP), Caloosahatchee NWR would be expanded to include Manatee Island, which was donated by Florida Power and Light Company to the "Ding" Darling Wildlife Society in 2001 because it was anticipated that it would be added to the acquisition boundary as part of the major expansion proposal in 2002, but the major expansion never received final approval.

Resource Protection Objective 2.b. Management Agreements

Resource Protection Objective 2.b(1): Within five years of CCP approval, work with the State of Florida to develop appropriate management agreements to implement refuge-managed closed area buffers around sensitive resources.

Discussion: The waters around the four refuges are state-owned sovereign submerged lands. In order to develop, post, and enforce closed area buffers to protect sensitive bird rookeries and serve shared goals and objectives between the Service and the state, the refuges would need to coordinate with the State to develop appropriate management agreements for these areas. Further, the refuges would also need to develop companion MEPs in order to include these areas under refuge management. Closed area buffers are proposed under Wildlife and Habitat Management objectives 2.a(2), 2.d(3), and 2.d(4) to minimize impacts and protect wood storks, roseate spoonbills, other wading and waterbirds, American oystercatchers, roseate terns, and other shorebirds and seabirds using these four refuges. These buffers would help protect nesting, resting, roosting, and foraging birds. Buffer size would depend on the species using each site. Current research (e.g., Rodgers and Schwikert 2002) would help determine the proper size needed to minimize negative impacts.

Resource Protection Objective 2.c. Additional Special Designations

Resource Protection Objective 2.c(1): Within 10 years of CCP approval, pursue the designation of lands and waters within the current management boundaries of Pine Island and Matlacha Pass NWRs for inclusion in the Western Hemisphere Shorebird Reserve Network and of all four refuges as RAMSAR Wetlands of International Importance, as part of the application for J.N. "Ding" Darling NWR. As lands and waters are added to the refuges, evaluate the applicability of these special designations to those additions.

Discussion: Two of the refuges (Pine Island and Matlacha Pass) appear to meet the criteria for designation as part of the Western Hemisphere Shorebird Reserve Network. The refuges would investigate the criteria used to qualify for inclusion in the Western Hemisphere Shorebird Reserve Network and, if warranted, resubmit stronger applications to receive these designations. Also, the refuges would apply for consideration as RAMSAR Wetlands of International Importance, as part of the potential J.N. "Ding" Darling NWR proposal, where all five refuges would be included in a single proposal and designation.

Resource Protection Goal 3: Island Bay NWR Wilderness Area

Protect the Island Bay NWR Wilderness Area and promote an understanding of its wilderness values among area visitors to preserve the opportunity for outstanding coastal wilderness experiences in southwest Florida.

Resource Protection Objectives 3.a. Island Bay NWR Wilderness Area

Resource Protection Objective 3.a(1): Within five years of CCP approval, work with the partners to provide information regarding the wilderness area, wilderness stewardship, and wilderness principles to area visitors and in environmental education and interpretation programs and materials.

Discussion: Wilderness areas generally provide opportunities for more primitive outdoor experiences and solitude. Although the Island Bay Wilderness Area is closed to public access, area visitors experience the wilderness area from adjacent waters. The Refuge Complex would provide information regarding wilderness areas, wilderness stewardship, and wilderness principles for both the Island Bay NWR Wilderness Area and the J.N. "Ding" Darling NWR Wilderness Area at the J.N. "Ding" Darling Education Center on Sanibel Island and in environmental education and interpretation programs and materials and would depict wilderness areas on refuge maps provided at both partner and refuge facilities.

Resource Protection Objective 3.a(2): Within five years of CCP approval, initiate coordination with the Charlotte County Environmental and Extension Services Department, Pest Management Division to ensure that no spraying of pesticides occurs within the Island Bay NWR Wilderness Area during mosquito control activities.

Discussion: Under the Wilderness Act, wilderness areas are to be managed with a least tool approach to ensure that the hand of man is not evident. This helps to protect and sustain the wilderness experience for current and future generations. However, the Refuge Complex would work with the partners to minimize the impacts to the Island Bay NWR Wilderness Area from mosquito control activities. The Refuge Complex regularly coordinates with the Lee County Mosquito Control District. This coordination effort needs to be expanded to include the Charlotte County Environmental and Extension Services Department, Pest Management Division to help minimize impacts on refuge resources from mosquito control activities, especially to the Island Bay NWR Wilderness Area.

VISITOR SERVICES

Visitor Services Goal 1: Welcome and Orient Visitors

Visitors will feel welcome and find accurate, timely, and appropriate orientation material and information on refuge programs and management activities.

Visitor Services Objectives 1.a. Welcome and Orient Visitors

Visitor Services Objective 1.a(1): During the life of the CCP, work with partners to provide welcome and orientation information about the refuges to area visitors.

Visitor Services Objective 1.a(2): Within 10 years of CCP approval, update the exhibits at the "Ding" Darling Education Center on Sanibel Island to highlight these four refuges and their roles in the landscape.

Discussion: These four refuges are closed to visitors. However, they exist within a larger estuarine ecosystem that does receive a lot of use. And the refuges are experienced in a visual way from adjacent waters. Although the refuges don't provide welcome and orientation, the partners do. The refuges are identified on visitor maps of the partners. Fishing and boating occur in state waters adjacent to the refuges. The refuges are part of the Great Calusa Blueway. The refuges would continue to work with the partners to update maps and information provided at area boat ramps and on partner web sites to identify the locations and extents of the refuges and their closed area statuses. And the refuges would work with the Randell Research Center on Pine Island to provide information on Pine Island and Matlacha Pass NWRs.

Visitor Services Goal 2: Adjacent Activities

Users participating in activities adjacent to the refuges will value Pine Island, Matlacha Pass, Island Bay, and Caloosahatchee NWRs and the resources they protect; will minimize impacts to the refuges and resources; and will support refuge management activities to protect them.

Visitor Services Objective 2.a. Adjacent Activities

Visitor Services Objective 2.a(1): Throughout the life of the CCP, work with partners to develop public awareness, understanding, and appreciation of Pine Island, Matlacha Pass, Island Bay, and Caloosahatchee NWRs; the wildlife and habitats they protect; and the refuges' roles in the landscape to help minimize impacts to refuge resources from adjacent activities and to improve the ethical behavior of area users.

Discussion: Although the refuges are closed to the public, they include islands and shorelines which are impacted by boating and fishing activities (e.g., disturbance of shorebirds and impacts of abandoned monofilament fishing line, cast nets, and crab traps). The refuges would work with the partners to provide information to the public to increase awareness and minimize disturbance and impacts, so members of the public would enjoy their boating, kayaking, fishing, wildlife watching and photographing experiences, while at the same time behaving ethically, valuing the diversity of area wildlife, and supporting Refuge Complex efforts to maintain optimal wildlife habitat (e.g., through habitat management activities and closed area buffers). The refuges would also work with partners to develop informational materials (e.g., brochures, websites, displays, kiosks, signs, and videos) on ethical behavior.

Visitor Services Goal 3: Environmental Education and Interpretation

Participants in quality environmental education and interpretation opportunities will develop an understanding and awareness of the values of Pine Island, Matlacha Pass, Island Bay, and Caloosahatchee NWRs; their natural resources; their roles in the landscape; and human influences on ecosystems.

Discussion: Human influences on ecosystems in this area include climate change and its associated impacts which can result in direct wildlife, habitat, and habitat functionality loss and disturbance, which are also impacted by human activities, such as development and landscape use and conversion. The associated impacts include declining wildlife and habitat; water quality, quantity, and timing impacts; invasion and spread of exotic, invasive, and nuisance species; and climate change and its associated impacts. Since J.N. "Ding" Darling NWR has high visibility and visitation, inclusion of these messages in environmental education and interpretation programs and activities is expected to help minimize impacts from human activities.

Visitor Services Objectives 3.a. Environmental Education and Interpretation Opportunities

Visitor Services Objective 3.a(1): During the life of the CCP, continue to work with the partners to provide quality curriculum-based programs with messages focused on the role and importance of the refuges in the landscape and the minimization of wildlife and habitat impacts from human activities. Incorporate the messages for these four refuges into the environmental education and interpretation programs and materials developed and provided by J.N. "Ding" Darling NWR.

Visitor Services Objective 3.a(2): Within 10 years of CCP approval, work with the partners to better incorporate migratory bird messages into their environmental education and interpretation programs and materials.

Visitor Services Objective 3.a(3): Within five years of CCP approval, expand the environmental education and interpretation program at J.N. "Ding" Darling NWR to more fully incorporate messages focused on the role and importance of the refuges in the landscape and the minimization of wildlife and habitat impacts from human activities.

Visitor Services Objective 3.a(4): Within 10 years of CCP approval, work with the partners to develop an annual event to be held in a local community near the refuges with messages focused on the role and importance of the refuges in the landscape and the minimization of wildlife and habitat impacts from human activities.

Visitor Services Objective 3.a(5): During the life of the CCP, continue to conduct regular interpretive programs at Pine Island Library with messages focused on the role and importance of the refuges in the landscape and the minimization of wildlife and habitat impacts from human activities.

Visitor Services Objective 3.a(6): Within 15 years of CCP approval, evaluate the feasibility of operating guided tours adjacent to Pine Island, Island Bay, and Matlacha Pass NWRs.

Discussion: Although not the primary focus, these four refuges are already included in the robust environmental education and interpretation programs at J.N. "Ding" Darling NWR. Programs are conducted at the J.N. "Ding" Darling NWR, in local schools, and at other off-site locations. The environmental education programs are linked to Florida standards. Environmental education and interpretation programs are conducted by Refuge Complex staff and volunteers, the "Ding" Darling Wildlife Society, and area teachers. Programs are also provided for home-school and Scout groups, as requested. In the summer of 2009, the Refuge Complex kicked off the Summer Teachers Assisting Refuge (STAR) program. The Refuge Complex also conducts "train the teacher" workshops. In 2006, the Refuge Complex began conducting regular interpretive programs at the Pine Island Library.

The Refuge Complex would expand the environmental education and interpretation programs at J.N. "Ding" Darling NWR to more fully incorporate messages focused on migratory birds, the role and importance of the refuges in the landscape, and the minimization of wildlife and habitat impacts from human activities. Further, staff, volunteers, and teachers would be trained to conduct education and interpretive programs. The refuges would work with partners to develop an annual event near the refuges to highlight them, contingent upon having sufficient staff to support this effort. Guided tours could interpret rookery islands, their historical importance, roles of the refuges in the landscape and the minimization of wildlife and habitat impacts from human activities. The refuges would coordinate with local eco-tour operators to incorporate refuge messages into their programs and materials.

Visitor Services Goal 4: Outreach

Communicate key messages and issues with off-site audiences to build support within the local communities and beyond for Pine Island, Matlacha Pass, Island Bay, and Caloosahatchee NWRs; their purposes; and their management.

Visitor Services Objectives 4.a. Outreach

Visitor Services Objective 4.a(1): Within five years of CCP approval, increase the outreach efforts and activities of the Refuge Complex staff, especially to the local communities with messages focused on the role and importance of the refuges in the landscape and the minimization of wildlife and habitat impacts from human activities.

Visitor Services Objective 4.a(2): Within three years of CCP approval, incorporate messages focused on the role and importance of the refuges in the landscape and the minimization of wildlife and habitat impacts from human activities into outreach materials developed for J.N. "Ding" Darling NWR.

Discussion: The refuges would increase participation in festivals and events held by the partners (e.g., at Mango Mania) to help increase outreach to the local communities. The annual refuge event proposed under Visitor Services Objective 3.a(4) would offer an excellent opportunity to also conduct outreach activities. Climate change and its associated impacts would be incorporated into refuge outreach activities to increase understanding and awareness and to increase support for management activities to respond to these impacts. The refuges will also coordinate with local schools to incorporate climate change curriculum and activities into their environmental education programs.

Visitor Services Objective 4.a(3): Within five years of CCP approval, develop a general brochure for all four refuges with an accompanying map.

Discussion: The general brochure would serve as another venue for outreach and would be made available at the J. N. "Ding" Darling NWR Education Center and at partner sites near the satellite refuges. The brochure would help highlight the importance of the refuges to migratory birds and in the landscape.

Visitor Services Objectives 4.b. Outreach Specific to Fishing Activities

Visitor Services Objective 4.b(1): Within five years of CCP approval, work with the partners to provide information to the fishing public utilizing the waters adjacent to the refuges regarding the impacts of fishing activities on migratory birds.

Visitor Services Objective 4.b(2): Within five years of CCP approval, work with the partners to evaluate the need to expand the existing monofilament recycling program.

Visitor Services Objective 4.b(3): Within five years of CCP approval, work with the partners to conduct cleanup events targeting abandoned monofilament fishing line, cast nets, and crab traps.

Discussion: Although fishing activities occur off the refuges, they do occur directly adjacent to them and they can have impacts (e.g., disturbance of shorebirds and impacts of abandoned monofilament fishing line, cast nets, and crab traps). To help increase outreach activities specific to fishing, Refuge Complex staff would coordinate with the local communities and recruit volunteers to participate in abandoned monofilament fishing line, cast net, and crab trap cleanup events as needed.

REFUGE ADMINISTRATION

Refuge Administration Goal 1: Refuge Operations and Management

Provide sufficient infrastructure, operations, volunteers, and staff to protect and manage refuge resources and the natural and cultural values of Pine Island, Matlacha Pass, Island Bay, and Caloosahatchee NWRs.

Refuge Administration Objectives 1.a. Staff

Refuge Administration Objective 1.a(1): During the life of the CCP, continue utilizing J.N. "Ding" Darling NWR staff to conduct minimal management at the satellite refuges, including periodic patrols of the refuges.

Refuge Administration Objective 1.a(2): During the life of the CCP, add five staff specific to these four refuges: Biological Science Technician, Law Enforcement Officer, Wildlife Refuge Specialist (Assistant Refuge Manager), Hydrologist, and a Park Ranger (environmental education).

Discussion: These four refuges are currently managed by staff of the J.N. "Ding" Darling NWR (Figure 22). To accomplish the outlined goals and objectives and to better serve the purposes for which the refuges were established, staff positions are needed specific to the refuges. With an estimated annual recurring cost of $443,368 (including a 25 percent operating margin), five positions are proposed to specifically serve these four refuges (Figure 23):

- Biological Science Technician – with a focus on Island Bay NWR;
- Law Enforcement Officer – with a focus on Matlacha Pass NWR;
- Wildlife Refuge Specialist (Assistant Refuge Manager) – with a focus on Pine Island NWR;
- Hydrologist – with a focus on Caloosahatchee NWR; and
- Park Ranger (environmental education) – with a focus on Pine Island NWR.

Refuge Administration Objectives 1.b. Administrative Facilities, Utilities, Equipment, and Signs

Refuge Administration Objective 1.b(1): During the life of the CCP, continue maintaining appropriate boundary signage for all four refuges.

Refuge Administration Objective 1.b(2): Within 10 years of CCP approval, work with the partners to evaluate and install interpretive information at partner sites.

Refuge Administration Objective 1.b(3): Within 15 years of CCP approval, evaluate the need to locate the staff proposed for the refuges within a local community.

Discussion: In the near term it is likely that any added staff would continue to be located at the Refuge Complex headquarters on Sanibel Island or at partner sites and facilities. As staff members are added to the refuges, the Service would evaluate the need to locate office facilities closer to the refuges.

Refuge Administration Goal 2: Intergovernmental Coordination and Other Partners

Foster strong and effective working relationships with existing and new governmental and nongovernmental partners for the purposes of accomplishing refuge management goals and protecting the natural and cultural resources of Pine Island, Matlacha Pass, Island Bay, and Caloosahatchee NWRs.

Refuge Administration Objective 2.a. Intergovernmental Coordination

Refuge Administration Objective 2.a(1): During the life of the CCP, continue to coordinate with existing governmental partners and develop new governmental partnerships to help serve common interests and to further the vision, purposes, goals, and objectives of these four refuges.

Discussion: Existing intergovernmental partners include: Lee County, Lee County Mosquito Control District, Charlotte County, Charlotte Harbor NEP, Charlotte Harbor Aquatic Preserves, West Coast Inland Navigation District, National Marine Fisheries Service (NOAA), FDEP, SWFWMD, SFWMD, USACE, USGS, and FWC. The refuges would increase and improve coordination with new governmental partners, including the local communities; Charlotte County Environmental and Extension Services

Figure 23. Proposed organizational chart for the J.N. "Ding" Darling NWR Complex.

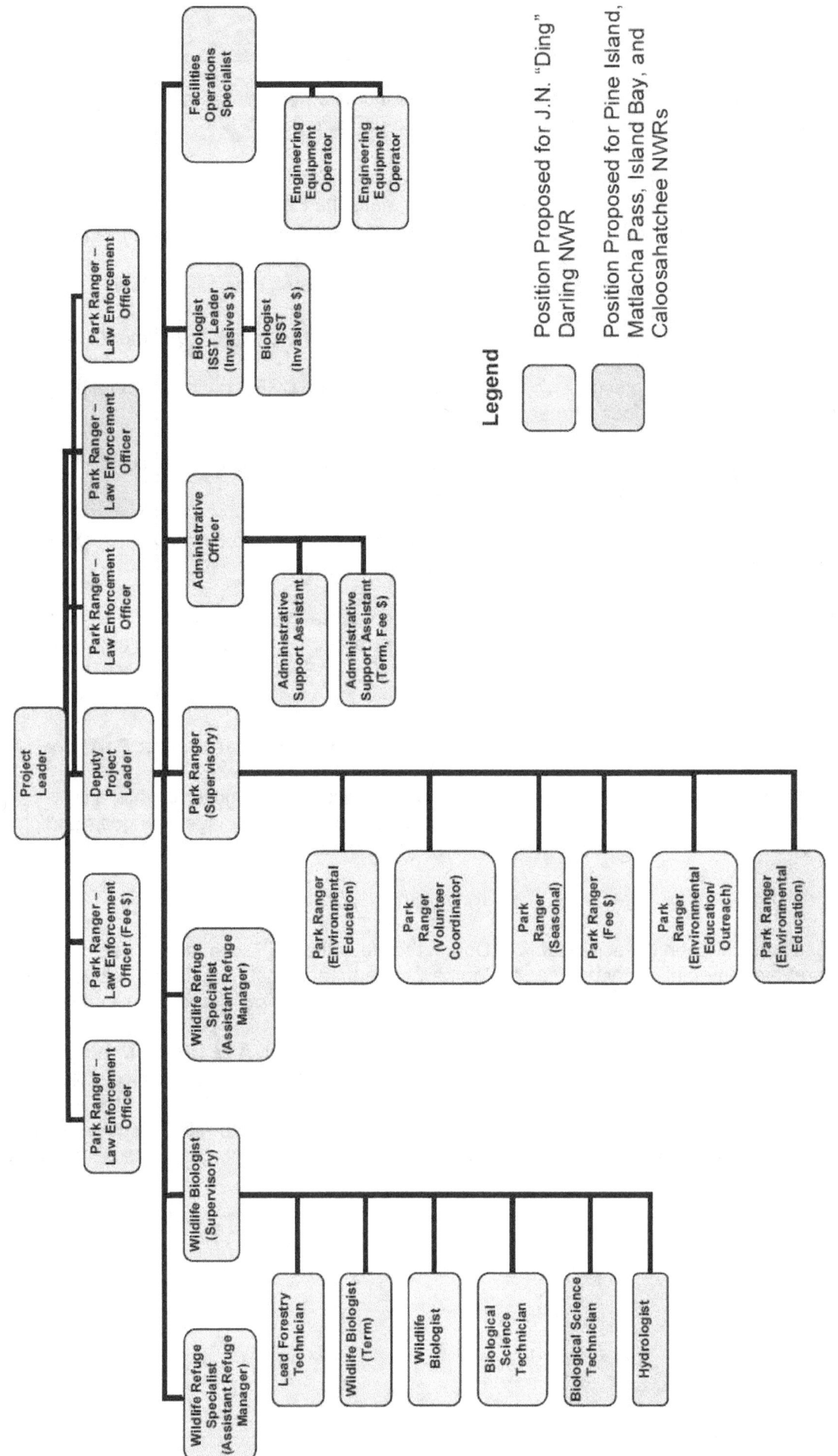

Department, Pest Management Division; Lee County Sea-Grant Program; Charlotte County Sea-Grant Program; Lee County School District; Charlotte County School District; and the city of Cape Coral.

Because the refuges exist within the larger estuarine landscape, they share numerous goals and objectives with the partners, especially with the Charlotte Harbor National Estuary Program and the Charlotte Harbor Aquatic Preserves, including protecting natural and cultural resources; supporting recovery of rare, threatened, and endangered species; conducting surveys; restoring and enhancing habitats; controlling exotic, invasive, and nuisance species; addressing water quality, quantity, and timing of flow concerns; understanding and ameliorating the impacts of climate change; increasing awareness and understanding of natural resource issues; minimizing human disturbance and impacts; and coordinating with the partners.

Refuge Administration Objective 2.b. Nongovernmental Partners, Volunteers, and Friends Group

Refuge Administration Objective 2.b(1): During the life of the CCP, continue to work with existing partners, including the "Ding" Darling Wildlife Society, Refuge Complex volunteers, Calusa Land Trust, Greater Pine Island Chamber of Commerce, Randell Research Center on Pine Island, Audubon of Southwest Florida, Mote Marine Laboratory, Peace River Audubon Society, SCCF, SWFL CISMA, and Florida Gulf Coast University and develop new partnerships to help serve common interests and to further the vision, purposes, goals, and objectives of these four refuges.

Discussion: In order to accomplish outlined goals and objectives, the refuges would need some assistance from existing and new partners. The "Ding" Darling Wildlife Society has continued to be a staunch supporter of these four refuges. And, the existing cadre of volunteers serves as a source or support and as a supporting workforce for the refuges. The refuges would also work with local guides and outfitters to help promote the refuges and build bridges to future partnerships. The refuges would also recruit new volunteers from the local area through outreach activities and events. New partners could include the Friends of the Charlotte Harbor Aquatic Preserves; Barrier Island Park Society; Charlotte Harbor Environmental Center; Florida Paddling Trails Association; Gasparilla Island Conservation and Improvement Association; Coastal Wildlife Club; Conservation Foundation of the Gulf Coast; and Society for Ethical Ecotourism of Southwest Florida. New partners for the refuges could also include such businesses as Tropic Star of Pine Island, Tarpon Lodge on Pine Island, Gulf Coast Kayaks of Matlacha, and Grande Tours of Placida.

Refuge Administration Goal 3: Service Visibility and Image

Members of the local communities will recognize and support Pine Island, Matlacha Pass, Island Bay, and Caloosahatchee NWRs.

Refuge Administration Objective 3.a. Service Visibility and Image

Refuge Administration Objective 3.a(1): Within five years of CCP approval, work with the partners and local communities to improve the visibility and image of the Service in the communities surrounding the refuges to increase their connections to the refuges and to build support for refuge management.

Discussion: The Refuge Complex recognizes that the refuges have limited visibility and a less than stellar image in the local area. To help increase the visibility and image of the refuges and the Service, Visitor Services Objective 3.a(4) proposes an annual event to be held in the local communities; Visitor Services objectives 1.a(1), 1.a(2), 3.a(1), 3.a(3),, 3.a(5), 3.a(6), 4.a(1), 4.a(3), and 4.b(1) propose to increase outreach, environmental education, and interpretation; and Refuge Administration objective 1.a(2) proposes to increase staff specific to the refuges. Further, Refuge

Administration objectives 2.a(1) and 2.b(1) seek to further existing and new partnerships to enhance management of the refuges and the resources protected. Working with the local communities is the key to future management of these resources.

V. Plan Implementation

INTRODUCTION

As required by the National Wildlife Refuge System Improvement Act, the Service will manage all refuges in accordance with an approved CCP, which, when implemented, will achieve the refuges' purposes; help fulfill the mission of the National Wildlife Refuge System; maintain and, where appropriate, restore the biological integrity, diversity, and environmental health of the refuges; help achieve the goals of the National Wilderness Preservation System; and meet other mandates.

This chapter summarizes the implementation strategy for achieving the purposes, vision, goals, and objectives outlined in the CCP. It addresses refuge projects; funding and personnel needs; volunteers and partnership opportunities; step-down management plans; a monitoring and adaptive management plan; and plan review and revision.

PROPOSED PROJECTS

The proposed projects reflect the basic needs identified by Service staff, the public, and the planning team members for the management of fish and wildlife populations, habitats, cultural resources, land protection, public use, outreach, and environmental education to address the identified priority issues and to serve the vision and goals developed for Pine Island, Matlacha Pass, Island Bay, and Caloosahatchee NWRs. Among these projects is a list of step-down management plans to be developed. Step-down plans are individual and specific and are the blueprint under which refuges operate. The step-down plans would provide more detail and specific tasks, stepping down from the CCP. Some existing plans would need revision, while others would need to be developed. The Service prepares step-down plans in conjunction with the provisions set forth in the National Environmental Policy Act of 1969.

Annual funding for staff, facilities, operations, and maintenance is an integral part of project implementation. The general cost estimates provided will be updated and adjusted annually. Essential needs are addressed, such as eliminating biological threats and problems, meeting Refuge System mission requirements, and fulfilling the purposes for which the refuges were established. There are no assurances that these projects will be either partially or fully funded. However, with the help and cooperation of conservation partners, the Service will use this CCP to focus attention on funding the operations and maintenance needs of the refuges.

Implementing the proposed management activities would result in increased protection for breeding, nesting, resting, roosting, foraging, and migrating birds on the refuges. Increased information on a variety of species, suites of species, and habitats would enhance decision-making for the refuges. Further benefits would be realized from increased control of exotic, invasive, and nuisance species. The refuges would coordinate with the partners to address concerns related to the impacts from water quality, quantity, and timing of flows and from climate change and sea level rise. Resource protection would be enhanced, including through increased information about cultural resources on the refuges, increased protection of cultural resources, additional special designations, improved management of the Island Bay NWR Wilderness Area, improved coordination with the partners to increase ethical outdoor behavior, and enhanced visitor services programs. To achieve this, the refuges would work with governmental and nongovernmental partners, area communities, the "Ding" Darling Wildlife Society, and local businesses and the refuges would pursue the addition of staff to address management concerns.

For the purpose of achieving the goals and objectives developed for the refuges, the CCP has grouped management strategies into specific projects. The CCP describes 21 projects for development and management. Additional staff would be needed to implement these projects. All projects would require the close coordination with partner agencies and organizations. Partnership agreements that would facilitate project implementation are also discussed.

WILDLIFE AND HABITAT MANAGEMENT

Project 1. Work with the partners to standardize survey and monitoring and to increase the scientific rigor of these efforts.

The refuges would work with the partners to conduct surveys and foster research to determine presence/absence, abundance, productivity, colony origins, foraging ranges, and other population information for wood storks, roseate spoonbills, roseate terns, black skimmers, American oystercatchers, snowy plovers, Wilson's plovers, red knots, piping plovers, mangrove forest birds, raptors, gopher tortoises, sea turtles, West Indian manatees, ornate diamondback terrapins, eastern indigo snakes, American alligators, American crocodiles, gopher tortoises, Gulf sturgeon, and smalltooth sawfish. Further, the refuges would work with the partners to increase the scientific rigor of these survey and monitoring efforts. Surveys based on standardized protocols would be conducted to determine presence and distribution of priority wildlife species and to provide baseline data to assist managers in habitat management practices. Information to be collected is the foundation for implementing the CCP, formulating habitat management, and developing adaptive management strategies for species of conservation concern.

Wildlife and Habitat Management Objectives: 1.a(1), 1.b(1), 1.c(3), 1.d(2)-(3), 1.e(1), 1.f(2), 1.g(1), 1.h(1), 1.j(1), 1.k(1),1.l(1), 2.a(1), 2.b(1), 2.c(1), 2.d(1), 3.a(1)-(2), 4.a(2), and 5.a(1)
Refuge Administration Objectives: 1.a(1)-(2), 2.a(1), and 2.b(1)

Project 2. Coordinate with the partners to address concerns related to water quality, quantity, and timing of flows.

This project is shared with all five refuges in the Refuge Complex. The Refuge Complex would work with partners on Lake Okeechobee regulation schedules to optimize water quality, quantity, and timing of flows to support the Caloosahatchee and Charlotte Harbor estuarine ecosystems in which the refuges exist. The Refuge Complex would work with the partners to address concerns on those activities impacting the refuge's ecology, with an emphasis on the needs of migratory birds. The Refuge Complex would also work with partners to install water quality monitoring station(s) at appropriate locations. Fish seining, seagrass surveys, and bird counts would be conducted in conjunction with water sampling activities to document any correlations.

Wildlife and Habitat Management Objectives: 1.a(1), 1.b(1), 1.i(2), 1.j(1), 1.k(1), 2.a(1), 2.b(1), 2.e(2), 2.e(4), 4.a(1)-(2)
Resource Protection Objectives: 2.b(1) and 2.c(1)
Visitor Services Objectives: 2.a(1), 3.a(1), 3.a(3)-(5), 4.a(1)-(2)
Refuge Administration Objective: 1.a(1)-(2), 2.a(1), and 2.b(1)

Project 3. Work with partners to provide appropriately sized closed area buffers around key nesting, roosting, resting, and foraging sites within Pine Island, Matlacha Pass, Island Bay, and Caloosahatchee NWRs.

The refuges would identify islands and areas in need of closed area buffers to minimize disturbance and impacts to protect nesting, roosting, resting, and foraging wildlife. Where necessary, the refuges would work with the partners to develop management agreements to implement appropriately sized refuge-managed closed area buffers around sensitive resources. The refuges would develop companion MEPs in order to include any of these areas not currently within the approved acquisition boundaries under refuge management. Key consideration for closed area buffers would be given to Pine Island NWR (including Lower Bird Island and Hemp Key) and Matlacha Pass NWR (including Skimmer Island, Lumpkin Island, Givney Key, Bird Rookery Key, Grackle Island, Big Smokehouse Key, and the Terrapin Creek Tract).

Wildlife and Habitat Management Objectives: 1.a(1), 1.b(1), 1.c(2)-(3), 1.d(1), 1.e(2), 1.f(1), 1.g(1), 2.a(2), 2.d(3) and 2.d(4)
Resource Protection Objectives: 2.a(2)-(4), 2.b(1), and 2.c(1)
Visitor Services Objectives: 2.a(1), 3.a(1), 3.a(3), 4.a(1)-(2), and 4.b(1)
Refuge Administration Objectives: 1.a(1)-(2), 1.b(1), 2.a(1), and 2.b(1)

Project 4. Work with the U.S. Army Corps of Engineers and other partners to create or enhance suitable nesting and foraging habitat for black skimmers, American oystercatchers, and roseate terns during area dredge and spoil activities.

Wildlife and Habitat Management Objectives: 1.c(1), 1.d(1), 2.d(2), 2.e(2), and 2.e(4)
Resource Protection Objective: 2.c(1)
Visitor Services Objectives: 3.a(1), 3.a(3), 4.a(1)-(2)
Refuge Administration Objectives: 1.a(1)-(2), 2.a(1), and 2.b(1)

Project 5. Develop and maintain a GIS database for vegetation within the acquisition boundaries of Pine Island, Matlacha Pass, Island Bay, and Caloosahatchee NWRs.

The refuges lack specific enough GIS vegetation data.

Wildlife and Habitat Management Objectives: 1.c(1), 1.d(1), 1.l(2), 2.b(1), 2.c(1), 2.c(2), 2.d(2), 2.e(1)-(4)
Refuge Administration Objectives: 1.a(1)-(2), 2.a(1), and 2.b(1)

Project 6. Work with partners to identify and address wildlife and habitat impacts associated with the proposed Interstate 75 widening project, including resolving any ownership and jurisdictional issues.

Interstate 75 passes directly over Caloosahatchee NWR. Further, the existing bridge stanchion is located on one of the islands of Caloosahatchee NWR. The Refuge Complex would work with the partners to resolve any ownership and jurisdictional issues associated Interstate 75 and Caloosahatchee NWR. Further, the Refuge Complex would work with the Florida Department of Transportation, the Service's Vero Beach Ecological Service's Field Office, and other partners to ensure that wildlife and habitat values are conserved and protected in relation to this project. Numerous options may be considered, including the addition of lands and waters to Caloosahatchee NWR or other area refuges.

Wildlife and Habitat Management Objectives: 1.a(1)-(2), 1.i(1), 1.l(1)-(2), 2.e(2), 2.e(4), 2.f(1), 4.a(1)-(2)
Resource Protection Objectives: 2.a(1) and 2.c(1)
Refuge Administration Objectives: 1.a(1)-(2), 1.b(1), 2.a(1), and 2.b(1)

Project 7. Continue to identify, locate, control, and eliminate where possible exotic, invasive, and nuisance plants and animals.

Work with the partners to identify and locate new infestations of Florida Exotic Pest Plant Council Category I and Category II exotic, invasive, and nuisance plants, focusing initial attack on eradication. Focus exotic plant control efforts on high-priority habitats for migratory birds. Work with the partners to increase education and awareness to build support for management activities to eradicate invasive exotic animals and to minimize impacts from nuisance animals. Increase management activities to address exotic, invasive, and nuisance species, including evaluating more effective means of trapping and euthanizing exotic, invasive, and nuisance species. Increase involvement and actively participate with Southwest Florida Cooperative Invasive Species Management Area (SWFL CISMA), including creating an alert network to notify partners of the presence and spread of exotic, invasive, and nuisance species, focusing efforts on early detection and rapid response.

Wildlife and Habitat Management Objectives: 2.b(1), 2.c(1)-(2), 2.d(3), 2.e(2)-(4), 3.a(1)-(2), 3.b(1)-(2)
Resource Protection Objective: 2.c(1)
Visitor Services Objectives: 3.a(1), 3.a(3), and 4.a(1)
Refuge Administration Objectives: 1.a(1)-(2), 2.a(1), and 2.b(1)

Project 8. Work with the partners to refine and run climate change models and foster needed research to understand the stressors, impacts on refuge resources, and their potential amelioration, with a focus on migratory birds.

Wildlife and Habitat Management Objectives: 1.a(1), 1.b(1), 1.c(1), 1.c(3), 1.d(1), 1.e(1), 1.f(2), 1.h(1), 1.j(1), 2.a(1), 2.b(1), 2.c(1), 2.d(1)-(2), 2.e(2)-(4), 3.a(1)-(2), 3.b(1)-(2), 4.a(1)-(2), and 5.a(1)
Resource Protection Objective: 1.a(2)
Visitor Services Objectives: 3.a(1), 3.a(3), 4.a(1)-(2)
Refuge Administration Objectives: 1.a(1)-(2), 2.a(1), and 2.b(1)

RESOURCE PROTECTION

Project 9. Protect archaeological resources through surveys and planning.

Coordinate with the Service's Regional Archaeologist and the State Historic Preservation Officer to develop a comprehensive survey of all cultural resources of the Pine Island, Matlacha Pass, Island Bay, and Caloosahatchee NWRs.

Resource Protection Objectives: 1.a(1)-(2)
Refuge Administration Objectives: 1.a(1)-(2), and 2.a(1)

Project 10. Review existing boundaries to ensure postable, identifiable, and defensible boundaries for all four refuges. Work with the Service's Southeast Region Realty Office to develop an accurate survey of the refuges' ownership boundaries. Work with partners to improve the posting of the piping plover critical habitat and other posting needs at Terrapin Creek on Matlacha Pass NWR.

Currently all four refuges have posted management boundaries. Over time, the refuges would repost these boundaries as needed. However, discrepancies exist regarding boundaries and ownership (e.g., at Caloosahatchee NWR). Due to various actions since the establishment of Caloosahatchee NWR in 1920 (e.g., dredging activities, shifting and erosion of islands, loss of islands, and islands claimed by the State), a BLM survey is needed to confirm Service ownership of the four remaining islands set aside by executive order, which are identified as part of the refuge's boundary (Figure 5), as well as the total acreage of the refuge. The Refuge Complex would work with the Service's Southeast Region Realty office, BLM, the State of Florida, and the Lee County Property Appraiser's office to confirm and recognize the proper boundary of Caloosahatchee NWR. To help resolve boundary and ownership discrepancies, the Refuge Complex would work with BLM to conduct legal boundary surveys and historical research. And, the Refuge Complex would evaluate the boundary and posting needs of the Terrapin Creek Tract of Matlacha Pass NWR.

Wildlife and Habitat Management Objectives: 1.a(1)-(2), 1.b(1), 1.c(1)-(3), 1.d(1), 1.e(2), 1.f(1), 2.a(2), 2.d(2)-(4), 2.e(1), and 2.f(1)
Resource Protection Objectives: 2.a(1)-(4), 2.b(1), and 2.c(1)
Visitor Services Objectives: 2.a(1), 3.a(1), 3.a(3), 4.a(1)-(2), and 4.b(1)
Refuge Administration Objectives: 1.a(1)-(2), 2.a(1), 2.b(1), and 3.a(1)

Project 11. Pursue the acquisition of Manatee Island from the "Ding" Darling Wildlife Society in Caloosahatchee NWR.

Under a Minor Expansion Proposal (MEP), Caloosahatchee NWR would be expanded to include Manatee Island, which was donated by Florida Power and Light Company (FPL) to the "Ding" Darling Wildlife Society in 2001 because FPL and other interested parties desired that it be managed by the Service. It was anticipated that Manatee Island would be added to the acquisition boundary as part of the major expansion proposal in 2002, but the major expansion never received final approval.

Wildlife and Habitat Management Objectives: 1.a(1), 1.b(1), 1.i(1), 1.j(1), 1.l(1), 2.a(1)-(2), 2.b(1), 2.c(1), 2.d(3), 2.e(2), 3.a(1)-(2), 3.b(1)-(2), 4.a(1)-(2), and 5.a(1)
Resource Protection Objectives: 2.a(1), 2.a(5), 2.b(1), and 2.c(1)
Refuge Administration Objectives: 1.a(1)-(2), 1.b(1), 2.a(1), and 2.b(1)

Project 12. Pursue the designation of lands and waters within the current management boundaries of Pine Island and Matlacha Pass NWRs for inclusion in the Western Hemisphere Shorebird Reserve Network.

Two of the refuges (Pine Island and Matlacha Pass) appear to meet the criteria for designation as part of the Western Hemisphere Shorebird Reserve Network. The refuges would investigate the criteria used to qualify for inclusion in the Western Hemisphere Shorebird Reserve Network and, if warranted, resubmit stronger applications to receive these designations.

Wildlife and Habitat Management Objectives: 1.c(1)-(3), 1.d(1)-(3), 1.e(1)-(2), 1.f(1)-(2), 2.d(1)-(4), 2.e(2)-(4)
Resource Protection Objectives: 2.b(1) and 2.c(1)
Visitor Services Objectives: 3.a(1), 3.a(3), 4.a(1)-(2), and 4.b(1)
Refuge Administration Objectives: 1.a(1)-(2), 1.b(1), 2.a(1), and 2.b(1)

Project 13. Pursue the designation of all five refuges in the Complex as RAMSAR Wetlands of International Importance, as part of the application for J.N. "Ding" Darling NWR.

The refuges would apply for consideration as RAMSAR Wetlands of International Importance, as part of the potential J.N. "Ding" Darling NWR proposal, where all five refuges would be included in a single proposal and designation.

Wildlife and Habitat Management Objectives: 1.a(1), 1.b(1), 1.c(1)-(3), 1.d(1)-(3), 1.e(1)-(2), 1.f(1)-(2), 1.(g), 1.h(1), 1.i(1)-(2), 1.j(1), 1.k(1), 1.l(1)-(2), 2.a(1)-(2), 2.b(1), 2.c(1)-(2), 2.d(1)-(4), 2.e(2)-(4), 4.a(1)-(2)
Resource Protection Objectives: 2.b(1) and 2.c(1)
Visitor Services Objectives: 3.a(1), 3.a(3), 4.a(1)-(2), and 4.b(1)
Refuge Administration Objectives: 1.a(1)-(2), 1.b(1), 2.a(1), and 2.b(1)

Project 14. Expand refuge management activities in relation to Island Bay NWR Wilderness Area.

Work with the partners to provide information regarding the J.N. "Ding" Darling NWR and Island Bay NWR wilderness areas, wilderness stewardship, and wilderness principles to area visitors and in environmental education and interpretation programs and materials and depict wilderness areas on refuge maps. Provide information about the two wilderness areas, wilderness stewardship, and wilderness principles to visitors at the "Ding" Darling Education Center and in environmental education and interpretation programs and materials. Update Refuge Complex materials (e.g., maps, brochures, and Internet) to include the two wilderness areas. Coordinate with the concessionaire to include wilderness information in its programs. Evaluate methods to improve the wilderness experience.

Resource Protection Objectives: 3.a(1)-(2)
Visitor Services Objectives: 3.a(1), 3.a(3), 4.a(1)-(2)
Refuge Administration Objectives: 1.a(1)-(2), and 2.b(1)

Project 15. Coordinate with the Charlotte County Environmental and Extension Services Department, Pest Management Division, to ensure that no spraying of pesticides occurs within the Island Bay NWR Wilderness Area during mosquito control activities.

Under the Wilderness Act, wilderness areas are to be managed with a least tool approach to ensure that the hand of man is not evident. This helps to protect and sustain the wilderness experience for current and future generations. However, the Refuge Complex would work with the partners to minimize the impacts to the Island Bay NWR Wilderness Area from mosquito control activities. The Refuge Complex regularly coordinates with the Lee County Mosquito Control District. This coordination effort needs to be expanded to include the Charlotte County Environmental and Extension Services Department, Pest Management Division to help minimize impacts on refuge resources from mosquito control activities, especially to the Island Bay NWR Wilderness Area.

Wildlife and Habitat Management Objectives: 1.a(1), 1.b(1), 1.c(2), 1.d(2)-(3), 1.e(2), 1.h(1), 1.l(1), 2.a(1), 2.b(1), 2.c(1), 2.d(1), 2.e(2), 2.e(4), 4.a(1)-(2)
Resource Protection Objectives: 3.a(2)
Refuge Administration Objectives: 1.a(1)-(2), 2.a(1), and 2.b(1)

Project 16. Protect refuge resources and area visitors.

An additional Law Enforcement Officer would help protect refuge resources and area visitors, helping improve safety. Regular law enforcement patrols would deter wildlife take, vandalism, trespass, and other illegal activities, also providing increased response to violations, complaints, and incidents when they occur.

Wildlife and Habitat Management Objectives: 1.c(2), 1.e(2), 1.f(1), 1.g(1), 1.i(1), 2.a(2), 2.d(3), and 2.d(4)
Resource Protection Objectives: 1.a(1), 2.a(1)-(4), and 2.b(1)
Visitor Services Objective: 2.a(1)
Refuge Administration Objectives: 1.a(1)-(2), 1.b(1), 2.a(1), and 3.a(1)

VISITOR SERVICES

Project 17. Update the exhibits at the "Ding" Darling Education Center at the J.N. "Ding" Darling NWR to highlight these four refuges and their role in the landscape.

These four refuges are closed to visitors. However, they exist within a larger estuarine ecosystem that does receive a lot of use and the refuges are experienced in a visual way from adjacent waters. The refuges would continue to work with the partners to update maps and information provided at area boat ramps and on partner web sites to identify the locations and extents of the refuges and their closed area statuses. And, the refuges would work with the Randell Research Center on Pine Island to provide information on Pine Island and Matlacha Pass NWRs.

Wildlife and Habitat Management Objectives: 1.a(1), 1.b(1), 1.c(2)-(3), 1.d(2)-(3), 1.e(2), 1.f(1), 1.g(1), 1.h(1), 1.i(2), 1.j(1), 1.k(1), 1.l(1), 2.a(1)-(2), 2.b(1), 2.c(1)-(2), 2.d(1), 2.d(3)-(4), 2.e(2)-(4), 3.a(1), 3.a(2), 3.b(1)-(2), 4.a(1)-(2), and 5.a(1)
Resource Protection Objectives: 2.c(1) and 3.a(1)
Visitor Services Objectives: 1.a(1)-(2), 2.a(1), 3.a(1), 3.a(3), and 4.b(1)
Refuge Administration Objectives: 1.a(1)-(2), 2.a(1), 2.b(1), and 3.a(1)

Project 18. Enhance the refuge's environmental education and interpretation programs and materials and work with the partners to better incorporate migratory bird messages into their environmental education and interpretation programs and materials.

Work with the partners to better incorporate migratory bird messages into their environmental education and interpretation programs and materials. Expand the environmental education and interpretation program at J.N. "Ding" Darling NWR to more fully incorporate messages focused on the roles and importance of the refuges in the landscape and the minimization of wildlife and habitat impacts from human activities.

Wildlife and Habitat Management Objectives: 1.a(1), 1.b(1), 1.c(2)-(3), 1.d(2)-(3), 1.e(2), 1.f(1), 1.g(1), 1.h(1), 1.i(2), 1.j(1), 1.k(1), 1.l(1), 2.a(1)-(2), 2.b(1), 2.c(1)-(2), 2.d(1), 2.d(3)-(4), 2.e(2)-(4), 3.a(1)-(2), 3.b(1)-(2), 4.a(1)-(2), and 5.a(1)
Resource Protection Objectives: 1.a(1), 2.b(1), 2.c(1) and 3.a(1)
Visitor Services Objectives: 1.a(1)-(2), 2.a(1), 3.a(1)-(6), and 4.b(1)
Refuge Administration Objectives: 1.a(1)-(2), 2.a(1), 2.b(1), and 3.a(1)

Project 19. Work with the partners to develop an annual event to be held in a local community near the refuges with messages focused on the role and importance of the refuges in the landscape and the minimization of wildlife and habitat impacts from human activities.

The Refuge Complex recognizes that the refuges have limited visibility and a less than positive image amongst some residents in the local area. An annual event in the local area would help increase visibility and image of the refuges and the Service. Working with the local communities is the key to future management of these resources.

Wildlife and Habitat Management Objectives: 1.c(2), 1.e(2), 1.f(1), 1.g(1), 1.i(1)-(2), 2.a(2), 2.d(3)-(4), 2.f(1), 3.a(1)-(2), 3.b(1)-(2), 4.a(1)-(2), and 5.a(1)
Resource Protection Objectives: 2.c(1) and 3.a(1)
Visitor Services Objectives: 1.a(1), 2.a(1), 3.a(4), 3.a(6), 4.a(1), and 4.b(1)
Refuge Administration Objectives: 1.a(1)-(2), 2.a(1), 2.b(1), and 3.a(1)

Project 20. Communicate key messages and issues with off-site audiences to build support within the local communities and beyond for Pine Island, Matlacha Pass, Island Bay, and Caloosahatchee NWRs; their purposes; and their management.

Increase the outreach efforts and activities of the Refuge Complex staff, especially to the local communities with messages focused on the role and importance of the refuges in the landscape and the minimization of wildlife and habitat impacts from human activities. Increase participation in festivals and events held by the partners (e.g., Mango Mania, Calusa Blueway Paddling Festival, and Charlotte Harbor Nature Festival) to help increase outreach to the local communities. Develop a general brochure for each refuge with an accompanying map. Work with the partners to provide information to the fishing public utilizing the waters adjacent to the refuges regarding the impacts of fishing activities on migratory birds; to evaluate the need to expand the existing monofilament recycling program; and to conduct cleanup events targeting abandoned monofilament fishing line, cast nets, and crab traps.

Wildlife and Habitat Management Objectives: 1.a(1), 1.b(1), 1.c(2), 1.e(2), 1.f(1), 1.g(1), 1.i(1)-(2), 1.j(1), 1.k(1), 2.a(2), 2.d(3)-(4), 2.f(1), 3.a(1)-(2), 3.b(1)-(2), 4.a(1)-(2), and 5.a(1)
Resource Protection Objectives: 1.a(1), 2.c(1) and 3.a(1)
Visitor Services Objectives: 1.a(1), 2.a(1), 3.a(4), 3.a(6), 4.a(1), and 4.b(1)
Refuge Administration Objectives: 1.a(1)-(2), 2.a(1), 2.b(1), and 3.a(1)

Project 21. Work with the partners to evaluate the need to expand the monofilament fishing line recycling program and to conduct cleanup events targeting abandoned monofilament fishing line, cast nets, and crab traps.

Although fishing activities occur off the refuges, they do occur directly adjacent to them and they can have impacts (e.g., disturbance of shorebirds and impacts of abandoned monofilament fishing line, cast nets, and crab traps). To help increase outreach activities specific to fishing, Refuge Complex staff would coordinate with the local communities and recruit volunteers to participate in abandoned monofilament, cast net, and crab trap cleanup events as needed to prevent entanglement of birds, manatees, sea turtles, and terrapins.

Wildlife and Habitat Management Objectives: 1.c(2), 1.e(2), 1.i(1)-(2), 1.j(1), 1.k(1), and 2.e(2)
Resource Protection Objective: 2.c(1)
Visitor Services Objectives: 2.a(1), 4.a(1), 4.b(1)-(3)
Refuge Administration Objectives: 1.a(1)-(2), 2.a(1), 2.b(1), and 3.a(1)

FUNDING AND PERSONNEL

Implementation of this CCP would require increased funding and personnel support from a variety of internal and external sources. New refuge projects are identified in the Refuge Operating and Needs System (RONS), while maintenance needs for existing facilities and projects are identified through Service Asset and Maintenance Management System (SAMMS). This plan outlines proposed projects that are substantially above current budget allocations. Once the final plan is approved, the refuges would update their RONS and SAMMS lists to account for the proposed management actions and outlined projects. The plan does not constitute a commitment (from Congress) for staffing increases, operational and maintenance increases, or funding for future land acquisition, but provides direction for future management, provides a basis for priorities, and represents wildlife resource needs based on sound biological science and input from the public.

To achieve the goals, objectives, and strategies and to complete the projects outlined in the CCP, additional personnel, operations, maintenance, facilities, and funds would be needed. These four refuges are currently managed by staff of the J.N. "Ding" Darling NWR. To support implementation of the CCP and to better serve the purposes for which the refuges were established, staff positions would be needed specific to the refuges. With an estimated annual recurring cost of $443,368 (including a 25 percent operating margin), five positions are proposed to specifically serve these four refuges:

- Biological Science Technician – with a focus on Island Bay NWR;
- Law Enforcement Officer – with a focus on Matlacha Pass NWR;
- Wildlife Refuge Specialist (Assistant Refuge Manager) – with a focus on Pine Island NWR;
- Hydrologist – with a focus on Caloosahatchee NWR; and
- Park Ranger (environmental education) – with a focus on Pine Island NWR.

The current budget for the salaries, benefits, and fixed costs for the 17.5 FTEs (not including the two Southeast Region Invasive Species Strike Team FTEs, but including the recreation fee, term appointment, and fire position) is $1,702,300. With the 25 percent operating margin, this total would be $2,065,000. The four refuges would add five staff (and five staff would be added for J.N. "Ding" Darling NWR) for a new Refuge Complex total of 27.5 FTEs (plus the two Southeast Region Invasive Species Strike Team FTEs for the refuges) (Figure 23): Biological Science Technician, Law Enforcement Officer, Wildlife Refuge Specialist, Hydrologist, and a Park Ranger (environmental education). The estimated annual recurring cost for these additional five positions, with the 25 percent operating margin, is $443,368. This increase in staff would also necessitate an increase in base funding above standard yearly increases that allow only for inflation.

PARTNERSHIP OPPORTUNITIES

Pine Island, Matlacha Pass, Island Bay, and Caloosahatchee NWRs function with the J.N. "Ding" Darling NWR as a partnership where a variety of partners help further the purposes, vision, goals, and objectives of the refuges through wildlife and habitat management activities, outreach, environmental education, cultural resource protection, law enforcement, and coordination. The Service will continue to work with existing and new partners including public, nonprofit, research-oriented, and private. The refuges would increase and improve coordination with new governmental partners, including the local communities; Charlotte County Environmental and Extension Services Department, Pest Management Division; and the city of Cape Coral.

STEP-DOWN MANAGEMENT PLANS

The refuges have several existing step-down plans, as follows:

- Oil Spill Response Plan (2010)
- Wildlife Inventory Plan (2001)
- Fire Management Plan (2001)
- Mosquito Control Operations Plan (2001)
- Exotic Plant Control Plan (1990)

To help serve the CCP's goals and objectives and to provide the details necessary for implementation of many of the proposed actions, the Service would prepare several additional step-down management plans. The needed step-down management plans and their anticipated completion dates are listed in Table 17.

Table 17. Step-down management plans to be developed during the 15-year life of the CCP.

Step-down Management Plan	Anticipated Completion Date
Refuge Complex Wildlife and Habitat Management Plan	2010
Refuge Complex Visitor Services Plan	2011
Refuge Complex Cultural Resources Management Plan	2013

MONITORING AND ADAPTIVE MANAGEMENT

Monitoring the Service's performance, while implementing this CCP, is critical to successful implementation of this CCP. Monitoring and evaluation allow the Service, other government agencies, the public, and the partners to measure and evaluate progress. Following approval of the final CCP and public notification of the decision, the Service would begin implementing the management actions identified in the CCP. The Service would monitor, evaluate, and determine whether or not progress is being made towards achieving the refuge's purposes, vision, and goals. Monitoring would address habitat or population objectives and the effects of management activities. Through adaptive management and evaluation of monitoring and research, results may indicate the need to modify objectives and/or strategies for the refuges.

PLAN REVIEW AND REVISION

The Service will review the final CCP annually to decide if it requires any revisions. The CCP will be modified along with associated management activities whenever this review or other monitoring and evaluation determine that changes are needed to achieve the purposes of the refuges, vision, and goals. The Service will revise the final CCP when significant new information becomes available, ecological conditions change, major refuge expansion occurs, or when the Service identifies the need to do so during CCP review. At a minimum, a CCP revision will occur every 15 years. All CCP revisions will follow the procedures outlined in current policy and will require compliance with the National Environmental Policy Act. The Service will conduct ongoing public involvement and continue informing and involving the public regarding management of the refuges.

APPENDICES

Appendix A. Glossary

Adaptive Management: Refers to a process in which policy decisions are implemented within a framework of scientifically driven experiments to test predictions and assumptions inherent in a management plan. Analysis of results helps managers determine whether current management should continue as is or whether it should be modified to achieve desired conditions.

Alluvial: Sediment transported and deposited in a delta or riverbed by flowing water.

Alternative: 1. A reasonable way to fix the identified problem or satisfy the stated need (40 CFR 1500.2). 2. Alternatives are different sets of objectives and strategies or means of achieving refuge purposes and goals, helping fulfill the Refuge System mission, and resolving issues (Service Manual 602 FW 1.6B).

Anadromous: Migratory fishes that spend most of their lives in the sea and migrate to fresh water to breed.

Biological Diversity: The variety of life and its processes, including the variety of living organisms, the genetic differences among them, and the communities and ecosystems in which they occur (Service Manual 052 FW 1. 12B). The System's focus is on indigenous species, biotic communities, and ecological processes. Also referred to as biodiversity.

Carrying Capacity: The maximum population of a species able to be supported by a habitat or area.

Categorical Exclusion: A category of actions that does not individually or cumulatively have a significant effect on the human environment and have been found to have no such effect in procedures adopted by a federal agency pursuant to the National Environmental Policy Act (40 CFR 1508.4).

CFR: Code of Federal Regulations.

Compatible Use: A proposed or existing wildlife-dependent recreational use or any other use of a national wildlife refuge that, based on sound professional judgment, will not materially interfere with or detract from the fulfillment of the National Wildlife Refuge System mission or the purpose(s) of the national wildlife refuge [50 CFR 25.12 (a)]. A compatibility determination supports the selection of compatible uses and identifies stipulations or limits necessary to ensure compatibility.

Comprehensive Conservation Plan:	A document that describes the desired future conditions of a refuge or planning unit and provides long-range guidance and management direction to achieve the purposes of the refuge; helps fulfill the mission of the Refuge System; maintains and, where appropriate, restores the ecological integrity of each refuge and the Refuge System; helps achieve the goals of the National Wilderness Preservation System; and meets other mandates (Service Manual 602 FW 1.6 E).
Concern:	See Issue
Cover Type:	The present vegetation of an area.
Cultural Resource Inventory:	A professionally conducted study designed to locate and evaluate evidence of cultural resources present within a defined geographic area. Inventories may involve various levels, including background literature search, comprehensive field examination to identify all exposed physical manifestations of cultural resources, or sample inventory to project site distribution and density over a larger area. Evaluation of identified cultural resources to determine eligibility for the National Register follows the criteria found in 36 CFR 60.4 (Service Manual 614 FW 1.7).
Cultural Resource Overview:	A comprehensive document prepared for a field office that discusses, among other things, its prehistory and cultural history, the nature and extent of known cultural resources, previous research, management objectives, resource management conflicts or issues, and a general statement on how program objectives should be met and conflicts resolved. An overview should reference or incorporate information from a field office's background or literature search described in Section VIII of the Cultural Resource Management Handbook (Service Manual 614 FW 1.7).
Cultural Resources:	The remains of sites, structures, or objects used by people in the past.
Designated Wilderness Area:	An area designated by the U.S. Congress to be managed as part of the National Wilderness Preservation System (Draft Service Manual 610 FW 1.5).
Disturbance:	Significant alteration of habitat structure or composition. May be natural (e.g., fire) or human-caused events (e.g., aircraft overflight).
Ecosystem:	A dynamic and interrelating complex of plant and animal communities and their associated nonliving environment.
Ecosystem Management:	Management of natural resources using system-wide concepts to ensure that all plants and animals in ecosystems are maintained at viable levels in native habitats and basic ecosystem processes are perpetuated indefinitely.

Endangered Species (Federal):	A plant or animal species listed under the Endangered Species Act that is in danger of extinction throughout all or a significant portion of its range.
Endangered Species (State):	A plant or animal species in danger of becoming extinct or extirpated in the state within the near future if factors contributing to its decline continue. Populations of these species are at critically low levels or their habitats have been degraded or depleted to a significant degree.
Environmental Assessment (EA):	A concise public document, prepared in compliance with the National Environmental Policy Act, that briefly discusses the purpose and need for an action, alternatives to such action, and provides sufficient evidence and analysis of impacts to determine whether to prepare an environmental impact statement or finding of no significant impact (40 CFR 1508.9).
Environmental Impact Statement (EIS):	A detailed written statement required by section 102(2)(C) of the National Environmental Policy Act, analyzing the environmental impacts of a proposed action, adverse effects of the project that cannot be avoided, alternative courses of action, short-term uses of the environment versus the maintenance and enhancement of long-term productivity, and any irreversible and irretrievable commitment of resources (40 CFR 1508.11).
Estuary:	The wide lower course of a river into which the tides flow. The area where the tide meets a river current.
Extirpation:	When a species can no longer survive in regions that were once part of its range.
Finding of No Significant Impact (FONSI):	A document prepared in compliance with the National Environmental Policy Act, supported by an environmental assessment, that briefly presents why a federal action will have no significant effect on the human environment and for which an environmental impact statement, therefore, will not be prepared (40 CFR 1508.13).
Goal:	Descriptive, open-ended, and often broad statement of desired future conditions that conveys a purpose but does not define measurable units (Service Manual 620 FW 1.6J).
Habitat:	Suite of existing environmental conditions required by an organism for survival and reproduction. The place where an organism typically lives.
Habitat Restoration:	Management emphasis designed to move ecosystems to desired conditions and processes, and/or to healthy ecosystems.
Habitat Type:	See Vegetation Type.

Hypoxia:	Hypoxia, or low oxygen, occurs when the levels of oxygen dissolved in water fall below levels necessary to support ocean and coastal life, and can lead to what is called a dead zone. Hypoxic waters have dissolved oxygen concentrations of less than two to three parts per million.
Improvement Act:	The National Wildlife Refuge System Improvement Act of 1997.
Informed Consent:	The grudging willingness of opponents to "go along" with a course of action that they actually oppose.
Issue:	Any unsettled matter that requires a management decision [e.g., an initiative, opportunity, resource management problem, threat to the resources of the unit, conflict in uses, public concern, or other presence of an undesirable resource condition (Service Manual 602 FW 1.6K)].
Management Alternative:	See Alternative
Management Concern:	See Issue
Management Opportunity:	See Issue
Migration:	The seasonal movement from one area to another and back.
Mission Statement:	Succinct statement of the unit's purpose and reason for being.
Monitoring:	The process of collecting information to track changes of selected parameters over time.
National Environmental Policy Act of 1969 (NEPA):	Requires all agencies, including the Service, to examine the environmental impacts of their actions, incorporate environmental information, and use public participation in the planning and implementation of all actions. Federal agencies must integrate NEPA with other planning requirements, and prepare appropriate NEPA documents to facilitate better environmental decision-making (40 CFR 1500).
National Wildlife Refuge System Improvement Act of 1997 (Public Law 105-57):	Under the Refuge Improvement Act, the Fish and Wildlife Service is required to develop 15-year comprehensive conservation plans for all national wildlife refuges outside Alaska. The Act also describes the six public uses given priority status within the Refuge System (i.e., hunting, fishing, wildlife observation, wildlife photography, and environmental education and interpretation).

National Wildlife Refuge System Mission: The mission is to administer a national network of lands and waters for the conservation, management, and where appropriate, restoration of the fish, wildlife, and plant resources and their habitats within the United States for the benefit of present and future generations of Americans.

National Wildlife Refuge System: Various categories of areas administered by the Secretary of the Interior for the conservation of fish and wildlife, including species threatened with extinction; all lands, waters, and interests therein administered by the Secretary as wildlife refuges; areas for the protection and conservation of fish and wildlife that are threatened with extinction; wildlife ranges; game ranges; wildlife management areas; or waterfowl production areas.

National Wildlife Refuge: A designated area of land, water, or an interest in land or water within the Refuge System.

Native Species: Species that normally live and thrive in a particular ecosystem.

Noxious Weed: A plant species designated by federal or state law as generally possessing one or more of the following characteristics: aggressive or difficult to manage; parasitic; a carrier or host of serious insect or disease; or nonnative, new, or not common to the United States. According to the Federal Noxious Weed Act (P.L. 93-639), a noxious weed is one that causes disease or had adverse effects on man or his environment and therefore is detrimental to the agriculture and commerce of the United States and to the public health.

Objective: A concise statement of what we want to achieve, how much we want to achieve, when and where we want to achieve it, and who is responsible for the work. Objectives derive from goals and provide the basis for determining strategies, monitoring refuge accomplishments, and evaluating the success of strategies. Making objectives attainable, time-specific, and measurable (Service Manual 602 FW 1.6N).

Plant Association: A classification of plant communities based on the similarity in dominants of all layers of vascular species in a climax community.

Plant Community: An assemblage of plant species unique in its composition; occurs in particular locations under particular influences; a reflection or integration of the environmental influences on the site such as soils, temperature, elevation, solar radiation, slope, aspect, and rainfall; denotes a general kind of climax plant community.

Preferred Alternative: This is the alternative determined (by the decision-maker) to best achieve the refuge purpose, vision, and goals; contributes to the Refuge System mission, addresses the significant issues; and is consistent with principles of sound fish and wildlife management.

Prescribed Fire:	The application of fire to wildland fuels to achieve identified land use objectives (Service Manual 621 FW 1.7). May occur from natural ignition or intentional ignition.
Priority Species:	Fish and wildlife species that require protective measures and/or management guidelines to ensure their perpetuation. Priority species include the following: (1) State-listed and candidate species; (2) species or groups of animals susceptible to significant population declines within a specific area or statewide by virtue of their inclination to aggregate (e.g., seabird colonies); and (3) species of recreation, commercial, and/or tribal importance.
Public Involvement Plan:	Broad long-term guidance for involving the public in the comprehensive conservation planning process.
Public Involvement:	A process that offers impacted and interested individuals and organizations an opportunity to become informed about, and to express their opinions on Service actions and policies. In the process, these views are studied thoroughly and thoughtful consideration of public views is given in shaping decisions for refuge management.
Public:	Individuals, organizations, and groups; officials of federal, state, and local government agencies; Indian tribes; and foreign nations. It may include anyone outside the core planning team. It includes those who may or may not have indicated an interest in service issues and those who do or do not realize that Service decisions may affect them.
Purposes of the Refuge:	"The purposes specified in or derived from the law, proclamation, executive order, agreement, public land order, donation document, or administrative memorandum establishing, authorizing, or expanding a refuge, refuge unit, or refuge sub-unit." For refuges that encompass congressionally designated wilderness, the purposes of the Wilderness Act are additional purposes of the refuge (Service Manual 602 FW 106 S).
Recommended Wilderness:	Areas studied and found suitable for wilderness designation by both the Director of the Fish and Wildlife Service and the Secretary of the Department of the Interior, and recommended for designation by the President to Congress. These areas await only legislative action by Congress in order to become part of the Wilderness System. Such areas are also referred to as "pending in Congress" (Draft Service Manual 610 FW 1.5).

Record of Decision (ROD):	A concise public record of decision prepared by the federal agency, pursuant to NEPA, that contains a statement of the decision, identification of all alternatives considered, identification of the environmentally preferable alternative, a statement as to whether all practical means to avoid or minimize environmental harm from the alternative selected have been adopted (and if not, why they were not), and a summary of monitoring and enforcement where applicable for any mitigation (40 CFR 1505.2).
Refuge Goal:	See Goal
Refuge Purposes:	See Purposes of the Refuge
Songbirds: (Also Passerines)	A category of birds that is medium to small, perching landbirds. Most are territorial singers and migratory.
Step-down Management Plan:	A plan that provides specific guidance on management subjects (e.g., habitat, public use, fire, and safety) or groups of related subjects. It describes strategies and implementation schedules for meeting CCP goals and objectives (Service Manual 602 FW 1.6 U).
Strategy:	A specific action, tool, technique, or combination of actions, tools, and techniques used to meet unit objectives (Service Manual 602 FW 1.6 U).
Study Area:	The area reviewed in detail for wildlife, habitat, and public use potential. For purposes of this CCP, the study area includes the lands within the currently approved refuge boundary and potential refuge expansion areas.
Threatened Species (Federal):	Species listed under the Endangered Species Act that are likely to become endangered within the foreseeable future throughout all or a significant portion of their range.
Threatened Species (State):	A plant or animal species likely to become endangered in the state within the near future if factors contributing to population decline or habitat degradation or loss continue.
Tiering:	The coverage of general matters in broader environmental impact statements with subsequent narrower statements of environmental analysis, incorporating by reference, the general discussions and concentrating on specific issues (40 CFR 1508.28).
U.S. Fish and Wildlife Service Mission:	The mission of the U.S. Fish and Wildlife Service is working with others to conserve, protect, and enhance fish and wildlife and their habitats for the continuing benefit of the American people.
Unit Objective:	See Objective

Vegetation Type, Habitat Type, Forest Cover Type: A land classification system based upon the concept of distinct plant associations.

Vision Statement: A concise statement of what the planning unit should be, or what we hope to do, based primarily upon the Refuge System mission and specific refuge purposes, and other mandates. We will tie the vision statement for the refuge to the mission of the Refuge System; the purpose(s) of the refuge; the maintenance or restoration of the ecological integrity of each refuge and the Refuge System; and other mandates (Service Manual 602 FW 1.6 Z).

Wilderness Study Areas: Lands and waters identified through inventory as meeting the definition of wilderness and undergoing evaluation for recommendation for inclusion in the Wilderness System. A study area must meet the following criteria:

- Generally appears to have been affected primarily by the forces of nature, with the imprint of man's work substantially unnoticeable;
- Has outstanding opportunities for solitude or a primitive and unconfined type of recreation; and
- Has at least 5,000 contiguous roadless acres or is sufficient in size as to make practicable its preservation and use in an unimpaired condition (Draft Service Manual 610 FW 1.5).

Wilderness: See Designated Wilderness

Wildfire: A free-burning fire requiring a suppression response; all fire other than prescribed fire that occurs on wildlands (Service Manual 621 FW 1.7).

Wildland Fire: Every wildland fire is either a wildfire or a prescribed fire (Service Manual 621 FW 1.3

ACRONYMS AND ABBREVIATIONS

°C	degrees Celsuis
°F	degrees Fahrenheit
AQI	Air Quality Index
BCR	Bird Conservation Region
BEBR	Bureau of Economic and Business Research (at the University of Florida)
BLM	Bureau of Land Management
BMP	Best Management Practice
CBRA	Coastal Barrier Resources Act
CBRS	Coastal Barrier Resources System
CCMCD	Charlotte County Mosquito Control District
CCMP	Comprehensive Conservation and Management Plan
CCP	Comprehensive Conservation Plan
CD	compact disk
CERP	Comprehensive Everglades Restoration Plan
CFR	Code of Federal Regulations
cfs	cubic feet per second
CHNEP	Charlotte Harbor National Estuary Program
CISMA	Cooperative Invasive Species Management Area
CO	carbon monoxide
CWA	Clean Water Act
CZMA	Coastal Zone Management Act
DBH	diameter at breast height
DDD	dichlorodiphenyldichloroethane
DDE	dichlorodiphenyldichloroethylene
DDT	dichlorodiphenyltrichloroethane
DM	Department Manual
DOI	Department of the Interior
EA	Environmental Assessment
EIS	Environmental Impact Statement
EO	Executive Order
EPA	U.S. Environmental Protection Agency
FAA	Federal Aviation Administration
FAC	Florida Administrative Code
FAS	Floridan Aquifer System
FBCI	Florida Bird Conservation Initiative
FCWCS	Florida's Comprehensive Wildlife Conservation Strategy
FDEP	Florida Department of Environmental Protection
FLEPPC	Florida Exotic Pest Plant Council
FNAI	Florida Natural Areas Inventory
FONSI	Finding of No Significant Impact
FPL	Florida Power and Light
FTE	full-time employee
FW	Fish and Wildlife Service Manual
FWC	Florida Fish and Wildlife Conservation Commission
FWS	U.S. Fish and Wildlife Service (also USFWS or Service)
FY	Fiscal Year
GEMS	Gulf Ecological Management Site
GIS	Geographic Information System
GMP	Gulf of Mexico Program

ha	hectares
I-75	Interstate 75
IBA	Important Bird Area
IFAS	Institute of Food and Agricultural Sciences (at the University of Florida)
IPCC	International Panel on Climate Change
IPMP	Integrated Pest Management Plan
LCC	Landscape Conservation Cooperative
LCH	Lower Charlotte Harbor
LCMCD	Lee County Mosquito Control District
LiDAR	Light Detecting and Ranging
LPP	Land Protection Plan
m	meters
mph	mile per hour
Max	Maximum
MEP	Minor Expansion Proposal
Min	Minimum
MIT	Massachusetts Institute of Technology
MLRA	Major Land Resource Area
MPA	Marine Protected Area
MSA	Metropolitan Statistical Area
NAAQS	National Ambient Air Quality Standards
NABCI	North American Bird Conservation Initiative
NAMS	National Ambient Monitoring Stations
NASA	National Aeronautics and Space Administration
NAWCP	North American Waterbird Conservation Plan
NAWMP	North American Waterfowl Management Plan
NEP	National Estuary Program
NEPA	National Environmental Policy Act
NMFS	National Marine Fisheries Service
NOAA	National Oceanic and Atmospheric Administration
NO_x	nitrogen oxides
NWPCP	National Wetlands Priority Conservation Plan
NWR	National Wildlife Refuge (also Refuge)
NWRS	National Wildlife Refuge System (also NWRS or Refuge System)
OCRM	Ocean and Coastal Resource Management
OFW	Outstanding Florida Water
ORV	Outstandingly Remarkable Value
PCB	polychlorinated biphenyls
PIF	Partners-in-Flight
PM	particulate matter
RA	Refuge Administration
RP	Resource Protection
RNA	Research Natural Area
ROD	Record of Decision
RONS	Refuge Operating Needs System
SAF	Southern American Foresters
SAMMS	Service Asset and Maintenance Management System
SAS	Surficial Aquifer System
SCCF	Sanibel-Captiva Conservation Foundation
SFWMD	South Florida Water Management District
SGCN	Species of Greatest Conservation Need

SLAMM	Sea Level Affecting Marshes Model
SLAMS	State and Local Ambient Monitoring Stations
SLOSH	Sea, Lake, and Overland Surges from Hurricanes
SO_2	sulfur dioxide
STAR	Summer Teachers Assisting Refuge
SWFFS	Southwest Florida Feasibility Study
SWFL	Southwest Florida
SWFRPC	Southwest Florida Regional Planning Council
SWFWMD	Southwest Florida Water Management District
SWIM	Surface Water Improvement and Management Program
TMDL	Total Maximum Daily Load
TWS	The Wildlife Society
U.S.	United States
UASCE	U.S. Army Corps of Engineers
USC	United States Code
USDA	U.S. Department of Agriculture
USFWS	U.S. Fish and Wildlife Service (also FWS or Service)
USGS	U.S. Geological Survey
VS	Visitor Services
WHM	Wildlife and Habitat Management

Appendix B. References and Literature Citations

AIRNow. 2009. "Air Quality Index (AQI) - A Guide to Air Quality and Your Health." April 24, 2009. U.S. Environmental Protection Agency, Office of Air Quality Planning and Standards. Research Triangle Park, NC. <http://www.airnow.gov/index.cfm?action=static.aqi>

Allen, Ginger M. and Martin Main. 2005. Florida's Geologic History. Fact Sheet WEC 189. Department of Wildlife Ecology and Conservation, Florida Cooperative Extension Service, Institute of Food and Agricultural Sciences, University of Florida. May 2005. Gainesville, FL. 3pp. <http://www.manatee.wateratlas.usf.edu/upload/documents/Florida_Geological_History.pdf>

Bailey, R. G. 1978. *Descriptions of the Ecoregions of the United States*. U.S. Department of Agriculture Forest Service, Misc. Publ. #1391. Washington, DC.

Beever III, James W., Whitney Gray, Daniel Trescott, Dan Cobb, Jason Utley, and Lisa B. Beever. 2009a. Comprehensive Southwest Florida/Charlotte Harbor Climate Change Vulnerability Assessment. September 15, 2009. Southwest Florida Regional Planning Council, Charlotte Harbor national Estuary Program, Technical Report 09-3. Fort Myers, FL. 296 pp. <http://www.swfrpc.org/content/ABM/Vulnerability_Assessment_Final.pdf> (Accessed July 16, 2010)

Beever III, James W., Whitney Gray, Daniel Trescott, Dan Cobb, Jason Utley, David Hutchinson, John Gibbons, Tim Walker, Moji Abimbola, Lisa B. Beeve, and Judy Utt. 2009b. City of Punta Gorda Adaptation Plan. November 18, 2009. Southwest Florida Regional Planning Council, Charlotte Harbor national Estuary Program, Technical Report 09-4. Fort Myers, FL. 409 pp. <http://www.swfrpc.org/content/ABM/Punta_Gorda_Adaptation_Plan.pdf> (Accessed July 19, 2010)

Bindoff, N.L., J. Willebrand, V. Artale, A, Cazenave, J. Gregory, S. Gulev, K. Hanawa, C. Le Quéré, S. Levitus, Y. Nojiri, C.K. Shum, L.D. Talley and A. Unnikrishnan. 2007: Observations: Oceanic Climate Change and Sea Level. In: Climate Change 2007: The Physical Science Basis. Contribution of Working Group I to the Fourth Assessment Report of the Intergovernmental Panel on Climate Change [Solomon, S., D. Qin, M. Manning, Z. Chen, M. Marquis, K.B. Averyt, M. Tignor and H.L. Miller (eds.)]. Cambridge University Press, Cambridge, United Kingdom and New York, NY, USA.

Boggess, D.H. and T.H. O'Donnell. 1982. Deep Artesian Aquifers of Sanibel and Captiva Islands, Lee County, Florida, USGS Open-file report 82-253. U.S. Geological Survey. Tallahassee FL. <http://sofia.usgs.gov/publications/ofr/82-253/ofr-82-253.pdf>

Browder, J., Alleman, R., Markley, S., Ortner, P. & Pitts, P. 2005. Biscayne Bay conceptual ecological model. Wetlands, 25,4: 854-869.

Bureau of Economic and Business Research. 1999. Florida Statistical Abstract. Janet Galvez, editor in chief; Susan Floyd, senior editor. University of Florida. University of Florida Press. Gainesville, FL.

Carver, Erin and James Caudill, Ph.D. 2007. Banking on Nature 2006: The Economica Benefits to Local Communities of National Wildlife Refuge Visitation. September 2007. Division of Economics. U.S. Fish and Wildlife Service. Washington, DC. 372 pp. <http://www.fws.gov/refuges/about/bankingonnature.html>

Caudill, J., and E. Henderson. 2005. *Banking on Nature 2004: The Economic Benefits to Local Communities of National Wildlife Visitation.* September 2005. U.S. Fish and Wildlife Service, Division of Economics. Washington, D.C.

Cervone, Sarah. 2003. Plant Management in Florida Waters: All you want to know about Florida's lakes, rivers, springs, marches, swamps, and canals. Center for Aquatic and Invasive Plants, Institute of Food and Agricultural Sciences, University of Florida, Gainesville, Fl, and Bureau of Invasive Plant Management, Florida Department of Environmental Protection, Tallahassee, FL. <http://aquat1.ifas.edu/guide/geology.html>

Chapman, F.M. "Autobiography of a Bird Lover." *Nature* 134, 719-720 (10 November 1934)

Chapman, F.M. "Autobiography of a Bird Lover." American Museum of Natural History, D. Appleton-Century Company, Inc., New York 1933.

City-Data.com. 2008. Charlotte County, Florida, Collier County, Florida, and Lee County, Florida. <http://www.city-data.com/county/Charlotte_County-FL.html>; <http://www.city-data.com/county/Collier_County-FL.html>; and <http://www.city-data.com/county/Lee_County-FL.html>

Charlotte County Visitor's Bureau. 2005. "Visitor's Bureau Releases Annual Report (2004 data)." November 29, 2005. Port Charlotte, FL. <http://www.charlotteharbortravel.com/press/original_releases/news68.htm>

Charlotte Harbor National Estuary Program. Undated. Charlotte Harbor National Estuary Plan. Program Overview. The Importance of Charlotte Harbor and its Tributaries. (Fact Sheet). <http://www.chnep.org/info/admin/NEP_overview.htm> (Accessed September 14, 2009)

Charlotte Harbor National Estuary Program. 2008. Committing to Our Future. A Comprehensive Conservation and Management Plan for the Greater Charlotte Harbor Watershed from Venice to Bonita Springs to Water Haven. Ft. Myers, FL. 170 pp.

Charlotte Harbor National Estuary Program and Southwest Florida Regional Planning Council. 2010. Charlotte Harbor Regional Climate Change Vulnerability Assessment. February 19, 2010. 59 pp. <http://www.chnep.org/projects/climate/VulnerabilityAssessment2-19-10.pdf> (Accessed July 19, 2010)

City of Sanibel. 2006a. "Impacts to the J.N. "Ding" Darling National Wildlife Refuge." Sanibel H_2O Matters Newsletter, Issue 2, March 2006. Sanibel, FL. <http://www.sanibelh2omatters.com/documents/Sanibel%20Newsletter%20Issue%202.pdf> (Accessed August 24, 2009).

City of Sanibel. 2006b. "Shellfish Epidemic Declared." Sanibel H_2O Matters Newsletter, Issue 3, August 2006. Sanibel, FL. <http://www.sanibelh2omatters.com/documents/Sanibel%20Newsletter%20Issue%203.pdf> (Accessed August 28, 2009).

City of Sanibel. 2007. Sanibel Water Quality Update. Sanibel H_2O Matters Newsletter, Issue 4, April 2007. Sanibel, FL. <http://www.sanibelh2omatters.com/documents/Sanibel%20Newsletter%20Issue%204.pdf> (Accessed August 28, 2009)

City of Sanibel. 2009a. Sanibel H_2O Matters, "Impacts of the 2004 & 2005 Hurricane Seasons". Sanibel, FL. <http://www.sanibelH2Omatters.com/crisis.cfm> (Accessed August 19 2009)

City of Sanibel. 2009b. Sanibel H_2O Matters, "Why Estuaries Are Important". Sanibel, FL. <http://www.sanibelH2Omatters.com/important.cfm> (Accessed August 19, 2009)

City of Sanibel. 2009c. Sanibel H_2O Matters, "What the City of Sanibel is already doing to protect Water Resources". Sanibel, FL. <http://www.sanibelH2Omatters.com/achievements.cfm> (Accessed August 28 2009)

City of Sanibel. 2009d. Sanibel H_2O Matters, "Maps". Sanibel, FL. <http://www.sanibelh20matters.com/maps.cfm> (Accessed August 28, 2009)

Clark, John. 1976. The Sanibel Report -- Formulation of a Comprehensive Plan Based on Natural Systems. The Conservation Foundation. Washington, D.C. <http://www.worldpolicy.newschool.edu/globalrights/environment/report/> and <https://www.sccf.org/content/122/SCCF-and-The-Sanibel-Report.aspx>

Clough, Jonathan S. 2008. Application of the Sea-Level Affecting Marshed Model (SLAMM 5.0) to Island Bay National Wildlife Refuge. Prepared for Dr. Brian Czech, Conservation Biology Program, Division of Natural Resources and Conservation Planning, U.S. Fish and Wildlife Service by Warrne Pinnacle Consulting, Inbc. Warren, VT. 26 pp.

Collier County Tourist Development Council. 2003. "Tourist Development Council" (2003 data). Naples, FL. <http://www.colliergov.net/Index.aspx?page=843>

Collins, M.E. 2009. "Key to Soil Orders in Florida." Document # SL-43. Soil and Water Science Department, Florida Cooperative Extension Service, Institute of Food and Agricultural Sciences, University of Florida. August 1985 (Reviewed March 2009). Gainesville, FL. <http://edis.ifas.ufl.edu/SS113>

Coppen, J. L. 2001. "J. N. "Ding" Darling National Wildlife Refuge Complex, Wildlife and Habitat Management Review (Biological Review)." May 3, 2001. U.S. Fish and Wildlife Service. Sanibel, FL.

Courtenay, W.R. 1994. Nonindigenous fishers in Florida. In *An Assessment of Invasive Nonindigenous Species in Florida's Public Lands.* D.C. Schmitz and T.C. Brown, eds. Technical Report TSS-94-100. Tallahassee, FL.: Florida Department of Environmental Protection, pp. 57-63.

Cox J., R. S. Kautz, M. MacLaughlin, and T. Gilbert. 1994. *Closing the Gaps in Florida's Wildlife Habitat Conservation System.* Florida Game and Freshwater Fish Commission, Office of Environmental Services. Tallahassee, FL.

"Ding" Darling Wildlife Society. 2009. "Sanibel Florida – Friends of the Refuge." Sanibel, FL. <http://dingdarlingsociety.org/>

Doyle, T.W. 1998. Modeling global change effects on coastal forests, in G.R. Guntenspergen and B.A. Vairin, eds., Vulnerability of coastal wetlands in the southeastern United States: Climate change research results, 1992-97: U.S. Geological Survey, Biological Resources Division Biological Science Report USGS/BRD/BSR-1998-0002, pp.105.

Drummond, M.A. 2008. Land Cover Trends, Southern Coastal Plain. U.S. Geological Survey. <http://landcovertrends.usgs.gov/east/eco75Report.html>

Dupree, A. Hunter. 1957. Science in the Federal Government: A History of Policies and Activities to 1940. Harvard University Press, Cambridge, Massachusetts. 460 pp.

Eaton, Chris, Erin McMichael, Blair Witherington, Allen Foley, Robert Hardy, and Anne Meylan. 2008. In-water Sea Turtle Monitoring and Research in Florida: Review and Recommendations. Technical Memorandum NMFS-OPR-38, June 2008. Florida Fish and Wildlife Conservation Commission for National Marine Fisheries Service, National Oceanic and Atmospheric Association, U.S. Department of Commerce. 233 pp.

Eisler, R. 1987. Mercury hazards to fish, wildlife, and invertebrates: Asynoptic review. Contaminant Hazard Reviews, report no. 10. Patuxent Wildlife Research Center, Laurel, Maryland, U.S. Fish Wildlife Service biological report 85: (1.10).

Emanuel, K. A. 1987. The dependence of hurricane intensity on climate. Nature, 326:483-485.

Emanuel, K. A. 2005. Increasing destructiveness of tropical cyclones over the past 30 years. Nature, 436; 686-688.

Erwin, R., Sanders, G. & Prosser, D. 2004. Changes in lagoonal marsh morphology at selected Northeastern Atlantic coast sites of significance to migratory waterbirds. Wetlands, 24,4: 891-903.

Fernald, E. A., and E. D. Purdum, eds. 1998. Water Resources Atlas of Florida. Florida State University, Tallahassee Institute of Science and Public Affairs.

Ferriter, Ann, Dan Thayer, Carole Goodyear, Bob Doren, Kan Langeland, and Jon Lane. 2005. Chapter 9: Invasive Exotic Species in the South Florida Environment Report. Volume I – The South Florida Environment- WY2004 – South Florida Water Management District. West Palm Beach, FL. 40 pp.

Field, J. et al. 2001. The potential consequences of climate variability and change on coastal areas and marine resources. U.S. National Assessment Synthesis Team, U.S. Global Change Research Program. Climate change impacts on the United States: The potential consequences of climate variability and change. <http://www.usgcrp.gov/usgcrp/Library/nationalassessment/foundation.htm> (Accessed 28 April 2006)

Florida Department of Agriculture and Consumer Services, Division of Aquaculture. 2004. "Shellfish Harvesting." Tallahassee, FL. <http://www.floridaaquaculture.com/SEAS/SEAS_intro.htm>

Florida Department of Environmental Protection. 2001. "Basin Status Report - Everglades West Coast – November 2001." Division of Water Resource Management, South District. <http://www.dep.state.fl.us/water/basin411/everwest/index.htm>

Florida Department of Environmental Protection. 2002a. "Basin Status Report - Charlotte Harbor – June 2002." Division of Water Resource Management, South District.
<http://www.dep.state.fl.us/water/basin411/charlotte/index.htm>

Florida Department of Environmental Protection. 2002b. "Basin Status Report-Charlotte Harbor (Pine Island Planning Unit)." Division of Water Resource Management, South District, Group 2 Basin. June 2002. <http://www.dep.state.fl.us/water/basin411/charlotte/p_units.htm>

Florida Department of Environmental Protection. 2002c. Gasparilla Island State Park Unit Management Plan. August 9, 2002. State of Florida, Department of Environmental Protection, Division of Recreation and Parks. Tallahassee, FL.
<http://www.dep.state.fl.us/parks/planning/plans/GasparillaIslandStatePark.pdf>

Florida Department of Environmental Protection. 2003. "Basin Status Report – Caloosahatchee – June 2003." Division of Water Resource Management, South District.
<http://www.dep.state.fl.us/water/basin411/caloosa/index.htm>

Florida Department of Environmental Protection. 2005a. Cayo Costa State Park Unit Management Plan. December 9, 2005. State of Florida, Department of Environmental Protection, Division of Recreation and Parks. Tallahassee, FL.
<http://www.dep.state.fl.us/parks/planning/plans/CayoCostaStatePark.pdf>

Florida Department of Environmental Protection. 2005b. "Water Quality Assessment Report - Charlotte Harbor." Division of Water Resource Management, South District.
<http://www.dep.state.fl.us/water/basin411/charlotte/index.htm>

Florida Department of Environmental Protection. 2006a. "Florida Air Monitoring Report, 2006." Division of Air Resource Management. Tallahassee, FL.
<http://www.dep.state.fl.us/air/air_quality/techrpt/amr06.pdf>

Florida Department of Environmental Protection. 2006b. "Florida Geological Survey - Geology Topics - Florida's Geologic History." January 4, 2006. Tallahassee, FL.
<http://www.dep.state.fl.us/geology/geologictopics/geohist.htm>

Florida Department of Environmental Protection. 2007. Charlotte Harbor Preserve State Park Unit Management Plan. June 15, 2007.. State of Florida, Department of Environmental Protection, Division of Recreation and Parks. Tallahassee, FL.
<http://www.dep.state.fl.us/parks/planning/plans/CharlotteHarborPreserveStatePark.pdf>

Florida Department of Environmental Protection. 2008. Florida's Gulf Ecological Management Sites (GEMS). Tallahassee, FL. <http://www.dep.state.fl.us/coastal/programs/gems.htm>

Florida Department of Environmental Protection. 2009a. Florida's Aquatic Preserves. Office of Coastal and Aquatic Managed Areas. Tallahassee, FL.
<http://www.dep.state.fl.us/coastal/programs/aquatic.htm>

Florida Department of Environmental Protection. 2009b. About the Charlotte Harbor Aquatic Preserves. Coastal and Aquatic Managed Areas. Tallahassee, FL.
<http://www.dep.state.fl.us/coastal/sites/charlotte/info.htm> (Accessed July 15, 2010)

Florida Department of Health, Division of Environmental Health. "2007 - Your Guide to Eating Fish Caught in Florida." Tallahassee, FL. <http://doh.state.fl.us/floridafishadvice/>

Florida Department of Natural Resources. 1983a. Charlotte Harbor Aquatic Preserves Management Plan: Cape Haze, Gasparilla Sound-Charlotte Harbor, Matlacha Pass and Pine Island Sound Aquatic Preserves. May 18, 1983. Florida Department of Natural Resources, Division of Recreation and Parks, Bureau of Environmental Land Management. Tallahassee, FL. <http://www.dep.state.fl.us/coastal/downloads/management_plans/aquatic/CharlotteHarbor.pdf>

Florida Department of Natural Resources. 1983b. Estero Bay Aquatic Preserve Management Plan. September 6, 1983. Florida Department of Natural Resources, Division of Recreation and Parks, Bureau of Environmental Land Management. Tallahassee, FL. <http://www.dep.state.fl.us/coastal/downloads/management_plans/aquatic/EsteroBay.pdf>

Florida Department of Natural Resources. 1992. Lemon Bay Aquatic Preserve Management Plan. April 17, 1992. Florida Department of Natural Resources, Division of State Lands, Bureau of Submerged Lands and Preserves. Tallahassee, FL. <http://www.dep.state.fl.us/coastal/downloads/management_plans/aquatic/LemonBay.pdf>

Florida Department of Transportation and University of South Florida. 2008. Trends and Conditions Report – 2008; Travel Demand: Visitors and Tourists. Office of Policy Planning of the Florida Department of Transportation and the Center for Urban Transportation Research at the University of South Florida. November 2008. 15 pp. <http://www.dot.state.fl.us/planning/trends/tc-report/Tourism112008.pdf>

Florida Exotic Pest Plant Council. 2007. List of Florida's Invasive Plant Species. Florida Exotic Pest Plant Council. <http://www.fleppc.org/list/07list.htm>

Florida Fish and Wildlife Conservation Commission. 2005. Florida's Wildlife Legacy Initiative. Florida's Comprehensive Wildlife Conservation Strategy. Tallahassee, FL. 472 pp. <http://myfwc.com/WILDLIFEHABITATS/Legacy_StrategyDownload.htm>

Florida Fish and Wildlife Conservation Commission. 2007. Boating Accidents: Statistical Report. Boating and Waterways Section. Division of Law Enforcement. Tallahassee, FL. 90 pp. < http://myfwc.com/law/boating/2007stats/Statbook.pdf. >

Florida Fish and Wildlife Conservation Commission. 2009a. Florida's Endangered Species, Threatened Species, and Species of Special Concern. Species Conservation Planning Section, Division of Habitat and Species Conservation, Florida Fish and Wildlife Conservation Commission. Tallahassee, FL. 6 pp. <http://www.myfwc.com/docs/WildlifeHabitats/Threatened_Endangered_Species.pdf>

Florida Fish and Wildlife Conservation Commission. 2009b. Roseate Spoonbill. Tallahassee, FL. < http://www.myfwc.com/WILDLIFEHABITATS/BirdSpecies_RoseateSpoonbill.htm>

Florida Fish and Wildlife Conservation Commission. 2009c. 2008 Manatee Mortality. Fish and Wildlife Research Institute, Florida Fish and Wildlife Conservation Commission. St. Petersburg, FL.

Florida Fish and Wildlife Conservation Commission. 2010a. Coastal Wildlife Conservation Initiative. Tallahassee, FL. <http://myfwc.com/Conservation/CWCI_index.htm> (Accessed February 23, 2010)

Florida Fish and Wildlife Conservation Commission. 2010b. Florida Bird Conservation Initiative. Tallahassee, FL. <http://myfwc.com/Conservation/FLBirdConservation_index.htm> (Accessed February 23, 2010)

Florida Fish and Wildlife Conservation Commission. Undated. Fish and Wildlife Research Institute. (Accessed 2009). "Red Tides in Florida." St. Petersburg, FL. <http://research.myfwc.com/features/view_article.asp?id=24936>

Florida Gulf Coast University, Regional Economic Research Institute. 2007. "2007 - Southwest Florida Regional Economic Indicators (October 2007)." Fort Myers, FL. <http://www.fgcu.edu/cob/reri/indicators/indicators200710a.pdf>

Florida Native Plant Society. 2005. "Climate." <http://www.fnps.org/pages/plants/climate.php>

Florida Natural Areas Inventory. Undated. "Conservation Lands". Florida State University. Tallahassee, FL. <http://www.fnai.org/conservationlands.cfm>

Florida Natural Areas Inventory. 2009. Florida Natural Areas Inventory. Florida State University. Tallahassee, FL. <http://www.fnai.org/>

Florida Oceans and Coastal Council. 2009. The Effects of Climate Change on Florida's Ocean and Coastal Resources. Revised June 2009. A special report to the Florida Energy and Climate Commission and the people of Florida. Tallahassee, FL. 34 pp. < http://www.floridaoceanscouncil.org/reports/Climate_Change_Report_v2.pdf > (Accessed August 6, 2010)

Francis, Mark. 2002. How Cities Use Parks for Community Engagement. City Parks Forum Briefing Papers. American Planning Association. Chicago, IL. 4 pp.

Gabrielson, Ira N. 1943. Wildlife Conservation. The Macmillan Company, New York, New York. 250 pp.

Galbraith, H., Jones, R., Park, R., Clough, J., Herrod-Julius, S., Harrington, B & Page, G. 2002. Global Climate Change and Sea Level Rise: Potential losses of intertidal habitat for shorebirds. *Waterbirds,* 25,2: 173-183.

Gelberg, Andy. 2009. Sanibel – Captiva Florida Island History—Gateway to the Gulf of Mexico. Sanibel, FL. <http://www.agentandygelberg.com/IslandsHistory>

Guentzel, J.L., W.M. Landing, G.A. Gill, and C.D. Pollman. 1995. Atmospheric deposition of mercury in Florida: The FAMS Project (1992 - 1996). Water, Air and Soil Pollution. 80: 373-382.

Hammond, E.A. 1970. "Sanibel Island and its Vicinity--A Document:" *Florida Historical Quarterly,* v. 48, 392-411.

Harris, L.D. and W.P. Cropper, Jr. 1992. Between the devil and the deep blue sea: Implications of climate change for wildlife in Florida. pp. 309-324 In: R. L. Peters and T.E. Lovejoy (eds.) Global warming and biological diversity. Yale Univ. Press, New Haven. 386 pp.

Hazen and Sawyer. 1998. "Charlotte Harbour National Estuary Program – Estimated Value of Resources." Environmental Scientists. Hollywood, FL. <http://www.chnep.org/info/EconEval1998.pdf>

Hiller, Herbert L. 1996. *Marketing the Real Florida. Florida Trends* in *The South Florida Ecosystem,* Multi-Species Recovery Plan for South Florida. U.S. Fish and Wildlife Service. <http://www.fws.gov/southeast/vbpdfs/ts.pdf>

Holland, G.J., and Webster, P.J. 2007. Heightened tropical cyclone activity in the North Atlantic: natural variability or climate trend? Phil. Trans. R. Soc. A doi:10.1098/rsta.2007.2083.

Hunter, W. C., with D. Allen, J. Collazo, M. Epstein, B. Harrington, B. Noffsinger, J.Saliva, and B. Winn. 2002. April 2000, Revised September 2002. *Southeastern Coastal Plains-Caribbean Region Report, U.S. Shorebird Conservation Plan.* U.S. Fish and Wildlife Service. Atlanta, GA. <http://www.fws.gov/shorebirdplan/RegionalShorebird/downloads/SECPCRRev02.pdf>

Hunter, W.C., W. Golder, S. Melvin, and J. Wheeler. 2006. *Southeast United States Regional Waterbird Conservation Plan.* September 2006. U.S. Fish and Wildlife Service and North Carolina Audubon Society. Atlanta, GA, and Arlington, VA. <http://www.waterbirdconservation.org/pdfs/regional/seusplanfinal906.pdf>

Inkley, D. B., M. G. Anderson, A. R. Blaustein, V. R. Burkett, B. Felzer, B. Griffith, J. Price, and T. L. Root. 2004. Global climate change and wildlife in North America. Wildlife Society Technical Review 04-2. The Wildlife Society (TWS), Bethesda, MD.

International Union for the Conservation of Nature. 2009. Red List of Threatened Species. Version 2009.1. Gland, Switzerland. <http://www.iucn.org/about/work/programmes/species/red_list/>

Intergovernmental Panel on Climate Change. 2007. Summary for Policymakers. In: Climate Change 2007: Impacts, Adaption, and Vulnerability. Contribution of Working Group II to the Fourth Assessment Report of the Intergovernmental Panel on Climate Change [Solomon, S., D. Quin, M. Manning, Z. Chen, M. Marquis, K.B. Averyt, M. Tignor, and H.L. Miller (editors)], Cambridge University Press, Cambridge, United Kingdom and New York, NY, USA.

J. N. "Ding" Darling Foundation. 2000. "J. N. "Ding" Darling National Wildlife Refuge." Sanibel, FL. <http://www.dingdarling.org/wildlife.html>

Krabill, W., W. Abdalati, E. Frederick, S. Manizade, C. Martin, J. Sonntag, R. Swift, R. Thomas, W. Wright, and J. Yungel. 2000. "Greenland Ice Sheet: High-elevation Balance and Peripheral Thinning." *Science.* July 21, 2000: pp. 428-430.

Laycock, George. 1965. The Sign of the Flying Goose: A Guide to the National Wildlife Refuges. The Natural History Press, Garden City, New York. 299 pp.

Lee County. 2009. Lee County's Watersheds: Then & Now. < http://www.lee-county.com/gov/dept/NaturalResources/WaterQuality/Pages/WatershedHistory.aspx> Lee County Natural Resources. Fort Myers, FL.

Lee County Visitors and Convention Bureau. 2005. "Lee County Government-Southwest Florida (2005 data)." <http://leevcb.com/statistics/20yearrecap.pdf>

Lewis, Megan. 2002. How Cities Use Parks for Economic Development. City Parks Forum Briefing Papers. American Planning Association. Chicago, IL. 4 pp.

Loveland, T.R. and W. Acevedo. 2008. Land Cover Trends, Land Cover Change in the Eastern United States. U.S. Geological Survey. <http://landcovertrends.usgs.gov/east/regionalSummary.html>

Main, M. B., and G. M. Allen. 2007. *Florida's Environment – Southwest Region.* Fact Sheet WEC 236. Florida's Environment Series. Department of Wildlife Ecology and Conservation, Florida Cooperative Extension Service, Institute of Food and Agricultural Sciences, University of Florida. July 2007. Gainesville, FL. <http://edis.ifas.ufl.edu/UW275>

Mann, M.E., and Emanuel, K.A. 2006. Atlantic hurricane trends linked to climate change, Eos Trans. AGU, 87(24), 233, 238, 241.

Matthews, S., R. O'Connor, L.R. Iverson, and A.M. Prasad. 2004. Atlas of Climate Change Effects in 150 Bird Species of the Eastern United States. Newton Square, PA: U.S. Fish and Wildlife Service, General Technical Report NE-GTR-318. <http://www.usgcrp.gov/usgcrp/Library/ocp2006/ocp2006-hi-eco.htm>

Meyers, J.M., C.A. Langtimm, T.J. Smith III, and K. Pednault-Willett. 2006. Wildlife and Habitat Damage Assessment from Hurricane Charley: Recommendations for Recovery of the J. N. "Ding" Darling National Wildlife Refuge Complex, Open File Report 2006-1126. U.S. Geological Survey, South Florida Information Access. <http://sofia.usgs.gov/publications/ofr/2006-1126/index.html>, <http://sofia.usgs.gov/publications/ofr/2006-1126/studyarea.html>, and <http://sofia.usgs.gov/publications/ofr/2006-1126/USGS_OFR_2006_1126_Finalv2.pdf>

McMahon, Sean. 2006. Rising Tides: A Summary of Projected Impacts of Sea Level Rise on Florida's Coasts and Ding Darling, Egmont Key, Pine Island and Pelican Island National Wildlife Refuges. Virginia Tech Independent Study Project Prepared for Dr. Brian Czech, U.S. Fish and Wildlife Service. October 25, 2006. 27 pp.

McNab, W. Henry and Peter E. Avers. 1994. "Ecological Subregions of the United States." July 1994. U.S. Forest Service. <http://www.fs.fed.us/land/pubs/ecoregions/>

Morton, R.A., and R.L. Peterson. 2003. Coastal Classification Atlas, Southwestern Florida Coastal Classification Maps - Venice Inlet to Cape Romano, Coastal Processes. USGS Open File Report 03-322. U.S. Geological Survey, Coastal and Marine Geology Program. <http://pubs.usgs.gov/of/2003/of03-322/process.html>

Mrosovsky, N., and J. Provancha 1992. Sex ratio of hatchling loggerhead sea turtles: Data and estimates from a five-year study. *Canadian Journal of Zoology* 70:530–538.

National Aeronautics and Space Administration. 2000. Goddard Space Flight Center. "NASA Scientists Detect Rapid Thinning Of Greenland's Coastal Ice." <http://svs.gsfc.nasa.gov/stories/greenland/> (July 20, 2000)

National Aeronautics and Space Administration. 2009. "Earth Observatory - Evidence for Global Warming."
<http://earthobservatory.nasa.gov/Features/GlobalWarming/global_warming_update3.php>
<http://sofia.usgs.gov/publications/ofr/2006-1126/studyarea.html>, and
<http://sofia.usgs.gov/publications/ofr/2006-1126/USGS_OFR_2006_1126_Finalv2.pdf>
(August 12, 2009)

National Oceanic and Atmospheric Administration. 2008. "Climate of 2007-Annual Report." National Climate Data Center.
<http://www.ncdc.noaa.gov/oa/climate/research/2007/ann/global.html#trends> (January 2008)

National Oceanic and Atmospheric Administration. 2009. The Office of Ocean and Coastal Resource Management. <http://coastalmanagement.noaa.gov/>

National Park Service, National Center for Recreation and Conservation. 2007. "National Rivers Inventory-Florida Segments." <http://www.nps.gov/ncrc/programs/rtca/nri/states/fl.html>

National Science and Technology Council, Committee on the Environment and Natural Resources, Interagency Working Group on Methylmercury. 2004. "Methylmercury in the Gulf of Mexico: State of Knowledge and Research Needs." June 2004. Washington, D.C.
<http://www.ostp.gov/pdf/methylmercurygulfmexiconstc04.pdf>

Natural Resources Defense Council. 2001. Feeling the Heat in Florida: Global Warming on the Local Level. 27 pp. <http://www.nrdc.org/globalwarming/florida/flainx.asp>

Nicholls, R.J., P.P. Wong, V.R. Burkett, J.O. Codignotto, J.E. Hay, R.F. McLean, S. Ragoonaden and C.D. Woodroffe. 2007. Coastal systems and low-lying areas. Climate Change 2007: Impacts, Adaptation and Vulnerability. Contribution of Working Group II to the Fourth Assessment Report of the Intergovernmental Panel on Climate Change, M.L. Parry, O.F. Canziani, J.P. Palutikof, P.J. van der Linden and C.E. Hanson, Eds., Cambridge University Press, Cambridge, UK, 315-356.

Ning, Z.H., R.E. Turner, T. Doyal, K. Abdollahi. 2003. "Preparing for a Changing Climate: The Potential Consequences of Climate Variability and Change – Gulf Coast Region, Findings of the Gulf Coast Regional Assessment." June 2003.
<http://www.usgcrp.gov/usgcrp/Library/nationalassessment/gulfcoast/gulfcoast-brief.pdf>

Ogden, J., Davis, S., Jacobs, K., Barnes, T., Fling, H. 2005. The use of conceptual ecological models to guide ecosystem restoration in South Florida. Wetlands, 25,4: 795-809.

Ogden, J.C., D.A. McCrimmon, Jr., G.T. Bancroft, and B.W. Patty. 1987. Breeding populations of the Wood Stork in the southeastern United States. Condor 89:752-759.

Rodgers, J. A., Jr. and S.T. Schwikert. 2002. Buffer zone distances to protect foraging and loafing waterbirds from disturbance by personal watercraft and outboard-powered boats. *Conservation Biology* Volume 16, Number 1: 216-224.

Rood, B.E., J.F. Gottgens, J.J. Delfino, C.D. Earle, and T.L. Crisman. 1995. Mercury Accumulation Trends in Florida Everglades and Savannas Marsh Flooded Soils. *Water, Air, and Soil Pollution* Volume 80, Numbers 1-4/February 1995: 981-990.

Ruth, J.M. 2006. Partners-in-Flight – U.S. Website. Served by the USGS Patuxent Wildlife Research Center, Laurel, Maryland. <http://www.partnersinflight.org/> and <http://www.partnersinflight.org/cont_plan/>

Roosevelt, T. "Harpooning Devilfish." 1917. Scribners Magazine. September 1917.

Roosevelt, T. "Notes on Florida Turtles." 1917a. American Museum Journal.

Sanibel and Captiva Islands Chamber of Commerce, Inc. 2009. "Sanibel & Captiva Islands Information." <http://www.sanibel-captiva.org/islands/history.asp>

Sanibel-Captiva Conservation Foundation. 2009. Sanibel-Captiva Conservation Foundation. Sanibel, FL. <http://www.sccf.org/>

Sanibel-Captiva Conservation Foundation. 2007. "Amphibians & Reptiles of Sanibel Island 2007." Sanibel, FL. <http://www.sccf.org/files/downloads/WildLProgReptilesList.pdf>

Sanibel-Captiva Conservation Foundation. (Date Unknown). "Birds of Sanibel." Sanibel, FL. <http://www.sccf.org/files/downloads/WildLProjSanibelBirds.pdf>

Schulte, S., S. Brown, and the American Oystercatcher Working Group. 2006. American Oystercatcher Conservation Plan for the Atlantic and Gulf Coasts of the United States" Version 1.0. April 2006. <www.ncsu.edu/project/grsmgis/AMOY/AMOYConservationPlan06_05_06.doc>

Scott, T.M. 2000. Geologic Map of the State of Florida. Map Series 147. Florida Geological Survey, Florida Department of Environmental Protection. Tallahassee, FL. <http://www.dep.state.fl.us/geology/gisdatamaps/state_geo_map_sim.htm>

Scott, T. M., K. M. Campbell, F. R. Rupert, J. D. Arthur, T. M. Missimer, J. M. Lloyd, J. W. Yon, and J. G. Duncan. 2001. *Geologic Map of the State of Florida.* Open file report # 80. Florida Geological Survey, Florida Department of Environmental Protection. Tallahassee, FL. <http://sofia.usgs.gov/publications/maps/florida_geology/index.html>

Southeast Regional Climate Center. 2007. "Historical Climate Summaries for Florida." <http://www.sercc.com/climateinfo/historical/historical_fl.html>

South Florida Water Management District. 2000. "Lower West Coast Water Supply Plan-Support Document, Chapter 3-Water Resources and System Overview." West Palm Beach, FL. <https://my.sfwmd.gov/portal/page?_pageid=1874,4166896,1874_4166893:1874_4165862&_dad=portal&_schema=PORTAL>

South Florida Water Management District. 2008. Lower Charlotte Harbor, Surface Water Improvement & Management Plan. February 2008. West Palm Beach, FL. <https://my.sfwmd.gov/pls/portal/docs/PAGE/PG_GRP_SFWMD_WATERSHED/PORTLET%20%20STORMWATER%20MANAGEMENT/TAB8996095/FINAL_PUBLISH_LCH_SWIM_.PDF>

South Florida Water Management District. 2009a. Northern Everglades & Estuaries Protection Program. March 2009. West Palm Beach, FL. <https://my.sfwmd.gov/pls/portal/docs/PAGE/COMMON/PDF/SPLASH/SPL_NORTHERN_EVERGLADES.PDF>

South Florida Water Management District. 2009b. Northern Everglades and Estuary Protection Program Caloosahatchee River Watershed Protection Plan. March 2009. West Palm Beach, FL.
<https://my.sfwmd.gov/pls/portal/docs/PAGE/COMMON/NEWSR/JTF_NE_CRWPP.PDF>

Southwest Florida Economic Development Office. 2009.
<http://www.labormarketinfo.com/Library/EP.htm> (Accessed September 4, 2009)

Southwest Florida Regional Planning Council. 2002. "Comprehensive Economic Development Strategy -- Southwest Florida Ecological Characterization Atlas, 1984; and Comprehensive Economic Development Strategy." Submitted to the Economic Development Administration by the Southwest Florida Regional Planning Council. June 2002. Fort Myers, FL. 144 pp.
<http://www.swfrpc.org/content/Publications/CEDS2002.pdf>

Starobin, M. 2000. Greenland's Receding Ice. NASA/Goddard Space Flight Center, Scientific Visualization Studio. Television Production NASA-TV/GSFC.
<http://svs.gsfc.nasa.gov/stories/greenland/index.html> (Accessed 2009)

Stout, B. 2008. "Ding Darling Days Returns." News-press.com of Fort Myers, Florida. October 16, 2008. Fort Myers, FL.
<http://www.news-press.com/apps/pbcs.d11/article?AID=/20081016/LIFESTYLES/810140> (Accessed November 20, 2008)

Sundlof, S.F., M.G. Spalding, J.D. Wentworth, and C.K. Steible. 1994. Mercury in livers of wading birds (Ciconiiformes) in Southern Florida.
Archives of Environmental Contaminants and Toxicology. 27: 299-305.

The Florida Legislature, Office of Economic and Demographic Research. 2007. "Florida Demographic Overview." Tallahassee, FL.
<http://www.csl.usf.edu/Florida%20Demographic%20Trends.ppt>

The Haskell Company. Undated. "Donax Water Reclamation Facility Upgrade & Expansion, City of Sanibel, Sanibel, FL. (Accessed 2008).
<http://www.thehaskellco.com/Portfolio/WaterWW/Sanibel_Donax/> and
<http://www.thehaskellco.com/upload/Portfolio/WaterWW/Additional%20Projects/Donax%20Water%20Reclamation%20Facility.pdf>

The Island Water Association, Inc. Undated. Sanibel, FL.
<http://www.islandwater.com/default.htm> (Accessed 2008)

Twilley, R.R., E.J. Barron, H.L. Gholz, M.A. Harwell, R.L. Miller, D.J. Reed, J.B. Rose, E.H. Siemann, R.G. Wetzel and R.J. Zimmerman. 2001. "Confronting Climate Change in the Gulf Coast Region: Prospects for Sustaninng Our Ecological Heritage". Union of Concerned Scientists and Ecological Society of America. <http://www.ucsusa.org/gulf/gcchallengereport.html>

U.S. Army Corps of Engineers, South Florida Water Management District, Water Resources Advisory Commission. 2006. "Southwest Florida Feasibility Study." September 7, 2006.
<http://my.sfwmd.gov/pls/portal/docs/PAGE/PG_GRP_SFWMD_WRAC/PORTLET_WRAC_ARCHIVE_REPORTSDOCS/TAB772049/WRAC_090606_STARNES.PDF>

U.S. Army Corps of Engineers and South Florida Water Management District. 2006. The Comprehensive Everglades Restoration Plan. http://www.evergladesplan.org/index.aspx, and http://www.evergladesplan.org/pm/pm_docs/cerp_2006_rpt_to_public.pdf (Accessed November 2008)

U.S. Army Corps of Engineers and South Florida Water Management District. 2007. "Caloosahatchee River [C-43] West Basin Storage Project – Facts & Information." <http://evergladesplan.org/docs/fact_sheet_c43_2007.pdf>

U.S. Army Corps of Engineers and South Florida Water Management District. 2003. C-43 Basin Storage Reservoir – Part 1. Jacksonville and West Palm Beach, FL. February 2003. 2 pp. <http://www.evergladesplan.org/docs/fs_c43.pdf>

U.S. Department of Agriculture. 2006a. Natural Resources Conservation Service. "Land Resources Regions and Major Land Resource Areas of the United States, the Caribbean, and the Pacific Basin." USDA Handbook # 296, 2006.

U.S. Department of Agriculture. 2006b. Soil Survey Staff. Keys to Soil Taxonomy, 10th ed. USDA-Natural Resources Conservation Service, Washington, DC. <http://soils.usda.gov/technical/classification/>

U.S. Department of Agriculture. 2008. Soil Survey Staff, Natural Resources Conservation Service, Official Soil Series Descriptions. <http://soils.usda.gov/technical/classification/osd/index.html> (Accessed 10 February 2008)

U.S. Department of Agriculture, Forest Service. 2008. "232 Outer Coastal Plain Mixed Province." <http://www.fs.fed.us/colormap/ecoreg1_provinces.conf?652,457>

U.S. Department of Commerce, National Oceanic and Atmospheric Administration, National Climate Data Center. Undated. Myers Page Field Airport FL, United States. <http://www4.ncdc.noaa.gov/cgi-win/wwcgi.dll?wwDI~StnSrch~StnID~10002008#ONLINE>

U.S. Department of Commerce, U.S. Census Bureau. 2006a. "American Community Survey-2006." <http://factfinder.census.gov/home/saff/main.html?_lang=en>

U.S. Department of Commerce, U.S. Census Bureau. 2006b. "Population Estimates for the 100 U.S. Counties with the Largest Numerical Increase." <http://www.census.gov/Press-Release/www/releases/archives/population/009756.html>

U.S. Department of Commerce, U.S. Census Bureau. 2007. "State and County Florida-QuickFacts." <http://quickfacts.census.gov/qfd/states/12000.html>

U.S. Department of Energy. 1999. "Carbon Sequestration Research and Development." <http://www.fossil.energy.gov/programs/sequestration/publications/1999_rdreport/>

U.S. Department of the Interior, Fish and Wildlife Service and U.S. Department of Commerce, U.S. Census Bureau. 2007. 2006 National Survey of Fishing, Hunting, and Wildlife-Associated Recreation. October 2007. Washington, DC. 164 pp. <http://library.fws.gov/pubs/nat_survey2006_final.pdf>

U.S. Environmental Protection Agency. Undated-a. Gulf of Mexico Program. Florida. <http://www.epa.gov/gmpo/about.html> (Accessed September 14, 2009)

U.S. Environmental Protection Agency. Undated-b. "Climate Change, Wildlife, and Wildlands Case Study – Everglades and South Florida." <http://www.epa.gov/climatechange/wycd/downloads/CS_Ever.pdf>

U.S. Environmental Protection Agency. 2004. "National Coastal Condition Report II (Chapter 5-Gulf of Mexico Coastal Condition)." Publication # EPA-620/R-03/002. December 2004. <http://www.epa.gov/owow/oceans/nccr/2005/>

U.S. Environmental Protection Agency. 2007a. Level III and IV Ecoregions of Florida <http://www.epa.gov/wed/pages/ecoregions/fl_eco.htm>

U.S. Environmental Protection Agency. 2007b. Level III Ecoregions. <http://www.epa.gov/wed/pages/ecoregions/level_iii.htm>

U.S. Environmental Protection Agency. 2007c. "National Estuary Program Coastal Condition Report (Chapter 5-Gulf Coast National Estuary Program Coastal Condition, Charlotte Harbor National Estuary Program)". Publication # EPA-842-B-06-001, June 2007. <http://www.epa.gov/owow/oceans/nepccr/>

U.S. Environmental Protection Agency. 2008. Air Quality Monitoring Information. <http://www.epa.gov/airtrends/factbook.html>

U.S. Environmental Protection Agency. 2009a. "Climate Change, Basic Information." <http://www.epa.gov/climatechange/basicinfo.html> (July 20, 2009)

U.S. Environmental Protection Agency. 2009b. "Climate Change, Science." <http://www.epa.gov/climatechange/science/index.html> (June 16, 2009)

U.S. Fish and Wildlife Service. 1984. Southwest Florida Ecological Characterization Atlas: Map Narratives (Biological Services Program). April 1984. FWS/OBS-82/47. 329 pp.

U.S. Fish and Wildlife Service, Southeast Region. 1998a. "South Florida Ecosystem Team's Ecosystem Plan. Ecosystem Management, June 1998." Vero Beach, FL. 90 pp. <http://www.fws.gov/southeast/ecosystems/southflecosystemplan.html>

U.S. Fish and Wildlife Service. 1998b. "J.N. "Ding" Darling National Wildlife Refuge Amphibian and Reptile List." July 1998. <http://library.fws.gov/Refuges/j.n.ding_darling_amphib_reptiles98.pdf>

U.S. Fish and Wildlife Service, Southeast Region. 1999. The South Florida Ecosystem – Multi-Species Recovery Plan for South Florida. <http://www.fws.gov/southeast/vbpdfs/ts.pdf> and <http://www.fws.gov/verobeach/images/pdflibrary/sf%20ecosystem.pdf>

U.S. Fish and Wildlife Service. 2000. J. N. "Ding" Darling National Wildlife Refuge Fishing and Boating Regulations. <http://www.fws.gov/dingdarling/VisitorInformation/Fishing%20and%20Boating%20Brochure.pdf>

U.S. Fish and Wildlife Service. 2001. Southeast Region, J. N. "Ding" Darling National Wildlife Refuge. "Public Use Review Report," July 2001. Atlanta, GA.

U.S. Fish and Wildlife Service. 2002. "Final Environmental Assessment and Land Protection Plan for the Proposed Expansion of the J. N. "Ding" Darling National Wildlife Refuge Complex, Lee and Charlotte Counties, Florida (Draft)." July 2002. Southeast Region. Atlanta, GA.

U.S. Fish and Wildlife Service. 2007a. Wood Stork (*Mycteria Americana*); 5-Year Review: Summary and Evaluation. Jacksonville Ecological Services Field Office, Southeast Region, U.S. Fish and Wildlife Service. Jacksonville, FL. 22 pp.
<http://ecos.fws.gov/docs/five_year_review/doc1115.pdf>

U.S. Fish and Wildlife Service. 2007b. West Indian Manatee (*Trichechus manatus*); 5-Year Review: Summary and Evaluation. Jacksonville Ecological Services Field Office and Caribbean Ecological Services Field Office, Southeast Region, U.S. Fish and Wildlife Service. Jacksonville, FL and Boqueron, Puerto Rico. 79 pp.
<http://ecos.fws.gov/docs/five_year_review/doc1042.pdf>

U.S. Fish and Wildlife Service. 2007c. "J. N."Ding" Darling National Wildlife Refuge Brochure." March 2007. <http://www.fws.gov/southeast/pubs/jndgen.pdf>

U.S. Fish and Wildlife Service. 2008. Recovery Plan for the Northwest Atlantic Population of the Loggerhead Sea Turtle (*Caretta caretta*) Second Revision, December 31, 2008.
<http://www.fws.gov/northflorida/SeaTurtles/2008_Recovery_Plan/20081231_Final%20NW%20Loggerhead%20Recovery%20Plan_signed.pdf>

U.S. Fish and Wildlife Service. 2008 "Ecosystem Units." <http://www.fws.gov/offices/ecounits.html> (Accessed September 16, 2009)

U.S. Fish and Wildlife Service. 2009a. "Endangered Species Program, September 8, 2009."
<http://www.fws.gov/endangered/>

U.S. Fish and Wildlife Service 2009b. North American Waterfowl Management Plan. Division of Bird Habitat Conservation. <http://www.fws.gov/birdhabitat/NAWMP/index.shtm> (Accessed September 16, 2009)

U.S. Fish and Wildlife Service. Undated. "Partners for Fish and Wildlife, Florida.-Factsheet." <http://www.fws.gov/southeast/pubs/facts/fpacon.pdf> (Accessed September 16, 2009)

U.S. Fish and Wildlife Service. Undated. The South Florida Ecosystem – Multi-Species Recovery Plan for South Florida.
<http://www.fws.gov/verobeach/images/pdflibrary/sf%20ecosystem.pdf and http://www.fws.gov/verobeach/index.cfm?Method=programs&NavProgramCategoryID=3&programID=107&ProgramCategoryID=3>

U.S. Fish and Wildlife Service. Undated. Pine Island National Wildlife Refuge. Southeast Region. <http://www.fws.gov/dingdarling/pineisland/> (Accessed September 11, 2009)

U.S. Fish and Wildlife Service. Undated. Caloosahatchee National Wildlife Refuge. Southeast Region. <http://www.fws.gov/dingdarling/caloosahatchee/> (Accessed September 11, 2009)

U.S. Fish and Wildlife Service. Undated. Island Bay National Wildlife Refuge. Southeast Region. <http://www.fws.gov/dingdarling/islandbay/> (Accessed September 11, 2009)

U.S. Fish and Wildlife Service. Undated. Matlacha Pass National Wildlife Refuge. Southeast Region. <http://www.fws.gov/dingdarling/matlachapass/> (Accessed September 11, 2009)

U.S. Geological Survey, Coastal and Marine Geology Program. 2003. "Coastal Classification Atlas, Southwestern Florida Coastal Classification Maps - Venice Inlet to Cape Romano, Coastal Processes." USGS Open File Report 03-322. <http://pubs.usgs.gov/of/2003/of03-322/process.html>

U.S. Geological Survey. 1982. "Deep Artesian Aquifers of Sanibel and Captiva Islands, Lee County, Florida, USGS Open-file report 82-253." <http://sofia.usgs.gov/publications/ofr/82-253/ofr-82-253.pdf>

U.S. Geological Survey. 2009. "Land Cover Trends, Land Cover and Ecoregions in the Eastern United States." <http://landcovertrends.usgs.gov/main/ecoIndex.html>

U.S. Geological Survey. 2008a. "Land Cover Trends, Land Cover Change in the Eastern United States." <http://landcovertrends.usgs.gov/east/eastResults.html> (Accessed August 21, 2009)

U.S. Geological Survey. 2008b. "Land Cover Trends, Southern Coastal Plain." http://landcovertrends.usgs.gov/east/eco75Report.html (Accessed August 21, 2009)

U.S. Geological Survey, Northern Prairie Wildlife Research Center. 2006a. "Bird Checklists of the United States – Ding Darling NWR." <http://www.npwrc.usgs.gov/resource/birds/chekbird/r4/dingdarl.htm> (Accessed August 21, 2009)

U.S. Geological Survey, Northern Prairie Wildlife Research Center. 2006b. "Bird Checklists of the United States – Pine Island, Matlacha Pass, Island Bay, Caloosahatchee National Wildlife Refuges." <http://www.npwrc.usgs.gov/resource/birds/chekbird/r4/pinendan.htm> (Accessed August 21, 2009)

U.S. Geological Survey, Northern Prairie Wildlife Research Center. 2006c. Mammal Checklists of the United States, Pine Island, Matlacha Pass, Island Bay, Caloosahatchee National Wildlife Refuges." <http://www.npwrc.usgs.gov/resource/birds/chekbird/r4/pinemam.htm> (Accessed August 21, 2009)

U.S. Geological Survey, Northern Prairie Wildlife Research Center. 2006d. "Miscellaneous Checklists of the United States, Pine Island, Matlacha Pass, Island Bay, Caloosahatchee National Wildlife Refuges." <http://www.npwrc.usgs.gov/resource/birds/chekbird/r4/pinefish.htm> (Accessed August 21, 2009)

U.S. Geological Survey, South Florida Information Access. 2006. "Wildlife and Habitat Damage Assessment from Hurricane Charley: Recommendations for Recovery of the J. N. "Ding" Darling National Wildlife Refuge Complex." <http://sofia.usgs.gov/publications/ofr/2006-1126/index.html> and <http://sofia.usgs.gov/publications/ofr/2006-1126/USGS_OFR_2006_1126_Finalv2.pdf>

U.S. North American Bird Conservation Initiative. 2007. "*Integrated Bird Conservation in the United States, Bird Conservation Plans*." Washington, D.C. <http://www.nabci-us.org/plans.html>

Ware, F.J. H. Royals, and T. Lange. 1990. Mercury contamination in Florida largemouth bass. Proceedings of the annual conference of southeast association of fish and wildlife agencies. 44: 5-12.

Webster, P.J., Holland, G.J., Curry, J.A., Chang, H.-R. 2005: Changes in Tropical Cyclone Number, Duration, and Intensity in a Warming Environment, Science, 309 (5742), 1844-1846.

Wikipedia. 2009. "Sanibel Island Light". <http://en.wikipedia.org/wiki/Sanibel_Island_Light> (accessed August 21, 2009)

Zhang, K., Douglas, B., Leatherman, S. 2004. Global Warming and Coastal Erosion. Climatic Change. 64: 41-58.

Zwick, Paul D., PhD. and Margaret H. Carr. 2006. Florida 2060: A Population Distribution Scenario for the State of Florida. GeoPlan Center, University of Florida for 1000 Friends of Florida. Gainesville, FL. 25 pp.
<http://www.1000friendsofflorida.org/PUBS/2060/Florida-2060-Report-Final.pdf>

Appendix C. Relevant Legal Mandates and Executive Orders

STATUTE	DESCRIPTION
Administrative Procedures Act (1946)	Outlines administrative procedures to be followed by federal agencies with respect to identification of information to be made public; publication of material in the Federal Register; maintenance of records; attendance and notification requirements for specific meetings and hearings; issuance of licenses; and review of agency actions.
American Antiquities Act of 1906	Provides penalties for unauthorized collection, excavation, or destruction of historic or prehistoric ruins, monuments, or objects of antiquity on lands owned or controlled by the United States. The Act authorizes the President to designate as national monuments objects or areas of historic or scientific interest on lands owned or controlled by the United States.
American Indian Religious Freedom Act of 1978	Protects the inherent right of Native Americans to believe, express, and exercise their traditional religions, including access to important sites, use and possession of sacred objects, and the freedom to worship through ceremonial and traditional rites.
Americans With Disabilities Act of 1990	Intended to prevent discrimination of and make American society more accessible to people with disabilities. The Act requires reasonable accommodations to be made in employment, public services, public accommodations, and telecommunications for persons with disabilities.
Anadromous Fish Conservation Act of 1965, as amended	Authorizes the Secretaries of Interior and Commerce to enter into cooperative agreements with states and other nonfederal interests for conservation, development, and enhancement of anadromous fish and contribute up to 50 percent as the federal share of the cost of carrying out such agreements. Reclamation construction programs for water resource projects needed solely for such fish are also authorized.
Archaeological Resources Protection Act of 1979, as amended.	This Act strengthens and expands the protective provisions of the Antiquities Act of 1906 regarding archaeological resources. It also revised the permitting process for archaeological research.
Architectural Barriers Act of 1968	Requires that buildings and facilities designed, constructed, or altered with federal funds, or leased by a federal agency, must comply with standards for physical accessibility.
Bald and Golden Eagle Protection Act of 1940, as amended	Prohibits the possession, sale or transport of any bald or golden eagle, alive or dead, or part, nest, or egg except as permitted by the Secretary of the Interior for scientific or exhibition purposes, or for the religious purposes of Indians.

STATUTE	DESCRIPTION
Bankhead-Jones Farm Tenant Act of 1937	Directs the Secretary of Agriculture to develop a program of land conservation and utilization in order to correct maladjustments in land use and thus assist in such things as control of soil erosion, reforestation, conservation of natural resources and protection of fish and wildlife. Some early refuges and hatcheries were established under authority of this Act.
Cave Resources Protection Act of 1988	Established requirements for the management and protection of caves and their resources on federal lands, including allowing the land managing agencies to withhold the location of caves from the public, and requiring permits for any removal or collecting activities in caves on federal lands.
Clean Air Act of 1970	Regulates air emissions from area, stationary, and mobile sources. This Act and its amendments charge federal land managers with direct responsibility to protect the "air quality and related values" of land under their control. These values include fish, wildlife, and their habitats.
Clean Water Act of 1974, as amended	This Act and its amendments have as its objective the restoration and maintenance of the chemical, physical, and biological integrity of the Nation's waters. Section 401 of the Act requires that federally permitted activities comply with the Clean Water Act standards, state water quality laws, and any other appropriate state laws. Section 404 charges the U.S. Army Corps of Engineers with regulating discharge of dredge or fill materials into waters of the United States, including wetlands.
Coastal Barrier Resources Act of 1982 (CBRA)	Identifies undeveloped coastal barriers along the Atlantic and Gulf Coasts and included them in the John H. Chafee Coastal Barrier Resources System (CBRS). The objectives of the act are to minimize loss of human life, reduce wasteful federal expenditures, and minimize the damage to natural resources by restricting most federal expenditures that encourage development within the CBRS.
Coastal Barrier Improvement Act of 1990	Reauthorized the Coastal Barrier Resources Act (CBRA), expanded the CBRS to include undeveloped coastal barriers along the Great Lakes and in the Caribbean, and established "Otherwise Protected Areas (OPAs)." The Service is responsible for maintaining official maps, consulting with federal agencies that propose spending federal funds within the CBRS and OPAs, and making recommendations to Congress about proposed boundary revisions.
Coastal Wetlands Planning, Protection, and Restoration (1990)	Authorizes the Director of the Fish and Wildlife Service to participate in the development of a Louisiana coastal wetlands restoration program, participate in the development and oversight of a coastal wetlands conservation program, and lead in the implementation and administration of a national coastal wetlands grant program.

STATUTE	DESCRIPTION
Coastal Zone Management Act of 1972, as amended	Established a voluntary national program within the Department of Commerce to encourage coastal states to develop and implement coastal zone management plans and requires that "any federal activity within or outside of the coastal zone that affects any land or water use or natural resource of the coastal zone" shall be "consistent to the maximum extent practicable with the enforceable policies" of a state's coastal zone management plan. The law includes an Enhancement Grants Program for protecting, restoring, or enhancing existing coastal wetlands or creating new coastal wetlands. It also established the National Estuarine Research Reserve System, guidelines for estuarine research, and financial assistance for land acquisition.
Emergency Wetlands Resources Act of 1986	This Act authorized the purchase of wetlands from Land and Water Conservation Fund moneys, removing a prior prohibition on such acquisitions. The Act requires the Secretary to establish a National Wetlands Priority Conservation Plan, required the states to include wetlands in their Comprehensive Outdoor Recreation Plans, and transfers to the Migratory Bird Conservation Fund amounts equal to import duties on arms and ammunition. It also established entrance fees at national wildlife refuges.
Endangered Species Act of 1973, as amended	Provides for the conservation of Threatened and Endangered species of fish, wildlife, and plants by federal action and by encouraging the establishment of state programs. It provides for the determination and listing of Threatened and Endangered species and the designation of critical habitats. Section 7 requires refuge managers to perform internal consultation before initiating projects that affect or may affect endangered species.
Environmental Education Act of 1990	This Act established the Office of Environmental Education within the U.S. Environmental Protection Agency to develop and administer a federal environmental education program in consultation with other federal natural resource management agencies, including the Fish and Wildlife Service.
Estuary Protection Act of 1968	Authorized the Secretary of the Interior, in cooperation with other federal agencies and the states, to study and inventory estuaries of the United States, including land and water of the Great Lakes, and to determine whether such areas should be acquired for protection. The Secretary is also required to encourage state and local governments to consider the importance of estuaries in their planning activities relative to federal natural resource grants. In approving any state grants for acquisition of estuaries, the Secretary was required to establish conditions to ensure the permanent protection of estuaries.

STATUTE	DESCRIPTION
Estuaries and Clean Waters Act of 2000	This law creates a federal interagency council that includes the Director of the Fish and Wildlife Service, the Secretary of the Army for Civil Works, the Secretary of Agriculture, the Administrator of the Environmental Protection Agency and the Administrator for the National Oceanic and Atmospheric Administration. The council is charged with developing a national estuary habitat restoration strategy and providing grants to entities to restore and protect estuary habitat to promote the strategy.
Food Security Act of 1985, as amended (Farm Bill)	The Act contains several provisions that contribute to wetland conservation. The Swampbuster provisions state that farmers who convert wetlands for the purpose of planting after enactment of the law are ineligible for most farmer program subsidies. It also established the Wetland Reserve Program to restore and protect wetlands through easements and restoration of the functions and values of wetlands on such easement areas.
Farmland Protection Policy Act of 1981, as amended	The purpose of this law is to minimize the extent to which federal programs contribute to the unnecessary conversion of farmland to nonagricultural uses. Federal programs include construction projects and the management of federal lands.
Federal Advisory Committee Act (1972), as amended	Governs the establishment of and procedures for committees that provide advice to the federal government. Advisory committees may be established only if they will serve a necessary, nonduplicative function. Committees must be strictly advisory unless otherwise specified and meetings must be open to the public.
Federal Coal Leasing Amendment Act of 1976	Provided that nothing in the Mining Act, the Mineral Leasing Act, or the Mineral Leasing Act for Acquired Lands authorized mining coal on refuges.
Federal-Aid Highways Act of 1968	Established requirements for approval of federal highways through national wildlife refuges and other designated areas to preserve the natural beauty of such areas. The Secretary of Transportation is directed to consult with the Secretary of the Interior and other federal agencies before approving any program or project requiring the use of land under their jurisdiction.
Federal Noxious Weed Act of 1990, as amended	The Secretary of Agriculture was given the authority to designate plants as noxious weeds and to cooperate with other federal, State and local agencies, farmers' associations, and private individuals in measures to control, eradicate, prevent, or retard the spread of such weeds. The Act requires each Federal land-managing agency, including the Fish and Wildlife Service, to designate an office or person to coordinate a program to control such plants on the agency's land and implement cooperative agreements with the states, including integrated management systems to control undesirable plants.

STATUTE	DESCRIPTION
Fish and Wildlife Act of 1956	Establishes a comprehensive national fish, shellfish, and wildlife resources policy with emphasis on the commercial fishing industry but also includes the inherent right of every citizen and resident to fish for pleasure, enjoyment, and betterment and to maintain and increase public opportunities for recreational use of fish and wildlife resources. Among other things, it authorizes the Secretary of the Interior to take such steps as may be required for the development, advancement, management, conservation, and protection of fish and wildlife resources including, but not limited to, research, development of existing facilities, and acquisition by purchase or exchange of land and water or interests therein.
Fish and Wildlife Conservation Act of 1980, as amended	Requires the Service to monitor nongame bird species, identify species of management concern, and implement conservation measures to preclude the need for listing under the Endangered Species Act.
Fish and Wildlife Coordination Act of 1958	Promotes equal consideration and coordination of wildlife conservation with other water resource development programs by requiring consultation with the Fish and Wildlife Service and the state fish and wildlife agencies where the "waters of a stream or other body of water are proposed or authorized, permitted or licensed to be impounded, diverted...or otherwise controlled or modified" by any agency under federal permit or license.
Improvement Act of 1978	This act was passed to improve the administration of fish and wildlife programs and amends several earlier laws, including the Refuge Recreation Act, the National Wildlife Refuge System Administration Act, and the Fish and Wildlife Act of 1956. It authorizes the Secretary to accept gifts and bequests of real and personal property on behalf of the United States. It also authorizes the use of volunteers on Service projects and appropriations to carry out volunteer programs.
Fishery (Magnuson) Conservation and Management Act of 1976	Established Regional Fishery Management Councils comprised of federal and state officials, including the Fish and Wildlife Service. It provides for regulation of foreign fishing and vessel fishing permits.
Freedom of Information Act, 1966	Requires all federal agencies to make available to the public for inspection and copying administrative staff manuals and staff instructions; official, published and unpublished policy statements; final orders deciding case adjudication; and other documents. Special exemptions have been reserved for nine categories of privileged material. The Act requires the party seeking the information to pay reasonable search and duplication costs.
Geothermal Steam Act of 1970, as amended	Authorizes and governs the lease of geothermal steam and related resources on public lands. Section 15 c of the Act prohibits issuing geothermal leases on virtually all Service-administrative lands.

STATUTE	DESCRIPTION
Lacey Act of 1900, as amended	Originally designed to help states protect their native game animals and to safeguard U.S. crop production from harmful foreign species, this Act prohibits interstate and international transport and commerce of fish, wildlife or plants taken in violation of domestic or foreign laws. It regulates the introduction to America of foreign species.
Land and Water Conservation Fund Act of 1948	This Act provides funding through receipts from the sale of surplus federal land, appropriations from oil and gas receipts from the outer continental shelf, and other sources for land acquisition under several authorities. Appropriations from the fund may be used for matching grants to states for outdoor recreation projects and for land acquisition by various federal agencies, including the Fish and Wildlife Service.
Marine Mammal Protection Act of 1972, as amended	The 1972 Marine Mammal Protection Act established a federal responsibility to conserve marine mammals with management vested in the Department of the Interior for sea otter, walrus, polar bear, dugong, and manatee. The Department of Commerce is responsible for cetaceans and pinnipeds, other than the walrus. With certain specified exceptions, the Act establishes a moratorium on the taking and importation of marine mammals, as well as products taken from them.
Migratory Bird Conservation Act of 1929	Established a Migratory Bird Conservation Commission to approve areas recommended by the Secretary of the Interior for acquisition with Migratory Bird Conservation Funds. The role of the commission was expanded by the North American Wetland Conservation Act to include approving wetlands acquisition, restoration, and enhancement proposals recommended by the North American Wetlands Conservation Council.
Migratory Bird Hunting and Conservation Stamp Act of 1934	Also commonly referred to as the "Duck Stamp Act," requires waterfowl hunters 16 years of age or older to possess a valid federal hunting stamp. Receipts from the sale of the stamp are deposited into the Migratory Bird Conservation Fund for the acquisition of migratory bird refuges.
Migratory Bird Treaty Act of 1918, as amended	This Act implements various treaties and conventions between the United States and Canada, Japan, Mexico, and the former Soviet Union for the protection of migratory birds. Except as allowed by special regulations, this Act makes it unlawful to pursue, hunt, kill, capture, possess, buy, sell, purchase, barter, export or import any migratory bird, part, nest, egg, or product.
Mineral Leasing Act for Acquired Lands (1947), as amended	Authorizes and governs mineral leasing on acquired public lands.

STATUTE	DESCRIPTION
Minerals Leasing Act of 1920, as amended	Authorizes and governs leasing of public lands for development of deposits of coal, oil, gas, and other hydrocarbons; sulphur; phosphate; potassium; and sodium. Section 185 of this title contains provisions relating to granting rights-of-way over federal lands for pipelines.
Mining Act of 1872, as amended	Authorizes and governs prospecting and mining for the so-called "hardrock" minerals (i.e., gold and silver) on public lands.
National and Community Service Act of 1990	Authorizes several programs to engage citizens of the U.S. in full- and/or part-time projects designed to combat illiteracy and poverty, provide job skills, enhance educational skills, and fulfill environmental needs. Among other things, this law establishes the American Conservation and Youth Service Corps to engage young adults in approved human and natural resource projects, which will benefit the public or are carried out on federal or Indian lands.
National Environmental Policy Act of 1969	Requires analysis, public comment, and reporting for environmental impacts of federal actions. It stipulates the factors to be considered in environmental impact statements, and requires that federal agencies employ an interdisciplinary approach in related decision-making and develop means to ensure that unqualified environmental values are given appropriate consideration, along with economic and technical considerations.
National Historic Preservation Act of 1966, as amended	It establishes a National Register of Historic Places and a program of matching grants for preservation of significant historical features. Federal agencies are directed to take into account the effects of their actions on items or sites listed or eligible for listing in the National Register.
National Trails System Act (1968), as amended	Established the National Trails System to protect the recreational, scenic, and historic values of some important trails. National recreation trails may be established by the Secretaries of Interior or Agriculture on land wholly or partly within their jurisdiction, with the consent of the involved state(s), and other land managing agencies, if any. National scenic and national historic trails may only be designated by Congress. Several national trails cross units of the National Wildlife Refuge System.
National Wildlife Refuge System Administration Act of 1966	Prior to 1966, there was no single federal law that governed the administration of the various national wildlife refuges that had been established. This Act defines the National Wildlife Refuge System and authorizes the Secretary of the Interior to permit any use of a refuge provided such use is compatible with the major purposes(s) for which the refuge was established.

STATUTE	DESCRIPTION
National Wildlife Refuge System Improvement Act of 1997	This Act amends the National Wildlife Refuge System Administration Act of 1966. This Act defines the mission of the National Wildlife Refuge System, establishes the legitimacy and appropriateness of six priority wildlife-dependent public uses, establishes a formal process for determining compatible uses of Refuge System lands, identifies the Secretary of the Interior as responsible for managing and protecting the Refuge System, and requires the development of a comprehensive conservation plan for all refuges outside of Alaska.
Native American Graves Protection and Repatriation Act of 1990	Requires federal agencies and museums to inventory, determine ownership of, and repatriate certain cultural items and human remains under their control or possession. The Act also addresses the repatriation of cultural items inadvertently discovered by construction activities on lands managed by the agency.
Neotropical Migratory Bird Conservation Act of 2000	Establishes a matching grant program to fund projects that promote the conservation of neotropical migratory birds in the united States, Latin America, and the Caribbean.
North American Wetlands Conservation Act of 1989	Provides funding and administrative direction for implementation of the North American Waterfowl Management Plan and the Tripartite Agreement on wetlands between Canada, the United States, and Mexico. The North American Wetlands Conservation Council was created to recommend projects to be funded under the Act to the Migratory Bird Conservation Commission. Available funds may be expended for up to 50 percent of the United States' share cost of wetlands conservation projects in Canada, Mexico, or the United States (or 100 percent of the cost of projects on federal lands).
Refuge Recreation Act of 1962, as amended	This Act authorizes the Secretary of the Interior to administer refuges, hatcheries, and other conservation areas for recreational use, when such uses do not interfere with the area's primary purposes. It authorizes construction and maintenance of recreational facilities and the acquisition of land for incidental fish and wildlife-oriented recreational development or protection of natural resources. It also authorizes the charging of fees for public uses.
Partnerships for Wildlife Act of 1992	Establishes a Wildlife Conservation and Appreciation Fund to receive appropriated funds and donations from the National Fish and Wildlife Foundation and other private sources to assist the state fish and game agencies in carrying out their responsibilities for conservation of nongame species. The funding formula is no more than 1/3 federal funds, at least 1/3 foundation funds, and at least 1/3 state funds.
Refuge Revenue Sharing Act of 1935, as amended	Provided for payments to counties in lieu of taxes from areas administered by the Fish and Wildlife Service. Counties are required to pass payments along to other units of local government within the county, which suffer losses in tax revenues due to the establishment of Service areas.

STATUTE	DESCRIPTION
Rehabilitation Act of 1973	Requires nondiscrimination in the employment practices of federal agencies of the executive branch and contractors. It also requires all federally assisted programs, services, and activities to be available to people with disabilities.
Rivers and Harbors Appropriations Act of 1899, as amended	Requires the authorization by the U.S. Army Corps of Engineers prior to any work in, on, over, or under a navigable water of the United States. The Fish and Wildlife Coordination Act provides authority for the Service to review and comment on the effects on fish and wildlife activities proposed to be undertaken or permitted by the Corps of Engineers. Service concerns include contaminated sediments associated with dredge or fill projects in navigable waters.
Sikes Act (1960), as amended	Provides for the cooperation by the Departments of Interior and Defense with state agencies in planning, development, and maintenance of fish and wildlife resources and outdoor recreation facilities on military reservations throughout the United States. It requires the Secretary of each military department to use trained professionals to manage the wildlife and fishery resource under his jurisdiction, and requires that federal and state fish and wildlife agencies be given priority in management of fish and wildlife activities on military reservations.
Transfer of Certain Real Property for Wildlife Conservation Purposes Act of 1948	This Act provides that upon determination by the Administrator of the General Services Administration, real property no longer needed by a federal agency can be transferred, without reimbursement, to the Secretary of the Interior if the land has particular value for migratory birds, or to a state agency for other wildlife conservation purposes.
Transportation Equity Act for the 21st Century (1998)	Established the Refuge Roads Program, requires transportation planning that includes public involvement, and provides funding for approved public use roads and trails and associated parking lots, comfort stations, and bicycle/pedestrian facilities.
Uniform Relocation and Assistance and Real Property Acquisition Policies Act (1970), as amended	Provides for uniform and equitable treatment of persons who sell their homes, businesses, or farms to the Service. The Act requires that any purchase offer be no less than the fair market value of the property.
Water Resources Planning Act of 1965	Established Water Resources Council to be composed of Cabinet representatives including the Secretary of the Interior. The Council reviews river basin plans with respect to agricultural, urban, energy, industrial, recreational and fish and wildlife needs. The act also established a grant program to assist States in participating in the development of related comprehensive water and land use plans.

STATUTE	DESCRIPTION
Wild and Scenic Rivers Act of 1968, as amended	This Act selects certain rivers of the nation possessing remarkable scenic, recreational, geologic, fish and wildlife, historic, cultural, or other similar values; preserves them in a free-flowing condition; and protects their local environments.
Wilderness Act of 1964, as amended	This Act directs the Secretary of the Interior to review every roadless area of 5,000 acres or more and every roadless island regardless of size within the National Wildlife Refuge System and to recommend suitability of each such area. The Act permits certain activities within designated wilderness areas that do not alter natural processes. Wilderness values are preserved through a "minimum tool" management approach, which requires refuge managers to use the least intrusive methods, equipment, and facilities necessary for administering the areas.
Youth Conservation Corps Act of 1970	Established a permanent Youth Conservation Corps (YCC) program within the Departments of Interior and Agriculture. Within the Service, YCC participants perform many tasks on refuges, fish hatcheries, and research stations.

EXECUTIVE ORDERS	DESCRIPTIONS
Executive Order (EO) 11593, Protection and Enhancement of the Cultural Environment (1971)	States that if the Service proposes any development activities that may affect the archaeological or historic sites, the Service will consult with Federal and State Historic Preservation Officers to comply with Section 106 of the National Historic Preservation Act of 1966, as amended.
EO 11644, Use of Off-road Vehicles on Public Land (1972)	Established policies and procedures to ensure that the use of off-road vehicles on public lands will be controlled and directed so as to protect the resources of those lands, to promote the safety of all users of those lands, and to minimize conflicts among the various uses of those lands.
EO 11988, Floodplain Management (1977)	The purpose of this Executive Order is to prevent federal agencies from contributing to the "adverse impacts associated with occupancy and modification of floodplains" and the "direct or indirect support of floodplain development." In the course of fulfilling their respective authorities, federal agencies "shall take action to reduce the risk of flood loss, to minimize the impact of floods on human safety, health and welfare, and to restore and preserve the natural and beneficial values served by floodplains."

EXECUTIVE ORDERS	DESCRIPTIONS
EO 11989 (1977), Amends Section 2 of EO 11644	Directs agencies to close areas negatively impacted by off-road vehicles.
EO 11990, Protection of Wetlands (1977)	Federal agencies are directed to provide leadership and take action to minimize the destruction, loss of degradation of wetlands, and to preserve and enhance the natural and beneficial values of wetlands.
EO 12372, Intergovernmental Review of Federal Programs (1982)	Seeks to foster intergovernmental partnerships by requiring federal agencies to use the state process to determine and address concerns of state and local elected officials with proposed federal assistance and development programs.
EO 12898, Environmental Justice (1994)	Requires federal agencies to identify and address disproportionately high and adverse effects of its programs, policies, and activities on minority and low-income populations.
EO 12906, Coordinating Geographical Data Acquisition and Access (1994), Amended by EO 13286 (2003). Amendment of EOs and other actions in connection with transfer of certain functions to Secretary of DHS.	Recommended that the executive branch develop, in cooperation with state, local, and tribal governments, and the private sector, a coordinated National Spatial Data Infrastructure to support public and private sector applications of geospatial data. Of particular importance to comprehensive conservation planning is the National Vegetation Classification System (NVCS), which is the adopted standard for vegetation mapping. Using NVCS facilitates the compilation of regional and national summaries, which in turn, can provide an ecosystem context for individual refuges.
EO 12962, Recreational Fisheries (1995)	Federal agencies are directed to improve the quantity, function, sustainable productivity, and distribution of U.S. aquatic resources for increased recreational fishing opportunities in cooperation with states and tribes.
EO 13007, Native American Religious Practices (1996)	Provides for access to, and ceremonial use of, Indian sacred sites on federal lands used by Indian religious practitioners and direction to avoid adversely affecting the physical integrity of such sites.
EO 13061, Federal Support of Community Efforts Along American Heritage Rivers (1997)	Established the American Heritage Rivers initiative for the purpose of natural resource and environmental protection, economic revitalization, and historic and cultural preservation. The Act directs Federal agencies to preserve, protect, and restore rivers and their associated resources important to our history, culture, and natural heritage.

EXECUTIVE ORDERS	DESCRIPTIONS
EO 13084, Consultation and Coordination With Indian Tribal Governments (2000)	Provides a mechanism for establishing regular and meaningful consultation and collaboration with tribal officials in the development of federal policies that have tribal implications.
EO 13112, Invasive Species (1999)	Federal agencies are directed to prevent the introduction of invasive species, detect and respond rapidly to and control populations of such species in a cost effective and environmentally sound manner, accurately monitor invasive species, provide for restoration of native species and habitat conditions, conduct research to prevent introductions and to control invasive species, and promote public education on invasive species and the means to address them. This EO replaces and rescinds EO 11987, Exotic Organisms (1977).
EO 13186, Responsibilities of Federal Agencies to Protect Migratory Birds. (2001)	Instructs federal agencies to conserve migratory birds by several means, including the incorporation of strategies and recommendations found in Partners in Flight Bird Conservation plans, the North American Waterfowl Plan, the North American Waterbird Conservation Plan, and the United States Shorebird Conservation Plan, into agency management plans and guidance documents.
EO 13443, Facilitation of Hunting Heritage and Wildlife Conservation (2007)	Directs federal agencies to facilitate the expansion and enhancement of hunting opportunities and the management of game species and their habitats.

Appendix D. Public Involvement

SUMMARY OF PUBLIC SCOPING COMMENTS

Through the Intergovernmental Coordination Planning Team, the State of Florida and other governmental partners (i.e., Seminole Tribe of Florida, Florida Fish and Wildlife Conservation Commission, Florida Department of Environmental Protection, Florida Department of Agriculture and Consumer Services, South Florida Water Management District, Southwest Florida Regional Planning Council, Lee County, Lee County Mosquito Control District, and the City of Sanibel) identified the top priority issues for the refuges to address over the 15-year life of the CCP.

- Need for Enhanced Habitat Management
- Need for Improved Water Quality, Quantity, and Flows
- Need to Control and Eliminate Exotic, Invasive, and Nuisance Species
- Need to address Existing and Increasing Wildlife and Habitat Impacts
- Need to Enhance Environmental Education
- Need for Improved Land Acquisition Efforts
- Need for Environmental Indicators and Models to Improve Refuge Management
- Declines in and Threats to Rare, Threatened, and Endangered Species
- Need for increased Staffing and Funding to Address Existing and Future Needs
- Need for Enhanced Intergovernmental Coordination and Management to Improve Management Activities across the Landscape
- Need for Continued Coordination Regarding Mosquito Control
- Need to Analyze Cumulative Impacts of Proposals
- Need to Integrate Cultural Resource Protection into all Refuge Management Activities

A representative of the Seminole Tribe of Florida participated in the Intergovernmental Coordination Planning Team. The main issues for future management of the refuges identified by the Seminole Tribe of Florida are:

- Need to Integrate Cultural Resource Protection into all Refuge Management Activities
- Need for Cultural Resource Training for Refuge Complex Staff
- Need for Baseline Cultural Resource Information
- Need for Comprehensive Inventory of all Cultural Resources
- Need for Enhanced Consultation in Relation to Cultural Resources

Three neighborhood public scoping meetings were conducted during the week of April 7, 2008: on April 8 at the Sanibel School, Sanibel Island, Florida; on April 9 at Cypress Lake Middle School, Fort Myers, Florida; and on April 10 at Pine Island Elementary School, Pine Island, Florida. The public meetings were attended by a total of over 40 individuals representing a variety of interests and organizations. Beyond the verbal comments recorded at these public meetings, over 90 written comments were also submitted by individuals, organizations, and governmental entities regarding future management of the refuges. Letters, faxes, email messages, and phone calls were received from across the country. The issues, ideas, concerns, and comments raised by the public addressed a wide range of topics, which are summarized below.

- Wildlife and Habitat Management – including controlling exotic, invasive, and nuisance species; keeping dogs off of key sites; minimizing take of alligators to restore the population and advocating a sensible control plan to the community; addressing water quality, water quantity, and flow concerns;

minimizing impacts from Lee County Mosquito Control activities; conducting a comprehensive inventory of flora and fauna on all five refuges; increasing closed areas to protect wildlife and habitat; and minimizing regulations

- Resource Protection – including addressing management of the future acquisition areas (from 2002 proposed Land Protection Plan); prioritizing land acquisition efforts, especially to protect the satellite island refuges; posting and buffering rookery areas; installing appropriate manatee zones; and increasing law enforcement presence and visibility, especially for the Terrapin Creek Tract and the satellite island refuges
- Visitor Services – including developing a required photographer's code of conduct; providing better access to key areas; providing more brochures and handouts, especially on key wildlife and plant species; developing interpretive signage to better explain key management activities (e.g., impoundment management); controlling high speed motor boating; providing recreational opportunities on Caloosahatchee, Pine Island, and Matlacha Pass NWRs; allowing only appropriate and compatible public use activities; determining whether or not visitation to J.N. "Ding" Darling NWR is overwhelming refuge resources; decreasing motorized traffic on the Wildlife Drive; increasing the Wildlife Drive closure; developing alternative parking for the Visitor Center and Wildlife Drive; developing alternative transportation (e.g., electric trams) for the Wildlife Drive; and addressing congestion on the J.N. "Ding" Darling NWR and Sanibel Island
- Refuge Administration – including increasing staff, especially in law enforcement, biology, and maintenance; increasing funding, especially for the unfunded satellite refuges; changing the name of the Refuge Complex to be more inclusive of all refuges in the Complex; improving the Service's image, especially in the communities surrounding the satellite refuges; enhancing intergovernmental coordination; and enhancing coordination with other partners

SUMMARY OF PUBLIC COMMENTS ON THE DRAFT CCP/EA AND THE SERVICE'S RESPONSES

All comments that were received on the Draft Comprehensive Conservation Plan and Environmental Assessment (Draft CCP/EA) for Pine Island, Matlacha Pass, Island Bay, and Caloosahatchee national wildlife refuges are summarized in this section. Public comments on the Draft CCP/EA were accepted from May 21 to June 22, 2010, while comments from the State of Florida were due from the State Clearinghouse by July 23, 2010. A total of seven responses submitting comments were received. One was from a private citizen; one was from Defenders of Wildlife, a nongovernmental organization; and five were from the following state and local governmental agencies: the Office of Coastal and Aquatic Managed Areas, Florida Department of Environmental Protection; Charlotte Harbor National Estuary Program; Division of Historical Resources, Florida Department of State; Lee County Mosquito Control District; and the Southwest Florida Regional Planning Council.

Under the State Clearinghouse review, the proposed activities, as updated, were found to be consistent with Section 106 of the National Historic Preservation Act of 1966, as amended and 36 CFR Part 800, Protection of Historic Properties for cultural resources; regionally significant and consistent with the Strategic Regional Policy Plan of the Southwest Florida Regional Planning Council; and consistent with the Florida Coastal Management Program.

Under the National Environmental Policy Act (NEPA), the Service must respond to substantive comments. For purposes of this CCP, a substantive comment is one that was submitted during the public review and comment period which is within the scope of the proposed action (and the other alternatives outlined in the EA), is specific to the proposed action, has a direct relationship to the proposed action, and includes reasons for the Service to consider it. (For example, a substantive comment might be that the document referenced 500 individuals of a particular species, but that current research found 600. In such a case, the Service would likely update the plan to reflect the 600, citing the current research. While a comment that would not be considered substantive would be: "We love the refuge.")

AFFILIATIONS OF COMMENTERS

The respondents who submitted comments and their affiliations are listed in the following table.

Commenter	Affiliation and Location
Lisa B. Beever, PhD, AICP	Director, Charlotte Harbor National Estuary Program, Fort Myers, Florida
Elizabeth Fleming and Julie Kates	Florida Associate and Refuge Associate, Federal Lands Program, respectively, Defenders of Wildlife
T. Wayne Gale	Executive Director, Lee County Mosquito Control District
Ken Heatherington, AICP	Executive Director, Southwest Florida Regional Planning Council
Laura A. Kammerer	Deputy State Historic Preservation Officer, Division of Historical Resources, Florida Department of State
Jean Public	Whitehouse Station, New Jersey
Heather Stafford and Melynda Brown	Program Manager for Pine Island Sound, Matlacha Pass, Cape Haze, Lemon Bay, Gasparilla Sound/Charlotte Harbor, and Estero Bay Aquatic Preserves and Environmental Specialist III for Pine Island Sound, Matlacha Pass, Cape Haze, Lemon Bay, and Gasparilla Sound/Charlotte Harbor Aquatic Preserves, respectively, Office of Coastal and Aquatic Managed Areas, Florida Department of Environmental Protection

SUMMARY OF CONCERNS AND THE SERVICE'S RESPONSES

The comments submitted during the public review and comment period were evaluated, summarized, and grouped into several categories: Wildlife and Habitat Management; Resource Protection; Visitor Services; Refuge Administration; and Other. Comments on like topics were grouped together. The Service's responses to the comments are provided, by category. The page numbers referenced relate to the original page numbers in the Draft CCP/EA that was released for public review and comment.

Wildlife and Habitat Management

Gopher Tortoise

Comment: Add management actions proposed under Alternative B to the preferred alternative (Alternative C) for gopher tortoises.

Service Response: Comment noted. The Service evaluated the management actions under all of the alternatives and selected Alternative C as the alternative that best met the purposes, vision, and goals of the refuges and the purpose and need for the proposed action. The management actions proposed under Alternative B for gopher tortoises would take additional resources that are not anticipated during the 15-year life of the plan. The Service supports partner efforts with state conservation agencies (e.g., FWC and FDEP) to better serve gopher tortoises on the refuges, including those listed under Alternative B.

Eastern Indigo Snake

Comment: Add management actions proposed under Alternative B to the preferred alternative (Alternative C) for eastern indigo snakes.

Service Response: Comment noted. The Service evaluated the management actions under all of the alternatives and selected Alternative C as the alternative that best met the purposes, vision, and goals of the refuges and the purpose and need for the proposed action. The management actions proposed under Alternative B for eastern indigo snakes would take additional resources that are not anticipated during the 15-year life of the plan. The Service supports partner efforts with state conservation agencies (e.g., FWC and FDEP) to better serve eastern indigo snakes on the refuges, including those listed under Alternative B.

Sanibel Island Rice Rat

Two comments were submitted regarding the Sanibel Island rice rat.

Comment: Add management actions proposed under Alternative B to the preferred alternative (Alternative C) for the Sanibel Island rice rat.

Service Response: Comment noted. The Service evaluated the management actions under all of the alternatives and selected Alternative C as the alternative that best met the purposes, vision, and goals of the refuges and the purpose and need for the proposed action. The management actions proposed under Alternative B for the Sanibel Island rice rat would take additional resources that are not anticipated during the 15-year life of the plan. The Service supports partner efforts with state conservation agencies (e.g., FWC and FDEP) to better serve Sanibel Island rice rats on the refuges, including those listed under Alternative B.

Comment: On page 160 of the Draft CCP: Given the habitat needs of the Sanibel Island rice rat, it is unlikely that it will be located on any of the islands of these four refuges.

Service Response: A rice rat was captured during the summer of 2008 in a large wire-mesh live trap on Skimmer Island in Matlacha Pass NWR. The animal was photographed and released. It was not identified until after the photograph was viewed by Refuge Biologist Joyce Mazourek Palmer, Refuge Manager Paul Tritaik, Biologist Jim Beever, and mammalogy professor emeritus Llewellyn M. Ehrhart. While not conclusive, the animal did not appear to be a roof rat (*Rattus rattus*) and had a similar appearance to rice rats (*Oryzomys palustris*). It was not determined whether it was a Sanibel Island rice rat (*Oryzomys palustris sanibeli*) or a Pine Island rice rat (*Oryzomys palustris planirostris*). Given this previous potential sighting, Alternative B proposed to survey for rice rats to determine presence/absence and to adapt management as necessary if the species was determined to be on any portion of the refuges.

Ornate Diamondback Terrapin

Comment: Add management actions proposed under Alternative B to the preferred alternative (Alternative C) for the ornate diamondback terrapin.

Service Response: Comment noted. The Service evaluated the management actions under all of the alternatives and selected Alternative C as the alternative that best met the purposes, vision, and goals of the refuges and the purpose and need for the proposed action. The management actions proposed under Alternative B for ornate diamondback terrapins would take additional resources that are not anticipated during the 15-year life of the plan. The Service supports partner efforts with state conservation agencies (e.g., FWC and FDEP) to better serve ornate diamondback terrapins on the refuges, including those listed under Alternative B.

Double-crested Cormorant

Comment: On page 77 of the Draft CCP, include cormorants as a typical common bird found nesting on Pine Island NWR islands.

Service Response: The list of birds for Pine Island NWR was updated on page 77 of the Draft CCP to include (the underlined text was added): double-crested cormorant (*Phalacrocorax auritus*).

Use of Dredge-spoil Materials

Comment: The American Oystercatcher Conservation Plan is referenced on 8 of the Draft CCP, which states, "creation of new habitat through carefully designed use of dredge-spoil materials." This activity could be a problematic issue if the spoil was placed on state-owned submerged lands. Coordination with the Charlotte Harbor Aquatic Preserves early in the planning stages would be recommended.

Service Response: Comment noted. The Service would coordinate with Charlotte Harbor Aquatic Preserves and other partners before pursuing the placement of dredge-spoil materials on state-owned submerged lands.

Preservation of Birds

Comment: All birds should be preserved.

Service Response: Comment noted. The concept of this comment provides the foundation of the Proposed Action (discussed in the EA and detailed in the Draft CCP) and the purposes of each of the refuges (provided in Chapter II of the Draft CCP), which established the refuges as preserves and breeding grounds for native birds. Further, nearly every goal and objective outlined in the Draft CCP provides for native birds on the refuges.

Exotic, Invasive, and Nuisance Species

Two comments were submitted concerning the control of exotic, invasive, and nuisance species.

Comment: The CCP should expand the scope of invasive species control. The effects of climate change are set to put additional pressure on ecosystems already challenged by habitat fragmentation, invasive species, pollution, overharvesting, and other threats. While natural systems and organisms exhibit a certain level of resiliency in the face of such challenges, the additional pressure of climate change threatens to push them toward thresholds beyond which they will be unable to recover (CCSP, *Thresholds of Climate Change in Ecosystems*, A Report by the U.S. Climate Change Science Program and the Subcommittee on Global Change Research. D.B. Fagre, C.W. Charles, C.D. Allen, C. Birkeland, F.S. Chapin III, P.M. Groffman, G.R. Guntenspergen, A.K. Knapp, A.D. McGuire, P.J. Mulholland, D.P.C. Peters, D.D. Roby, and G. Sugihara, U.S. Geological Survey, Reston, VA. [2009]). Examples of the synergistic effects of climate and other stressors have already been documented, and there is evidence that multiple stressors can produce ecosystem change of a greater magnitude than would be expected by summing their individual effects (see Rachel Przeslawski et al., *Synergistic Effects Associated with Climate Change and the Development of Rocky Shore Molluscs*, 11 GLOBAL CHANGE BIOLOGY 515-522 [2005]; Bayden D. Russell et al., *Synergistic Effects of Climate Change and Local Stressors: CO2 and Nutrient-driven Change in Subtidal Rocky Habitats*, 15 GLOBAL CHANGE BIOLOGY 2153-2162 [2009]). Limiting such stressors serves to reduce pressure on ecosystems and will increase the resiliency of the refuges' species and habitats to climate change. Defenders of Wildlife supports a plan to control exotic, invasive, and nuisance species on the refuges. Defenders recommends, however, that control be carried out where it will be of greatest benefit of native wildlife and habitat diversity. By limiting control to those activities that benefit only migratory birds, as proposed in Alternative C, the Service may forgo actions that would better promote resiliency.

Service Response: Comment noted. Although Alternative C has a focus on controlling exotic, invasive, and nuisance species for those high priority habitats serving migratory birds, the CCP, through Wildlife and Habitat Management Goal 3 and objectives 3.a(1), 3.a(2), 3.b(1), and 3.b(2), recognizes the need to control these species for all impacted habitats and native wildlife. The management focus of migratory birds and the objectives provide a means for the refuges to set priorities in addressing exotic, invasive, and nuisance species. However, all of the habitats found on the refuges serve migratory birds, as well as native wildlife. Wildlife and Habitat Goal 3 is clear: Eradicate existing and future exotic, invasive, and nuisance species within Pine Island, Matlacha Pass, Island Bay, and Caloosahatchee NWRs to maintain and enhance the biological integrity of their upland, transitional, and estuarine habitats. This will benefit a greater diversity of wildlife, including migratory birds, and will serve to enhance the resiliency of each of the refuges.

Comment: It is stated in the plan that the use of herbicides for the control of exotics will be employed on the rookery islands. When will this occur? Again, there is concern about flushing the birds during the nesting seasons and the negative effects to the birds and water quality as the islands are relatively small in size. Could hand removal be considered during the nonnesting season (November-December) to be conservative?

Service Response: Comment and questions noted. All exotic control activities, including the use of herbicides, will continue to be performed on rookery islands either during the nonnesting season or on a part of the island that does not cause disturbance. Hand removal is performed when appropriate, but in some cases it is not practical, as is the case with Australian pines (*Casuarina equisetifolia*).

Predator Control Activities

Comment: Predator control will also be a management activity on the rookery islands. How and when will this occur and how invasive is this activity? What were the success rates and associated impacts from the activity from previous predatory control efforts?

Service Response: Questions noted. All predator control activities will continue to be performed on rookery islands either during the nonnesting season or on a part of the island that does not cause disturbance. Minimal predator control efforts have been conducted in the recent past, but those efforts performed had mixed success and negligible disturbance.

Mosquito Control Activities

Comment: The Appropriate Use and Compatibility Determinations are missing from the Draft CCP for the refuges. They were included for the Draft CCP for J.N. "Ding" Darling NWR and should be applicable to the refuges.

The Mosquito Control Compatibility Determination for the J.N. "Ding" Darling NWR would need to be modified if it were appended to this CCP. Modifications suggested for the J.N. "Ding" Darling NWR Draft CCP are as listed (the page numbers refer to the Draft CCP for J.N. "Ding" Darling NWR).

Page 350, paragraph 3: This paragraph is in the Appropriate Use Determination for mosquito control. It contains language relative to specific chemicals to be used for mosquito control activities. This level of specificity on how mosquito control will be conducted on the refuge is more appropriate for the annual Special Use Permit process. Developments in technology, changes in product formulation and product packaging, etc. are very dynamic and need review yearly. A ten-year plan document such as this lacks the flexibility needed. Also, this paragraph contradicts the current Special Use Permit.

Page 350, paragraph 4, line 1: The statement, "Adulticiding does not occur on the refuge..." could become problematic under conditions of health and environmental emergency. By inserting a statement indicating that "Under periods of wide spread health threats or disaster recovery, the refuge may allow adulticiding," the refuge retains the option to allow adulticiding.

Page 350, paragraph 4, next to last line: Aerial adulticide is actually performed between 9 p.m. and 2 a.m., not between 10 p.m. and 2 a.m. Hourly trapping studies performed in 2009 indicated that flight activity of the *Aedes teahiorhynchus*, salt marsh mosquito, is highest between 9 p.m. and 1 a.m.

Service Response: Mosquito control activities for the Refuge Complex have historically been handled together in one compatibility determination. A new Appropriate Use form and a new compatibility determination were added to the Draft CCP to cover mosquito control activities for the satellite refuges separately. The Appropriate Use form and the compatibility determination are nearly exactly the same at the ones prepared for J.N. "Ding" Darling NWR and included in the public review and comment for that CCP. The compatibility determinations for both the satellite refuges and J.N. "Ding" Darling NWR were updated to address the listed comments.

Comment: The Mosquito Control Compatibility Determination for the J.N. "Ding" Darling NWR would need to be modified if it were appended to this CCP. Modifications suggested for the J.N. "Ding" Darling NWR Draft CCP are as listed (the page numbers refer to the Draft CCP for J.N. "Ding" Darling NWR). Page 351: Stipulations Necessary to Ensure Compatibility, item #8: This item goes into the details of obtaining permission to treat for larval mosquitoes. This description is too specific for a plan that is updated on a 10-year basis. This item should be a more general statement, such as: "Prior approval is necessary for any larvicide applications. The specifics of larvicide notification are contained in a step-down management plan." Also, this item contradicts the current Special Use Permit. Modifications suggested for the J.N. "Ding" Darling NWR Draft CCP are as listed (the page numbers refer to the Draft CCP for J.N. "Ding" Darling NWR).

Service Response: Comment noted. This comment refers to the compatibility determination on mosquito control found on pages 349-352 of the Draft CCP for J.N. "Ding" Darling NWR. This compatibility determination has historically covered all five refuges in the Refuge Complex. This is a current requirement of the existing compatibility determination for mosquito control and will continue to be a requirement. Although the CCP is a 15-year plan and although the compatibility determination for mosquito control activities is for 10 years, the compatibility determination can be updated as needed.

Protection of Estuarine Habitat

Comment: Defenders of Wildlife supports the plan to expand protection of estuarine habitat. Among the threats to the estuarine waters surrounding the refuges are the freshwater releases from the Caloosahatchee River, the largest source of pollution and disturbance in these estuaries. The natural flow regimes have long been severely altered by the impoundment of Lake Okeechobee and the connection of the lake to the Caloosahatchee River via a system of canals and locks. Artificial freshwater releases intended to lower Lake Okeechobee have disturbed the delicate natural balance between fresh and marine water— which is the essence of a healthy estuary—by sending huge slugs of freshwater into the estuary. Nutrients from agricultural areas drain into the lake, adding pollutants to the estuaries during releases. Conversely, in times of little rainfall, the water is withheld in the lake and the estuary becomes hypersaline. These regulated releases are not sustainable. The Comprehensive Everglades Restoration Plan (CERP) efforts may eventually address these serious problems, but implementation of the proposed solutions may be decades away. Defenders appreciates the level of concern and degree of commitment the Draft CCP conveys, and Defenders supports the approach outlined in Alternative C to address these freshwater releases and generally protect these habitats.

Service Response: Comment noted. Protection of the estuarine system resources is key to management of the refuges. The estuarine system and its values and functions serve numerous species of management concern to the refuges. Further, water quality, quantity, and timing impact the vast majority of the refuges' wildlife and habitat management goals and objectives.

Surveys

Two comments were submitted regarding surveys.

Comment: Page 12 of the Draft CCP states: "Colonial bird roost surveys are conducted quarterly on Bird Island and the nearby Broken Islands (off the refuge). Colonial nesting surveys are conducted annually from April through August on Bird Island and Hemp Key on the refuge and on the nearby Broken Islands (off the refuge)." What actually happens currently is that in partnership with Charlotte Harbor Aquatic Preserves, the colonial bird nest surveys are conducted monthly from January to October on Broken Islands, Hemp Key, and several other refuge and State owned islands in Matlacha Pass and Pine Island Sound.

Service Response: Page 12 of the Draft CCP was updated by deleting the two referenced sentences, as listed (the underlined text was added).

> Colonial bird <u>nest</u> surveys are conducted <u>monthly from January to October on Broken Islands, Hemp Key, and several other refuge and State owned islands in Matlacha Pass and Pine Island Sound</u>.

Comment: Pages 77 and 104 of the Draft CCP state: "The partners currently conduct rookery surveys from February through July on Matlacha Pass NWR and in Pine Island Sound (Charlotte Harbor Aquatic Preserve). Change the dates to January to October. Make Aquatic Preserve plural.

Service Response: Pages 77 and 104 of the Draft CCP were updated to reflect these changes.

Baseline Data

Comment: As noted in the CCP, however, "the refuges are unable to evaluate the status and trends of many fish and wildlife species and their habitats within the refuges due to the lack of sufficient baseline data and the lack of a comprehensive habitat management plan to help guide management, monitor results, and adapt management as necessary to achieve outlined goals and objectives" (on page 91 of the Draft CCP). Defenders of Wildlife therefore urges the Service to make the collection of baseline data a priority for the diversity of species on the refuges. Although resources may not be available to conduct ongoing monitoring of all documented species, baseline information will provide at least one point of reference by which to track change at a future point in time.

Service Response: Comment noted. The collection of baseline data on species diversity is a priority for the refuges and will be reflected in the Habitat Management Plan when it is finished, which is anticipated in 2013.

Proposed I-75 Widening

Comment: With respect to the proposed I-75 widening project, Defenders of Wildlife encourages the Service to work with partners to minimize impacts not only to migratory birds, but also to native habitat and rare, threatened, and endangered species.

Service Response: Comment noted. This comment is addressed under Wildlife and Habitat Management Objective 2.f(1): During the planning phases for the proposed Interstate 75 widening project, work with partners to identify and address wildlife and habitat impacts associated with the proposed project.

Buffers for Rookery Islands

Comment: Coordination with Charlotte Harbor Aquatic Preserves is requested when discussing and implementing the protection buffers for the rookery islands.

Service Response: Comment noted. This comment is addressed under Resource Protection Objective 2.b(1), which says that the Service would coordinate with the state to develop and implement these buffers. As an important partner for the refuges, Charlotte Harbor Aquatic Preserves would be included in these efforts.

Climate Change

Two commenters submitted comments on climate change.

Comment: Defenders of Wildlife applauds the U.S. Fish and Wildlife Service for recognizing the magnitude of the challenges imposed by climate change and working to substantively address this threat to the refuges' ecological integrity and wildlife resources. The CCP includes an appropriate level of detail in describing the potential impacts of climate change on the refuges' habitats and wildlife, and Defenders supports many of the strategies proposed to address these impacts, including those listed:

- Research and Monitoring. Research and monitoring activities will provide essential information about the status of resources and will allow the Service to document how those resources respond to climatic changes. They will also allow the Service to evaluate the success of management actions and make adjustments. Data obtained from these efforts should be used to inform the more detailed management strategies put forth in future step-down management plans for the "Ding" Darling Complex.
- Closed Area Buffers. Providing buffers around sensitive resources will limit disturbance to these species and habitats and increase their resiliency to climate change.
- Partnerships. Collaboration with other institutions will allow the refuges to more effectively address climate change impacts by working at a larger geographic scale, and by increasing capacity and support.

Defenders supports an adaptation approach that provides species the space and time to adapt to changing conditions. Defenders encourages the Service to undertake management activities that facilitate, rather than impede, the transition of wildlife and habitats to new areas in response to climate change. Helping wildlife and habitat adapt to the effects of climate change, including sea-level rise, warming atmospheric and ocean temperatures, unpredictable water availability and weather patterns, and the spread of invasive species will all be central to sustaining American wildlife and the environmental health of the Refuge System.

Service Response: Comment noted. Climate change is discussed in numerous places in the documents, including specifically under goals and objectives addressing black skimmer, American oystercatcher, snowy plover, Wilson's plover, red knot, piping plover, and climate change. Further, other goals and objectives seek to decrease impacts from other stressors to increase resiliency of systems and populations, including goals and objectives addressing decreasing disturbance, developing closed area buffers around sensitive resources, increasing outreach and education, increasing ethical outdoor behavior, increasing protection, monitoring species and habitats, and increasing information to aid decision making, as well as restoring, enhancing, and managing habitats; controlling exotic, invasive, and nuisance plants and animals; and addressing water quality, quantity, and timing of flows concerns. Adaptive management, coordination with the partners, shared data and information, and monitoring, and a larger landscape scale focus will benefit the natural resources protected at the refuge.

Comment: On page 44 of the Draft CCP: Hurricane Charley had significantly more impacts to the refuges than the No-name storm.

Service Response: Hurricane Charley was added to the second paragraph under the Potential Effects of Climate Change section on page 44 of the Draft CCP.

Comment: On p. 44 of the Draft CCP: It is inaccurate to say that direct impacts of climate change on the refuges are currently unknown given the documented sea level rise for the region, the effects of hurricanes, and the effects of the recent cold snap. Climate change is more than global warming and more extreme temperature shifts, both cold and hot, are climate change signatures.

On page 48 of the Draft CCP: There is significantly more information on the current and potential effects of climate change in Southwest Florida. The Southwest Florida Regional Planning Council and Charlotte Harbor National Estuary Program have several climate change and sea level rise documents completed. Completed copies can be found at:

- http://www.swfrpc.org/content/ABM/Vulnerability_Assessment_Final.pdf,
- http://www.swfrpc.org/content/ABM/Punta_Gorda_Adaptation_Plan.pdf, and
- http://www.chnep.org/projects/climate/VulnerabilityAssessment2-19-10.pdf.

The Southwest Florida Regional Planning Council is currently working on a Lee County Resiliency study and has a draft Lee County Vulnerability Assessment that could be shared with the Service upon request if Lee County agrees. There is also a study that was done on the potential sea level rise effects on the Southwest Florida Feasibility Study in a PowerPoint presentation. Currently the Southwest Florida Regional Planning Council is working on a project looking at sea level impacts and effect on Southwest Florida salt marshes.

Service Response: As discussed in the Draft CCP on pages 44-45, pages 48-50, and Wildlife and Habitat Goal 5 and Objective 5.a(1) on pages 109-110, the Service and the Draft CCP recognize the variety of impacts that are likely to be felt by the refuges from climate change and associated changes and stressors, including alterations in wildlife populations and ranges, increased storm intensity, increased drought severity and persistence, and increased density and diversity of exotic and invasive species. And these are likely to exacerbate other stressors, resulting in decreased water quality, altered water quantity and timing of flows, and increased pollution.

The Regional Conservation Plans and Initiatives section of the Draft CCP was expanded, beginning on page 40, to include a new subsection, as listed (the underlined text was added).

Area Climate Change Plans

The Service and the partners recognize the need to respond to the impacts of climate change, including through the development of the Peninsular Florida LCC, the development and refinement of various modeling efforts, and the development of management plans. The Charlotte Harbor National Estuary Program and the Southwest Florida Regional Planning Council have several very recent climate change related plans that are useful for the refuges, including the Comprehensive Southwest Florida/Charlotte Harbor Climate Change Vulnerability Assessment (Beever et al. 2009a), Charlotte Harbor Regional Climate Change Vulnerability Assessment (Charlotte Harbor National Estuary Program and Southwest Florida Regional Planning Council 2010), and City of Punta Gorda Adaptation Plan (Beever et al. 2009b). Further, Lee County is currently working on a Climate Change Vulnerability Report and a Climate Change Resiliency Plan. The Service is committed to working with these and other partners to understand and ameliorate the impacts of climate change in the Charlotte Harbor area.

Comprehensive Southwest Florida/Charlotte Harbor Climate Change Vulnerability Assessment

The Comprehensive Southwest Florida/Charlotte Harbor Climate Change Vulnerability Assessment examined climate change in Southwest Florida, identifying 246 climate change adaptations that could be utilized to address various vulnerabilities in the region. The document emphasizes the need for monitoring, especially to establish threshold indicators; prescriptive actions that can be adaptively managed as additional information becomes available; and the need to act now to avoid, mitigate, minimize, and adapt to the negative effects of climate change. (Beever et al. 2009a)

The Refuge Complex assisted the Charlotte Harbor Climate Change Vulnerability Assessment by participating in the selection of climate change indicators as part of the Climate Change Indicators Workgroup.

Charlotte Harbor Regional Climate Change Vulnerability Assessment

The Charlotte Harbor Regional Climate Change Vulnerability Assessment addresses potential climate changes in air and water and the effects of those changes on climate stability, sea level, hydrology, geomorphology, natural habitats and species, land use changes, economy, human health, human infrastructure, and variable risk projections, in the Charlotte Harbor Region. The Assessment identifies priority vulnerabilities facing the Charlotte Harbor region, including changes related to drought, flood, hurricane severity, land area, habitats, biological cycles, and uncertainty in environmental models. (Charlotte Harbor National Estuary Program and Southwest Florida Regional Planning Council 2010)

City of Punta Gorda Adaptation Plan

The City of Punta Gorda Adaptation Plan identifies the alternative adaptations that could be undertaken to address the identified climate change vulnerabilities for the City of Punta Gorda, including adaptive management and subsequent monitoring. Eight major areas of climate change vulnerability were identified for the City of Punta Gorda: fish and wildlife habitat degradation; inadequate water supply; flooding; unchecked or unmanaged growth; water quality degradation; education and economy and lack of funds; fire; and availability of insurance. The top agreed upon adaptations for each area of vulnerability include: protecting and restoring seagrass; using xeriscaping and native plant landscaping; explicitly indicating in the comprehensive plan which areas will retain natural shorelines; constraining locations for certain high risk infrastructure; restricting fertilizer use; promoting green building alternatives through education, taxing incentives, and green lending; and conducting drought preparedness planning. (Beever et al. 2009b)

The Potential Effects of Climate Change Section starting on page 44 of the Draft CCP was updated with a new paragraph three, as listed (the underlined text was added).

In the Comprehensive Southwest Florida/Charlotte Harbor Climate Change Vulnerability Assessment, the Southwest Florida Regional Planning Council and the Charlotte Harbor National Estuary Program examine current and ongoing climate change. Southwest Florida is currently experiencing climate change. The natural setting of southwest Florida coupled with extensive overinvestment in the areas closest to the coast have placed the region at the forefront of geographic areas that are among the first to suffer the negative effects of a changing climate. More severe tropical storms and hurricanes with increased wind speeds and storm surges have already severely damaged both coastal and interior communities of southwest Florida. Significant losses of mature mangrove forest, water quality degradation, and barrier island geomorphic changes have already occurred. Longer, more severe dry season droughts coupled with shorter duration wet seasons consisting of higher volume precipitation have generated a pattern of drought and flood impacting both natural and man-made ecosystems. Even in the most probable, lowest impact future climate change scenario predictions, the future for southwest Florida will include increased climate instability; wetter wet seasons; drier dry seasons; more extreme hot and cold events; increased coastal erosion; continuous sea level rise; shifts in fauna and flora with reductions in temperate species and expansions of tropical invasive exotics; increasing occurrence of tropical diseases in plants, wildlife and humans; destabilization of aquatic food webs including increased harmful algae blooms; increasing strains upon and costs in infrastructure; and increased uncertainty concerning variable risk assessment with uncertain actuarial futures (Beever et al. 2009a).

In the same section, the introduction to the old paragraph three/new paragraph four on page 44 of the Draft CCP was updated (the underlined text was added): Since the refuges lack even baseline data, measured impacts to refuge resources are currently unknown.

Resource Protection

Land Acquisition Strategy

Comment: The CCP should commit to a strategy for land acquisition. Climate change will increasingly reduce the suitability of habitats for species that have historically depended upon them. As ecosystem components shift in different directions, hydrological and disturbance regimes change, and land is lost to rising seas, land acquisition will be critical to ensuring the refuges' continued existence and to facilitating the transition of wildlife to more suitable locations. The "Ding" Darling Complex protects very little upland habitat, and what does exist will be at risk of inundation.

The CCP states that minor expansion proposals (MEPs) would be developed for managing closed buffer areas around sensitive resources in the event that the buffer areas fall outside of the refuges' current acquisition boundaries (page 111 of the Draft CCP). Defenders of Wildlife supports the development of MEPs and encourages the Service to include in the CCP a commitment to develop MEPs regardless of whether they are needed to manage closed buffer areas. Expanding the refuges' boundaries would allow the Service to acquire additional land in the future, thereby protecting more habitat and offsetting the loss of coastal acreage due to sea-level rise. Because the Service lacks data on many species inhabiting the refuges, Defenders cautions against a firm commitment to prioritize acquisition of lands important to migratory birds. Instead, climate change models and species vulnerability assessments should guide acquisition prioritization.

Service Response: Comment noted. Land acquisition was not a major component of the CCP and EA when written. However, as additional information and models become available, the Service would consider the addition of lands and waters that would further the goals for climate change adaptation. As the Peninsular Florida LCC becomes active, the Service, the State of Florida, and other conservation partners will evaluate the long-term prognosis of existing conservation lands and the need for increasing, shifting, and connecting conservation lands potentially impacted by climate change.

Refuges' Boundaries

Two comments were submitted regarding the boundaries of the refuges.

Comment: The plan indicates that there are discrepancies over some of the acquisition boundaries. Some boundaries are unclear, and some have shifted with erosion, attenuation, and dredging. Defenders of Wildlife suggests that the planning team provide in the CCP a more detailed explanation of the current boundaries. Defenders also supports the plan to clearly define and mark boundaries, as proposed in Alternative C.

Service Response: Although Resource Protection Objective 2.a(1) on page 111 of the Draft CCP addresses the boundary discrepancies, a new Resource Protection Objective 2.a(2) was added, as listed (the underlined text was added) and the remaining objectives under 2.a were renumbered.

<u>Objective 2.a(2): Within five years of plan approval, work with the Service's Southeast Region Realty Office to develop an accurate survey of the refuges' ownership boundaries.</u>

And the listed text was added to the discussion on page 111 of the Draft CCP (the underlined text was added).

<u>The refuges need complete, clearly defined surveys to help minimize issues associated with ownership, encroachment from adjoining private properties, and expansion of adjacent rights-of-way.</u>

Project 10 on page 124 of the Draft CCP was modified to overtly outline the needed surveys, as listed (the underlined text was added).

Project 10. Review existing boundaries to ensure postable, identifiable, and defensible boundaries for all four refuges. <u>Work with the Service's Southeast Region Realty Office to develop an accurate survey of the refuges' ownership boundaries.</u> Work with partners to improve the posting of the piping plover critical habitat and other posting needs at Terrapin Creek on Matlacha Pass NWR.

Comment: On page 92 of the Draft CCP the report states, "Island Bay NWR lacks surveyed and posted boundaries." However, the report states that "Currently all four refuges have posted management boundaries" (pages 111 and 124). This inconsistency should be addressed.

Service Response: Paragraph 4 on page 92 of the Draft CCP was updated to replace the Island Bay NWR sentence with (the underlined text was added): <u>Island Bay NWR has some boundary posts, but lacks a complete posted boundary.</u>

Cultural Resources

Comment: The State Historic Preservation Officer concurs that additional cultural resource surveys will be necessary prior to any new construction or excavation on refuge lands and that such projects would require review by the State Historic Preservation Officer.

Service Response: Comment noted. This comment is addressed more specifically on pages 110, 124, and 130 and more generally on pages 5, 11, 21, 95, 109, 118, and 121 of the Draft CCP.

Visitor Services

Environmental Education, Interpretation, and Outreach

Comment: Environmental education and interpretation are priority public uses of the Refuge System and, when compatible, support the Refuge System's mission by building public understanding and support for wildlife conservation. According to the Service Manual, recreational uses should provide "an opportunity to make visitors aware of resource issues, management plans, and how the refuge contributes to the Refuge System and Service mission" (605 FW 1 General Guidelines for Wildlife-Dependent Recreation (2006)). Because Pine Island, Matlacha Pass, Island Bay, and Caloosahatchee NWRs are closed to the public, Defenders of Wildlife supports the expansion of environmental education, interpretation, and outreach through "Ding" Darling NWR. However, Defenders recommends that the CCP include specific provisions for incorporating information about climate change impacts into these programs and materials. The Service is well positioned to educate and inform the visiting public about the climate-driven changes impacting the entire "Ding" Darling Complex and its wildlife, and measures the public can take to help protect them.

Service Response: Existing goals and objectives for environmental education and interpretation (pages 114-115 of the Draft CCP) and for outreach (pages 115-116 of the Draft CCP) generally discuss human impacts to natural systems, as follows:

- Visitor Services Goal 3 (environmental education and interpretation): Participants in quality environmental education and interpretation opportunities will develop an understanding and awareness of the values of Pine Island, Matlacha Pass, Island Bay, and Caloosahatchee NWRs; their natural resources; their roles in the landscape; and human influences on ecosystems.
    - Under Visitor Services Goal 3, Visitor Services objectives 3.a(1), 3.a(3), 3.a(4), and 3.a(5) also include the minimization of wildlife and habitat impacts from human activities.
- Visitor Services objectives 4.a(1) and 4.a(2) (outreach) also include the minimization of wildlife and habitat impacts from human activities.

However, the Service agrees with Defenders of Wildlife that climate change and its associated impacts should be more specifically addressed and included in refuge outreach activities and environmental education and interpretation programs and activities. To that end, a discussion was added under Goal 3, as listed (the underlined text was added).

Human influences on ecosystems in this area include climate change and its associated impacts which can result in direct wildlife, habitat, and habitat functionality loss and disturbance, which are also impacted by human activities, such as development and landscape use and conversion. The associated impacts include declining wildlife and habitat; water quality, quantity, and timing impacts; invasion and spread of exotic, invasive, and nuisance species; and climate change and its associated impacts. Since J.N. "Ding" Darling NWR has high visibility and visitation, inclusion of these messages in environmental education and interpretation programs and activities is expected to help minimize impacts from human activities.

Further, the discussion under Visitor Services objectives 4.a(1) and 4.a(2) on page 115 of the Draft CCP was expanded, as listed (the underlined text was added).

The refuges would increase participation in festivals and events held by the partners (e.g., at Mango Mania) to help increase outreach to the local communities. The annual refuge event proposed under Visitor Services Objective 3.a(4) would offer an excellent opportunity to also conduct outreach activities. Climate change and its associated impacts would be incorporated into refuge outreach activities to increase understanding and awareness and to increase support for management activities to respond to these impacts. The refuges will also coordinate with local schools to incorporate climate change curriculum and activities into their environmental education programs.

Adjacent Activities and Unauthorized Access

Comment: On page 20 of the Draft CCP: An area of management concerns that do not appear to be well addressed in the document are the significant issues of unauthorized access to the refuges and the high public use levels and activities adjacent to the refuges in area waters, particularly at Caloosahatchee NWR and the southern islands of the Matlacha Pass NWR that are at the mouth of the Caloosahatchee River. There appears to be significant human use of some of these islands, including recreational boat anchoring very close to and landing on the refuges and the use by the public of the islands of the Caloosahatchee NWR and the southern islands of Matlacha Pass NWR that are at the mouth of the Caloosahatchee River. On these islands humans have left trash, waste, and debris, including abandoned monofilament. Propeller dredging occurs when boats approach and leave the islands and shallow waters. Human use may be discouraging the use of these islands for wading and shorebird nesting.

Service Response: Comment noted. These concerns are recognized on pages 20, 84, 87, and 91-92 of the Draft CCP and specifically addressed on page 95 and under Resource Protection Objective 1.a(1) (cultural resource protection); Resource Protection objectives 2.a(1), 2.a(2), 2.a(3), and 2.a(4) (boundaries); Resource Protection objectives 2.b(1) (closed area buffers) and 3.a(1) (Island Bay NWR Wilderness Area); Visitor Services objectives 3.a(1), 3.a(3), 3.a(4), and 3.a(5) (environmental education and interpretation); Visitor Services objectives 4.a(1) and 4.a(2) (outreach); Visitor Services objectives 4.b(1), 4.b(2), and 4.b(3) (outreach specific to fishing activities); and Refuge Administration objectives 1.a(1) (staffing, including law enforcement), 2.a(1) (governmental partners), 2.b(1) (nongovernmental partners), and 3.a(1) (Service visibility and image) of the Draft CCP. Since the Service does not control these areas off of the refuges, access to these areas, or these adjacent activities, coordination with the partners, increased visibility and presence of the Service, and increased awareness and understanding by area users are needed to address the impacts of these activities.

Refuge Administration

Staffing

Two comments were submitted regarding staffing.

Comment: The employees need to be downsized.

Service Response: Comment noted. The four refuges are currently unstaffed. They are currently managed as a collateral duty by staff of the J.N. "Ding" Darling NWR. During the public scoping period, increased staffing was identified by governmental partners, individual members of the public, and organizations as an important need to be addressed in the CCP. During the development and analysis of alternatives, the Service determined that staff members were needed to serve the purposes of the refuges, to address the priority issues and ecological threats and problems facing the refuges, and to manage the refuges and the resources they protect. Refuge Administration Objective 1.a(2) on page 116 of the Draft CCP and Figure 23 on page 117 of the Draft CCP outline the five positions proposed to support these four refuges.

Comment: Defenders of Wildlife supports hiring a Biological Science Technician for inputting and maintaining data in a GIS system.

Service Response: Comment noted. The Biological Science Technician proposed in Refuge Administration Objective 1.a(2) would have a variety of duties. GIS will likely be one of those duties.

Funding

Comment: The employees need to stop looking to turn every dollar spent here into their own benefit.

Service Response: Comment noted. The refuges are currently unstaffed and unfunded. They are currently managed as a collateral duty by staff of the J.N. "Ding" Darling NWR. During the public scoping period, increased funding was identified by governmental partners, individual members of the public, and organizations as an important need to be addressed in the CCP. During the development and analysis of alternatives, the Service determined that funding was needed to serve the purposes of the refuges, to address the priority issues and ecological threats and problems facing the refuges, and to manage the refuges and the resources they protect. Refuge Administration Objective 1.a(2) on page 116 of the Draft CCP and Figure 23 on page 117 of the Draft CCP outline the five positions proposed to support these four refuges. Further, Chapter V of the Draft CCP outlines proposed projects to meet the basic needs of the refuges.

Partners

Multiple comments were submitted regarding partners.

Comment: I do not favor working with partners. Far too often partners are after money and power for themselves by using the resources that belong to all of us.

Service Response: Comment noted. The Service has a long and successful history of working with governmental and private partners to further the mission of the Service and the purposes of refuges. Since the refuges have historically been unstaffed and due to their distance from the staff of J.N. "Ding" Darling NWR, the Service has relied upon the partners, with limited support from the Service, to conduct wildlife surveys; protect cultural resources; conduct law enforcement patrol and enforcement activities; provide outreach and environmental education activities; and control invasive, exotic species on and around the refuges to help protect the refuges and serve their designated purposes. Partners will continue to play a key role in future management of the refuges and are addressed in various locations in the Draft CCP/EA, including under a variety of goals and objectives.

Comment: Refuge Administration Objective 2.a(1) should also include the Lee County Sea-Grant Program, Charlotte County Sea-Grant Program, Lee County School District, Charlotte County School District, West Coast Inland Navigation District, and National Marine Fisheries Service (NOAA).

Service Response: The Discussion under Refuge Administration Objective 2.a(1) on page 118 of the Draft CCP was updated to add these organizations to the list of partners. The West Coast Inland Navigation District and National Marine Fisheries Service were added to the list of existing partners, while the rest were added to the list of new partners.

Comment: Refuge Administration Objective 2.b(1) should also include Mote Marine Laboratory, Friends of the Charlotte Harbor Aquatic Preserves, Barrier Island Park Society, Charlotte Harbor Environmental Center, Florida Paddling Trails Association, Gasparilla Island Conservation and Improvement Association, Coastal Wildlife Club, Conservation Foundation of the Gulf Coast, and Society for Ethical Ecotourism of Southwest Florida.

Service Response: Refuge Administration Objective 2.b(1) on page 118 of the Draft CCP was updated to add these organizations to the list of partners, volunteers, and friends groups. Mote Marine Laboratory was added to the list of existing partners and the remaining were added to the list of new partners.

Comment: As a partner, Charlotte Harbor Aquatic Preserves looks forward to continuing to coordinate with the Refuge Complex on monthly colonial bird nest counts on the refuges and state-owned islands in Matlacha Pass and Pine Island Sound and on other ongoing projects. Further, we see other partnering opportunities as outlined in several of the 21 proposed projects.

Service Response: Comment noted. The refuges are committed to working with the partners to further resource protection goals and objectives.

Partners – Management Plans

Comment: State Aquatic Preserves (page 39): Add reference to the Charlotte Harbor Aquatic Preserves Management Plan, which was approved in 1983 and remains in effect. [NOTE: Within the Draft CCP/EA, when referring to the four aquatic preserves with a single name, Charlotte Harbor Aquatic Preserves should be plural.] The 1983 Charlotte Harbor Aquatic Preserves Management Plan should be added to the list of references.
http://www.dep.state.fl.us/coastal/downloads/management_plans/aquatic/CharlotteHarbor.pdf

Comment: Only four aquatic preserves are located within the area of these four refuges: Pine Island Sound, Matlacha Pass, Cape Haze, and Gasparilla Sound/Charlotte Harbor aquatic preserves. Two additional aquatic preserves are located nearby: Lemon Bay and Estero Bay aquatic preserves.

Service Response: Page 20 of the Draft CCP was updated to include this sentence (the underlined text was added): Further, six state aquatic preserves are located in the larger landscape area and the area is part of the Charlotte Harbor National Estuary Program. The State Aquatic Preserves subsection on page 39 of the Draft CCP was updated to reflect the Charlotte Harbor Aquatic Preserves Management Plan, the Lemon Bay Aquatic Preserve Management Plan, and the Estero Bay Aquatic Preserve Management Plan and applicable citations for these plans, as listed. It was also updated to reflect four aquatic preserves in the area of the four refuges with two additional aquatic preserves nearby, as listed. The underlined text was added.

In 1975 Florida adopted the Aquatic Preserve Act to protect state-owned submerged lands for those areas with exceptional biological, aesthetic, and scientific value to set them aside forever as aquatic preserves or sanctuaries for the benefit of future generations. Today, Florida has 46 aquatic preserves on nearly 2 million acres (Florida Department of Environmental Protection 2009). Four aquatic preserves totaling over 157,000 acres are located in the area of these four refuges: Pine Island Sound (designated in 1970, 54,000 acres), Matlacha Pass (designated in 1972, 12,500 acres), Cape Haze (designated in 1978, 11,000 acres), and Gasparilla Sound/Charlotte Harbor (designated in 1979, 80,000 acres) (Florida Department of Environmental Protection 2009). Covering the Cape Haze, Gasparilla Sound, Matlacha Pass, and Pine Island Sound aquatic preserves, the Charlotte Harbor Aquatic Preserves Management Plan was approved in 1983 (Florida Department of Natural Resources 1983a). The Charlotte Harbor Aquatic Preserves Management Plan covers over 200 square miles, which is 90% of the surface water area in the Charlotte Harbor system (Florida Department of Natural Resources 1983a). These four aquatic preserves were designated and are managed as wilderness preserves to maintain their wilderness condition (Florida Department of Natural Resources 1983a). Beyond these four aquatic preserves, two additional aquatic preserves totaling about 19,000 acres are located nearby: Lemon Bay (designated in 1986, 8,000 acres) and Estero Bay Aquatic Preserve (designated in 1983, 11,000 acres) (Florida Department of Environmental Protection 2009). Covering 7,667 acres and as outlined in its management plan, the Lemon Bay Aquatic Preserve was established to preserve marine and estuarine areas in essentially natural or restored conditions so that the aesthetic, biologic, and scientific values shall endure for the enjoyment of present and future generations (Florida Department of Natural Resources 1992). Covering over 15 square miles of surface water area, the Estero Bay Aquatic Preserve was designated and is managed as a wilderness preserve to maintain the wilderness condition (Florida Department of Natural Resources 1983b). The resources of these four refuges benefit from protection and management of all of these aquatic preserves.

Comment: Implementation of Proposed Alternative C in the Draft CCP/EA should be coordinated with existing management plans for the Aquatic Preserves and State Parks within the boundaries of the Complex. Insert State Parks and Preserve State Park on page 40 immediately before Wild and Scenic Rivers. Cayo Costa State Park, Gasparilla Island State Park, and Charlotte Harbor Preserve State Park all have approved management plans. (See http://www.dep.state.fl.us/parks/planning/plans.htm for more information.)

Service Response: The Service will continue coordinating with these and other applicable plans. State aquatic preserves are addressed under the Regional Conservation Plans and Initiatives section on pages 39-40 of the Draft CCP. The Charlotte Harbor National Estuary Program is addressed under the Regional Conservation Plans and Initiatives section on page 34 and pages 38-39 of the Draft CCP. State parks are initially addressed under the Relationship to State Wildlife Agency section on pages 9-10 of the Draft CCP. Page 40 of the Draft CCP was updated to add a new subsection entitled: State Parks and Preserves. This new subsection cites and summarizes the management plans for Cayo Costa State Park, Gasparilla Island State Park, and Charlotte Harbor Preserve State Park, as listed (the underlined text was added).

Management plans for Cayo Costa State Park, Gasparilla Island State Park, and Charlotte Harbor Preserve State Park also relate to and benefit these four refuges. Located north of North Captiva Island between Pine Island Sound and the Gulf of Mexico, Cayo Costa State Park is near Pine Island NWR and includes portions of four islands, totaling 2,656 acres (Florida Department of Environmental Protection 2005a). Cayo Costa State Park is designated as a public outdoor recreation site (Florida Department of Environmental Protection 2005a). Located just north of Cayo Costa State Park between Charlotte Harbor and the Gulf of Mexico and north of Boca Grande Pass, Gasparilla Island State Park is near Island Bay NWR and is 128 acres in size (Florida Department of Environmental Protection 2002c). Gasparilla Island State Park is also designated as a public outdoor recreation site (Florida Department of Environmental Protection 2002c). Encompassing 42,598 acres along Charlotte Harbor, Charlotte Harbor Preserve State Park is close to Island Bay NWR with portions in Punta Gorda and Cape Coral (Florida Department of Environmental Protection 2007). Designated for public outdoor recreation and conservation, Charlotte Harbor Preserve State Park includes 70 miles of shoreline and numerous islands (Florida Department of Environmental Protection 2007).

Comment: Management issues in the Charlotte Harbor Aquatic Preserves Management Plan that are consistent with and address management goals in the CCP/EA should be identified.

Service Response: The discussion under Refuge Administration 2.a(1) on page 118 of the Draft CCP was updated to include the listed text (the underlined text was added).

Since the refuges exist within the larger estuarine landscape, they share numerous goals and objectives with the partners, especially with the Charlotte Harbor National Estuary Program and the Charlotte Harbor Aquatic Preserves, including protecting natural and cultural resources; supporting recovery of rare, threatened, and endangered species; conducting surveys; restoring

<u>and enhancing habitats; controlling exotic, invasive, and nuisance species; addressing water quality, quantity, and timing of flow concerns; understanding and ameliorating the impacts of climate change; increasing awareness and understanding of natural resource issues; minimizing human disturbance and impacts; and coordinating with the partners.</u>

Step-down Management Plans

Comment: The Service is faced with the challenge of addressing a number of major threats to the refuges, including impacts from nearby development; high public use; climate change impacts such as sea level rise; water quality, quantity, and timing issues; and invasive species. Defenders of Wildlife supports the general management direction proposed in the CCP, and Defenders looks forward to reviewing more specific details on management strategies in the anticipated step-down management plans.

Service Response: Comment noted. Step-down management plans are addressed in Chapter V on pages 129-130 of the Draft CCP. Three step-down management plans are anticipated to be developed for the Refuge Complex during the 15-year life of the plan: Visitor Services Plan, Habitat Management Plan, and Cultural Resources Management Plan.

Other

CCP in General

Comment: Overall, the CCP is quite comprehensive and does an admirable job of summarizing past, present, and future management challenges and opportunities, as well as identifying staffing and other administrative shortcomings and needs. It identifies many opportunities for synergy with other plans and planning efforts affecting the refuges, their habitats, and their wildlife.

Overall, the plan is comprehensive, outlining the major threats and goals over the next 15 years with a guiding directive on migratory birds.

Service Response: Comments noted.

Alternatives

Multiple comments were submitted regarding the alternatives.

Comment: Alternative C is acceptable. It is consistent with the Charlotte Harbor National Estuary Program (CHNEP) Comprehensive Conservation and Management Plan's (CCMP's) quantifiable objectives relating to water quality, hydrology, fish and wildlife habitat, and stewardship gaps. The CHNEP supports Alternative C's primary management goal of focusing on the needs of migratory birds.

Comment: Defenders of Wildlife supports the overall management direction of Alternative C, the alternative preferred by the Service. Although this alternative focuses on migratory bird management, it generally does a good job of balancing management of other wildlife.

Service Response: Comments noted. The primary purpose for each of the four refuges is as a ". . . preserve and breeding ground for native birds". The Draft CCP/EA, including the alternatives, was developed with input from a variety of governmental agencies, organizations, businesses, and the public. The Draft CCP/EA, including the alternatives, was developed following the National Environmental Policy Act and the National Wildlife Refuge System Improvement Act, with guidance provided by the Service's planning policy (602 FW1-4), the Service's policy on biological integrity, diversity, and environmental health (601 FW3), and other applicable and related mandates. Further, the Service evaluated applicable management plans such as the CHNEP CCMP in the development and analysis of alternatives and proposed future management actions.

Comment: The agency should stop picking alternatives of their design and enrichment for the American public. The American public has been telling this agency for some time and this agency doesn't want to talk or listen to the American public.

Service Response: Comment noted. The Draft CCP/EA, including the alternatives, was developed with input from a variety of governmental agencies, organizations, businesses, and the public. The Draft CCP/EA, including the alternatives, was developed following the National Environmental Policy Act and the National Wildlife Refuge System Improvement Act, with guidance provided by the Service's planning policy (602 FW1-4), the Service's policy on biological integrity, diversity, and environmental health (601 FW3), and other applicable and related mandates. Chapter I of the Draft CCP summarizes the legal and policy context for the planning effort. Further, Appendix C outlines relevant legal mandates and executive orders. Chapter III of the Draft CCP summarizes the public scoping activities and the issues, concerns, and opportunities that were raised during the public scoping period. Further, Appendix D summarizes public involvement in the planning process. The issues, concerns, and opportunities raised during public scoping were used to help the Service determine the priority issues to be addressed in the CCP, develop and analyze alternatives, and fully develop the future management actions that are outlined in the Draft CCP. Chapter V of the EA summarizes the consultation and coordination activities of the planning process. In addition, comments received during this public review of the Draft CCP/EA have resulted in some changes to the plan, corrections, and updates. Every public comment received was appreciated and considered in the development of the final CCP.

Oil Spill

Comment: The CCP should outline a plan for addressing oil spill impacts. Spilled or leaking oil can be devastating to estuaries and to mangrove, marsh, and seagrass habitats. Because these are vitally important nurseries for young fish, invertebrates such as shellfish, and other marine organisms, and because these habitats provide important feeding, roosting, and nesting habitat for wading birds and shorebirds, it is important to keep spilled oil out of estuaries whenever possible. Once the oil reaches an estuary, cleanup is very difficult. Research on previous spills suggests that marshes and mangroves can be further damaged by well intentioned cleanup efforts (NOAA Ocean Servs., Nat'l Oceanic and Atmospheric Admin., OIL SPILLS IN MANGROVES: PLANNING AND RESPONSE CONSIDERATIONS [R. Hoff ed. 2002]). The research also shows that these habitats are very slow to recover from the damage of an oil spill (J. B. Culbertson et al., *Long-term Consequences of Residual Petroleum on Salt Marsh Grass*, 45 JOURNAL OF APPLIED ECOLOGY 1284 [2008]). The recent BP Deepwater Horizon disaster underscores the potential for oil spills to impact America's national wildlife refuges, and the risk could be heightened by hurricane activity. The CCP should include a contingency plan for dealing with oil spills, including measures that can be employed to prevent oil from reaching the refuges' waters and shores.

Service Response: Comment noted. Oil spill response plans were developed in May 2010 for several national wildlife refuges, including Pine Island, Matlacha Pass, Island Bay, and Caloosahatchee NWRs, in response to the Deepwater Horizon event. The list of existing step-down management plans on page 129 of the Draft CCP in Chapter V was updated to include this new step-down plan for the refuges.

Number of State Aquatic Preserves

Comment: Page 10 of the Draft CCP states that the Florida Department of Environmental Protection manages 57 coastal and aquatic managed areas, while there are only 46.

Service Response: Pages 10 and 39 of the Draft CCP were updated to reflect 46.

Clarification on State Aquatic Preserves

Comment: On page 21 of the Draft CCP, please add "through the Florida Department of Environmental Protection's Office of Coastal and Aquatic Managed Areas" to the second sentence of paragraph three so that it reads: "In addition, Lemon Bay Aquatic Preserve (also administered under the Charlotte Harbor Aquatic Preserves through the Florida Department of Environmental Protection's Office of Coastal and Aquatic Managed Areas) …".

Service Response: The sentence on page 21 was updated to read as listed (the underlined text was added).

> In addition, Lemon Bay Aquatic Preserve (also administered under the Charlotte Harbor Aquatic Preserves through the Florida Department of Environmental Protection's Office of Coastal and Aquatic Managed Areas) is near Island Bay NWR and Estero Bay Aquatic Preserve is near Matlacha Pass NWR.

Comment: Table 1 on page 22 of the Draft CCP needs to be updated. Change Camp Haze State Aquatic Preserve to Cape Haze Aquatic Preserve and change Charlotte Harbor State Buffer Preserve to Charlotte Harbor Preserve State Park. Add Estero Bay Preserve State Park to the Lee County part of the list.

Service Response: Table 1 on page 22 of the Draft CCP was updated to make these changes.

Map Clarifications Needed

Comment: On page 27 on the Draft CCP, Figure 6 (8): There is an error on the map that indicates the entire Southwest Florida International Airport is a local conservation land. Portions of the area indicated are, but the operating airport and associated aviation facilities are not.

On page 27 of the Draft CCP, Figure 6 (8): The category "other" has a combination of real conservation lands, such as private conservation easements that are fully preserved and managed as mitigation for DRIs and lands that are proposed, but not yet secured for conservation such as lands in the CREW boundary that are not yet acquired and protected.

Service Response: Figure 8 on page 27 of the Draft CCP shows the area conservation lands. This map was updated to reflect a smaller conservation land area for the Airport. The legend was also updated to indicate that the "Other" category included acquisition boundaries.

Comment: On page 71 of the Draft CCP, Figure 20: The Figure 20 should indicate the date of the seagrass coverage data.

Service Response: Figure 20 on page 71 of the Draft CCP was updated with 2004.

Typographical Errors and Updates

Comment: On page 32 of the Draft CCP, hammocks is misspelled as hummocks.

Service Response: Page 32 of the Draft CCP was updated to reflect this correction.

Comment: Page 32 of the Draft CCP states that average temperature is 68-75°F. In the Ding Darling plan, it was around 74-75; 68 may be the average winter temperature.

Service Response: Page 32 of the Draft CCP was updated with data from Table 5 (the underlined text was added): Based on data from the Fort Myers Airport, annual average temperatures range from 64.6°F to 84°F, while monthly average temperatures range from 53.5°F in January to 91.4°F in August (Southeast Regional Climate Center 2007).

Appendix E. Appropriate Use Determinations

Pine Island, Matlacha Pass, Island Bay, and Caloosahatchee National Wildlife Refuges Appropriate Use Determinations

An appropriate use determination is the initial decision process a refuge manager follows when first considering whether or not to allow a proposed use on a refuge. The refuge manager must find that a use is appropriate before undertaking a compatibility review of the use. This process clarifies and expands on the compatibility determination process by describing when refuge managers should deny a proposed use without determining compatibility. If a proposed use is not appropriate, it will not be allowed and a compatibility determination will not be undertaken.

Except for the uses noted below, the refuge manager must decide if a new or existing use is an appropriate refuge use. If an existing use is not appropriate, the refuge manager will eliminate or modify the use as expeditiously as practicable. If a new use is not appropriate, the refuge manager will deny the use without determining compatibility. Uses that have been administratively determined to be appropriate are:

- Six wildlife-dependent recreational uses - As defined by the National Wildlife Refuge System Improvement Act of 1997, the six wildlife-dependent recreational uses (hunting, fishing, wildlife observation, wildlife photography, and environmental education and interpretation) are determined to be appropriate. However, the refuge manager must still determine if these uses are compatible.
- Take of fish and wildlife under state regulations - States have regulations concerning take of wildlife that includes hunting, fishing, and trapping. The Service considers take of wildlife under such regulations appropriate. However, the refuge manager must determine if the activity is compatible before allowing it on a refuge.

Statutory Authorities for this policy:

National Wildlife Refuge System Administration Act of 1966, as amended by the National Wildlife Refuge System Improvement Act of 1997, 16 U.S.C. 668dd-668ee. This law provides the authority for establishing policies and regulations governing refuge uses, including the authority to prohibit certain harmful activities. The Act does not authorize any particular use, but rather authorizes the Secretary of the Interior to allow uses only when they are compatible and "under such regulations as he may prescribe." This law specifically identifies certain public uses that, when compatible, are legitimate and appropriate uses within the Refuge System. The law states ". . . it is the policy of the United States that . . .compatible wildlife-dependent recreation is a legitimate and appropriate general public use of the System . . .compatible wildlife-dependent recreational uses are the priority general public uses of the System and shall receive priority consideration in refuge planning and management; and . . . when the Secretary determines that a proposed wildlife-dependent recreational use is a compatible use within a refuge, that activity should be facilitated . . . the Secretary shall . . . ensure that priority general public uses of the System receive enhanced consideration over other general public uses in planning and management within the System . . . ." The law also states "in administering the System, the Secretary is authorized to take the following actions: . . . issue regulations to carry out this Act." This policy implements the standards set in the Act by providing enhanced consideration of priority general public uses and ensuring other public uses do not interfere with our ability to provide quality, wildlife-dependent recreational uses.

Refuge Recreation Act of 1962, 16 U.S.C. 460k. The Act authorizes the Secretary of the Interior to administer refuges, hatcheries, and other conservation areas for recreational use, when such uses do not interfere with the area's primary purposes. It authorizes construction and maintenance of recreational facilities and the acquisition of land for incidental fish and wildlife oriented recreational development or protection of natural resources. It also authorizes the charging of fees for public uses.

Other Statutes that Establish Refuges, including the Alaska National Interest Lands Conservation Act of 1980 (ANILCA) (16 U.S.C. 410hh - 410hh-5, 460 mm - 460mm-4, 539-539e, and 3101 - 3233; 43 U.S.C. 1631 et seq.).

Executive Orders. The Service must comply with Executive Order 11644 when allowing use of off-highway vehicles on refuges. This order requires the Service to designate areas as open or closed to off-highway vehicles in order to protect refuge resources, promote safety, and minimize conflict among the various refuge users; monitor the effects of these uses once they are allowed; and amend or rescind any area designation as necessary based on the information gathered. Furthermore, Executive Order 11989 requires the Service to close areas to off-highway vehicles when it is determined that the use causes or will cause considerable adverse effects on the soil, vegetation, wildlife, habitat, or cultural or historic resources. Statutes, such as ANILCA, take precedence over executive orders.

Definitions:

Appropriate Use
A proposed or existing use on a refuge that meets at least one of the following four conditions.
1) The use is a wildlife-dependent recreational use as identified in the Improvement Act.
2) The use contributes to fulfilling the refuge purpose(s), the Refuge System mission, or goals or objectives described in a refuge management plan approved after October 9, 1997, the date the Improvement Act was signed into law.
3) The use involves the take of fish and wildlife under state regulations.
4) The use has been found to be appropriate as specified in section 1.11.

Native American. American Indians in the conterminous United States and Alaska Natives (including Aleuts, Eskimos, and Indians) who are members of federally recognized tribes.

Priority General Public Use. A compatible wildlife-dependent recreational use of a refuge involving hunting, fishing, wildlife observation, wildlife photography, and environmental education and interpretation.

Quality. The criteria used to determine a quality recreational experience include:
- Promotes safety of participants, other visitors, and facilities.
- Promotes compliance with applicable laws and regulations and responsible behavior.
- Minimizes or eliminates conflicts with fish and wildlife population or habitat goals or objectives in a plan approved after 1997.
- Minimizes or eliminates conflicts with other compatible wildlife-dependent recreation.
- Minimizes conflicts with neighboring landowners.
- Promotes accessibility and availability to a broad spectrum of the American people.
- Promotes resource stewardship and conservation.
- Promotes public understanding and increases public appreciation of America's natural resources and the Service's role in managing and protecting these resources.

- Provides reliable/reasonable opportunities to experience wildlife.
- Uses facilities that are accessible and blend into the natural setting.
- Uses visitor satisfaction to help define and evaluate programs.

Wildlife-Dependent Recreational Use. As defined by the Improvement Act, a use of a refuge involving hunting, fishing, wildlife observation, wildlife photography, and environmental education and interpretation.

FINDING OF APPROPRIATENESS OF A REFUGE USE

Refuge Name: Pine Island, Matlacha Pass, Island Bay, and Caloosahatchee National Wildlife Refuges

Use: Research

This form is not required for wildlife-dependent recreational uses, take regulated by the State, or uses already described in a refuge CCP or step-down management plan approved after October 9, 1997.

Decision Criteria:	YES	NO
(a) Do we have jurisdiction over the use?	X	
(b) Does the use comply with applicable laws and regulations (Federal, State, tribal, and local)?	X	
(c) Is the use consistent with applicable Executive orders and Department and Service policies?	X	
(d) Is the use consistent with public safety?	X	
(e) Is the use consistent with goals and objectives in an approved management plan or other document?	X	
(f) Has an earlier documented analysis not denied the use or is this the first time the use has been proposed?	X	
(g) Is the use manageable within available budget and staff?	X	
(h) Will this be manageable in the future within existing resources?	X	
(i) Does the use contribute to the public's understanding and appreciation of the refuge's natural or cultural resources, or is the use beneficial to the refuge's natural or cultural resources?	X	
(j) Can the use be accommodated without impairing existing wildlife-dependent recreational uses or reducing the potential to provide quality (see section 1.6D, 603 FW 1, for description), compatible, wildlife-dependent recreation into the future?	X	

Where we do not have jurisdiction over the use ["no" to (a)] there is no need to evaluate it further as we cannot control the use. Uses that are illegal, inconsistent with existing policy, or unsafe ["no" to (b), (c), or (d)] may not be found appropriate. If the answer is "no" to any of the other questions above, we will generally not allow the use.

If indicated, the refuge manager has consulted with State fish and wildlife agencies.   Yes X   No ____

When the refuge manager finds the use appropriate based on sound professional judgment, the refuge manager must justify the use in writing on an attached sheet and obtain the refuge supervisor's concurrence.

Based on an overall assessment of these factors, my summary conclusion is that the proposed use is:

Not Appropriate ____   Appropriate X

Refuge Manager: _Signed_   Date: 7/28/2010

If found to be **Not Appropriate**, the refuge supervisor does not need to sign concurrence if the use is a new use.
If an existing use is found Not Appropriate outside the CCP process, the refuge supervisor must sign concurrence.
If found to be Appropriate, the refuge supervisor must sign concurrence.

Refuge Supervisor: _Signed_   Date: 8/5/10

A compatibility determination is/required before the use may be allowed.

FINDING OF APPROPRIATENESS OF A REFUGE USE

Refuge Name: Pine Island, Matlacha Pass, and Caloosahatchee National Wildlife Refuges

Use: Mosquito Control

This form is not required for wildlife-dependent recreational uses, take regulated by the State, or uses already described in a refuge CCP or step-down management plan approved after October 9, 1997.

Decision Criteria:	YES	NO
(a) Do we have jurisdiction over the use?	X	
(b) Does the use comply with applicable laws and regulations (Federal, State, tribal, and local)?	X	
(c) Is the use consistent with applicable Executive orders and Department and Service policies?	X	
(d) Is the use consistent with public safety?	X	
(e) Is the use consistent with goals and objectives in an approved management plan or other document?	X	
(f) Has an earlier documented analysis not denied the use or is this the first time the use has been proposed?	X	
(g) Is the use manageable within available budget and staff?	X	
(h) Will this be manageable in the future within existing resources?	X	
(i) Does the use contribute to the public's understanding and appreciation of the refuge's natural or cultural resources, or is the use beneficial to the refuge's natural or cultural resources?	X	
(j) Can the use be accommodated without impairing existing wildlife-dependent recreational uses or reducing the potential to provide quality (see section 1.6D, 603 FW 1, for description) compatible, wildlife-dependent recreation into the future?	X	

Where we do not have jurisdiction over the use ("no" to (a)), there is no need to evaluate it further as we cannot control the use. Uses that are illegal, inconsistent with existing policy, or unsafe ("no" to (b), (c), or (d)), may not be found appropriate. If the answer is "no" to any of the other questions above, we will generally not allow the use.

If indicated, the refuge manager has consulted with State fish and wildlife agencies.   Yes X   No ____

When the refuge manager finds the use appropriate based on sound professional judgment, the refuge manager must justify the use in writing on an attached sheet and obtain the refuge supervisor's concurrence.

Based on an overall assessment of these factors, my summary conclusion is that the proposed use is:

Not Appropriate ____   Appropriate   X

Refuge Manager: _Signed_   Date: 7/28/2010

If found to be **Not Appropriate**, the refuge supervisor does not need to sign concurrence if the use is a new use.
If an existing use is found **Not Appropriate** outside the CCP process, the refuge supervisor must sign concurrence.
If found to be **Appropriate**, the refuge supervisor must sign concurrence.

Refuge Supervisor: _Signed_   Date: 8/5/10

A compatibility determination is required before the use may be allowed.

Appendix F. Compatibility Determinations

COMPATIBILITY DETERMINATIONS FOR THE PINE ISLAND, MATLACHA PASS, ISLAND BAY, AND CALOOSAHATCHEE NATIONAL WILDLIFE REFUGES

Uses: The following uses were evaluated to determine their compatibility with the mission of the National Wildlife Refuge System and the purposes of the refuges.

- Research
- Mosquito Control

Refuge Names: Pine Island, Matlacha Pass, Island Bay, and Caloosahatchee National Wildlife Refuges (NWRs)

Dates Established:

Pine Island, Matlacha Pass, and Island Bay NWRs – 1908
Caloosahatchee NWR – 1920

Establishing and Acquisition Authorities:
- Pine Island NWR – Executive Order 939
- Matlacha Pass NWR – Executive Order 043
- Island Bay NWR – Executive Order 958
- Caloosahatchee NWR – Executive Order 3299

Refuges' Purposes:

Pine Island NWR
- "…as a preserve and breeding ground for native birds" Executive Order 939
- "…suitable for (1) incidental fish and wildlife-oriented recreational development, (2) the protection of natural resources, (3) the conservation of endangered species or threatened species" 16 U.S.C. 460k-1 (Refuge Recreation Act) "…the Secretary…may accept and use…real…property. Such acceptance may be accomplished under the terms and conditions of restrictive covenants imposed by donors" 16 U.S.C. 460k-2 (Refuge Recreation Act)
- "…for the development, advancement, management, conservation, and protection of fish and wildlife resources" 16 U.S.C. 742f(a)(4) (Fish and Wildlife Act) "…for the benefit of the United States Fish and Wildlife Service, in performing its activities and services. Such acceptance may be subject to the terms of any restrictive or affirmative covenant, or condition of servitude" 16 U.S.C. 742f(b)(1) (Fish and Wildlife Act)

Matlacha Pass NWR
- "…as a preserve and breeding ground for native birds" Executive Order 943

Island Bay NWR
- "…as a preserve and breeding ground for native birds" Executive Order 958

- "...wilderness areas...shall be administered for the use and enjoyment of the American people in such manner as will leave them unimpaired for future use and enjoyment as wilderness, and so as to provide for the protection of these areas, the preservation of their wilderness character, and for the gathering and dissemination of information regarding their use and enjoyment as wilderness..." 16 U.S.C. 1131 (Wilderness Act)

Caloosahatchee NWR
- "...as a preserve and breeding ground for native birds" Executive Order 3299

National Wildlife Refuge System Mission:

The mission of the National Wildlife Refuge System, as defined by the National Wildlife Refuge System Improvement Act of 1997, is:

... to administer a national network of lands and waters for the conservation, management, and where appropriate, restoration of the fish, wildlife and plant resources and their habitats within the United States for the benefit of present and future generations of Americans.

Other Applicable Laws, Regulations, and Policies:
Antiquities Act of 1906 (34 Stat. 225)
Migratory Bird Treaty Act of 1918 (15 U.S.C. 703-711; 40 Stat. 755)
Migratory Bird Conservation Act of 1929 (16 U.S.C. 715r; 45 Stat. 1222)
Migratory Bird Hunting Stamp Act of 1934 (16 U.S.C. 718-178h; 48 Stat. 451)
Criminal Code Provisions of 1940 (18 U.S.C. 41)
Bald and Golden Eagle Protection Act (16 U.S.C. 668-668d; 54 Stat. 250)
Refuge Trespass Act of June 25, 1948 (18 U.S.C. 41; 62 Stat. 686)
Fish and Wildlife Act of 1956 (16 U.S.C. 742a-742j; 70 Stat.1119)
Refuge Recreation Act of 1962 (16 U.S.C. 460k-460k-4; 76 Stat. 653)
Wilderness Act (16 U.S.C. 1131; 78 Stat. 890)
Land and Water Conservation Fund Act of 1965
National Historic Preservation Act of 1966, as amended (16 U.S.C. 470, et seq.; 80 Stat. 915)
National Wildlife Refuge System Administration Act of 1966 (16 U.S.C. 668dd, 668ee; 80 Stat. 927)
National Environmental Policy Act of 1969, NEPA (42 U.S.C. 4321, et seq; 83 Stat. 852)
Use of Off-Road Vehicles on Public Lands (Executive Order 11644, as amended by Executive Order 10989)
Endangered Species Act of 1973 (16 U.S.C. 1531 et seq; 87 Stat. 884)
Refuge Revenue Sharing Act of 1935, as amended in 1978 (16 U.S.C. 715s; 92 Stat. 1319)
National Wildlife Refuge Regulations for the Most Recent Fiscal Year
(50 CFR Subchapter C; 43 CFR 3101.3-3)
Emergency Wetlands Resources Act of 1986 (S.B. 740)
North American Wetlands Conservation Act of 1990
Food Security Act (Farm Bill) of 1990 as amended (HR 2100)
The Property Clause of the U.S. Constitution Article IV 3, Clause 2
The Commerce Clause of the U.S. Constitution Article 1, Section 8
The National Wildlife Refuge System Improvement Act of 1997 (Public Law 105-57, U.S.C. 668dd)
Executive Order 12996, Management and General Public Use of the National Wildlife Refuge System. March 25, 1996
Title 50, Code of Federal Regulations, Parts 25-33
Archaeological Resources Protection Act of 1979
Native American Graves Protection and Repatriation Act of 1990

Public Review and Comment:

The compatibility determinations for Pine Island, Matlacha Pass, Island Bay, and Caloosahatchee NWRs were made available for public review and comment as part of the refuges' Draft Comprehensive Conservation Plan and Environmental Assessment. The methods used to solicit public review and comment included a notice of availability of the Draft CCP/EA for public review and comment, published in the *Federal Register* on May 21, 2010 (volume 75, number 98); notices and updates posted at the J.N. "Ding" Darling National Wildlife Refuge Complex's Educational Center and on the refuge's Internet website; postcards mailed to individuals on the refuges' CCP mailing list; news releases and articles published in area newspapers; notices posted on the Service's Southeast Regional Planning website; and copies of the Draft CCP/EA sent to the Ding Darling Wildlife Society, adjacent landowners, the general public, nongovernmental organizations, and local, state, and federal agencies.

The descriptions and anticipated impacts of each use are considered separately. However, for brevity, the preceding "Uses" through "Public Review and Comment" sections and the "Approval of Compatibility Determinations" section apply to each use. If any one of these uses is considered outside of the Comprehensive Conservation Plan, then those sections become part of that compatibility determination.

Description of Use: *Research*

Research is the planned, organized, and systematic gathering of data to discover or verify facts. In principle, research conducted on the refuges by universities, cooperative units, nonprofit organizations, and other research entities furthers refuge management and serves the purposes, vision, and goals of the refuges. The refuges can host research from a variety of research institutions, including various universities and private research institutions. All research activities, whether conducted by governmental agencies, public research entities, universities, private research groups, or any other entity, shall be required to obtain special use permit from the Refuge Complex. All research activities will be overseen by the Refuge Biologist and Refuge Manager of the Refuge Complex. Projects that are fish and wildlife management-oriented, which will provide needed information to refuge operation and management, will receive priority consideration.

Availability of Resources: Other than the administration of associated special use permits, no refuge resources are generally required for this use.

Anticipated Impacts of the Use: Generally, adverse impacts from research are minimal. Slight or temporary wildlife or habitat disturbances may occur (e.g., minor trampling of vegetation may occur when researchers access monitoring plots). However, these impacts are not significant, nor are they permanent. Also, a small number of individual plants or animals might be collected for further scientific study, but these collections are anticipated to have minimal impact on the populations from which they came. All collections will adhere to the Service's specimen collection policy (Director's Order 109, dated March 28, 2005).

Determination:

_____ Use is Not Compatible

__X__ Use is Compatible with Following Stipulations

Stipulations Necessary to Ensure Compatibility: All research conducted on the refuges must further the purposes of the refuges and the mission of the National Wildlife Refuge System. All research will adhere to established Refuge Complex and Service policies on research and on collecting specimens (Director's Order Number 109). To ensure that research activities are compatible, the refuges requires that a refuge special use permit be obtained from the Refuge Complex before any research activity may occur. Research proposals and/or research special use permit applications must be submitted in advance of the activity to allow for review by refuge staff to ensure minimal impacts to the resources, staff, and programs of the refuges. Each special use permit may contain conditions under which the research will be conducted. Each special use permit holder will submit annual reports or updates to the refuge on research activities, progress, findings, and other information. Further, each special use permit holder will provide copies of findings, final reports, publications, and/or other documentation at the end of each project. The refuge will deny permits for research proposals that are determined to not serve the purposes of the refuge and the mission of the National Wildlife Refuge System. The refuge will also deny permits for research proposals that are determined to negatively impact resources or that materially interfere with or detract from the purposes of the refuge. All research activities are subject to the conditions of their permits.

Justification: Research activities provide important benefits to the refuges and to the natural resources supported by the refuges. Supporting management, research conducted on the refuges can lead to new discoveries, new facts, verified information, and increased knowledge and understanding of resource management, as well as track current trends in fish and wildlife habitat and populations to enable better management decisions. Research has the potential to further the purposes of the refuges and the mission of the National Wildlife Refuge System.

NEPA Compliance for Refuge Use Description:

_____ Categorical Exclusion without Environmental Action Statement
_____ Categorical Exclusion and Environmental Action Statement
__X__ Environmental Assessment and Finding of No Significant Impact
_____ Environmental Impact Statement and Record of Decision

Mandatory 10-year Re-evaluation Date: 09/16/2020

Description of Use: *Mosquito Control*

Mosquito control activities occur on Pine Island, Matlacha Pass, and Caloosahatchee NWRs and around all four refuges in both Lee and Charlotte counties. The Refuge Complex annually works with the Service's Regional and national pest management coordinators and with the Lee County Mosquito Control District to review and update the list of approved chemicals for mosquito control activities. The focus is to find the safest, yet effective chemicals for use on the refuge. Larviciding is allowed on the three refuges, but adulticiding is not. However, under periods of wide spread health threats or disaster recovery, the Refuge Complex will review proposals for treatments with approved chemicals or may coordinate with the Service's Regional and national pest management coordinators and with the Lee County Mosquito Control District to consider allowing proposed new chemicals.

The Lee County Mosquito Control District (LCMCD) conducts mosquito control activities through an integrated pest management approach on the three refuges and throughout Lee County. The mission of the LCMCD is that the Lee County Mosquito Control District is committed to improving the quality of life, facilitating outdoor activities and protecting the public health in our community by implementing environmentally sound practices that control mosquitoes throughout Lee County.

The LCMCD conducts surveillance on the three refuges. Mosquito traps may be deployed to determine mosquito population levels. Sentinel chickens may be used with the approval of the Refuge Manger. LCMCD helicopter and fixed wing aircraft will comply with the flight restrictions listed in the Special Conditions section of the Special Use Permit. LCMCD are required to notify the Refuge Biologist prior to any mosquito control treatments.

The LCMCD focuses on larviciding. Larviciding refers to the control of mosquitoes in the larval, aquatic stage. Its efforts are focused toward controlling mosquitoes in this stage, because the insects are confined to the aquatic environment and can be efficiently targeted with minimal effect on other organisms. Mosquitoes remain in the larval stage for as little as four days, which requires an intense effort to locate and treat them before they become adults. Larval inspections are conducted by trained LCMCD personnel capable of identifying mosquitoes to genera and larval stage. Aircraft are used to expedite locating and treating larval mosquitoes in remote areas and large acreages, while ground inspections and treatments are performed in residential and small areas using vehicle-mounted spraying equipment. All larvicide applications are based on a demonstrated presence of mosquito larvae. Aerial and ground larviciding by helicopter, truck, and boat are conducted on and around the three refuges.

The LCMCD also uses adulticiding treatments to control mosquitoes. Adulticiding does not occur on the three refuges, but does occur near them. Adulticiding refers to the control of mosquitoes in the adult, terrestrial flying stage. Despite all efforts to prevent adult mosquito populations from reaching annoyance levels, it is inevitable that outbreaks will occur. All of LCMCD adulticiding activity is based on surveillance data and no adulticide spraying is performed on a scheduled basis. Each weekday, LCMCD inspectors are busy monitoring Lee County's adult mosquito populations. Ground adulticiding trucks use Ultra-Low-Volume technology with equipment that atomizes or creates many tiny droplets which drift through the air and contact a mosquito in flight. The method achieves excellent results in areas with a good network of roads. Aerial adulticiding is conducted by helicopters or fixed-wing aircraft with Ultra-Low-Volume spray systems, usually between 10:00 pm and 2:00 am or at sunrise.

After the U.S. Environmental Protection Agency (EPA) determines that an insecticide can be registered for use in the United States, the Florida Department of Agriculture and Consumer Services (FDACS) determines which pesticides can be registered and applied in the State of Florida. The primary aerial adulticide material used by the LCMCD is Naled. FDACS states the Naled, sold under the name Dibrom, when applied in accordance with the label, can be used to kill mosquitoes without posing unreasonable risks to human health or the environment. FDACS further notes that the EPA recently conducted preliminary risk assessments for Naled. These assessments calculated risks under a number of different scenarios, including assumptions of several Naled spraying events over a period of weeks and toddlers ingesting some Naled in soil and grass along with exposure through the skin and inhalation exposure. Because of the very small amount of active ingredient released per acre of ground, the EPA found that for all scenarios considered, exposures were hundreds or even thousands of times below an amount that might pose a health concern. FDACS further states that when applied for mosquito control in accordance with the label, Naled is not harmful to animals.

Availability of Resources: The Lee County Mosquito Control District funds and implements these mosquito control activities. Thus, no refuge resources are required to administer this use, other than reviewing management plans and the operations and pesticides to be used. Staff to administer this use includes the Refuge Complex Biologist and Refuge Manager. Salaries for these positions come from the Refuge Complex operating budget, which is adequate to sustain the existing program.

Anticipated Impacts of the Use: Mosquito control activities have the potential for a variety of impacts. Potential impacts of chemicals on nontarget organisms are a concern and are considered prior to mosquito control operations. Potential negative impacts to invertebrates from chemical applications may result in decreases in density and diversity of insects, arachnids, and/or crustaceans, thus negatively impacting food sources for various birds. Further, temporary wildlife or habitat disturbances may occur during actual operations (e.g., wildlife disturbance and temporary trampling of vegetation during pesticide applications by ground vehicles).

Determination (check one below):

_____ Use is Not Compatible

_X_ Use is Compatible with the Listed Stipulations

Stipulations Necessary to Ensure Compatibility: Stipulations to help ensure compatibility of this use are listed.
- A Refuge Complex special use permit is required and must be renewed annually.
- No mosquito control activities can occur within Island Bay NWR. No flights shall be conducted over the Island Bay NWR Wilderness Area.
- Overflights are restricted to areas with low migratory bird use.
- Larval control may only be conducted when breeding is widespread, as documented by sampling conducted by the LCMCD and/or CCMCD.
- Priority for treatments will be given to those chemicals with the least effect on nontarget organisms.
- The Refuge Manager has final approval for all pesticide treatments.
- The LCMCD and CCMCD shall each submit to the Refuge Complex a final report at the end of each year.
- The LCMCD and CCMCD shall notify the Refuge Manager or Refuge Complex Biologist by phone of all pesticide applications, including areas and acreages to be treated, pesticide to be applied, date and time of planned treatment, method of application, and data supporting the need for treatment.
- In developing approaches to specific treatments, consideration will be given to avoiding or minimizing impacts to the resources of the refuges.
- Refuge staff shall be allowed to inspect operations at any time.
- All pesticides used must be included in the Refuge Complex Pesticide Use and Disposal Management Plan. If a pesticide proposed for use is not included in this step-down plan, the Refuge Manager must review and approve its use before any application occurs.
- The LCMCD and the CCMCD shall immediately notify the Refuge Manager of any chemical spills, threats to human safety on the refuge, human disturbance, or wildlife disturbance that may occur as a consequence of its mosquito control operations.

The Refuge Complex will modify or eliminate any use that results in unacceptable impacts.

Justification: Under the right environmental conditions, areas of the refuges are productive habitats for population explosions of mosquitoes. The refuges exist within a developed human landscape, where mosquitoes represent a potential disease threat to public health, as well as to wildlife. Mosquito control activities address health safety issues for the refuges and the community. The use, with the listed stipulations, does not materially interfere with the purposes of the refuges.

NEPA Compliance for Refuge Use Description:

_____ Categorical Exclusion without Environmental Action Statement
_____ Categorical Exclusion and Environmental Action Statement
__X__ Environmental Assessment and Finding of No Significant Impact
_____ Environmental Impact Statement and Record of Decision

Mandatory 10-year Re-evaluation Date: 09/16/2020

Approval of Compatibility Determinations

The signature of approval is for the compatibility determinations considered within the Comprehensive Conservation Plan for Pine Island, Matlacha Pass, Island Bay, and Caloosahatchee National Wildlife Refuges.

Refuge Manager: _Signed_ 7/28/2010
(Signature/Date)

Regional Compatibility Coordinator: _Signed_ 8/10/10
(Signature/Date)

Refuge Supervisor: _Signed_ 8/16/10
(Signature/Date)

Regional Chief, National Wildlife Refuge System, Southeast Region: _Signed_ 8-18-10
(Signature/Date)

Appendix G. Intra-Service Section 7 Biological Evaluation

SOUTHEAST REGION
INTRA-SERVICE SECTION 7 BIOLOGICAL EVALUATION FORM

Originating Person: Paul Tritaik, Wildlife Refuge Manager (Project Leader), J.N. "Ding" Darling NWR Complex

Telephone Number: 239/472-1100 X 223   **E-Mail:** paul_tritaik@fws.gov

Date: 9/28/2009

PROJECT NAME: Comprehensive Conservation Plan for Pine Island, Matlacha Pass, Island Bay, and Caloosahatchee NWRs

I. **Service Program:**

  ___ Ecological Services

  ___ Federal Aid

   ___ Clean Vessel Act

   ___ Coastal Wetlands

   ___ Endangered Species Section 6

   ___ Partners for Fish and Wildlife

   ___ Sport Fish Restoration

   ___ Wildlife Restoration

  ___ Fisheries

  _X_ Refuges/Wildlife

II. **State/Agency:**
n/a

III. **Station Name:**
Pine Island, Matlacha Pass, Island Bay, and Caloosahatchee National Wildlife Refuges (refuges), FL (satellite refuges of the J.N. "Ding" Darling National Wildlife Refuge Complex [Refuge Complex])

IV. **Description of Proposed Action:**
The proposed project is to implement the refuges' Comprehensive Conservation Plan (CCP) as required under the National Wildlife Refuge System Improvement Act of 1997. The purpose of a CCP is to describe the desired future conditions of a refuge and provide long-range guidance and management direction to accomplish the purposes of a refuge, to contribute to the mission of the Refuge System, and to meet other relevant mandates.

The CCP details the preferred action to improve refuge management in the following areas: wildlife and habitat management, resource protection, visitor services, and refuge administration. The preferred action (Alternative C) focuses refuge management actions on the needs of migratory birds.

Wildlife and Habitat Management

Under Alternative C, the refuges would expand wildlife and habitat management activities, with a focus on migratory birds to address rare, Threatened, and Endangered species; wildlife and habitat diversity; exotic, invasive, and nuisance species; water quality, quantity, and timing concerns; and climate change impacts. The needs of migratory birds would be prioritized in all management and restoration plans.

Rare, Threatened, and Endangered Species
Twelve federally listed species and 24 State listed species occur on and around the refuges. This list includes species that are of management concern to the refuges, including the wood stork, roseate spoonbill, roseate tern, black skimmer, American oystercatcher, snowy plover, Wilson's plover, red knot, piping plover, bald eagle, mangrove cuckoo, black-whiskered vireo, gray kingbird, Florida prairie warbler, West Indian manatee, ornate diamondback terrapin, loggerhead sea turtle, green sea turtle, Kemp's Ridley sea turtle, gopher tortoise, American alligator, American crocodile, eastern indigo snake, gulf sturgeon, and smalltooth sawfish. Wildlife surveys conducted by the partners and refuge staff have shown a decline in several wildlife populations in recent years. An up-to-date, geographically referenced, wildlife database inventory (including all refuge flora and fauna) will be developed and implemented to monitor long-term status and trends and to proactively protect refuge species and habitat, with particular attention for:

- migratory bird populations;
- habitat and land and water use, improvements, management practices, and changes;
- rare, threatened, and endangered species;
- native fish populations (as a food source for wildlife and to support recreational fishing); and
- exotic, invasive, and nuisance species.

The refuges would work with the partners to support recovery of wood storks, including improving, protecting, and restoring habitat and decreasing disturbance. Further, the refuges would foster research to develop an understanding of wood stork colony origin and foraging range and locations. For roseate spoonbills, the refuges would work with the partners to better document usage of the refuges by spoonbills and to foster research to identify colony origin. For both wood storks and roseate spoonbills, the refuges would work with the partners to increase public awareness and understanding of the impacts of disturbance to foraging and nesting of these species. To benefit black skimmers, American oystercatchers, roseate turns, snowy and piping plovers, Wilson's plovers, and red knots, as well as other birds using shorelines of the refuges, the refuges would monitor the beach profile changes over time in relation to climate change and sea level rise and the refuges would better understand and manage beach habitats and disturbances. Over the long term, the refuges would work with the U.S. Army Corps of Engineers (USACE) and other partners to continually create or enhance suitable nesting and foraging habitat for black skimmers, American oystercatchers, and roseate terns during dredge and spoil activities. The Terrapin Creek Tract of Matlacha Pass NWR would be monitored for black skimmer use. Also, the refuges would increase efforts and work with the partners to minimize human access to Skimmer Island and/or to other sites found to be used by black skimmers. The refuges would work with the partners to develop appropriate closed area buffers around rookeries and other nesting sites (e.g., for wood storks, roseate spoonbills, American oystercatchers, roseate terns, and snowy plovers). The refuges would work with the partners to also minimize disturbances to snowy and piping plovers, ensuring no human disturbances to snowy plover nesting areas and piping plover wintering areas. The refuges would evaluate the development of a formal survey to monitor the population status and trends for American oystercatchers. To benefit piping and Wilson's plovers and red knots, the refuges would conduct surveys to monitor for their presence/absence, adapting management as necessary to minimize disturbances. Surveys would also be conducted to better understand population status and trends for mangrove cuckoos, black-whiskered vireos, gray kingbirds, and Florida prairie warblers. The refuges would research the effectiveness of survey protocols with nesting cycles and timing. And, the refuges would maintain mangrove and uplands used by mangrove forest birds. For West Indian manatees, the partners take the lead in law enforcement of speed zones and in the Marine Mammal Stranding Network. The refuges would increase intergovernmental coordination and habitat protection to better serve manatees. And, the refuges would work with the partners to evaluate the Turtle Bay area of Island Bay NWR for designation as a Manatee Sanctuary, since it is an important manatee natality area within Charlotte Harbor. The refuges would initiate management activities to benefit the ornate diamondback terrapin, including coordinating with the partners on surveys to determine population status and trends. The refuge staff would work with partners to determine the relative abundance of in-water populations of juvenile sea turtles around the refuges and evaluate potential trends. The refuge staff would work with partners to survey gopher tortoise presence/absence on the refuges and estimate density and habitat carrying capacity, where applicable.

Wildlife and Habitat Diversity
Alternative C would also provide management actions to benefit wildlife and habitat diversity, including for wading and water birds, raptors and birds of prey, nearctic-neotropical migratory birds, shorebirds and seabirds, mangroves, uplands, interior grasslands and wetlands, and seagrass beds, as well as address impacts from the proposed widening of Interstate 75 (I-75). To benefit a variety of birds, the refuges would work with the partners to identify, protect, restore, and enhance rookeries, foraging areas, and roosting habitats and to increase understanding and awareness of the impacts of disturbances to rookeries and foraging and roosting areas. The establishment of buffer zones around known rookery locations, other nesting sites, and key foraging and resting areas would benefit a variety of birds, including at the Terrapin Creek Tract at Matlacha Pass NWR. Where seagrass beds are included in these buffers, the refuges would work with the partners to protect and maintain them. Including raptors and birds of prey, nearctic-neotropical migratory birds, shorebirds, and seabirds in other surveys would increase information to enhance refuge decision-making. To also benefit raptors and birds of prey, the refuges would identify the nesting, breeding, roosting, and foraging habitat needs on the refuges, working with the partners to restore and maintain these habitats. The refuges would also identify and manage for the habitat needs of nearctic-neotropical migratory birds using the refuges, selecting for certain shrubs and trees as food sources and potential migration and nesting habitats. Over the long term, the refuges would work with USACE and other partners to continually create or enhance suitable nesting habitat for shorebirds and seabirds during dredge and spoil activities. Additional information to enhance refuge decision-making would come from an inventory of wetland species. To benefit a variety of species, the Terrapin Creek Tract at Matlacha Pass NWR and islands within all four refuges would be evaluated for potential restoration opportunities. In relation to the proposed widening of I-75, the refuge would work with the partners to identify and address wildlife and habitat impacts associated with the proposed project with an emphasis on minimizing impacts to wildlife and habitat diversity. The U.S Fish and Wildlife Service (Service) would consider offsetting these impacts with the addition of lands to Caloosahatchee NWR or other area refuges.

Exotic, Invasive, and Nuisance Species
Under Alternative C, the refuges would expand exotic, invasive, and nuisance species control activities with a focus on migratory birds. The refuges would update the list of priority species of exotic, invasive, and nuisance plants to be controlled. And, they would identify and locate new infestations of Florida Exotic Pest Plant Council (FLEPPC) Category I and Category II invasive upland plants (FLEPPC 2009).

Exotic plant control activities would focus initial attack on elimination. Control of existing exotic, invasive, and nuisance plants would focus on reducing negative impacts to migratory birds. Further, the refuges would work with the partners to control and eradicate monitor lizards, feral hogs, black rats, and green iguanas and would coordinate with the partners to increase the public's awareness of the negative impacts of exotic, invasive, and nuisance animals. In all these efforts, the refuges would adapt management as necessary to eradicate new invasive species and increase active participation in the Southwest Florida Cooperative Invasive Species Management Area.

Water Quality, Quantity, and Timing of Flows
Under Alternative C, the refuges would increase management and coordination activities related to water quality, quantity, and timing of flow concerns. Focusing on migratory birds, such management efforts would be expected to benefit a variety of species and habitats, including wood storks, roseate spoonbills, black skimmers, American oystercatchers, bald eagles, West Indian manatees, wading and water birds, raptors and birds of prey, shorebirds, seabirds, mangroves, and seagrass beds. The refuges would evaluate the need to expand the existing water quality monitoring stations to cover all four refuges.

Climate Change
And, the refuges would increase management activities under Alternative C to better identify and understand climate change impacts. The refuges would work with the partners to foster and conduct research to better understand the impacts of climate change on resources of the refuges and to refine and run appropriate climate change models (e.g., rerun the Sea Level Affecting Marshes Model (SLAMM) with higher resolution Light Detection and Ranging (LIDAR) data) to better predict sea level change impacts on resources of the refuges with a focus on migratory birds. Further, the refuges would work with the partners to establish benchmarks to record sea level rise and beach profiles and shoreline changes, which could potentially impact a variety of species, including black skimmers, American oystercatchers, snowy plovers, piping plovers, Wilson's plovers, and red knots. Refuge management activities could be adapted as necessary to respond to the impacts associated with climate change and sea level rise.

Resource Protection

Resource protection management activities would be expanded under Alternative C, including addressing cultural resources, boundary issues, future acquisitions, special designations, and the Island Bay NWR Wilderness Area.

Alternative C would allow the refuges to better protect the archaeological and historical resources of the refuges by coordinating with the State Historic Preservation Officer and the Regional Archaeologist to conduct a complete archaeological and historical survey of the satellite refuges and to protect any newly identified sites. Management activities would be adapted as necessary to protect any newly identified sites.

To resolve boundary and ownership discrepancies, the refuges would conduct legal boundary surveys and historical research. Boundaries would be posted to ensure that they are identifiable and enforceable. To serve the purposes of the refuges and wildlife and habitat management goals and objectives, the refuges would work with the partners to develop agreements to establish closed area buffers to protect key resources. And, the boundary and posting needs would be evaluated for the Terrapin Creek Tract at Matlacha Pass NWR.

The refuges would pursue the designation of lands and waters within the current management boundaries of Pine Island and Matlacha Pass NWRs for inclusion in the Western Hemisphere Shorebird Reserve Network and of all four refuges as Ramsar Convention Wetlands of International Importance, as part of the application for J.N. "Ding" Darling NWR. As lands and waters are added to the refuges, evaluate the applicability of these special designations to those additions.

To improve management of the Island Bay NWR Wilderness Area, Alternative C would initiate coordination with the Charlotte County Environmental and Extension Services Department, Pest Management Division to eliminate the use of larvicides in the wilderness area during mosquito control activities. To increase understanding and awareness regarding the wilderness area, the Refuge Complex would incorporate Island Bay NWR Wilderness Area information, wilderness stewardship, and wilderness principles into programs and materials delivered at the "Ding" Darling Education Center and at the proposed annual event for the refuges. Further, if/when the refuges are expanded they would evaluate the appropriateness of expanding the Island Bay NWR Wilderness Area to these areas.

Visitor Services

Although the refuges would likely remain closed throughout the life of the CCP, Alternative C would expand the Visitor Services program of the refuges through coordination with the partners, expanded environmental education and interpretation opportunities, and increased outreach efforts and activities. Visitor services programs and activities would be focused on migratory birds.

Although the refuges themselves are closed, the area receives high use and numerous activities occur in the waters adjacent to the refuges. Ensuring that the public is aware of the refuges would be a key element to future management and protection of the resources. To help provide additional welcome and orientation, the refuges would expand existing activities. Since numerous area visitors also visit the nearby J.N. "Ding" Darling NWR, the Refuge Complex would update the exhibits and activities at the "Ding" Darling Education Center to highlight the refuges and provide wilderness stewardship principles. The refuges would also work with the partners to develop public awareness, understanding, and appreciation of the refuges and their purposes, the resources protected by the refuges, and the role that the refuges play in the landscape.

Since numerous uses occur adjacent to the refuges, the refuges would work with the partners to minimize the impacts to resources of the refuges from these adjacent activities (e.g., impacts from monofilament and fishing activities on migratory birds) and to improve the ethical outdoor behavior of area users. Closed area buffers would be established to protect key resources (e.g., a closed area buffer might be created around an already closed bird rookery, helping to minimize impacts to the nesting, resting, and foraging birds and only removing a small area from direct public access).

Under Alternative C, the refuges would expand environmental education and interpretation programs and activities. The Refuge Complex would incorporate messages that focus on migratory birds, the role and importance of the refuges in the landscape, and the importance of minimizing the impacts of human activities into on-site (at the "Ding" Darling Education Center) and off-site curriculum-based environmental education programs, as well as into interpretive and outreach materials developed for all refuges in the Refuge Complex. The Refuge Complex would train volunteers, teachers, and staff to conduct educational and interpretive programs; increase outreach efforts and activities to the local communities (e.g., at Mango Mania); and work with partners to develop an annual satellite refuges event in one of the local communities. The refuges would also work with the partners to provide information to the fishing public regarding the impacts of fishing activities on migratory birds and to evaluate the need to expand the monofilament recycling program.

The potential exists for additional lands and/or waters to be added to these four refuges. At a minimum, this might include closed area buffers to protect sensitive resources (e.g., rookeries). The refuges would evaluate the appropriateness and compatibility of opening portions of the refuges as they are expanded. However, it is likely that they will remain closed throughout the life of the CCP.

Refuge Administration

To protect and manage the natural and cultural resources of the refuges, Alternative C would expand upon the refuge administration activities of Alternative A. Alternative C would create five staff positions specific to the refuges: Biological Science Technician, Law Enforcement Officer, Wildlife Refuge Specialist (Assistant Refuge Manager), Hydrologist, and a Park ranger (environmental education). The estimated annual recurring costs of these five positions, with a 25 percent operating margin, would total $443,368. The lead Biologist at the J.N. "Ding" Darling NWR would continue to design and oversee the biological program and activities at the satellite refuges. The refuges would work with the partners to evaluate and install interpretive signage at partner sites. And, the refuges would expand partnerships, including improving and increasing coordination with governmental entities (e.g., city of Cape Coral and Charlotte County Environmental and Extension Services Department, Pest Management Division) and developing new partnerships (e.g., Audubon Society). And, a key refuge administration activity would be to work to improve the visibility and image of the Service in communities around the refuges to build support for refuge management, including through the development of an annual event in one of the local communities to highlight the refuges.

V. **Pertinent Species and Habitat:**

A. **Refuge Location and Habitats:**
Critical habitat maps are provided in the CCP for the piping plover (around Lee County's Bunche Beach and the Matlacha Pass NWR's Terrapin Creek Tract) and the West Indian manatee. General species occurrence maps are included in the South Florida Multi-Species Recovery Plan (Service 1999). The proposed project area is located on Pine Island, Matlacha Pass, Island Bay, and Caloosahatchee NWRs in Lee and Charlotte counties, on the southwest coast of Florida. Refuge habitats include mangrove islands, and vegetated and unvegetated wetlands.

B. **Federally Listed Species:**
The refuge currently serves 13 federally Threatened or Endangered species, as listed.

SPECIES	CRITICAL HABITAT	STATUS
West Indian manatee (*Trichechus manatus*)	designated / present	Endangered
Atlantic green sea turtle (*Chelonia mydas*)	designated / not present	Endangered
Hawksbill sea turtle (*Eretmochelys imbricata*)	designated / not present	Endangered
Kemp's ridley sea turtle (*Lepidochelys kempii*)	none designated	Endangered
Loggerhead sea turtle	none designated	Threatened

SPECIES	CRITICAL HABITAT	STATUS
(*Caretta caretta*)		
Eastern indigo snake (*Drymarchon corais copueri*)	none designated	Threatened
American alligator (*Alligator mississippiensis*)	none designated	Threatened (s/a)
American crocodile (*Crocodylus acutus*)	designated / not present	Threatened
Piping plover (*Charadrius melodus*)	designated / present	Threatened
Wood stork (*Mycteria americana*)	designated / not present	Endangered
Roseate tern (*Sterna dougallii dougallii*)	none designated	Threatened
Smalltooth sawfish (*Pristis pectinata*)	designated / present	Endangered
Gulf sturgeon (*Acipenser oxyrinchus oxyrinchus*)	designated / not present	Threatened

VI. Location:

    A. **Ecoregion Number and Name:**
        Ecoregion 75b, Southwestern Florida Flatwoods Sub-Ecoregion

    B. **County and State:**
        Lee and Charlotte Counties, Florida.

    C. **Latitude and longitude:**
        Pine Island = North 26° 40' 02" West 82° 13' 40"
        Matlacha Pass = North 26° 30' 45" West 82° 01' 59"
        Island Bay = North 26° 46' 26" West 82° 11' 22"
        Caloosahatchee = North 26° 41' 54" West 81° 47' 50"

    D. **Distance and direction to nearest town:**
        Pine Island is less than 5 miles north of Sanibel, FL
        Matlacha Pass is less than 5 miles west of Cape Coral, FL
        Island Bay is less than 10 miles southwest of Punta Gorda, FL
        Caloosahatchee is less than 5 miles northeast of Fort Myers, FL

    E. **Species/habitat occurrence:**

Wood Stork

Wood storks are known to have used the refuges for roosting and foraging, while nesting is known to occur on Caloosahatchee NWR. The refuges would continue coordinating with the partners to survey rookeries to determine presence/absence of wood storks and to help support wood stork recovery. And the refuges would coordinate with the Service's lead on wood storks (at the Service's Jacksonville Ecological Services Office) to help develop an understanding of the colony origin and the foraging range and locations for the wood storks using the refuges. Adaptive management activities could include assessing valuable foraging wetlands used by the wood storks for protection, assessing valuable roosting and nesting sites used by the wood storks for protection, and forming or enhancing collaboration with other agencies managing areas used by the wood storks. The refuges would work with the State to implement closed area buffers to protect nesting wood storks and other wading birds and waterbirds. Rodgers and Schwikert (2002) recommended a minimum buffer size for wood storks of 118 meters to minimize impacts from outboard-powered boats and personal watercraft. And, the refuges would work with the partners to address water quality, quantity, and timing concerns to benefit a variety of resources, including wood storks.

Buzzard Roost of Caloosahatchee NWR includes a wood stork rookery. However, discrepancies exist it is whether this island is reflected in some maps as part of the Caloosahatchee NWR. Further discrepancies exist in relation to the official management boundary for Caloosahatchee NWR. The refuges would work with the Service's Southeast Region Realty office, the State of Florida, and the Lee County Property Appraiser's office to recognize the actual boundary for Caloosahatchee NWR and ownership of the known wood stork nesting island at the refuge.

Piping Plover

The refuges would continue protecting the designated piping plover wintering critical habitat as a closed area at Terrapin Creek in Matlacha Pass NWR to support recovery of the species. The refuges would develop a winter surveying program to document the presence/absence of piping plovers. The refuges would increase survey efforts to document presence, abundance, and locations used during the winter for all four refuges. All refuges would adapt management as necessary to minimize disturbances and support recovery of this species. The refuges would support recovery goals, including by conducting winter surveys, minimizing impacts and disturbances, and increasing public awareness. The refuges would work with the partners to minimize disturbances and impacts to piping plovers from humans and dogs on the beach and to minimize disturbances to beach habitats. And, the refuges would monitor beach profile changes over time in relation to climate change and sea level rise. To provide better protection and to help minimize disturbance, the refuges would work with the partners to establish seasonal closed areas buffers around known piping plover roost areas. And, the refuges would post boundaries for the piping plover critical habitat designated at Terrapin Creek at Matlacha Pass NWR.

West Indian Manatee

The refuges would continue working with the partners to conduct regular law enforcement patrols of speed zones to minimize threats and impacts to West Indian manatees in and around Pine Island, Matlacha Pass, Island Bay, and Caloosahatchee NWRs. To help minimize watercraft collisions with manatees, the refuges would continue to work with the partners to conduct regular law enforcement patrols of speed zones and no-motor zones, including the Service's Office of Law Enforcement, Florida Fish and Wildlife Conservation Commission (FWC), Lee County Sheriff's Office, and the Sanibel Police Department. The refuges would continue to participate in the Florida Marine Mammal Stranding Network – Southwest and with the Mote Marine Laboratory to facilitate quick response, care, and rehabilitation of injured manatees. The refuges would continue to coordinate with the National Atmospheric and Oceanic Administration's National Marine Fisheries Service (NOAA Fisheries) and FWC on necropsies, potentially using the Gavin Site, if necessary. Critical habitat for manatees was designated by the Service in 1976 to include: "all U.S. territorial waters adjoining the coast and islands of Lee County," which includes the waters around the Pine Island and Matlacha Pass refuge islands (note: the waters around the Pine Island refuge islands are mostly unregulated, but the waters around the Matlacha Pass NWR islands are Slow Speed All Year, 25 MPH in Channel); "Charlotte Harbor north of the Charlotte – Lee County line," which includes the waters around the Island Bay NWR's islands (note: these waters are a combination of unregulated, 25 MPH, Idle Speed Zones); and "Caloosahatchee River downstream from the Florida State Highway 31 bridge, Lee County," which includes the waters around the Caloosahatchee NWR's islands (note: these waters are all regulated as Idle Speed Outside Channel All Year, ICW Idle Speed Nov 15 - Mar 31, ICW 25 MPH Apr 1 - Nov 14).

The refuges will continue working with the partners to support recovery of the West Indian manatee, including providing and supporting environmental education, interpretation, and outreach. To help develop public awareness, understanding, and appreciation for manatees and related management activities, the refuges would continue working with Lee County's Manatee Park by providing interpretative assistance on manatees and information on the refuges. The refuges will also work with the partners to increase removal of monofilament fishing line.

Sea Turtles

The refuges will work with the partners to determine the relative abundance of in-water populations of juvenile sea turtles around the refuges and evaluate potential trends.

In-water populations of sea turtles have been monitored in the greater Charlotte Harbor area since 2003, by Mote Marine Laboratory. Mote Marine and partners have been conducting set netting and visual surveys of the Charlotte Harbor area, including Island Bay, Pine Island, and Matlacha Pass NWRs, to evaluate species composition, developmental migrations, habitat use, and feeding ecology. So far, the survey results have yielded sightings and captures of loggerheads, Kemp's ridleys, and greens. In order of abundance, loggerheads are typically found near tidal passes, ridleys congregate close to creek or bay mouths, and greens are often observed in seagrass pastures in six to eight feet of water. Annual catch per unit effort rates for visual transect sightings range from 0.011-0.021 turtles/hour and sighting densities drop during the winter months (Eaton et al. 2008). Another goal of this project is to evaluate post-hurricane effects on turtle foraging ecology in Charlotte Harbor. Surveys conducted after Hurricane Charley in 2004 reported hypoxic conditions and a massive horseshoe crab die-off in that same area. Disturbances to seagrass beds and changes in crustacean populations after hurricanes are also being evaluated as having possible effects on sea turtle foraging ecology. This information would enable the refuge to adapt management as necessary to protect these turtles.

Two hawksbill sea turtles were found in the waters of the refuges in early 2010 following a period of colder than normal temperatures, and were suffering from cold stress. Prior to this event, hawksbills had not been observed within the refuges.

Gopher Tortoise

The refuges will work with the partners to survey gopher tortoise presence/absence and estimate population density and habitat carrying capacity, where applicable. Gopher tortoises are under review for listing in Florida by the Service under the Endangered Species Act and are listed by the State of Florida as a Threatened species (Florida Fish and Wildlife Conservation Commission 2009a). There is recent and historic evidence of gopher tortoise activity on islands in Island Bay, Pine Island, and Caloosahatchee NWRs. And, the Terrapin Creek Tract of Matlacha Pass NWR is expected to support gopher tortoises. The refuges will enhance upland habitat islands where gopher tortoises are known to occur and work with partners to continue removing invasive exotic vegetation and thin understory.

Indigo Snake

In conjunction with gopher tortoise surveys conducted on the refuges, additional surveys in suitable habitats would help determine the presence or absence of the eastern indigo snake.

VII. **Determination of Effects:**

    A. **Explanation of effects:**
        The impacts to all the listed species occurring on the refuge (listed in Table V.B) are anticipated to be beneficial over the long-term. The Draft CCP/EA for the refuges includes a table that summarizes the environmental consequences of plan implementation

SPECIES/ CRITICAL HABITAT	IMPACTS TO SPECIES/CRITICAL HABITAT
Wood Stork	Positive. Increased habitat quantity and quality. Potential for stable to increased numbers of wood storks using the refuges. Increased information to enhance decision-making. Decreased disturbance. Increased coordination to minimize impacts from water quality, quantity, and timing of flows.
Piping Plover	Positive. Potential for stable to increased numbers of piping plovers using the refuges. Increased information to enhance decision-making. Decreased disturbances. Managed beach habitats.
Roseate Tern	Positive. Stable to increased numbers of roseate terns using the refuges. Increased habitat quality and quantity. Increased information to enhance decision-making. Increased coordination to minimize impacts from water quality, quantity, and timing of flows. Decreased disturbances. Managed beach habitats.
West Indian Manatee	Positive. Increased habitat on the refuges due to the designation of closed area buffers (e.g., for rookeries). Potential for increased habitat and protection due to designation of Manatee Sanctuary. Increased protection. Decreased disturbances. Increased coordination to minimize impacts from water quality, quantity, and timing of flows.

SPECIES/ CRITICAL HABITAT	IMPACTS TO SPECIES/CRITICAL HABITAT
Sea Turtles (Loggerhead, Green, Hawksbill, and Kemp's Ridley)	Neutral to positive. Increased information to enhance decision-making and coordination. Increased habitat on the refuges due to the designation of closed area buffers (e.g., for rookeries). Decreased disturbances. Increased coordination to minimize impacts from water quality, quantity, and timing of flows.
Eastern Indigo Snake	Neutral to positive. Increased information to enhance decision-making.
American Crocodile	Neutral to positive. Increased habitat on the refuges due to the designation of closed area buffers (e.g., for rookeries). Decreased disturbances. Increased coordination to minimize impacts from water quality, quantity, and timing of flows.
Smalltooth Sawfish	Neutral to positive. Increased habitat on the refuges due to the designation of closed area buffers (e.g., for rookeries). Decreased disturbances. Increased coordination to minimize impacts from water quality, quantity, and timing of flows.
Gulf Sturgeon	Neutral to positive. Increased habitat on the refuges due to the designation of closed area buffers (e.g., for rookeries). Decreased disturbances. Increased coordination to minimize impacts from water quality, quantity, and timing of flows.

B. **Explanation of actions to be implemented to reduce adverse effects:**
The implementation of all goals, objectives, and strategies outlined in the CCP will follow the refuge's best management practices and will pursue avoidance and minimization of impacts to federally Threatened and Endangered species, to the extent possible and practicable. Whenever and wherever prudent, the avoidance and minimization measures outlined in Table VII.B will be incorporated into the implementation of the CCP to minimize the effect to federally Threatened or Endangered species.

SPECIES/ CRITICAL HABITAT	ACTIONS TO MINIMIZE IMPACTS
All federally Threatened and Endangered species on the refuge	**Fire Management Activities** Fire management is a tool employed for the benefit of wildlife, including improving habitat, controlling wildfires, and controlling or removing exotic plants. The refuge will make all efforts possible and practicable to limit long-term wildlife impacts of management activities. Measures employed to limit wildlife impacts related to fire management activities include scheduling fire preparation and burns around nesting seasons and other periods of increased wildlife activity. Fire management activities are implemented according to the refuge's Fire Management Plan which had a section 7 review prior to its implementation. Future plan revisions will also receive a section 7 review. **Exotic Plant Control and Removal Activities** The refuge provides orientation information regarding federally Threatened and Endangered species found on the refuge to all new employees, volunteers, and contractors involved in controlling and removing exotic plants. All pesticides and herbicides are approved through the Service's Pesticide Use Proposal process and applied in accordance with label directions. The refuge will make all efforts possible and practicable to limit long-term wildlife impacts from management activities. Measures to limit wildlife impacts during the control and removal of exotic plants include preliminary assessments by qualified individuals to avoid burrows, nests, and other obvious signs of wildlife activity. Exotic plant control and removal activities are guided by an exotic control plan which had a section 7 review prior to implementation. Future plan revisions will also receive a section 7 review. **Research Activities** All researchers on the refuge must obtain all applicable permits, including a refuge special use permit before the commencement of research activities on the refuge. During the application for permits, conditions may be imposed to eliminate or minimize any impacts that may be anticipated from a research proposal. The refuge provides orientation information regarding federally Threatened and Endangered species found on the refuge to all researchers.

VIII. Effect Determination and Response Requested:

SPECIES / CRITICAL HABITAT	DETERMINATION[1]			RESPONSE[1] REQUESTED
	NE	NA	AA	
West Indian manatee (*Trichechus manatus*)		X		Concurrence
Atlantic green sea turtle (*Chelonia mydas*)		X		Concurrence
Hawksbill sea turtle (*Eretmochelys imbricata*)		X		Concurrence
Kemp's ridley sea turtle (*Lepidochelys kempii*)		X		Concurrence
Loggerhead sea turtle (*Caretta caretta*)		X		Concurrence
Eastern indigo snake (*Drymarchon corais copueri*)		X		Concurrence
American crocodile (*Crocodylus acutus*)		X		Concurrence
Piping plover (*Charadrius melodus*)		X		Concurrence
Wood stork (*Mycteria americana*)		X		Concurrence
Roseate tern (*Sterna dougallii dougallii*)		X		Concurrence
Smalltooth sawfish (*Pristis pectinata*)				Consulted with NOAA Fisheries
Gulf sturgeon (*Acipenser oxyrinchus oxyrinchus*)		X		Concurrence

Appendices

[1]DETERMINATION/ RESPONSE REQUESTED:

NE = no effect. This determination is appropriate when the proposed action will not directly, indirectly, or cumulatively impact, either positively or negatively, any listed, proposed, candidate species or designated/proposed critical habitat. Response Requested is optional, but a "Concurrence" is recommended for a complete Administrative Record.

NA = not likely to adversely affect. This determination is appropriate when the proposed action is not likely to adversely impact any listed, proposed, candidate species or designated/proposed critical habitat or there may be beneficial effects to these resources. Response Requested is a "Concurrence."

AA = likely to adversely affect. This determination is appropriate when the proposed action is likely to adversely impact any listed, proposed, candidate species or designated/proposed critical habitat. Response Requested for listed species is "Formal Consultation." Response requested for proposed and candidate species is "Conference."

Literature Cited:

Eaton, C., E. McMichael, B. Witherington, A. Foley, R. Hardy, and A. Meylan. 2008. In-water Sea Turtle Monitoring and Research in Florida: Review and Recommendations. Technical Memorandum NMFS-OPR-38, June 2008. Florida Fish and Wildlife Conservation Commission for National Marine Fisheries Service, National Oceanic and Atmospheric Administration, U.S. Department of Commerce.

Florida Fish and Wildlife Conservation Commission. 2009b. Florida's Endangered Species, Threatened Species, and Species of Special Concern [Internet]. Tallahassee, Florida [modified July 2009; cited Sept 8, 2009]. Available from: http://www.myfwc.com/docs/WildlifeHabitats/Threatened_Endangered_Species.pdf

Rodgers, J.A., Jr. and S.T. Schwikert. 2002. Buffer zone distances to protect foraging and loafing waterbirds from disturbance by personal watercraft and outboard-powered boats. Conservation Biology 16 (1):216-224.

U.S. Fish and Wildlife Service. 1999. The South Florida Ecosystem – Multi-Species Recovery Plan for South Florida [Internet]. Vero Beach, Florida [cited Sept 8, 2009]. Available from: http://www.fws.gov/verobeach/index.cfm?method=PDFLibrary

Signed _____ 3/30/2010
Signature (originating station)   Date

Wildlife Refuge Manager
Title

IX. Reviewing Ecological Services Office Evaluation:

   A. Concurrence __X__ Non-concurrence _____

   B. Formal consultation required _____

   C. Conference required _____

   D. Informal conference required _____

   E. Remarks (attach additional pages as needed):

Signed _____ 3/31/2010
Signature   Date

Supervisory Fish & Wildlife Biologist   _SFESO, Vero Beach_
Title   Office

Appendix H. Wilderness Review

The Wilderness Act of 1964 defines a wilderness area as an area of federal land that retains its primeval character and influence, without permanent improvements or human inhabitation, and is managed so as to preserve its natural conditions and which:

1. generally appears to have been influenced primarily by the forces of nature, with the imprint of man's work substantially unnoticeable;
2. has outstanding opportunities for solitude or primitive and unconfined types of recreation;
3. has at least 5,000 contiguous roadless acres (2,023 ha) or is of sufficient size to make practicable its preservation and use in an unimpeded condition; or is a roadless island, regardless of size;
4. does not substantially exhibit the effects of logging, farming, grazing, or other extensive development or alteration of the landscape, or its wilderness character could be restored through appropriate management at the time of review; and
5. may contain ecological, geological, or other features of scientific, educational, scenic, or historic value.

The lands within Pine Island, Matlacha Pass, Island Bay, and Caloosahatchee NWRs were reviewed for their suitability in meeting the criteria for wilderness, as defined by the Wilderness Act of 1964.

In review of the federally owned lands and waters within the boundary of J.N. "Ding" Darling NWR Complex, no additional areas were found suitable for designation as Wilderness. The lands and waters of the refuge:

- do not meet the Wilderness minimum size requirement of 5,000 contiguous roadless acres (2,023 ha);
- do not contain any units of sufficient size for preservation as Wilderness;
- have been altered by historic and ongoing human activities;
- do not include outstanding opportunities for solitude or for primitive recreation; and
- are fragmented by roadways and human development.

Therefore, no units of Pine Island, Matlacha Pass, Island Bay, and Caloosahatchee NWRs are suitable for designation as Wilderness at this time and the designation of Wilderness is not further analyzed in the CCP.

Appendix I. Refuge Biota

BIRDS OF THE J.N. "DING" DARLING NATIONAL WILDLIFE REFUGE COMPLEX

LOONS
Common Loon *Gavia immer*

GREBES
Pied-billed Grebe *Podilymbus podiceps*
Horned Grebe *Podiceps auritus*

PELICANS AND ALLIES
American White Pelican *Pelecanus erythrorhynchos*
Brown Pelican *Pelecanus occidentalis*
Double-crested Cormorant *Phalacrocorax auritus*
Anhinga *Anhinga anhinga*
Magnificent Frigatebird *Fregata magnificens*

HERONS, EGRETS AND ALLIES
American Bittern *Botaurus lentiginosus*
Least Bittern *Ixobrychus exilis*
Great Blue Heron *Ardea Herodias*
Great Egret *Ardea alba*
Snowy Egret *Egretta thula*
Little Blue Heron *Egretta caerulea*
Tricolored Heron *Egretta tricolor*
Reddish Egret *Egretta rufescens*
Cattle Egret *Bubulcus ibis*
Green Heron *Butorides virescens*
Black-crowned Night-Heron *Nycticorax nycticorax*
Yellow-crowned Night-Heron *Nyctanassa violacea*

IBISES, SPOONBILL AND STORKS
Glossy Ibis *Plegadis falcinellus*
White Ibis *Eudocimus albus*
Roseate Spoonbill *Platalea ajaja*
Wood Stork *Mycteria americana*

WATERFOWL
Green-winged Teal *Anas crecca*
Mottled Duck *Anas fulvigula*
Northern Pintail *anas acuta*
Blue-winged Teal *Anas discors*
Northern Shoveler *Anas clypeata*
American Wigeon *Anas americana*
Lesser Scaup *Aythya affinis*
Hooded Merganser *Lophodytes cucullatus*
Red-breasted Merganser *Mergus serrator*

VULTURES, HAWKS AND ALLIES
Black Vulture *Coragyps atratus*
Turkey Vulture *Cathartes aura*
Osprey *Pandion haliaetus*
American Swallow-tailed Kite *Elanoides forficatus*
Bald Eagle *Haliaeetus leucocephalus*
Northern Harrier *Circus cyaneus*
Sharp-shinned Hawk *Accipiter striatus*
Cooper's Hawk *Accipiter cooperii*
Red-shouldered Hawk *Buteo lineatus*
Broad-winged Hawk *Buteo platypterus*
Red-tailed Hawk *Buteo jamaicensis*
American Kestrel *Falco sparverius*
Merlin *Falco columbarius*
Peregrine Falcon *Falco peregrinus*
Short-tailed Hawk *Buteo brachyurus*

RAILS, GALLINULES AND COOTS
Clapper Rail *Rallus longirostris*
King Rail *Rallus elegans*
Virginia Rail *Rallus limicola*
Sora *Porzana carolina*
Common Moorhen *Gallinula chloropus*
American Coot *Fulica americana*

PLOVERS, SANDPIPERS AND ALLIES
Black-bellied Plover *Pluvialis squatarola*
Snowy Plover *Charadrius alexandrinus*
Wilson's Plover *Charadrius wilsonia*
Semipalmated Plover *Charadrius semipalmatus*
Piping Plover *Charadrius melodus*
Killdeer *Charadrius vociferus*
American Oystercatcher *Haematopus palliates*
Black-necked Stilt *Himantopus mexicanus*

Greater Yellowlegs *Tringa melanoleuca*
Solitary Sandpiper *Tringa solitaria*
Spotted Sandpiper *Actitis macularius*
Ruddy Turnstone *Arenaria interpres*
Sanderling *Calidris alba*
Western Sandpiper *Calidris mauri*
Dunlin *Caldris alpine*
Short-billed Dowitcher *Limnodromus griseus*

Lesser Yellowlegs *Tringa flavipes*
Willet *Catoptrophorus semipalmatus*
Marbled Godwit *Limosa fedoa*
Red Knot *Calidris canutus*
Semipalmated Sandpiper
Least Sandpiper *Calidris minutilla*
Stilt Sandpiper *Calidris himantopus*
Common Snipe *Capella gallinago*

GULLS, TERNS AND SKIMMERS
Laughing Gull *Larus atricilla*
Ring-billed Gull *Larus delawarensis*
Caspian Tern *Sterna caspia*
Sandwich Tern *Sterna sandvicencis*
Least Tern *Sterna antillarum*
Black Skimmer *Rynchops niger*

Bonaparte's Gull *Larus philadelphia*
Herring Gull *Larus argentatus*
Royal Tern *Sterna maxima*
Forster's Tern *Sterna fosteri*
Black Tern *Chlidonias niger*

PIGEONS AND DOVES
Eurasian Collared-Dove *Streptopelia decaocto*
Mourning Dove *Zenaida macroura*

Ringed Turtle-Dove *Streptopelia risoria*
Common Ground-Dove *Columbina passerina*

CUCKOOS
Yellow-billed Cuckoo *Coccyzus americanus*

Mangrove Cuckoo *Coccyzus minor*

OWLS
Barn Owl *Tyto alba*
Great Horned Owl *Bubu virginianus*

Eastern Screech-Owl *Megascops asio*

GOATSUCKERS
Common Nighthawk *Chordeiles minor*
Whip-poor-will *Caprimulgus vociferous*

Chuck-will's-widow *Caprimulgus carolinensis*

SWIFTS
Chimney Swift *Chaetura pelagica*

HUMMINGBIRDS
Ruby-throated Hummingbird *Archilochus colubris*

KINGFISHERS
Belted Kingfisher *Ceryle alcyon*

WOODPECKERS
Red-bellied Woodpecker *Melanerpes carolinus*
Downy Woodpecker *Picoides pubescens*
Pileated Woodpecker *Dryocopus pileatus*

Yellow-bellied Sapsucker *Sphyrapicus varius*
Northern Flicker *Colaptes auratus*

FLYCATCHERS
Eastern Phoebe *Syornis phoebe*
Western Kingbird *Tyrannus verticalis*
Gray Kingbird *Tyrannus dominicensis*

Great Crested Flycatcher *Myiarchus crinitus*
Eastern Kingbird *Tyrannus tyrannus*
Scissor-tailed Flycatcher *Tyrannus forficatus*

MARTINS AND SWALLOWS
Purple Martin *Progne subis*
Bank Swallow *Riparia ripaira*
Northern Rough-winged Swallow *Stelgidopteryx serripennis*

Tree Swallow *Tachycineta bicolor*
Barn Swallow *Hirundo rustica*

JAYS AND CROWS
Blue Jay *Cyanocitta cristata*
Fish Crow *Corvus ossifragus*
American Crow *Corvus brachyrhynchos*

WRENS
Carolina Wren *Thryothorus ludovicianus*
House Wren *Troglodytes aedon*

GNATCATCHERS
Blue-gray Gnatcatcher *Polioptila caerulea*

THRUSHES
American Robin *Turdus migratorius*
Gray-cheeked Thrush *Catharus minimus*
Wood Thrush *Hylocichla mustelina*
Swainson's Thrush *Catharus ustulatus*
Veery *Catharus fuscescens*

MOCKINGBIRDS, THRASHERS AND ALLIES
Gray Catbird *Dumetella carolinensis*
Brown Thrasher *Toxostoma rufum*
Northern Mockingbird *Mimus polyglottos*

WAXWINGS
Cedar Waxwing *Bombycilla cedrorum*

STARLINGS
European Starling *Sturnus vulgaris*

VIREOS
White-eyed Vireo *Vireo griseus*
Red-eyed Vireo *Vireo olivaceus*
Solitary Vireo *Vireo solitarius*
Black-whiskered Vireo *Vireo altiloquus*

WARBLERS
Orange-crowned Warbler *Vermivora celata*
Tennessee Warbler *Vermivora peregrine*
Blue-winged Warbler *Vermivora pinus*
Yellow Warbler *Dendroica petechia*
Black-throated Green Warbler *Dendroica virens*
Black-throated Blue Warbler *Dendroica caerulescens*
Blackburnian Warbler *Dendroica fusca*
Prairie Warbler *Drendroica discolor*
Blackpoll Warbler *Dendroica striata*
American Redstart *Setophaga ruticilla*
Bay-breasted Warbler *Dendroica castanea*
Ovenbird *Seiurus aurocapilla*
Louisiana Waterthrush *Seiurus motacilla*
Hooded Warbler *Wilsonia citrina*
Nashville Warbler *Vermivora ruficapilla*
Golden-winged Warbler *Vermivora chrysoptera*
Northern Parula *Parula americana*
Magnolia Warbler *Dendroica magnolia*
Cape May Warbler *Dendroica tigrina*
Yellow-rumped Warbler *Dendroica coronata*
Yellow-throated Warbler *Dendroica dominica*
Palm Warbler *Dendroica palmarum*
Black-and-white Warbler *Mniotilta varia*
Prothonotary Warbler *Protonotaria citrea*
Worm-eating Warbler *Helmitheros vermivorum*
Northern Waterthrush *Seiurus noveboracensis*
Common Yellowthroat *Geothlypis trichas*

TANAGERS
Summer Tanager *Piranga rubra*
Scarlet Tanager *Piranga olivacea*

NEW WORLD FINCHES
Northern Cardinal *Cardinalis cardinalis*
Indigo Bunting *Passerina cyanea*
Rose-breasted Grosbeak *Pheucticus ludovicianus*
Blue Grosbeak *Passerina caerulea*
Painted Bunting *Passerina ciris*

SPARROWS
Rufous-sided Towhee *Pipilo erythrophthalmus*
Swamp Sparrow *Melospiza georgiana*

BLACKBIRDS, GRACKLES, COWBIRDS AND ORIOLES
Bobolink *Dolichonyx oryzivorus*
Boat-tailed Grackle *Quiscalus major*
Shiny Cowbird *Molothrus bonariensis*
Orchard Oriole *Icterus spurious*
Red-winged Blackbird *Agelaius phoeniceus*
Common Grackle *Quiscalus quiscula*
Brown-headed Cowbird *Molothrus ater*
Northern Oriole *Icterus galbula*

NORTHERN FINCHES
American Goldfinch *Carduelis tristis*

OLD WORLD SPARROWS
House Sparrow *Passer domesticus*

ACCIDENTALS
(Birds seen only once or twice during the past eight years)
Northern Gannet *Morus bassanus*
Greater Flamingo *Phoenicopterus ruber*
Fulvous Whistling-Duck *Dendrocygna bicolor*
Wood Duck *Aix sponsa*
Mallard *Anas platyrhynchos*
Savannah Sparrow *Passerculus sandwichensis*
White-crowned Pigeon *Columba leucocephala*
Eurasian Wigeon *Anas penelope*
Canvasback *Aythya valisineria*
Hairy Woodpecker *Picoides villosus*
Ring-necked Duck *Aythya collaris*
Bufflehead *Bucephala albeola*
Ruddy Duck *Oxyura jamaicensis*
Swainson's Hawk *Buteo swainsoni*
Black Rail *Laterallus jamaicenis*
Purple Gallinule *Porphyrio martinica*
Roseate Tern *Sterna dougallii*
Common Tern *Sterna hirundo*
American Avocet *Recurvirostra americana*
Whimbrel *Numenius phaeopus*
Chestnut-sided Warbler *Dendroica pensylvanica*
White-rumped Sandpiper *Calidris fuscicollis*
Parasitic Jaeger *Stercorarius parasiticus*
Pectoral Sandpiper *Calidris melanotos*
Black-billed Cuckoo *Coccyzus erythropthalmus*
Red-headed Woodpecker *Melanerpes erythrocephalus*
Great Black-backed Gull *Larus marinus*
Common Black-headed Gull *Larus ridubundis*
Monk Parakeet *Myiopsitta monachus*
Green Parakeet *Aratinga holochlora*
Canary-winged Parakeet
Rose-ringed Parakeet
Sandhill Crane *Grus canadensis*
Smooth-billed Ani *Crotophaga ani*
Barred Owl *Strix varia*
Short-eared Owl *Asio flammeus*
Redhead *Aythya americana*
Eastern Meadowlark *Sturnella magna*
Vermilion Flycatcher *Pyrocephalus rubinus*
Sedge Wren *Cistothorus platensis*
Marsh Wren *Cistothorus palustris*
Ruby-crowned Kinglet *Regulus calendula*
Eastern Bluebird *Sialia sialis*
White-winged Dove *Zenaida asiatica*
Loggerhead Shrike *Lanius ludovicianus*
Yellow-throated Vireo *Vireo flavifrons*
Philadelphia Vireo *Vireo philadelphicus*
Snow Goose *Chen caerulescens*
Gadwall *Anas strepera*
Pine Warbler *Dendroica pinus*
Kentucky Warbler *Oporornis formosus*
Wilson's Warbler *Wilsonia pusilla*
Yellow-breasted Chat *Icteria virens*
Gull-billed Tern *Sterna nilotica*
Limpkin *Aramus guarauna*
Rock Dove *Columbo columbo*

ADDITIONAL Birds of Sanibel Island
Hermit Thrush *Catharus guttatus*
Cerulean Warbler *Dendroica cerulean*
Connecticut Warbler *Oporornis agilis*
Dickcissel *Spiza Americana*
Grasshopper Sparrow *Ammodramus savannarum*
Le Conte's Sparrow *Ammodramus leconteii*
Seaside Sparrow *Ammodramus maritimus*
White-throated Sparrow *Zonotrichia albicollis*
Purple Finch *Carpodacus purpureus*
Black Scoter *Melanitta nigra*
Bridled Tern *Sterna anaethetus*
White-winged Parakeet *Brotogeris versicolurus*
Bay-breasted Warbler *Dendroica castanea*
Swainson's Warbler *Limnothlypis swainsonii*
Mourning Warbler *Oporornis Philadelphia*
Field Sparrow *Chondestes grammacus*
Henslow's Sparrow *Ammodramus henslowii*
Sharp-tailed Sparrow *Ammodramus caudacutus*
Song Sparrow *Melospiza melodia*
White-crowned Sparrow *Zonotrichia leucophrys*
Cinnamon Teal *Anas cyanoptera*
Wilson's Snipe *Gallinago delicate*
White-crowned Pigeon *Patagioenas leucocephala*
Eastern Wood-Pewee *Contopus virens*

Acadian Flycatcher *Empidonax virescens* Bridled Tern *Sterna anaethetus*
Yellow-headed Blackbird *Xanthocephalus xanthocephalus*

Sources:
"Birds of Sanibel", Sanibel-Captiva Conservation Foundation, http://www.sccf.org/files/downloads/WildLProjSanibelBirds.pdf
"Bird Checklists of the United States, J.N. "Ding" Darling National Wildlife Refuge," Northern Prairie Wildlife Research Center, USGS, http://www.npwrc.usgs.gov/resource/birds/chekbird/r4/dingdarl.htm

AMPHIBIANS AND REPTILES OF J.N. "DING" DARLING NATIONAL WILDLIFE REFUGE COMPLEX

AMPHIBIANS

Frogs
Southern Toad *Bufo terrestris*
Oak Toad *Bufo quercicus*
Eastern Narrowmouth Toad *Gastrophryne c. carolinensis*
Pig Frog *Rana grylio*
Southern Leopard Frog *Rana sphenocephala*
Green Tree Frog *Hyla cinerea*
Squirrel Tree Frog *Hyla squirella*
Cuban Tree Frog *Osteopilus septentrionalis*
Greenhouse Frog *Eleutherodactylus planirostris planirostris*
Florida Cricket Frog *Acris gryllus*
Florida Chorus Frog *Pseudacris nigrita*
Little Grass Frog *Pseudacris ocularis*

REPTILES

Crocodilians
American Alligator *Alligator mississippiensis*
American Crocodile *Crocodylus acutus*

Lizards
Green Anole *Anolis carolinensis*
Brown Anole *Anolis sagrei*
Six-lined Racerunner *Cnemidophorus sexlineatus*
Southeastern Five-lined Skink *Eumeces inexpectatus*
Ground Skink *Scincella lateralis*
Eastern Glass Lizard *Ophisaurus ventralis*
Indo-pacific Gecko *Hemidactylus garnotii*
Tropical House Gecko *Hemidactylus mabouia*
Tokay Gecko *Gekko gecko*
Green Iguana *Iguana iguana*
Nile Monitor *Varanus niloticus*
Eastern Glass Lizard *Ophisaurus ventralis*
Red-headed Agama *Agama agama Africana*

Snakes
Yellow Rat Snake *Elaphe obsoleta quadrivittata,{ E. alleganiensis}*
Corn Snake *Elaphe guttata guttata*
Southern Black Racer *Coluber constrictor priapus*
Eastern Coachwhip Snake *Masticophis flagellum flagellum*

Southern Ringneck Snake *Diadophis punctatus punctatus*
Florida Brown Snake *Storeria victa*
Peninsula Ribbon Snake *Thamnophis sauritus sackenii*
Florida Water Snake *Nerodia fasciata pictiventris*
Mangrove Water Snake *Nerodia clarki compressicauda*
Eastern Indigo Snake *Drymarchon corais couperi*
Southern Ringneck Snake *Diadophis punctatus punctatus*
Florida Brown Snake *Storeria victa*
Peninsula Ribbon Snake *Thamnophis sauritus sackenii*
Florida Water Snake *Nerodia fasciata pictiventris*
Mangrove Water Snake *Nerodia clarki compressicauda*
Eastern Indigo Snake *Drymarchon corais couperi*
Brahminy Blind Snake *Rhamphotyphlops braminus*
Eastern Coral Snake *Micrurus fulvius fulvius*
Eastern Diamondback Rattlesnake *Crotalus adamanteus*
Brown Water Snake *Nerodia taxispilota*
Green Water Snake *Nerodia floridana*
Eastern Garter Snake *Thamnophis sirtalis sirtalis*
Florida Cottonmouth *Agkistrodon piscivorus conanti*
Dusky Pigmy Rattlesnake *Crotalus miliarius barbouri*
Red Rat Snake
Everglades Racer

Turtles
Peninsula Cooter Turtle *Pseudemys peninsularis*
Florida Redbelly Turtle *Pseudemys nelsoni*
Yellowbelly Slider *Trachemys scripta scripta*
Florida Chicken Turtle *Deirochelys reticularia chrysea*
Ornate Diamondback Terrapin *Malaclemys terrapin macrospilota*
Florida Mud Turtle *Kinosternon subrubrum steindachneri*
Striped Mud Turtle *Kinosternon bauri*
Florida Box Turtle *Terrapene carolina bauri*
Gopher Tortoise *Gopherus polyphemus*
Loggerhead Turtle *Caretta caretta*
Green Turtle *Chelonia mydas*
Kemp's Ridley Turtle *Lepidochelys kempii*
Florida Snapping Turtle *Chelydra serpentina osceola*
Florida Softshell Turtle *Apalone ferox*
Red-eared Slider *Trachemys scripta elegans*
Leatherback Sea Turtle *Dermochelys coriacea*
Hawksbill Sea Turtle *Eretmochelys imbricata*

Sources:
"J.N. "Ding" Darling National Wildlife Refuge Amphibian and Reptile List", U.S. Fish and Wildlife Service,
   http://library.fws.gov/Refuges/j.n.ding_darling_amphib_reptiles98.pdf

"Amphibians & Reptiles of Sanibel Island 2007", Sanibel-Captiva Conservation Foundation,
   http://www.sccf.org/files/downloads/WildLProgReptilesList.pdf

MAMMALS IN THE VICINITY OF J.N. "DING" DARLING NATIONAL WILDLIFE REFUGE COMPLEX

Florida Bonneted Bat *Eumops floridanus*
Atlantic Bottle-nosed Dolphin *Tursiops truncatus*
West Indian Manatee *Trichechus manatus*
Virginia Opossum *Dilelphis virginiana*
Southern Short-tailed Shrew *Blarina brevicauda peninsulae*
Least Shrew *Cryptotis parva floridana*
Southeastern Shrew *Sorex longirostris*
Eastern Mole *Scalopus aquaticus*
Eastern Yellow Bat *Lasiurus intermedius*
Big Brown Bat *Eptesicus fuscus*
Seminole Bat *Nycteris seminolus*
Evening Bat *Nycticeius humeralis*
Brazilian Free-tailed Bat *Tadarida brasiliensis*
Nine-banded Armadillos *Dasypus novemcinctus*
Eastern Cottontail Rabbit *Sylvilagus floridanus floridanus*
Marsh Rabbits *Sylvilagus palustris*
Southeastern Pocket Gopher *Geomys pinetis*
Gray Squirrel *Sciurus carolinensis*
Big Cypress Fox Squirrel *Sciurus niger avicennia*
Sherman's Fox Squirrel *Sciurus niger shermani*
Southern Flying Squirrel *Glaucomys volans*
Marsh Rice Rat *Oryzomys palustris coloratus*
Eastern Harvest Mouse *Reithrodontomys humilis*
Eastern Woodrat *Neotoma floridana*
Golden Mouse *Ochrotmys nuttalli*
Florida Cotton Mouse *Peromyscus gossypinus palmarinus*
Collier Cotton Mouse *Peromyscus gossypinus temaphilus*
Oldfield Mouse *Peromyscus polionotus*
Florida Mouse *Podomys floridanus*
Florida Hispid Cotton Rat *Signodon hispidus floridanus*
Round-tailed Muskrat *Neofiber alleni*
House Mouse *Mus musculus*
Gray Fox *Urocyon cinereoargenteus floridanus*
Red Fox *Vulpes vulpes fulva*
Florida raccoon *Procyon lotor elucus*
Long-tailed Weasel *Mustela frenata peninsulae*
Spotted Skunk *Spilogale putorius ambarvalus*
Striped Skunk *Mephitis mephitis elongata*
River Otter *Lutra canadensis*
Bobcat *Lynx rufus*
White-tailed Deer *Odocoileus virginianus seminola*
Wild Hog *Sus scrofa*

Source:
"Mammal Checklists of the United States, Pine Island, Matlacha Pass, Island Bay, Caloosahatchee National Wildlife Refuges", Northern Prairie Wildlife Research Center, USGS, http://www.npwrc.usgs.gov/resource/birds/chekbird/r4/pinemam.htm

FISH IN THE VICINITY OF J.N. "DING" DARLING NATIONAL WILDLIFE REFUGE COMPLEX

Florida Gar *Lepisosteus platyrhincus*
Nurse Shark *Ginglymostoma cirratum*
Bull Shark *Carcharhinus leucas*
Blacktip Shark *Carcharhinus limbatus*
Spinner Shark *Carcharhinus maculipinnis*
Sandbar Shark *Carcharhinus plumbeus*
Dusky Shark *Carcharhinus obscurus*
Tiger Shark *Galeocerdo cuvieri*
Lemon Shark *Negaprion brevirostis*
Atlantic Sharpnose Shark *Rhizoprionodon terraenovae*
Great Hammerhead *Sphyrna mokarran*
Bonnethead Shark *Sphyrna tiburo*
Atlantic Guitarfish *Rhinobatos lentiginosus*
Lesser Electric Ray *Narcine brasiliensis*
Clearnose Skate *Raja eglanteria*
Southern Stingray *Dasyatis americana*
Atlantic Stingray *Dasyatis sabina*
Smooth Butterfly Ray *Gymnura micura*
Spotted Eagle Ray *Aetobatus narinari*
Southern Eagle Ray *Myliobatis goodei*
Cownose Ray *Rhinoptera bonasus*
Ladyfish *Elops saurus*
Tarpon *Megalops atlantica*
American Eel *Anguilla rostrata*
Gulf Menhaden *Brevoortia patronus*
Atlantic Thread Herring *Opisthonema oglinum*
Scaled Sardine *Harengula jaguana*
Bay Anchovy *Anchoa mitchilla*
Inshore Lizardfish *Synodus foetens*
Gafftopsail Catfish *Bagre marinus*
Hardhead Catfish *Arius felis*
Gulf Toadfish *Opsanus beta*
Skilletfish *Goiesox strumosus*
Polka-dot Batfish *Ogcocephalus radiatus*
Houndfish *Tylosurus crocodilus*
Sheepshead minnow *Cyprinodon variegatus*
Gulf Killifish *Fundulus confluentus*
Longnose Killifish *Fundulus similis*
Rainwater Killifish *Lucania parva*
Mosquitofish *Gambusia affinis*
Sailfin Molly *Poecilia latipinna*
Dwarf Seahorse *Hippocampus zosterae*
Gulf Pipefish *Syngnathus hildebrandi*
Common Snook *Centropomus undecimalis*
Spotted Jewfish *Epinephelus itajara*
Red Grouper *Epinephelus morio*
Gag Grouper *Mycteroperca microlepis*
Black Seabass *Centropristis striata*

Bluefish *Pomatomus saltatrix*
Cobia *Rachycentron canadum*
Remora *Remora remora*
Yellow Jack *Caranx bartholomaei*
Crevalle Jack *Caranx hippos*
Atlantic bumper *Chloroscombrus chrysurus*
Leatherjacket *Oligoplites saurus*
Greater Amberjack *Seriola setapinnis*
Florida pompano *Trachinotus carolinus*
Lane Snapper *Lutjanus synagris*
Mangrove Snapper *Lutjanus griseus*
Tripletail *Lobotes surinamensis*
Striped Mojorra *Diapterus plumieri*
Silver Jenny *Eucinostomus gula*
Mottled Mojarra *Ulaema lefroyi*
Pigfish *Orthopristis chrysoptera*
White Grunt *Haemulon plumieri*
Sheepshead *Archosargus probatocephalus*
Pinfish *Lagodon rhomboides*
Grass Porgy *Calamus arctifrons*
Cubbyu *Equetus umbrosus*
Southern Kingfish *Menticirrus americanus*
Gulf Kingfish *Menticirrhus littoralis*
Black Drum *Pogonias cromis*
Red Drum *Sciaenops ocellata*
Silver *Cynoscion nothus*
Spotted Seatrout *Cynoscion nebulosus*
Atlantic Spadefish *Chaetodipterus faber*
Striped Mullet *Mugil cephalus*
White Mullet *Mugil curema*
Great Barracuda *Sphyraena barracuda*
Highfin Blenny *Lupinoblennius nicholsi*
Spanish Mackerel *Scomberomorus maculatus*
Bighead Searobin *Prionotus tribulus*
Barbfish *Scorpaena brasiliensis*
Gulf Flounder *Paralichthys albigutta*
Southern Flounder *Paralichthys lethostigma*
Hogchoker *Trinectes maculatus*
Tonguefish *Symphurus sp.*
Plainhead Filefish *Monachnthus hispidus*
Queen Triggerfish *Balistes vetula*
Southern Puffer *Sphoeroides nephelus*
Striped Burrfish *Chilumycterus schoepfi*

Source: "Miscellaneous Checklists of the United States, Pine Island, Matlacha Pass, Island Bay, Caloosahatchee National Wildlife Refuges."
http://www.npwrc.usgs.gov/resource/birds/chekbird/r4/pinefish.htm

Appendix J. Budget Requests

The refuges' budget requests are contained in the Refuge Operating Needs System (RONS) and Service Asset and Maintenance Management System (SAMMS) databases that include a wide variety of new and maintenance refuge projects.

The RONS and SAMMS lists are constantly updated and include priority projects. Please contact the Refuge Complex for the most current RONS and SAMMS lists. Chapter V, Plan Implementation, describes the key budget requests associated with the proposed projects and staffing. Chapter V includes 21 proposed projects, which are linked to the related objectives, and a summary of funding to support the existing and proposed staffing levels.

Appendix K. List of Preparers

A variety of local, state, and federal agencies; nongovernmental organizations; area residents and landowners; and local businesses, as well as the general public played a role in the development of this CCP (see Appendix L for an overview of consultation and coordination). The actual preparers of the documents are:

U.S. Fish and Wildlife Service

- Paul Tritaik, Project Leader, J.N. "Ding" Darling NWR Complex
- Cheri M. Ehrhardt, AICP, Natural Resource Planner
- Patrick Martin, Deputy Project Leader, J.N. "Ding" Darling NWR Complex
- Kevin Godsea, Supervisory Park Ranger, J.N. "Ding" Darling NWR Complex
- Joyce Mazourek Palmer, Biologist, J.N. "Ding" Darling NWR Complex Tara Wertz, Biologist, J.N. "Ding" Darling NWR Complex
- Toni Westland, Park Ranger-Environmental Education and Supervisory Park Ranger, J.N. "Ding" Darling NWR Complex
- Jeff Combs, Park Ranger-Volunteer Coordinator, J.N. "Ding" Darling NWR Complex
- Spencer Simon, Ecological Services, Vero Beach Field Office

Contractor to the U.S. Fish and Wildlife Service

- Charles McEntyre, Tennessee Valley Authority
- Patricia Hamlett, Tennessee Valley Authority

Appendix L. Consultation and Coordination

OVERVIEW

This chapter summarizes the consultation and coordination that has occurred to date in identifying the issues, alternatives, and proposed alternative, which are presented in the Draft CCP/EA. It lists the meetings that have been held with the various agencies, organizations, and individuals who were consulted in the preparation of the Draft CCP/EA. Appendix D provides a list of those entities that submitted comments on the Draft CCP/EA.

The comprehensive planning process for Pine Island, Matlacha Pass, Island Bay, and Caloosahatchee NWRs involved a wide variety of participants, including federal, state, and local governments; tribal governments; universities and other researchers; private nonprofit groups; and the "Ding" Darling Wildlife Society, as well as a wide variety of local residents, local businesses, concerned citizens, local schools, and state and national organizations. The list of participants, beyond those individuals, agencies, and organizations providing comments during the public scoping process, includes the Core CCP Team, the Wildlife and Habitat Management Review Team, the Wilderness Review Team, and the Intergovernmental Coordination Planning Team.

CORE CCP TEAM

The Core CCP Team included representatives from the Service and the CCP contractor, the Tennessee Valley Authority. The Team met as a whole to review the all the issues, determine the priority issues, and identify potential solutions or approaches.

U.S. Fish and Wildlife Service
- Paul Tritaik, Wildlife Refuge Manager (Project Leader), J.N. "Ding" Darling NWR Complex
- Cheri M. Ehrhardt, AICP, Natural Resource Planner
- Patrick Martin, Deputy Project Leader, J.N. "Ding" Darling NWR Complex
- Kevin Godsea, Supervisory Park Ranger, J.N. "Ding" Darling NWR Complex
- Joyce Mazourek Palmer, Biologist, J.N. "Ding" Darling NWR Complex
- Tara Wertz, Biologist, J.N. "Ding" Darling NWR Complex
- Toni Westland, Park Ranger-Environmental Education and Supervisory Park Ranger, J.N. "Ding" Darling NWR Complex
- Jeff Combs, Park Ranger-Volunteer Coordinator, J.N. "Ding" Darling NWR Complex
- Spencer Simon, Ecological Services, Vero Beach Field Office

Contractor to the U.S. Fish and Wildlife Service
- Charles McEntyre, Tennessee Valley Authority

WILDLIFE AND HABITAT MANAGEMENT REVIEW TEAM

The Wildlife and Habitat Management Review Team included a core group of Service staff with invited participants. The invited participants included local and regional experts, researchers, and individuals with intimate knowledge of and expertise with the resources of the refuge. The wildlife and habitat management review for Pine Island, Matlacha Pass, Island Bay, and Caloosahatchee NWRs was conducted during April of 2000, concurrently with the review for J.N. "Ding" Darling NWR.

U.S. Fish and Wildlife Service
- Frank Bowers, Southeast Regional Office, Atlanta, GA
- Chuck Hunter, Southeast Regional Office, Atlanta, GA
- David Brownlie, Fire Ecologist, Tallahassee, FL
- Doug Fruge, Southeast Region, Gulf Coast Fisheries Resource Office
- Mark Musaus, A.R.M. Loxahatchee NWR

U.S. Fish and Wildlife Service (Refuge Staff)
- Lou Hinds, Wildlife Refuge Manager, J.N. "Ding" Darling NWR Complex
- Layne Hamilton
- Jorge L. Coppen
- Allison Baker
- Susan Trokey
- Steve Alvarez
- Mike Ward
- Carol Pratt

State and Local Agency and Nongovernmental Officials
- Jim Beever, Florida Fish and Wildlife Conservation Commission, Office of Environmental Services
- Jeff McGrady, Florida Fish and Wildlife Conservation Commission
- Dave Ceilley, Sanibel-Captiva Conservation Foundation
- Rob Loflin, City of Sanibel, Natural Resources Department
- George Wichterman, Lee County Mosquito Control District
- Doug Carlson, Indian River Mosquito Control District

VISITOR SERVICES REVIEW TEAM

None of the refuges (Pine Island, Matlacha Pass, Island Bay, or Caloosahatchee NWR) are open to the public. Therefore, the visitor services review, which was completed for J.N. "Ding" Darling NWR in 2001, did not address the refuges.

WILDERNESS REVIEW TEAM

The Wilderness Review Team involved the Wildlife Refuge Manager and the Natural Resource Planner. The review was completed in 2008.

U.S. Fish and Wildlife Service
- Paul Tritaik, Project Leader, J.N. "Ding" Darling NWR Complex
- Cheri M. Ehrhardt, AICP, Natural Resource Planner
- Patrick Martin, Deputy Project Leader, J.N. "Ding" Darling NWR Complex
- Joyce Mazourek Palmer, Biologist, J.N. "Ding" Darling NWR Complex

INTERGOVERNMENTAL COORDINATION PLANNING TEAM

The Intergovernmental Coordination Planning Team included local, State, and federal government field staff representatives involved with the resources at the local level. A letter inviting participation by the Florida Fish and Wildlife Conservation Commission (FWC) in the CCPs for the Refuge Complex was sent to the FWC Director in January 2008. Additional invitation letters were also sent to: Seminole Tribe of Florida, Miccosukee Tribe of Indians of Florida, Seminole Nation of Oklahoma, Poarch Band of Creek Indians, Muscogee (Creek) Nation of Oklahoma, United South and Eastern Tribes, Charlotte Harbor National Estuary Program, South Florida Water Management District, Florida Department of Environmental Protection, Florida Department of Agriculture and Consumer Services, Southwest Florida Regional Planning Council, Lee County, Lee County Mosquito Control District, and City of Sanibel. To gather together the various local, State, and federal agencies, an Intergovernmental Coordination Planning Team meeting was conducted in April 2008 with attendees representing 11 local, State, and federal agencies and a Tribal government, as listed.

U.S. Fish and Wildlife Service
- Cheri M. Ehrhardt, AICP, Natural Resource Planner
- Kevin Godsea, Supervisory Park Ranger
- Laura Housh, Regional Planner
- Patrick Martin, Deputy Project Leader, J.N. "Ding" Darling NWR Complex
- Joyce Mazourek Palmer, Wildlife Biologist, J.N. "Ding" Darling NWR Complex
- Bill Miller, Fish and Wildlife Biologist
- Jim Serfis, Acting Project Leader, J.N. "Ding" Darling NWR Complex
- Paul Tritaik, Project Leader, J.N. "Ding" Darling NWR Complex

Contractor to the U.S. Fish and Wildlife Service
- Charlie McEntyre, Tennessee Valley Authority

Seminole Tribe of Florida
- Marion Smith, Tribal Historic Preservation Office

Florida Fish and Wildlife Conservation Commission
- Ron Mezich, Biological Scientist IV, Aquatic Habitat Restoration and Conservation Section, Marine Habitat Management

Florida Department of Environmental Protection
- Jennifer L. Nelson, Environmental Manager, Watershed Projects/Biological Monitoring & Research
- Heather Stafford, Manager, Charlotte Harbor Aquatic Preserves and Estero Bay Aquatic Preserve

South Florida Water Management District
- Judith Nothdurft, Project Manager, Lower West Coast Service Center

Florida Department of Agriculture and Consumer Services
- Michael Weston, County Forester, Caloosahatchee District, Florida Division of Forestry

Southwest Florida Regional Planning Council
- Jim Beever, Senior Planner

Lee County
- Steve Boutelle, Operations Manager, Marine Services, Division of Natural Resources
- Roger Clark, Land Stewardship Manager, Parks and Recreation

Lee County Mosquito Control District
- T. Wayne Gale, Executive Director
- Katie Heggemeir, Manager, Mosquito Control
- Bryan Smith, Supervisor, Aerial Larviciding

City of Sanibel
- Robert J. Duffy, AICP, Planning Director
- Robert K. Loflin, PhD, Natural Resources Director

PUBLIC SCOPING MEETINGS

The Core Planning Team hosted open houses and public scoping meetings in Lee and Charlotte counties in April 2008 at the Sanibel School, the Cypress Lake Middle School in Fort Myers, and the Pine Island Elementary School. The Refuge Complex's draft vision, goals, and issues were presented and public input was requested. Comment forms were made available at the meetings as well as at the J.N. "Ding" Darling NWR Visitor Center and the Tarpon Bay Concessionaire headquarters. The completed forms were submitted to the Service by mail or e-mail. Public input is greatly appreciated and was incorporated into the CCP.

"DING" DARLING WILDLIFE SOCIETY – FRIENDS OF THE REFUGE

The "Ding" Darling Wildlife Society, a nonprofit Friends of the Refuge organization, was established in 1982. It supports environmental education and services at J.N. "Ding" Darling NWR. The "Ding" Darling Wildlife Society currently has over 1,400 members. Many members of the "Ding" Darling Wildlife Society have participated in the CCP in some capacity, but the entire "Ding" Darling Wildlife Society has regularly provided input on a variety of issues that have been incorporated into the CCP.

COMMENTERS ON THE DRAFT CCP/EA

A total of seven responses submitting comments were received. One was from a private citizen; one was from Defenders of Wildlife, a nongovernmental organization; and five were from other governmental agencies. The commenters and their affiliations are listed in the following table.

Commenter	Affiliation and Location
Lisa B. Beever, PhD, AICP	Director, Charlotte Harbor National Estuary Program, Fort Myers, Florida
Elizabeth Fleming and Julie Kates	Florida Associate and Refuge Associate, Federal Lands Program, respectively, Defenders of Wildlife
T. Wayne Gale	Executive Director, Lee County Mosquito Control District
Ken Heatherington, AICP	Executive Director, Southwest Florida Regional Planning Council

Commenter	Affiliation and Location
Laura A. Kammerer	Deputy State Historic Preservation Officer, Division of Historical Resources, Florida Department of State
Jean Public	Whitehouse Station, New Jersey
Heather Stafford and Melynda Brown	Program Manager for Pine Island Sound, Matlacha Pass, Cape Haze, Lemon Bay, Gasparilla Sound/Charlotte Harbor, and Estero Bay Aquatic Preserves and Environmental Specialist III for Pine Island Sound, Matlacha Pass, Cape Haze, Lemon Bay, and Gasparilla Sound/Charlotte Harbor Aquatic Preserves, respectively, Office of Coastal and Aquatic Managed Areas, Florida Department of Environmental Protection

Appendix M. Finding of No Significant Impact

INTRODUCTION

The U.S. Fish and Wildlife Service proposes to protect and manage certain fish and wildlife resources in Lee and Charlotte counties, Florida, through the Pine Island, Matlacha Pass, Island Bay, and Caloosahatchee National Wildlife Refuges (NWRs). An Environmental Assessment was prepared to inform the public of the possible environmental consequences of implementing the Comprehensive Conservation Plan (CCP) for Pine Island, Matlacha Pass, Island Bay, and Caloosahatchee NWRs. A description of the alternatives, the rationale for selecting the preferred alternative, the environmental effects of the preferred alternative, the potential adverse effects of the action, and a declaration concerning the factors determining the significance of effects, in compliance with the National Environmental Policy Act of 1969, are outlined below. The supporting information can be found in the Environmental Assessment, which was Section B of the Draft Comprehensive Conservation Plan.

ALTERNATIVES

In developing the Comprehensive Conservation Plan for Pine Island, Matlacha Pass, Island Bay, and Caloosahatchee NWRs, the Fish and Wildlife Service evaluated four alternatives with different focuses for future management:

Alternative A – Current Management (No Action Alternative)
Alternative B – Native Wildlife and Habitat Diversity
Alternative C – Migratory Birds (Preferred Alternative)
Alternative D – Rare, Threatened, and Endangered Species

The different management focuses of the action alternatives (i.e., B, C, and D) represent different philosophies and approaches to refuge management, messages delivered, priority setting, and decision-making.

The Service adopted Alternative C, the Preferred Alternative, as the CCP for guiding the direction of the Pine Island, Matlacha Pass, Island Bay, and Caloosahatchee NWRs for the next 15 years. The overriding concern reflected in this plan is that wildlife conservation assumes first priority in refuge management; wildlife-dependant recreational uses are allowed if they are compatible with wildlife conservation. The refuges are currently closed to general public access and they will likely remain so throughout the 15-year life of the plan.

ALTERNATIVE A: CURRENT MANAGEMENT (NO ACTION)

Alternative A represents no change from current management of the refuges. Under this alternative, limited refuge management activities would continue to be conducted as collateral duty by the staff of J.N. "Ding" Darling NWR. The refuges would continue to rely on partners for the bulk of refuge management activities, including surveys, monitoring, outreach, and patrol and law enforcement. The refuges would remain closed. Violations of closed areas would continue to occur. Wildlife and habitat disturbance from adjacent uses would continue to occur, with some of these activities spilling over onto closed refuge areas. The Service's image would likely remain poor in the local communities.

ALTERNATIVE B: NATIVE WILDLIFE AND HABITAT DIVERSITY

Alternative B would increase refuge management and cultural and natural resource protection activities with a focus on native wildlife and habitat diversity. Coordination with the partners would continue to be a key aspect of future management. Proposed wildlife and habitat management activities would focus on native wildlife and habitat diversity, spreading management activities across a broad range of species; expanding the number of species of management concern to the refuges; establishing closed area buffer zones around certain rookeries and key foraging and resting areas; expanding exotic, invasive, and nuisance species control activities; working with the partners to address water quality, quantity, and timing concerns affecting a broad range of species; and working with the partners to understand and ameliorate the impacts of climate change. The refuges would likely remain closed, while environmental education, interpretation, and outreach activities would increase, with messages focused on native wildlife and habitat diversity and the minimization of human impacts. The refuges would develop an annual event in one of the local communities and would work with the partners to improve ethical outdoor behavior. Five positions would be added to support these refuge management activities, while staff from J.N. "Ding" Darling NWR would continue to provide support. Management activities would work to improve the Service's visibility and image in the local communities.

ALTERNATIVE C: MIGRATORY BIRDS (PREFERRED ALTERNATIVE)

Where Alternative B serves a broad range of species to support native wildlife and habitat diversity, Alternative C focuses on migratory birds. The preferred alternative, Alternative C, is considered to be the most effective management action for meeting the purposes of the refuges by focusing future management on migratory birds. This alternative addresses the management needs of all birds covered under the Migratory Bird Treaty Act, including resident species of native birds that are found using the refuge year round. Coordination with the partners would continue to be a key aspect of future management. Proposed wildlife and habitat management activities would focus on migratory birds, expanding the number of species of management concern to the refuges; establishing closed area buffer zones around rookeries and key foraging and resting areas; expanding exotic, invasive, and nuisance species control activities; working with the partners to address water quality, quantity, and timing concerns affecting migratory birds; and working with the partners to understand and ameliorate the impacts of climate change. The refuges would likely remain closed, while environmental education, interpretation, and outreach activities would increase, with messages focused on migratory birds and the minimization of human impacts. The refuges would develop an annual event in one of the local communities and would work with the partners to improve ethical outdoor behavior. Five positions would be added to support these refuge management activities, while staff from J.N. "Ding" Darling NWR would continue to provide support. Management activities would work to improve the Service's visibility and image in the local communities. Although the refuges would also serve rare, threatened, and endangered species and native and wildlife and habitat diversity, migratory birds would be the focus for refuge management, messages, priorities, and decision making.

ALTERNATIVE D: RARE, THREATENED, AND ENDANGERED SPECIES

Where Alternative B serves native wildlife and habitat diversity, Alternative D focuses on management actions that promote the recovery of rare, threatened, and endangered species. Coordination with the partners would continue to be a key aspect of future management. Proposed wildlife and habitat management activities would focus on rare, threatened, and endangered species, expanding the number of species of management concern to the refuges; establishing closed area buffer zones around certain rookeries and key foraging and resting areas serving rare, threatened, and endangered species;

expanding exotic, invasive, and nuisance species control activities; working with the partners to address water quality, quantity, and timing concerns affecting rare, threatened, and endangered species; and working with the partners to understand and ameliorate the impacts of climate change. The refuges would likely remain closed, while environmental education, interpretation, and outreach activities would increase, with messages focused on rare, threatened, and endangered species and the minimization of human impacts. The refuges would develop an annual event in one of the local communities and would work with the partners to improve ethical outdoor behavior. Five positions would be added to support these refuge management activities, while staff from J.N. "Ding" Darling NWR would continue to provide support. Management activities would work to improve the Service's visibility and image in the local communities. Rare, threatened, and endangered species would be the focus for refuge management, messages, priorities, and decision making.

SELECTION RATIONALE

Alternative C is selected for implementation because it directs the development of programs to best achieve the purposes and goals of Pine Island, Matlacha Pass, Island Bay, and Caloosahatchee NWRs; emphasizes migratory birds in refuge management activities; collects habitat and wildlife data; and ensures long term achievement of objectives of the refuges and the Service. At the same time, the Service evaluated compatible public use opportunities consistent with existing laws, Service policies, and sound biological principles. Alternative C provides the best mix of program elements to achieve desired long-term conditions.

Under this alternative, all lands under the management and direction of the Pine Island, Matlacha Pass, Island Bay, and Caloosahatchee NWRs will be protected, maintained, and enhanced to best achieve national, ecosystem, and refuge specific goals and objectives within anticipated funding and staffing levels. In addition, the alternative positively addresses priority issues and concerns expressed by the public.

ENVIRONMENTAL EFFECTS

Implementation of the Service's management action is expected to result in environmental, social, and economic effects as outlined in the Draft CCP/EA. Habitat management, population management, land conservation, and visitor service management activities for Pine Island, Matlacha Pass, Island Bay, and Caloosahatchee NWRs would result in increased management and protection of natural and cultural resources, increased awareness and understanding, and improved ethical outdoor behavior. These effects are detailed as listed.

Implementing the preferred alternative is anticipated to result in increased protection for breeding, nesting, resting, roosting, foraging, and migrating birds on these four refuges. Increased information on a variety of species, suites of species, and habitats will enhance decision-making for the refuges. Further benefits will be realized from increased control of exotic, invasive, and nuisance species. The refuges will coordinate with the partners to address concerns related to the impacts from water quality, quantity, and timing of flows and from climate change and sea level rise. Resource protection will be enhanced, including through increased information about cultural resources on the refuges, resolved boundary issues, additional special designations, improved management of the Island Bay Wilderness Area, improved coordination with the partners to increase awareness and understanding of area residents and area visitors of these closed refuges, and minimized impacts from adjacent uses. To achieve this and to help improve the Service's visibility and image in the local communities, the refuges will work with governmental and nongovernmental partners, area communities, the "Ding" Darling Wildlife Society, and local businesses and the refuges will pursue the addition of refuge-specific staff to address management concerns.

Potential Adverse Effects and Mitigation Measures

Effect on Water Quality from Soil Disturbance and Use of Herbicides

Soil and sediment disturbances and/or siltation due to prop wash from visitor exploration of the area; area fishing activities; management activities related to habitat restoration and management; and exotic, invasive, and nuisance plant control and removal activities are expected to be minor and of short duration. To further reduce potential impacts, the refuges would use best management practices to minimize the erosion of soils and nearshore sediment disturbances.

Foot traffic is expected to have a negligible impact on soil erosion, since the refuges are closed to public visitation. To minimize the impacts from adjacent public use activities, the proposed buffer zones would include informational signs that clearly mark refuge boundaries to minimize disturbances and to avoid causing potential erosion problems and the proposed increased activities of the refuges would help increase awareness and understanding of the refuges and would help increase ethical outdoor behavior.

Long-term herbicide use to control exotic plants could result in a slight decrease in water quality. Through proper application of select herbicides and adjuvants appropriate to site specific conditions, herbicidal control of exotic plants seeks to benefit the environmental health and integrity of the refuge. Appropriately used herbicides and adjuvants may have a minimal, short term impact on water quality in the immediate vicinity of the application where significant and unexpected rain events or high winds may move recently applied, highly mobile herbicides. The use of site appropriate herbicides is a proven, standard methodology to control and manage exotic plant infestations presently degrading native plant and wildlife habitats throughout Florida and proper application following label requirements greatly reduces risks to water quality. Every effort will be employed to ensure proper and appropriate application of herbicides to control noxious weeds throughout the refuge. Through the proper application of herbicides, it is expected to have a minor impact on the environment, with the benefit of reducing or eliminating exotic plant infestations.

Wildlife Disturbance

Disturbance to wildlife is an unavoidable consequence of any public use program, regardless of the activity involved. While some activities such as wildlife observation may be less disturbing than others, all of the public use activities occurring under the Proposed Action would be planned and coordinated to avoid unacceptable levels of impacts, including from adjacent public use activities.

Since all four of the refuges are closed to visitors, the known and anticipated levels of disturbance from the Proposed Action are not considered to be significant. Nevertheless, the refuges would work with the partners to address adjacent public use activities to reduce impacts to the refuges. Posting buffer zones around sensitive rookeries and nesting sites, providing informational signs that clearly mark refuge boundaries, increasing awareness and understanding of the refuges, and increasing ethical outdoor behavior can provide for adjacent public use opportunities without adversely impacting migratory birds and their habitats. General wildlife observation may result in minimal disturbance to wildlife. If the refuges determine that impacts to the refuges from area visitors are above the levels that are deemed appropriate, the refuges would work with the partners and the users to minimize or eliminate these impacts.

Native Vegetation Disturbance

Negative impacts could result from the control and elimination of exotic, invasive, and nuisance plants. However, this is expected to be a minor, short-term, and discrete impact.

Without visitor use, the potential for the introduction of new exotic species would be decreased. The refuges would enforce regulations that restrict access to the refuges by posting buffers signage around sensitive areas and by installing informational signs that prohibit refuge access. Regular patrol and enforcement activities would help limit illegal access to the refuges.

User Group Conflicts

As public use increases in the area, unanticipated conflicts between different user groups could occur, having negative impacts on the refuges. If this should happen, the refuges would coordinate with the partners to address these conflicts and minimize their impacts.

Effects on Adjacent Landowners

Implementation of the management actions is not expected to negatively affect the owners of private lands adjacent to the refuge. In contrast, positive impacts would be expected, including higher property values, increased aesthetics, less intrusion of invasive exotic plants, and increased opportunities for viewing more diverse wildlife.

Land Ownership and Site Development

Land acquisition efforts by the Service could lead to changes in land use and recreational use patterns. However, most of the non-Service-owned lands within the refuges' approved acquisition boundaries are currently undeveloped. If these lands are acquired as additions to the refuges, they would be maintained in a natural state; managed for native wildlife populations; and evaluated for appropriateness and compatibility of wildlife-compatible public uses, where feasible.

The management action is not expected to have significant adverse effects on wetlands and floodplains, pursuant to Executive Orders 11990 and 11988.

COORDINATION

The management action has been thoroughly coordinated with all interested and/or affected parties. Parties contacted include those listed.

All affected landowners
Congressional representatives
Seminole Tribe of Florida
Charlotte Harbor National Estuary Program
Governor of the State of Florida
Florida Fish and Wildlife Conservation Commission
Florida State Historic Preservation Officer
Florida Department of Environmental Protection
South Florida Water Management District
Florida Department of Agriculture and Consumer Services
Southwest Florida Regional Planning Council
Lee County

Lee County Mosquito Control District
City of Sanibel
Local community officials
"Ding" Darling Wildlife Society
Interested citizens
Conservation organizations
Area media

FINDINGS

It is my determination that the management action does not constitute a major federal action significantly affecting the quality of the human environment under the meaning of Section 102(2)(c) of the National Environmental Policy Act of 1969 (as amended). As such, an Environmental Impact Statement is not required. This determination is based on the listed factors (40 C.F.R. 1508.27), as addressed in the Environmental Assessment of the Draft Comprehensive Conservation Plan for Pine Island, Matlacha Pass, Island Bay, and Caloosahatchee national wildlife refuges.

1. Both beneficial and adverse effects have been considered and this action will not have a significant effect on the human environment. (Environmental Assessment, pages 179-206).

2. The actions will not have a significant effect on public health and safety. (Environmental Assessment, pages 179, 182).

3. The project will not significantly affect any unique characteristics of the geographic area such as proximity to historical or cultural resources, wild and scenic rivers, or ecologically critical areas. (Environmental Assessment, pages 181-182, 188, 195-196).

4. The effects on the quality of the human environment are not likely to be highly controversial. (Environmental Assessment, pages 179-182, 188, 193, 197-199, 200-201, 202-206).

5. The actions do not involve highly uncertain, unique, or unknown environmental risks to the human environment. (Environmental Assessment, pages 179-206).

6. The actions will not establish a precedent for future actions with significant effects nor do they represent a decision in principle about a future consideration.
(Environmental Assessment, pages 179-206).

7. There will be no cumulatively significant impacts on the environment. Cumulative impacts have been analyzed with consideration of other similar activities on adjacent lands, in past action, and in foreseeable future actions. (Environmental Assessment, pages 203-205).

8. The actions will not significantly affect any site listed in, or eligible for listing in, the National Register of Historic Places, nor will they cause loss or destruction of significant scientific, cultural, or historic resources. (Environmental Assessment, pages 181-182, 195, 197, 198, 200-201).

9. The actions are not likely to adversely affect threatened or endangered species, or their habitats. (Environmental Assessment, pages 184, 186-189, 191-205).

10. The actions will not lead to a violation of federal, state, or local laws imposed for the protection of the environment. (Environmental Assessment, pages 179-206).

SUPPORTING REFERENCES

U.S. Fish and Wildlife Service. 2010. Draft Comprehensive Conservation Plan and Environmental Assessment for Pine Island, Matlacha Pass, Island Bay, and Caloosahatchee National Wildlife Refuges, Lee and Charlotte Counties, Florida. U.S. Department of the Interior, Fish and Wildlife Service, Southeast Region. 291 pp.

DOCUMENT AVAILABILITY

The Environmental Assessment was Section B of the Draft Comprehensive Conservation Plan for Pine Island, Matlacha Pass, Island Bay, and Caloosahatchee National Wildlife Refuges. The document was made available for public review and comment from May 21 to June 22, 2010, while comments from the State of Florida were due from the State Clearinghouse by July 23, 2010. Additional copies are available by writing: Project Leader, J.N. "Ding" Darling NWR Complex, 1 Wildlife Drive, Sanibel, FL 33957.

Signed   SEP 16 2010

Cynthia K. Dohner   Date
Regional Director, Southeast Region

www.ingramcontent.com/pod-product-compliance
Lightning Source LLC
Chambersburg PA
CBHW081059290526
45795CB00006B/1915